music

music

A SUBVERSIVE HISTORY

TED GIOIA

BASIC BOOKS

New York

Basic Books
Hachette Book Group
1290 Avenue of the Americas, New York, NY 10104
www.basicbooks.com

Printed in the United States of America
First Edition: October 2019

Published by Basic Books, an imprint of Perseus Books, LLC, a subsidiary of Hachette Book Group, Inc. The Basic Books name and logo is a trademark of the Hachette Book Group.

The Hachette Speakers Bureau provides a wide range of authors for speaking events. To find out more, go to www.hachettespeakersbureau.com or call (866) 376-6591.

The publisher is not responsible for websites (or their content) that are not owned by the publisher.

Print book interior design by Jeff Williams.

Library of Congress Cataloging-in-Publication Data
Names: Gioia, Ted, author.
Title: Music : a subversive history / Ted Gioia.
Description: First edition. | New York : Basic Books, 2019. | Includes bibliographical references and index.
Identifiers: LCCN 2019001627 | ISBN 9781541644366 (hardcover : alk. paper) | ISBN 9781541617971 (ebook)
Subjects: LCSH: Music–Social aspects–History. | Music–Political aspects–History.
Classification: LCC ML3916 .G59 2019 | DDC 780.9–dc23

LC record available at https://lccn.loc.gov/2019001627

ISBNs: 978-1-5416-4436-6 (hardcover), 978-1-5416-1797-1 (ebook)

LSC-C

10 9 8 7 6 5 4 3 2 1

For Tara, Michael, and Thomas

Contents

Contents

Music, to create harmony, must investigate discord.
PLUTARCH

I accept chaos. I'm not sure whether it accepts me.
BOB DYLAN

Introduction

'll admit it. I cringe when I hear the term *music history*. The phrase summons up images of long-dead composers, smug men in wigs and waistcoats. I hear the refrain of a stately dance in waltz meter performed for some decrepit king and his court. People are dancing without touching, merely making stiff bows and curtsies in each other's direction. Even the musicians struggle to stifle their yawns.

You may have similar notions about music history. But why? In all fairness, the institutions that preserve and propagate the inherited traditions of our musical culture don't *intend* to be boring. But they do crave respectability, and this zeal to present an image of stiff decorum imparts a palpable sense of tedium to almost everything they touch. Music is drained of its vitality, and at times even becomes a chore. Just as you go to the dentist to take care of your teeth, you show up dutifully at the symphony to burnish your cultural street cred. But look around you at your next visit to the concert hall, and count how many people appear to be sleeping in their high-priced seats.

This pervasive ennui is a symptom of a deeper problem with music history. Boredom, in itself, is no crime. Many subjects are inherently boring, and their exponents even pride themselves on their monotonous routines. I once took a class in cost accounting, and Shakespeare himself, brought back to life and given a CPA certificate, couldn't have made that textbook enjoyable. My statistics class was worse, situating itself more than two standard deviations outside the realm of the mildly interesting. Even in the arts and humanities—spheres of human endeavor whose very destiny is to delight and astonish—many academic journals will kill any submission in peer review if it fails to achieve a mandated level of obstinate dreariness. These fields *cultivate* boredom the same way a farmer grows tobacco—who cares if the crop is deadening, so long as it sells? No one expects otherwise.

So I don't object to the boredom of conventional music history because I demand excitement. I object, rather, to the false notions that undergird the tedium. When we celebrate the songs of previous eras, the respectable music of cultural elites gets almost all the attention, while the subversive efforts of outsiders and rebels fall from view. The history books downplay or hide essential elements of music that are considered disreputable or irrational—for example, its deep connections to sexuality, magic, trance and alternative mind states, healing, social control, generational conflict, political unrest, even violence and murder. They whitewash key elements of a four-thousand-year history of disruptors and insurgents creating musical revolutions, instead celebrating assimilators within the mainstream power structure who borrowed these innovations while diluting their impact and disguising their sources. More than historical accuracy is lost in the process. The very sources from which creativity and new techniques arise are distorted and misrepresented. A key theme of this book is that the *shameful* elements of songs—their links to sex, violence, magic, ecstatic trance, and other disreputable matters—are actually sources of power, serving as the engines of innovation in human music-making. When we cleanse the historical record of their presence, we lose our grasp on how our most cherished songs arose in the first place.

The real history of music is not respectable. Far from it. Neither is it boring. Breakthroughs almost always come from provocateurs and insurgents, and they don't just change the songs we sing, but often shake up the foundations of society. When something genuinely new and different arrives on the music scene, those in positions of authority fear it and work to repress it. We all know this because it has happened in our own lifetimes. We have seen firsthand how music can challenge social norms and alarm upholders of the status quo, whether political bosses, religious leaders, or just anxious parents fretting about some song bellowing ominously from behind a teenager's bedroom door. Yet this same thing has been happening since the dawn of human history, and maybe even longer—although you won't get told that side of the story in Music 101, or from the numerous well-funded music institutions devoted to protecting their respectability and the highbrow pretensions of their mission statements.

Those fretting parents are delighted with this kind of sanitized approach to music appreciation, as are those within the cultural ecosystem who see their own status rising in tandem with the prestige and authority of the traditions they uphold. They gain a kind of secondhand luster from the cleansed, purified vision of music-making they promote. Even rude and vulgar songs are made dignified as part of this process. But the whole endeavor is a distortion, no less a lie for the pleasing patina of respectability it imparts to the dangerous soundtracks of the past. At every stage in human history, music has been a catalyst for change, challenging conventions and conveying coded messages—or, not infrequently, delivering blunt, unambiguous ones. It has given voice to individuals and groups denied access to other platforms for expression, so much so that, in many times and places, freedom of song has been as important as freedom of speech, and far more controversial.

Yet there's a second stage to this process, and it is just as interesting and deserving of study. This is the mechanism by which these disruptive musical intrusions into the social order enter the mainstream. The dangerous rebel gets turned, after a few years or decades, into a respected tribal elder. We have lived through this

3

process, too, but even those of us who have seen it firsthand may struggle to explain how it happened. When Elvis Presley appeared on TV in 1956, CBS was reluctant to show what he was doing with his hips—those gyrating movements were too dangerous for mainstream audiences to see. Yet just a few years later, in 1970, Elvis not only got invited to the White House, but even received a badge from the hand of President Richard Nixon making him an unofficial agent for the Federal Bureau of Narcotics. (Adding to the bizarre tenor of the event, Presley may have been stoned when he received this dubious honor.) Parents were shocked by their first encounters with the Beatles and the Rolling Stones, but those bad boys would eventually get knighted and turn into *Sir* Paul McCartney and *Sir* Mick Jagger. Bob Dylan was a leader of the counterculture in 1966, but honored as the Nobel laureate in literature in 2016. *Straight Outta Compton*, by hip-hoppers N.W.A., got banned by many retailers and radio stations in 1988, and was even denounced by the FBI, but that same album was chosen by the Library of Congress for preservation in the National Recording Registry for its cultural merit in 2017. What strange social evolution allows a radical outsider to turn into an official hero of the mainstream? Yet this process has been repeated throughout history. In fact, this very insistence on mainstreaming and assimilating radical music is the single biggest reason why the historical accounts are so misleading. The officially 'cleansed' public image is promulgated—whether we are dealing with the Beatles, or back in a previous day, Sappho or the troubadours or Bach—while the disreputable past is shuffled offstage and out of view.

Musical innovation happens from the bottom up and the outside in, rather than vice versa; those with power and authority usually oppose these musical innovations, but with time, whether through co-optation or transformation, the innovations become mainstream, and then the cycle begins again. The authority figures who impose their preferred meanings on our messy music have changed over the centuries. In the past, they might have been kings or prophets or esteemed philosophers. In the current day, they can often seem nameless and faceless, at least from the perspective of most music fans—for example, the marketing department for the local symphony, designers of school curricula, or judges at music competitions. But in every case, the tools they employ to prevent the incursion of disruptive new ways of music-making follow a predictable path, starting with exclusion, if not outright censorship, and when that fails—as it so often does—shifting to more devious methods of containment and repurposing. Upholders of the status quo really have no choice except to push back. The songs of outsiders and the underclass have always posed a threat, and thus must be purified or reinterpreted. The power of music, whether to put listeners into a trance or rouse them to action, has always been feared, and thus must be controlled. The close connection of songs to sex and violence has always shocked, and thus must be regulated. And the narratives that chronicle and define our musical lives are inevitably written and rewritten in recognition of these imperatives.

The scope of this book is the full history of music, even beginning in the pre-human natural soundscapes, whose danger and power prefigure so much to come, all the way to the reality show singing contests and viral videos of the current day. In this kind of history, there's room for both Mozart and Sid Vicious, and everything in between—along with minstrels, rappers, holy rollers, shamans, troubadours, courtesans, singing cowboys, Homeric bards, chanting street vendors, and many others outside the concert hall tradition. I'm not trying to be flashy or fashionably eclectic: we need to cast our net wide in order to grasp the forces at work. My approach is roughly chronological, but the connections across eras will become increasingly clear as we proceed. The early chapters will provide opportunities for me to share conceptual tools and insights that will be pressure-tested in subsequent sections of the book, and will, I hope, prove their value in resolving long-standing debates about key figures in music history as different as Ludwig van Beethoven and Robert Johnson. If I am correct, these methodologies can also assist us in the present day, both in predicting how songs might evolve in the future and in creating a healthy musical ecosystem in a digital age that often seems intent on devaluing artists and their works.

As these comments might suggest, the subversive forces remain largely the same over time, despite shifting tastes and technologies. They are both shameful *and* powerful, as well as ever present in human society, if sometimes unspoken or pushed out to the fringes. They can't be halted, nor can they really be exiled permanently from the mainstream. Yet misleading narratives can be constructed around them, and again and again those deceptions enter into the official accounts. In this book I attempt to cut through these sanctioned interpretations and recover the fractious reality too often excluded from our view.

These inquiries will bring us into the heart of a profound mystery: Where do these changes in music come from? Why are the sources of innovation so closely linked to shame and secrecy? Why do power brokers need to turn, again and again, to outsiders and excluded groups for the songs that eventually define norms and behavior for the broader society? What is it about music that makes its historical evolution and pedigree so different from what we find in other modes of cultural expression? And why does the cycle repeat with such brutal persistence over such broad expanses of time and geography? These are vital questions, and I hope to answer them before bringing this expansive study to a conclusion.

What we learn will also force us to revise our notions of the aesthetics of music, its capacities and consequences. Old-fashioned concepts of the role of song in our lives, emphasizing its transcendence or purposeless beauty, will be tested and found wanting. In fact, we will learn that many of the most influential philosophical systems about music came about as part of persistent attempts by elites to halt the spread of innovation and enervate the inherent power of song. As we uncover the actual course of causes and effects, our grasp of what music really does and means will be permanently altered.

More than ever, we need a subversive history of music. We need it both to subvert the staid accounts that misrepresent the past as well as to grasp the subversive quality inherent in these catalytic sounds in our own time. This book aims to provide that alternative narrative. But the goal isn't to be iconoclastic or controversial. I have no interest in adopting a provocative revisionist pose so I can stand out from the crowd. I simply want to do justice to the subject. I want to tell the real story of music as a change agent, as a source of disruption and enchantment in human life.

I started work on an alternative approach to music history more than twenty-five years ago, but back then I didn't realize the scope of what I would uncover. My starting point was much simpler than where I ended up. My core belief back then—unchanged today, so many years later—was that music is a force of transformation and empowerment, a catalyst in human life. My curiosity was piqued by the many ways songs had enhanced and altered the lives of individuals throughout history, and especially the great masses of people who don't get much visibility in surviving accounts. I didn't exclude kings and lords, or popes and patrons, from my purview. But I was perhaps even more interested in peasants and plebeians, slaves and bohemians, renegades and outcasts. What did their music sound like? Even better, what did it *do*?

To answer these questions, I had to uncover a whole range of different sources outside the realm of academic music history. During the first decade of my research, I floundered in my attempts to circumscribe these issues. To answer even simple questions, I found I had to immerse myself, at a surprisingly deep level, in primary documents and academic literature from folklore, mythology, classics, philosophy, theology and scriptural exegesis, social history, anthropology, archaeology, sociology, psychology, neuroscience, Egyptology, Sinology, Assyriology, medieval studies, travel literature, and various other fields and topics, as well as a formidable amount of literature produced by music historians and musicologists. As a result, more than fifteen years elapsed from the start of my research until I published the first fruits—my two books *Work Songs* and *Healing Songs*, both released in 2006. Another decade elapsed before I completed the third book in my trilogy on the music of everyday life, *Love Songs*.

But by this time I saw that a general history of music needed to be written that encompassed the full range of surprising findings I had uncovered during this twenty-five-year endeavor. I won't try to summarize here the unexpected and sometimes disturbing things I learned on my long, strange trip. But my goals are simple ones and ought to be shared here at the outset. My aim is to celebrate music as a source of creation, destruction, and transformation. I affirm songs as a source of artistry, but will also insist on taking them seriously as a social force and conduit of power, even as a kind of technology for societies that lack microchips and space-ships. I want to cast light on the neglected spheres of music that survive outside the realms of power brokers, religious institutions, and social elites, and explore how songs enrich the day-to-day lives of small communities, families, and individuals. Above all, I hope to show how music can topple established hierarchies and rules, subverting tired old conventions and asserting bold new ones.

Put another way, music is not just a soundtrack in the back-ground of life, but has repeatedly entered the foreground, even altering social and cultural currents that would seem resistant to something as elusive and intangible as a song. It almost seems like magic, and maybe it really is.

All these things have happened repeatedly in the past, as well as in our own lifetimes, and will recur again in the future. This is their story.

1

The Origin of Music as a Force of Creative Destruction

'm not surprised the whole thing started with a huge bang, not just a big downbeat in bar one, but the biggest one of them all. How fitting that this initial pulse of rhythm came as part of an explosion both destructive and creative. That's a symbol for all the later musical outbursts charted in these pages, those unruly sounds that shatter the existing order, cause turbulence and even chaos, only gradually coalescing into a new stability.

Our original downbeat took place some 13.7 billion years ago, the proverbial Big Bang in a still unfolding composition. But if matter explodes in the universe and no one is around to hear it—maybe couldn't hear it, if it took place in a surrounding vacuum—is it really a bang? Do our histories even falsify this first beat, which really possessed no bang at all, not even an intergalactic whimper? Perhaps we should consider this opening galaxy-forming gambit as akin to the silent wave of the conductor's baton before the concert begins. A look, a nod, a quick movement, and we are off . . .

That universal symphony continues even today, but as cosmic background microwave radiation, an almost silent echo, barely detectable even with the most finely tuned instruments. Yet it still makes music, even in a vacuum. I note that the scientists who discovered the faint reverberations of the Big Bang first heard it over the radio. A lot of strange things happened on the radio in 1964—from the British Invasion to Louis Armstrong topping the chart with "Hello Dolly"—but this was the strangest of them all: *Tune in to the right station and you can hear the origin of the universe!* These late-arriving listeners for the longest-running live musical broadcast wisely realized that a hit song needs a suitable title, and their new—but very old—discovery finally received one when they published their findings the following year: "A Measurement of Excess Antenna Temperature at 4080 Megacycles per Second." That title, announcing the strange fact that somebody finally heard the bang a few billion years after it banged, was too long to fit on a jukebox label, but sufficient to earn a Nobel Prize for Arno Penzias and Robert Wilson.

But what modern science tells us simply repeats the *Nada Brahma*—that affirmation that the *world is sound*—of ancient Indian spirituality. In Hindu iconography, Shiva is even depicted as holding a *damaru*, or hourglass-shaped drum, in the moment of creation, a little bang doing the work of the big one surmised by physicists. This same vision of musical genesis is supported by countless creation myths around the world, with their tracing of ultimate origins back to cosmological compositions. More than one thousand references to music can be found in the Bible—in Judeo-Christian tradition, no physical icon or relic can come close to matching the potency of sound as a pathway to the divine and a source of transformative energy. Sometimes the power of music is brutally destructive—for example, the trumpet blasts of the Israelites sending the walls of Jericho tumbling to the ground—but more often, sound, in the Bible and in other traditions, is associated with creation and transformation. "In the Hebrew 'Genesis' the creating word is *spoken*," explains Natalie Curtis, one of the first scholars to write about Native American songs. "In nearly every Indian myth the creator *sings* things into life." In Australia, writes Bruce Chatwin in *The Songlines*, "Aboriginal creation myths tell of the legendary totemic beings who had wandered over the continent in the Dreamtime, singing out the name of everything that crossed their path—birds, animals, plants, rocks, waterfalls—and so singing the world into existence." Pythagoras turned this almost universal mythology into philosophy when, holding up a stone, he told his students: "This is frozen music."[1]

It's worth noting how rarely myths describe music originating as entertainment or works of artistic expression. Those categories may describe how we view songs in the current day, but our oldest ancestors knew something we ought to remember and which should be the starting point for all histories of song: music is power. Sound is the ultimate source of genesis, broadly defined, as well as metamorphosis and annihilation. A song can contain a cataclysm.

Science tells the same story, whether we peer into the depths of the universe or study the world at hand. From the start, waves of sound came not just from a primal explosion, but from the smallest particles of matter. In the heart of the atom we find vibrations of extraordinary speed—up to one hundred trillion times per second—creating a tone some twenty octaves above the range of our hearing. Over the years, a host of serious researchers and borderline crackpots—Ernst Chladni, Fabre d'Olivet, Charles Kellogg, Hans Jenny, Robert Monroe, Alfred Tomatis, and others—have demonstrated surprising and sometimes enchanting relations between our intangible music and the surrounding physical world. And in 1934, scientists at the University of Cologne discovered that sound waves sent through fluid can create flashes of light inside bubbles, visible to the naked eye and bearing an uncanny resemblance to the stars in the heavens. This property of sound—now known as *sonoluminescence*—is accompanied by intense pressure and high temperature coinciding with bubble collapse and the release of energy. Here is the littlest bang of all, if you will. As with the creation myths, sound has become visible.

As matter coalesced and cooled following that inaugural Big Bang, larger sounds and rhythms were superimposed on this microscopic chorus. Just as the cosmos offers its astral soundscape, the earth below supplies a terrestrial rhythm section. This is the ultimate ground beat: the movements of terra firma are not haphazard rumblings, but follow set rhythms—even today our seismographs can detect ongoing and consistent periods of vibration lasting between 53.1 and 54.7 minutes, producing a tone twenty octaves below the capacity of the human ear to hear. Indeed, each of the four ancient elements—earth, air, fire, water—conveys its own particular musical personality, made manifest in the crack of thunder, the roar of waves, the steady drone of the waterfall, the sporadic crash of a falling boulder or tree, and other natural events large and small.

These inanimate sounds were matched by their earliest organic counterpoints, a living orchestra constructed from the rich vocalizations of animals, birds, and insects. "Each creature appears to have its own sonic niche (channel, or space) in the frequency spectrum . . . occupied by no others at that particular moment," writes musical ecologist Bernie Krause, who sees this aural territoriality as the foundation for the earliest human musical compositions. The first hunting and gathering societies must have paid close attention to this ever-changing aural tapestry—shifting every few meters, every few minutes. Long before aesthetic considerations came to the fore, the Darwinian struggle for survival ensured that our progenitors were careful listeners of their ambient soundscape.[2]

Krause describes a memorable encounter with an elder of the Nez Perce tribe named Angus Wilson, who chided him one day: "You white people know nothing about music. But I'll teach you something about it if you want." The next morning, Krause found himself led to the bank of a stream in northeastern Oregon, where he was motioned to sit quietly on the ground. After a chilly wait, a breeze picked up, and suddenly his surroundings were filled with the sound of a pipe organ chord—a remarkable occurrence, since no instrument was in sight. Wilson brought him over to the water's edge and pointed to a group of reeds, broken at different lengths by wind and ice. "He took out his knife," Krause later recalled, "and cut one at the base, whittled some holes, brought the instrument to his lips and began to play a melody. When he stopped, he said, 'This is how we learned our music.'"[3]

Lynne Kelly, an Australian researcher, encountered a similar surprise when her friend Nungarrayi of the Warlpiri tribe explained that even trees, bushes, and grasses can be identified by their songs. "I found this hard to believe," Kelly later explained, "but was assured that if I gave it a try I would discover that it is possible." That afternoon, when she began listening to vegetation, she found that the passing breeze imparted a distinctive aural soundscape to the trees around her. "The eucalypt to my left, the acacias in front, and the grasses to the right all made distinctly different sounds. I could not accurately convey these sounds in writing. In subsequent sessions, I've been able to distinguish between different species of eucalypt. . . . The experience convinced me that the sound of plants, animals, moving water, rock types when struck and many other aspects of the environment can be taught through song in a way that is impossible in writing."[4]

Biologist David George Haskell has trained students how to hear this tree music, and as an entry point he advises them to wait until a rainstorm, when the melodies are easiest to discern. Some present the listener with "a splatter of metallic sparks," others "a low, clean, woody thump," or "a speed-typist's clatter." When teaching ornithology, he issues a challenge to the class: "Okay, now that you've learned the songs of 100 birds, your task is to learn the sounds of 20 trees. Can you tell an oak from a maple by ear?" Their homework is to "go out, pour their attention into their ears, and harvest sounds." For him, "it's an almost meditative experience. And from that, you realize that trees sound different, and they have *amazing* sounds coming from them." Moreover, the music of nature guides us through life cycles and seasonal patterns. "Our unaided ears can hear how a maple tree changes its voice," Haskell explains, especially when the soft spring leaves grow stiff and brittle with the approach of winter.[5] As we shall soon see, this same cyclical process from life to death (and back again) has shaped human music-making for thousands of years.

These stories make clear that a natural history of sound preceded its social or aesthetic history. You simply can't understand the latter without paying close attention to the former. For our earliest ancestors, this was a matter of survival, plain and simple. If they paid attention to the wrong soundscape, they might not survive another day.

I emphasize these facts because to grasp the developments ahead of us in this chronicle it is essential to understand how different music is from other art forms. Movies, novels, figurative art, comic books, dramas, and most other forms of cultural expression were invented by human beings, and they possess only the power invested in them by individuals and social institutions. But humans evolved in an ecosystem that already contained formidable sounds, melodies, and rhythms. As part of that evolution, they seized this power for themselves—at least as much of it as they could. The birth of song can almost be viewed as akin to Prometheus stealing fire from the gods in the famous Greek myth. It was a matter of usurping quasi-divine energy, an exemplary moment of empowerment. Natural sounds may have inspired the first strains of human music, as early societies imitated what they experienced in their various habitats. Or, perhaps more likely, the organization of sound into music was intended to subdue the natural world, reduce its ever-present dangers, bring it within the span of social control. In either case, sounds were weaponized.

The songs and dances of hunting societies, for example, often mimic the sounds and movements of the animals they hunt—an example of what is known as sympathetic magic, where people imitate what they hope to influence. To conquer the beast, one borrows its music. We find this in the turtle-hunting song of the Andaman Islanders, the buffalo dance of the Mandan tribe of the Dakotas, the elephant-hunting music of the Hehe people of Tanzania, the opossum dance of the Aboriginal settlers of southeastern Australia, and a host of other settings. In far-flung spots on the globe, wherever human communities lived in symbiotic relationship with their prey, hunters emulated the soundspaces of the hunted.

Experts have offered dozens of theories about the origins of music among our hunting ancestors, many of them fanciful or absurd, but the most persuasive hypotheses usually boil down to matters of sex or violence. That should hardly surprise us, if only because songs always seem to gravitate to those two subjects. Listen to the most highbrow music genre, grand opera, and you discover that sex and violence are the two dominant themes of the most popular works. Consider the populist folk ballad, and you find the same obsession. And you will also encounter a fixation with sex and violence in hip-hop and punk rock, ballads and blues, country and metal. You can feel those forces in the air, propelling the dance music at the disco and the electronic grooves at the rave. Even religious music, seemingly hostile to these fierce imperatives, cannot resist them. The oldest song in the Bible, found in the Book of Exodus, taunts the defeated Egyptian army after God has drowned the Israelites' enemies in the Red Sea. On the other hand, the most famous song in the Bible—it's called the Song of Songs, if you had any doubts—couches praise of God in the erotic language of a love poem. Perhaps some extraterrestrials in another galaxy possess songs that have nothing to do with these primal forces, but no human society has been able to make music without their guidance.

Charles Darwin, in fact, saw sex as the source of *all* music-making, claiming that the songs of human societies grew out of the mating calls of birds and other creatures. "Musical tones and rhythms," he declared, "were used by our half-human ancestors, during the season of courtship, when animals of all kinds are excited not only by love, but by the strong passions of jealousy, rivalry, and triumph." Darwin asserted in 1871 that "love is still the commonest theme of our songs," and little has changed in that regard since his day. Not just our performances of music as participants, but also our preferences as consumers of recordings, reveal a linkage with procreation. In 2006, researcher Geoffrey Miller surveyed six thousand recent recordings and found that 90 percent of them were made by males, most of them during their peak years of sexual activity. That gender discrepancy may surprise current-day listeners, given the chart-topping successes of female pop singers in recent years, but the voices of men dominated airplay during most of the second half of the twentieth century—a period when rock, punk, and early hip-hop set a macho tone for commercial music. And even after the balancing out of the last decade, the ages of the most popular singers, regardless of gender, still coincide with heightened biological fertility.[6]

If you still have doubts about the linkage between songs and procreation, just pay attention to the lyrics. A recent study of songs that made the top ten on the *Billboard* chart found that 92 percent refer to sex—"with a mention [on average] of 10.49 reproductive phrases per song." Almost every playlist tells the same story: music is not only life-changing, but actually *life-creating*. Just consider, many of us might not be here today if our parents had not heard one of these songs with "reproductive phrases" at the right time and place.[7]

But there's just as much reason to believe that music arose (reversing the hippie dictum) to make war, not love. Strange to say, some of the most persuasive evidence for this view comes from the same songbirds that Darwin studied, but drawing on findings unavailable to him. We now know that birdsong plays a key role in asserting territorial claims. A mere recording of avian melodies, played over a loudspeaker, is sufficient to deter other birds from entering an area. In contrast, a male bird surgically deprived of his singing ability soon finds rivals intruding on his turf, but he will sometimes still mate even without the benefit of his courtship songs. In some instances, birds will even cooperate in using songs to defend their territory, providing an uncanny counterpart to human military alliances.

Our own musical traditions, many of them shaped by violence, reinforce this alternative theory of the birth of song. Sometimes these origins survive in symbolic form—for example, in the fight songs of sports teams, or the countless singing competitions on television—but in other cases they show up in actual confrontations. I am told that Inuit culture preserves a tradition of song duels to settle disputes. But you only need to observe schoolchildren for confirmation of this process at work in the modern day. Their bullying and fights are often accompanied by semi-musical chants filled with taunts, boasts, and ridicule. I'm sure it happened in Darwin's day too.

Yet violent music isn't always accompanied by violent behavior. A 2018 study showed that death metal fans, a mix of both men and women, extract feelings of joy and peace from listening to "Hammer Smashed Face" (by Cannibal Corpse) and "Waiting for Screams" (by Autopsy), among other songs selected by the researchers. Perhaps these aficionados have been desensitized by repeated exposure to such music, or maybe some kind of Aristotelian catharsis takes place in the listening process. There are millions of people who listen to songs of this sort without descending into the barbarism implied by the lyrics. We need to take seriously at least the possibility that violent tendencies get channeled and transformed in constructive, or at least neutral, directions through music.[8]

So which of these is the main impetus behind music: sex or violence? Are songs aligned with creation or destruction? In fact, we don't need to choose, because both aspects of music seem to arise from the same biological foundations. A large and growing body of research confirms that singing in groups—or even just listening to music—causes the release of the hormone oxytocin. This change in our body chemistry makes us more trusting of those around us, more willing to cooperate with them in pairs or teams. This obviously explains why songs can lead both to sexual unions and the formation of military units. They are flip sides of the same coin. Music creates group cohesion for both creative and destructive purposes. In other words, hypotheses about both of the proposed sources for our earliest songs—sex and violence— find validation here.

The same findings lend support to other conjectures about early music, some of them so far-fetched as to defy belief. The eighteenth-century social philosopher Giambattista Vico claimed that the first legal codes were *sung* before they were spoken or written down. Many have laughed at this notion, but if singing actually brings about cooperation and helps settle disputes, Vico may have been onto something. Back in 1896, economist Karl Bücher theorized that music originated when communities turned to song and rhythm as a way of organizing the labor necessary for social survival and advancement—in essence, early music was a kind of *management tool.* Few scholars today give much credence to Bücher's views, but he may also have captured part of the truth. The same can be said of philosopher Carl Stumpf, who argued that music was invented for the purpose of communication, since songs can be heard over greater distances than the spoken word. Songs thus served as invaluable signaling tools for early human societies. I also call attention to the work of current-day scientists Edward Hagen and Gregory Bryant, who have focused on the role of song in forming coalitions in human society. Each of these thinkers has expanded our notions of the wide-ranging power of song. Although sex and violence may be the most awe-inspiring forces it channels, they are merely at the top of a long list. Songs are repositories for many kinds of power.

Yet theory can only take us so far. Researchers have also learned a considerable amount by digging into the remains of prehistoric communities. In 1995, paleontologist Dr. Ivan Turk excavated a bear's thighbone from a site in Slovenia. This femur was perforated with four holes in a straight alignment, which suggests conscious design rather than arbitrary markings. In appearance, the object resembles the bone flutes found at other European and Asian excavations. But there is one important difference: whereas other bone flutes had been dated as far back as thirty-five thousand years, and were remnants of human culture, the specimen retrieved by Dr. Turk came from hunting areas occupied by Neanderthals. Radiocarbon dating indicates that this artifact, allegedly the oldest known musical instrument, is between forty-three thousand and eighty-two thousand years old. Although some have tried to explain away the apparent finger holes as random teeth marks, their placement suggests an intention to create the notes of a diatonic scale. The implications are surprising, but clear: Neanderthals, who many researchers doubt even had language or any kind of articulate speech, may have soothed the anxieties and celebrated the modest successes of their arduous lives with the dulcet tones of a flute. But how fitting, given our speculations above, that the creator of the oldest surviving musical instrument had to kill a bear first before relaxing with a song.[9]

Popular science has intruded into these matters with enthusiasm. Many recent best-selling books have explored music as something that takes place *inside the brain*. Who could have imagined, back in the days of Lester Bangs and the rise of *Rolling Stone*, that a time would come when so many leading music writers would be neurologists and neuroscientists? Yet Dr. Daniel Levitin has given us *This Is Your Brain on Music* (more than one million copies sold), the late Dr. Oliver Sacks followed up with *Musicophilia: Tales of Music and the Brain*, another best-seller still going strong more than a decade after publication, and hardly a week passes without some team of scientists gaining mainstream press coverage for their latest research findings on music. I have some sympathy for the agendas pursued by these experts, and often learn from them, but remain troubled at the reductionist perspectives they have occasionally fostered. Biology lays the foundation for music, but it cannot comprehend the superstructure. Even the most complete mapping of brain functions or body chemistry, with every neuron and synapse found and tracked, will never fully encompass the *Jupiter Symphony*, a Bach fugue, or the call-and-response antiphony of a work song.

In other words, biology deals the cards, but social conditions dictate how the game is played. This is the starting point for our history of music, as it should be for *all* histories of music. There may be an organic imperative to music-making that is hardwired into our DNA—and we will need to grapple with biological issues many times during the course of this work. Yet the way this universal impulse gets turned into actual songs is shaped by countless other factors every bit as complex as the human genome. Technological innovations, political structures, economic conditions, cultural institutions, belief systems, and a host of other intersecting variables play their parts, helping to shape the ever-shifting soundscapes of human history. No, it's not just sex and violence, but what we make of them. On the other hand, ignoring these powerful forces, and their recurring role as constituent elements of our songs, is hardly an option. The pages ahead are filled with case studies of those who underestimated their sway and were swept aside in the aftermath.

2

Carnivores at the Philharmonic

W e cannot begin to grasp the first stirrings of human music without placing it within its ecosystem. The instruments themselves began as part of the food chain. Wind instruments—such as the aforementioned Neanderthal flute, constructed from a bear's femur—came from the bones of prey. Hides got made into drums. And the first 'horns' were literally animal horns, an ancient tradition mentioned in the Psalms of David and preserved even today in the blowing of the shofar, or ram's horn, on Rosh Hashanah and Yom Kippur. The power of the animal now resided in the music, but only because of this physical appropriation of its subdued body.

And when the instruments didn't come from the dead animal, they evolved from the weapons used to kill it. Our earliest stringed instrument was the hunter's bow: only gradually did its structure change to make it more suitable for music-making than slaughter. Even a simple visual inspection of harps from traditional hunting societies reveals the connection with weaponry—"as if someone had straightened the bow," writes ethnomusicologist Eric Charry, "and added a few more strings." The same sticks and stones that dealt

death in the chase could also serve as sources of percussion. Everywhere bloodshed and music showed their intimate connections.[1]

"In the *Iliad*, the *kithara* is not a cithara [a lyre, and the forerunner of our guitar]: it is still a bow," French writer Pascal Quignard reminds us in his provocative book *The Hatred of Music*. When
Apollo shows up with his bow, you may be treated to a musical
performance—or you might be killed. By the same token, when
Odysseus tightens his bow in preparation for murdering the suitors at the conclusion of the *Odyssey*, Homer explicitly compares
him to a musician tuning an instrument. For the modern listener,
these two spheres—musical performance and killing—seem to
have nothing in common, but for our ancestors, they frequently
overlapped.[2]

That moment of bending the bow is ambiguous at first glance.
It stores potential energy for later use—but how will it be applied,
for beauty or for massacre? I note that Homer shows no mercy in
killing off the suitors in the most dramatic scene in the *Odyssey*, but
Odysseus does allow one person to leave the premises unscathed:
the musician who had performed songs for the victims. I can't help
thinking that Homer saw something of himself in that singing bard
who survives the carnage.

At a certain point in human history, weapons of mass destruction
became primarily instruments of mass entertainment—perhaps the
striking sex-role shift in fifth century BC Greek art, when women
replaced men as the primary performers of stringed instruments,
gives us an approximate time frame for this transition. This overlap
between the hunting bow and the musical bow has been traced
in Africa, South America, and Oceania. Eventually the instrument
evolves in ways to facilitate music-making, and becomes worthless
as a weapon. The Book of Isaiah offers an oft-cited description of
peaceful times: the sword is beaten into the new shape of a plough-
share and the spear turned into a pruning hook. But let's give full
credit to the equally poetic transformation of the killing bow into
the thrilling guitar.

Yet this association of musical performance with weaponry
never completely disappears. A surviving list of requirements for

minstrels in medieval Germany includes the peculiar demand that the musician know how "to acquit himself well as a swordsman," along with other odd skills (the minstrel must also "know how to throw up little apples and to catch them on the point of a knife; to imitate the songs of birds, perform tricks with cards and jump through hoops"). Even today, I find it odd how often I read articles in the news about someone getting assaulted by a musical instrument. My favorite story relates to blues musician John Lee Hooker, whose longtime companion Maude Mathis drove all the way from Detroit to Toledo to confront her fickle lover onstage. She grabbed the guitar from his hands and slammed it on his head. Hooker later said he was glad he was playing a hollow-body acoustic and not his solid-body Les Paul at the gig. In modern times, as in antiquity, choice of the wrong instrument could be a matter of life or death.[3]

Even the most respectable of all musical institutions, the symphony orchestra, carries inside its DNA this legacy of the hunt. The various instruments in the orchestra can be traced back to these primitive origins—their earliest predecessors were made either from the animal (horn, hide, gut, bone) or the weapons employed in subduing the animal (stick, bow). Are we wrong to hear this history in the music itself, in the formidable aggression and awe-inspiring assertiveness of those monumental symphonies that remain the core repertoire of the world's leading orchestras? Listening to Beethoven, Brahms, Mahler, Bruckner, Berlioz, Tchaikovsky, Shostakovich, and other canonic composers, I can easily summon up images of bands of men embarking on the hunt, using sound as a source and symbol of dominance, an expression of the will to predatory power (although, with Shostakovich, it is sometimes hard to tell whether he is extending that tradition or merely satirizing it).

I'm not referring merely to the specific use of hunting themes in the Western classical music repertory, although it's worth considering how often these come to the forefront—for example, in Mahler's First Symphony, or Bruckner's Fourth, or at various places in Haydn, or Mozart's prolific orchestral output. Brahms, for his part, actually learned how to play the valveless hunting horn as a youngster—his father taught him—and he retained such fondness for its sound that he later composed music for it. But even more striking than these sounds and motifs is the pervasive declamatory tribalism that seems to propel these works forward. I sometimes wonder whether the ease with which the symphony embraced the impulses of nationalism during its period of ascendancy wasn't made all the easier by this long lineage going back to the musical lives of our prey-seeking ancestors. After all, wasn't the symphony the most nationalistic of all the Romanticist art forms? Could painting, poetry, or fiction ever match its tribal fervor?

If you only judged matters from the musical instruments, you might conclude that orchestras were built out of the remnants of the primitive dinner table or the leftovers of a sacrificial killing. Only the reed instruments might have appeared in a vegetarian community. Most other instruments—of horn, bone, gut, and hide—should remind us that our songs, like the musicians themselves, are descended from carnivores. Such is the bloody history behind our stately evenings at the philharmonic.

Even today, classical music enjoys a widespread reputation as a tool of territorial assertion, not just for nations but for far lesser domains as well. Back in 1985, after a 7-Eleven manager discovered the value of Mozart and Beethoven in dispersing vagrants and panhandlers from the parking lot, around 150 other franchisees started blasting classical music through loudspeakers. Today, this practice is widespread. Law enforcement agencies, transit authorities, and business owners use it to repel unwanted parties, ranging from criminal gangs to the homeless, from public spaces. When West Palm Beach police tested this technique in a neighborhood infested by drug dealers, "the officers were amazed when at 10 o'clock at night there was not a soul on the corner," according to detective Dena Kimberlin. "We talked to people on the street, and they said, 'We don't like that kind of music.'" Soon they were fielding requests from other police departments on how to implement a similar program, and which classical works had proven most effective. In perhaps the strangest example of all, Tesla CEO Elon Musk announced in early 2019 his company's test of a car security system that plays Bach's Toccata and Fugue in D minor at high volume when a robber tries to break into an automobile. The various case studies suggest that Bach, Mozart, and Beethoven possess a special efficacy in establishing territorial dominance, but in the world of criminology, the avant-garde also finds a place, most notably in a 2018 experiment to dispel drug dealers from a Berlin train station with modern atonal music. Many in the music community complain about these measures—the Berlin program was even canceled in response to criticisms from arts organizations about the weaponization of culture—but few go so far as to claim that they don't work.[4]

Musicologists rarely dwell on the connection between music and war, or on the tribal elements of an orchestral performance. They are aware, of course, that military organizations always seem to have bands, although the scope of this investment might surprise them. The United States supports 130 military bands, spending three times as much on military music as on the National Endowment for the Arts. This makes military music the single largest commitment to artistic performance in the entire government. That may seem like a curio to most observers, or perhaps a prime example of government waste. Yet music throughout its long history, as we shall see in the pages ahead, has always had a close relationship with aggressive tribal behavior, whether the hunt, warfare, labor strikes, political protests, or just athletic contests. (It's hardly a coincidence that the only other place one finds large institutional investment in live band music is at sporting events.)

And here's the strangest part of the story: even when music doesn't express a tribal allegiance, the fans create it. Just watch how devotees of heavy metal, country, hip-hop, punk, or any other genre employ their musical tastes as a source of group identity, expressed with the most intense demonstrations of solidarity and loyalty. This simply doesn't happen in other cultural arenas. You never see aficionados of, say, mystery stories or crossword puzzles bonding together with the fervor of attendees at a musical event. The music itself serves as sufficient cause for tribal loyalty.

There are good reasons for this. As we saw in Chapter 1, when we perform or listen to music, our bodies release the hormone oxytocin, which makes us more trusting of the people around us. That's why music often plays such an important role in a romantic evening with a loved one. Songs can actually serve as a kind of glue bonding a couple together. Even our body rhythms become synchronized with those around us during a musical performance. Brainwaves adjust to the rhythm of the music, as does respiration and pulse—"the hearts of the singers accelerate and decelerate simultaneously," researchers have determined. Our hearts may literally *beat as one*, as in the old cliché. But there must be other evolutionary factors at play here as well. Not only does our DNA seem hardwired with a tendency to use song as a tool in protecting our turf, just as birds and other creatures do, but music may also play a role in solving the so-called free-rider problem, which occurs when individuals decide to let others in the group do the hard work (whether fighting, farming, or some other task essential for group survival), while they sit on the sidelines and avoid the struggle. By synchronizing the bodies and spirits of the participants, songs bind individuals to the task at hand. Yet a final, and purely pragmatic, consideration explains why music so often serves as a tool in group formation and cohesion, namely, its universality. When the first US labor unions brought workers together to sing songs, the tactic had little to do with music appreciation or entertainment, but came from a realization that the working class at the time contained immigrants from many nations where English was not the native language. Many of these workers had limited education and even less knowledge of the American vernacular. For this reason, a speech or pamphlet might not influence them, but a song could stir their emotions and inspire their allegiance to the larger cause.[5]

We even have a word for a song that creates loyalty and bonding: it is an anthem. But perhaps all songs are anthems, to some degree, each tying us to the larger tribe, even if that tribe is nothing more than other people at a rock concert or dance partners at a disco.

Each of these factors played a key role in the musical lives of early hunting societies, but another element was also involved in these settings, one that is largely forgotten nowadays, or perhaps considered too embarrassing to mention. I am referring to the powerful and persistent belief in traditional societies—some might call it a *superstition*—that music possesses a kind of magic. Those who played the first musical instruments understood that they continued to channel the power of the natural forces and organisms that had served as their raw materials. The animal still resided in the drum and horn and flute.

In the current day, many (perhaps most) listeners have little grasp of the connection between music and its organic origins. I often flummox students by asking them to identify what is creating the sound they hear on a record—is it a saxophone? a trumpet? a synthesizer? a sample? They simply shrug their shoulders, unable to answer. Most of us have lost the ability to listen to songs in this way. Music has become an abstract art, consumed as though it existed as pure sound, disconnected from the realm of physical objects and the process of living-in-the-world. The *performance* has evolved into a *track*, a file, created not by flesh-and-blood humans but by compressed data. Yet even in a digital age, cultivating a deeper way of hearing is more than a pedagogical exercise in ear training; it opens up an entry point into the inner life of music. If we can't even identify the instrument, how can we hope to comprehend the natural forces that these objects once possessed for their users, or—an even more elusive goal—recapture those powers for ourselves?

Can they be recaptured? Grateful Dead drummer Mickey Hart forced his students at a summer camp into a queasy understanding of the hidden power of the drum in an unconventional way. He decided they would construct their own musical instruments—a process that was much more fraught with anxiety and difficulty than any of them expected. And how do you make your own drum? Here's the opening step: *Obtain the hide of two-year-old steer.* "That's a simple sentence to read," Hart later observed, "but it doesn't even begin to convey the reality of a sixty-pound hunk of steerhide, dripping with blood, with big gobs of fat still clinging to it." In a world of digital music, this was the ultimate analog truth—one those students would never forget. The flute may soothe and the drum may enliven, but blood and guts are inextricably linked to their origins, perhaps even to their efficacy.[6]

The very word "instrument" is revealing, signifying not just a sound-making device, but a tool for adaptation and survival. Music in early human societies not only drew on the surrounding habitat, but attempted to tame and transform it. Both song and instrument were sources of power and authority, means for tilting the balance in the battle for survival. For our forebears, music may well have been a source of pleasure and delight, but it was equally a form of mastery, a force for subduing nature.

Can we identify a moment of intersection where this sonic tool of survival first took on a resonance of artistry and expression, a starting point for music as a platform for human culture? It's worth noting that cultural historian Arnold Hauser begins his magisterial multivolume study of the social history of visual art with the remarkable Paleolithic cave paintings in the south of France, where the vivid realism of the animal images—almost one thousand creatures are depicted in just the Lascaux cave complex—has startled onlookers since their discovery. Oddly enough, our search for the origins of human music takes us to this same locale, where we find intriguing connections between the early history of music and painting.

Here researchers in the 1980s were startled to learn that these prehistoric images were located in the parts of these caves with the *greatest resonance*. Iegor Reznikoff, an expert in the acoustics of European churches of the late Middle Ages, had developed a habit of humming when he entered enclosed spaces in order to gauge the aural properties of his surroundings. He was startled during his 1983 visit to the caves in Le Portel in France to find the sound grew markedly clearer and louder when he came into the vicinity of the animal paintings. Subsequent research at ten different caves in the region confirmed his hypothesis: that the placement of these images must have been determined, at least in part, by acoustical considerations. Again and again, he and other researchers encountered this unexpected correlation. In the caves of Niaux in Ariège, Arcy-sur-Cure in Burgundy, and elsewhere, the same linkage between sound properties and visual images was eventually documented. Not only were the most sonorous parts of the caves preferred for illustrations, but the density of painted images was directly proportional to the level of resonance. In some narrow tunnels, so small that one must crawl to move through them, no paintings were found, but red marks were placed on the cave walls at precisely the points of maximum resonance—suggesting that the primitive inhabitants were mapping the acoustics of their shelter. In other instances, paintings appeared at locations where the acoustical properties made it easy for onlookers to mimic with their voices the sounds of the animals depicted.[7]

Our conclusion is inescapable: the early inhabitants of these caves must have gathered around the images for chanting or singing. Steven Errede has called these imagined Paleolithic performances "the world's first 'rock' concerts." My own research into the music of hunting societies persuades me that the singers hoped to secure some supernatural advantage over the animals depicted, taking on the beasts' totemic power for themselves and thus ensuring success in capturing prey. Some of the paintings depict strange creatures—part animal and part human—and thus reinforce this view of a mystical merging or usurpation of powers. The fact that many of the animals are portrayed as wounded or killed further confirms the hypothesis that the cave paintings and the music made in their presence served to empower the hunters in their bloody pursuits.[8]

How many songs about animals do you have in your music collection or on your playlists? What's that you're saying? You don't have any? You probably think the very notion of a music 'genre' devoted to animals is bizarre. What about stories? Have you read any novels lately with animals as the main protagonist? None, you say? But if I were asking a young child, I'd get a very different response. You might be puzzled by the strange cave paintings that mix human and animal figures, or by songs celebrating this fusion, but a child would grasp their significance immediately.

Look at the best-known fairy tales, nursery rhymes, and children's songs, and you will find that the 'animal genre' is the most popular of all. In fact, these songs and rhymes are often attributed to a mysterious woman called Mother Goose—one of the most puzzling figures in cultural history. Even today, scholars can't quite agree on the origins of this personage, whose very name suggests a merging of animal and human qualities, just like those creatures depicted in the cave paintings. Later in this book, I will look at the primitive sources of fairy tales and explore what they might tell us about the early history of music. But you don't need to be a folklorist to comprehend that the songs and stories we tell children today re-create the rituals of shamans and hunter-gatherers in the prehistoric age.

The shaman could talk with animals. If you were looking today for people who communicated in the language of animals, you would turn to children's stories. And the more popular the author—Dr. Seuss, Lewis Carroll, A. A. Milne, Beatrix Potter, C. S. Lewis—the more likely you are to find cross-species dialogue. Look at the most popular animated films among the preteen demographic, and count how many involve talking animals. And the songs—"Itsy Bitsy Spider," "Baa Baa Black Sheep," "Old McDonald's Farm," "Mary Had a Little Lamb," and others—present a veritable menagerie of animal spirits. You can't help concluding that we are all born shamans, although society expects us to grow out of it. But something is lost in this process of growing up. "We human beings have made a world reduced to ourselves and our artifacts," author Ursula K. Le Guin reminded us. "But we weren't made for it, and we have to teach our children to live in it." Songs and stories are a reaction against this narrowing of experience. "Our children must learn poverty and exile: to live on concrete among endless human beings, seeing a beast now and then through bars."[9]

Yet if you want to grasp the origins of music, *you must change and become like little children*, as the evangelist tells us. The relations between primitive man and animals, writes scholar Mircea Eliade, "are spiritual in nature and of a mystical intensity that a modern, desacralized mentality finds it difficult to imagine." At Lascaux, for example, around one hundred intact paintings of animals have survived, but only one of a human figure—and that person is depicted with a bird's head. Another famous cave painting, at Les Trois Frères, shows a man jumping, perhaps in a trance state, with antlers on his head and a tail hanging behind. "We have seen that even today," Eliade remarks, "shamans believe that they can change themselves into animals. . . . We have reason to believe that this magical transformation resulted in a 'going out of the self' that very often found expression in ecstatic experience."[10]

And wherever we find ecstatic experience, we also find music. In every part of the world, at every stage of history (and prehistory), the two come together synergistically, the music heightening the ecstasy, and the ecstasy shaping the music. Those suspicious of transcendental experiences have tried to debunk and ridicule the causative chain between sound and spirit, applying a hardheaded empiricism that, they believe, leaves no wiggle room for shamans and seers. "Music has often been thought of as endowed with the mysterious power of triggering possession," ethnomusicologist Gilbert Rouget explains in his flawed but influential book *Music and Trance*—then adds, in a sweeping statement of remarkable audacity: "There is no truth whatsoever in this assumption." Rouget prefers to see these incidents as theatrical performances or nervous fits, and certainly not as demarcating a musical pathway to "altered states of consciousness" (a phrase he derides as "not a concept at all").[11]

Could this be true? Are these altered states bogus, and the musical pathways to them a fraud? The biggest obstacle for those trying to dismiss the transformational power of music on the basis of hardheaded empirical evidence is, strange to say, a growing body of empirical evidence drawn from our hard heads proving the exact opposite. Researcher Andrew Neher changed the rules of music theory with a pathbreaking 1961 article on rhythms and brainwaves published in *Electroencephalography and Clinical Neurophysiology*—not previously considered a must-read periodical by music scholars. But soon they would need to pay close attention to medical journals, which now became surprising sources of learning on music-making. Neher's paper, "Auditory Driving Observed with Scalp Electrodes in Normal Subjects," shared the results of his study of the brain activity of test subjects exposed to repetitive rhythms. He followed it up the next year with a bold attempt to apply his findings to ethnomusicology, in a paper titled "A Physiological Explanation of

Unusual Behavior in Ceremonies Involving Drums." Fast-forward to the present day, and recall how many recent best-selling books on music are written by scientists (I have cited a few already, but there are many others). When Rouget, our trance skeptic, battled with Neher, he claimed that the latter was the author of the only research in the field—another sweeping claim, which wasn't true even at the time—and announced that such work was "unfortunately devoid of all scientific value." But Rouget's heirs have a whole library of research with which to contend. The skeptics who deny the connection between music and trance have simply lost the argument; instead of debunking the shamans, they themselves have been debunked.[12]

In truth, even the ancients pursued scientific research linking repetitive rhythms to altered states of consciousness. More than two thousand years ago, Ptolemy discovered that when he placed a spoked spinning wheel in front of a light source, the repeating visual pattern produced feelings of euphoria in an observer. The stimulus was visual, but the cause was clearly *rhythmic*. The same connection has been observed in the animal kingdom: chimpanzees, for example, have been known to travel long distances to watch sunlight reflected off a waterfall. Neuroscientists nowadays call this phenomenon *entrainment*, the technical term for the tendency of brainwaves to match their frequency to the recurring pattern of an external stimulus. Neher found that repeating sound patterns caused similar adaptations in the brains of test subjects. Put simply, the human organism aligns itself to the rhythms of the world, whether musical or visual. From this perspective, the shaman's drum and the mystic's chant are practical technologies, real tools that, however primitive they may seem to some observers, produce demonstrable and repeatable results.

Since Neher's time, we've learned a great deal more about the cause-and-effect connection between musical stimulus and biological response. A new theory of consciousness, formulated by philosopher Tam Hunt and psychologist Jonathan Schooler, goes so far as to identify rhythm as the mysterious missing link between mind and matter. In a universe in which every subject and object is vibrating and oscillating, our very sense of self and grasp of reality may be grounded in the beat. Yet music not only changes our brains, but alters our body chemistry as well. Participants in a drum circle, for example, show higher T-cell counts and strengthened immune systems after only one hour of music-making. Even drummers are puzzled to learn that Remo, the largest supplier of drumheads in the world, has established a health science department. Why is a musical instrument supplier dabbling in medicine? Drumming skeptics—who are usually unfamiliar with the scientific literature on the subject—laugh at the incongruity. But there isn't as big a leap as they might assume between the traditional healer's drum and various current-day tools of the doctor's trade, many of which also rely on rhythms and sonic properties. In fact, the more we learn, the more it seems that songs are not just human constructs, as are so many works of art and imagination, but a genuine channeling of an external power. Nowadays sound waves are used to break up cataracts and kidney stones, to detect cysts and tumors, to treat tendonitis and joint inflammation, and sometimes even to fight cancer. We still use 'songs' to cure; we just prefer to give them a different name. *Phacoemulsification* or *lithotripsy* sound so much more impressive than 'healing song,' but these medical procedures could very well be described as branches in our growing science of therapeutic music. In 2016, scientists at the University of California at Los Angeles even managed to wake a man from a coma just through the use of ultrasound, emitted from a small 'instrument' about the size of a coffee cup. The similarity with ancient myths about journeys to the underworld, where music is also used to revive the departed, is uncanny.[13]

As our focus is on history, not physiology, we must leave this fascinating subject behind. But historians do have something unique and vital to offer here—you cannot reduce the cultural resonance and aesthetic richness of music to descriptions of "your brain on music," no matter how detailed. Even so, as we return to our consideration of the role of music in the earliest hunter-gatherer societies, we do well to acknowledge biological forces—along with economic, communal, spiritual, and artistic ones—as part of the vital conjunction of imperatives that formed the basis of human music-making.

All these elements are at play in even the 'simplest' prehistoric songs. In fairness to our cave-dwelling predecessors, let's admit that our modern songs, geared almost entirely toward diversion and entertainment, are paltry things by comparison. As I envision them, the songs of the hunters who assembled before these images might well be considered work songs—solicitations for magical powers that would assist them in their pursuit of prey. But they were also spiritual songs, attempting to create a bridge between the here-and-now and the spirit realm. In addition, the very act of singing or chanting must also have strengthened the emotional bonds between the members of the community, much as social sing-alongs do even today. Some pedagogical element may also have figured in these songs—core knowledge is almost always communicated in musical form in traditional societies. And finally, almost as an afterthought, let's admit that music also entertained—although perhaps *entranced* and *entrained* may be better words. Does any modern song achieve half as much? Can even our greatest songwriters match their prehistoric predecessors in the multifaceted ways they served their community?

Note that I haven't used the word *audience* yet. Perhaps there wasn't an audience in these settings, at least not in the modern sense of the term. Certainly there were participants—there always are in rituals, where even those who remain silent are integrated into the proceedings, constitutive of the unfolding events. In contrast, the concept of an 'audience' for a musical performance is foreign to many traditional cultures. The hierarchies of modern-day entertainment, which radically separate performer from spectator, rarely apply to these situations, in which everyone is invited to contribute, to some degree, in the musical life of the community. It is hardly a coincidence that call-and-response forms are so common in such settings, because these arise from the social structure as much as they define a musical structure. For this same reason, music is frequently connected to dance in traditional societies—so much so that any attempt to isolate a 'song' and assess it in the same way a musicologist studies a movement of a Beethoven symphony is often an exercise in futility and self-deception.

This participative approach must have defined music-making in the hunter-gatherer cultures, and we can see its lingering influence well into historic times, and even in the modern day. The earliest documented concert halls in the Western world were the *odeons* of ancient Greece—the name derived from *aeidein*, meaning "to sing." In other words, the odeon was literally a "singing place," not an auditorium, our modern equivalent, which signifies a "listening place." Even in situations where a clear distinction between performer and audience was essential to the proceedings—for example, at public performances of Homer's epics—the dividing line between the two was very different from that found at our modern-day concerts. The rhapsode Ion, in Plato's dialogue of the same name, notes that he weeps when he performs, and that he can look out at those around him and see them weeping as well. Socrates responds by insisting that the audience is the last link in a chain that starts with the Muse inspiring the poet—the performer, under this interpretation, serves as a mere intermediary. Can you imagine any pundit describing the millionaire megastars of pop music in such a derisory manner?

The 'audience' not only participated in these rituals, but must have been empowered in the process. I'm not talking merely about the magical powers implicit in the shamanic proceedings of hunter-gatherers, but something more measurable, more predictable: the actual power conferred by sound upon those who wield it and whose songs change the world around them—whether in preparing for the hunt, or organizing labor, or infusing ritual with solemnity and efficacy, or in myriad other ways. Music itself defined a relationship of dominion and authority to a degree that a modern city-dweller can hardly imagine.

In those preindustrial times before electronic amplification, early humans and their prey rarely encountered loud sounds. With few exceptions, perhaps when they were in the presence of a thunderstorm or large waterfall, their aural environments were subtly differentiated and yielded their riches only to the careful

35

listener. Primitive hunters could live their entire lives without hearing anything in nature that matched the volume and force of their own collective singing, especially when it took place in a resonant, enclosed place such as those special cave 'hot spots' described above. The first humans who gathered in these locations to sing or chant must have felt tremendously empowered by the results. And their prey must have felt a commensurate fear at the reverberations.

The power balance on our planet shifted at this moment—the animals now fleeing before the hunter, ceding territory to the song-equipped human settlers. I am reminded of the story of anthropologist James Woodburn, who brought a Hadza hunter to a nature preserve in Kenya, and noted the astonishment with which this seasoned outdoorsman witnessed, for the first time in his life, wild animals up close. Never before had the hunter been in the presence of creatures of this sort that didn't retreat at his approach. His wonder testifies to the animals' adaptive practice of taking flight at the *sound* that precedes the *appearance* of the hunter, and reminds us that, in the state of nature, even a musical performance, especially one amplified by collective organization or a special acoustic setting, can serve as an assertion of territorial rights. Today, a piece of paper, the so-called *title*, gives us dominion over our property; in an earlier day, it could have been something as simple as a song.[14]

This view becomes all the more persuasive when we consider that early human beings may have been scavengers as well as hunters and gatherers. The scavenger must scare away other predators— a dangerous job, in most circumstances. But what if songs allowed you to do this without actually confronting other animals? What if music—in this instance, choral music, because the louder the better, and more voices mean more volume—were an even more powerful tool than spear or stone in securing the calories required for survival? Such songs would serve as our first dinner music, not subdued and soothing like the background tracks at a fancy restaurant, but noisy and threatening, designed to dissuade other diners from lingering over their meal.

Renegade music scholar Joseph Jordania goes so far as to claim that our ancestors were "very slow and bad hunters." The weapons available to them were inadequate. Do you really think you can kill a lion or a tiger with a stone or spear or bow and arrow? Ah, that hardly mattered to early *Homo sapiens,* because these primitive hunters had something more potent, the terror inspired by their collective voices. "They lacked natural weapons to kill a prey, but they became excellent at scaring away all other competitors," Jordania explains, "including the strongest of the African predators, the lion." Rather than hunting with traditional weapons, they preferred to wait until a lion or other large beast had made a kill. At that moment, they began their evening concert, the loud rhythmic sounds that would force the killer to leave before all the food was consumed.[15]

If Jordania is right, it would help explain one of the great mysteries of early human society, namely, why evolution made it so difficult for our ancestors to hide from predators. Instead, changes in physiology gradually made early humans bigger, taller, louder, more obvious. They stood up on two legs, rather than crouching, slinking, and slithering like the more elusive creatures in the wild. Almost everything about human beings made it hard to practice *crypsis*—the technical term for an animal's skill at hiding. So the only alternative available was to adopt the opposite approach: to make the biggest songs possible. If humans couldn't match the lion's strength, they could at least roar louder—so long as they cooperated in their singing or chanting.

Could this be why our folklore is filled with stories and superstitions about confronting hostile parties with music? Is this why we are taught to whistle when walking by a graveyard to keep away the ghosts? Jordania recalls a Georgian folk singer who told him: "If you have to go through the dangerous places, there are two options how to do this. You can choose to be as silent as possible, in order to stay out of bears and wolves; but you can also go through the dangerous places loudly singing, as if saying 'I am not afraid! Keep away!'" Folktales from many cultures celebrate this practice: a hero travels to the underworld, or some other perilous realm, and overcomes dark forces by means of a magical song.[16]

In any event, the songs from primitive hunting cultures that have survived long enough to be studied and documented make one thing clear: in these groups, music is deeply integrated into their relationship with the animal kingdom. These communities rely on special songs and rituals in preparation for the hunt, or for the celebration afterward, or to praise illustrious hunters, or to communicate while actually stalking prey. Yet these songs are not always adversarial. In a symbiotic process that might puzzle the modern mind, these hunting societies again and again reveal their close *identification* with the same creatures they kill. Songs of propitiation, seeking the forgiveness or intercession of the animal slaughtered, are well documented in hunting communities. In other cases, we find songs invoking higher powers, in order to secure the preservation and propagation of animals of prey—an understandable concern, given the interdependence of these early societies and their sources of food, and a useful reminder that our simplistic us-versus-them attitudes, drawn from purely human conflicts, miss nuances understood by these earlier societies. Here the functional considerations coexist with a more mystical undercurrent, a deliberate blurring of the role of hunter and hunted.[17]

These considerations provide us with the starting point in our alternative history of human music-making. At the moment of origin, songs possessed both functional value and magical properties. They brought communities together, and they helped ensure their long-term survival. They created a pathway to the divine, but they also put food on the table tonight. They served as a source of transformation and enchantment for individuals and communities. They forged a tapestry of myth and meaning, becoming embodiments of best practices in a way that could be handed down from generation to generation. These aspects of song are now mostly forgotten, given the dominant music-as-entertainment paradigm of the current day. But these powers still exist in our music, mostly as latent potential, sometimes actualized in surprising ways. As we trace the subsequent history of music, we will find each of these aspects recurring, even in situations where we least expect to encounter them.

3

In Search of a Universal Music

A t this point we run into a tricky issue—a controversy that threatens to topple our history almost at the very start. As we uncover the patterns and connections that define human music-making, we face a powerful entrenched dogma that denies they even exist. Even as we chart a course of inclusivity, we need to address a long tradition of exclusivity, almost a bunker mentality, that challenges the very underpinnings of the project at hand. This prickly problem goes by many names, depending on whether you arrive at it through Jungian psychology or comparative anthropology or neuroscience or some other discipline. I prefer to call it the *problem of musical universals.*

We will run into it at many junctures in our study, and it will usually present itself via unusual and seemingly inexplicable coincidences. Musical traditions and rituals in one part of the world will bear an astonishing resemblance to similar practices halfway around the globe. In my studies of love songs, for example, I was hardly surprised to find that the ethos of courtly romance spread from France into Germany and Italy. But how do I explain its appearance in *The Knight in the Panther's Skin*, the Georgian epic composed by

Shota Rustaveli in the Caucasus (four thousand kilometers from Provence) around the end of the twelfth century? "This could not be due to Western influence—it is scarcely conceivable that Provence should have traveled into the Caucasus," declared the brilliant but befuddled medievalist Peter Dronke when confronted with this anomaly. He was forced to conclude: "Georgia makes her own Provence freshly and unaided." By the same token, why does the Celtic story of lovers Tristan and Iseult, featured in so many French lyrics, seem to echo the eleventh-century Persian epic about the lovers Vis and Rāmin by Fakhruddin As'ad Gorgani? Why do I find such marked similarities in the musical cultures of herding societies that are separated by large land masses and oceans? Why do I detect a convergence in the rituals of healing music, or the lullaby, or war songs in cultures isolated from one another?[1]

We must address this issue before proceeding further in our history because these similarities are already noticeable in the musical practices of hunter-gatherer societies. The shamanistic musical rituals of Siberia are echoed again and again in the practices of Native American tribes—and here, perhaps, we can trace an actual migration, one that took place more than fifteen thousand years ago. Genetic evidence confirms kinship between Native American and Siberian populations. But how do we explain the congruence between these same musical practices and those found among the Aboriginals of Australia, or the San people of southern Africa, or practitioners in other parts of the globe? Some 40 percent of San hunters experienced trances, for example, and not only do these altered mental states resemble those of our Siberian shamans—twelve thousand kilometers distant!—but even the associated musical practices are eerily congruent. The mesmerizing rhythms, ritualistic dancing, and intercession with animal spirits seem to come from the exact same playbook. And the same can be said of the Australian shamans, those tribal elders that scholar A. P. Elkin calls "Aboriginal men of high degree," and whose body of wisdom, musical practice, and sacred ritual bear uncanny similarities to those found half a world away in the Americas. Even at the heart of Western civilization, in the supposedly rationalistic worldview of ancient Greece, we encounter the Orphic tradition, discussed below, which clearly represents a variant of shamanistic practice. Did Siberian shamans really impart their teachings to the ancestors of Plato and Aristotle, or vice versa? The mind boggles at such a path of transmission, but resists even more vehemently the notion that mere coincidence can explain such convergences.[2]

I could cite numerous other examples, but the conclusion we reach would be the same in every instance. Our theories of dispersion and migration break down, and we are left with a seemingly unsolvable puzzle. Sometimes we speak casually of music as a universal language, but this oft-repeated catchphrase contains a profound truth. Those who study the multiplicity of musical practices arrive at too many commonalities for it to be just a matter of chance.

Are the similarities rooted in human biology? Perhaps we make love songs or sing lullabies in certain ways because our DNA programs us to do so. Or do these musical practices possess Darwinian survival value, and thus eventually come to the forefront of societies and communities that have no direct contact with each other? Or was Jung correct, in hypothesizing the existence of psychological archetypes, universal concepts that we all share, but not consciously? Or did these musical practices actually spread over these enormous distances?—a theory that raises a litany of questions about how, when, and why.

Normally we would turn to ethnomusicologists to solve this problem for us. These are scholars who devote their careers to the study of the diverse musical practices of human societies, and they ought to serve as the leading investigators into the commonalities and congruencies in song styles and types. But the exact opposite has been the case. The leading scholars in this field have preferred to emphasize the differences between musical cultures, and treat with suspicion—and sometimes even disdain—those who seek out convergences. "When I was a student," ethnomusicologist Bruno Nettl has reflected, "I was taught that any attempt to generalize about the music of the world should be countered by an example falsifying that generalization." Even while acknowledging that the question of universals deserves attention from scholars, Nettl notes his field's apparent "temporary abandonment of it" well into the twenty-first century. "Many decades of skepticism have prevented the field of musicology from embracing the importance of musical universals," researchers Steven Brown and Joseph Jordania conclude in a recent survey. On the few occasions when the question is explicitly addressed, they add, it is almost always in the form of "meta-critiques about the concept of universals," rather than actual consideration of empirical evidence. The topic seems to produce a marked anxiety among musicologists, almost as if they wish it would go away.[3]

This rejection of universals has been driven by the best of motives. Many ethnomusicologists believe that they raise the dignity of their field by emphasizing the uniqueness and incommensurability of each and every musical tradition. This attitude is understandable—in fact, commendable—when presented in these terms as a mindset built on openness and respect. But when pushed to an extreme and turned into a rigid methodological imperative, this doctrine of difference and exclusivity exacts too heavy a cost. The insistence that other groups are *so* different that an unbridgeable gulf separates their cultures from ours makes many of us uneasy in the current day, and it's not hard to see that this worldview can lead to unpleasant decisions and consequences. But it's also, put simply, a flawed platform for research and scholarship. Imagine if the study of linguistics had never gone through its Chomskian, structuralist, and later phases. Consider the impact if scholars still insisted on grasping language from the perspective of social relativity models from the past, struggling to explain matters with the moldy old Sapir-Whorf hypothesis from the 1920s—which avoided cross-cultural linkages and held that the world's many languages imposed incompatible (and often stereotypical) behavior patterns on members of a community—while ignoring more recent research that challenged their assumptions. Today that way of looking at people and culture is considered a shameful part of the past history of linguistics. Yet it's not dissimilar to how ethnomusicology has typically been taught and practiced over the past century.

This has created a troubling divide in music research, with most scholars within the field of ethnomusicology going in one direction, and almost every expert outside the field taking an opposite tack. Many old-school ethnomusicologists complained bitterly after a group of Harvard scientists recently announced their discovery that people in sixty countries, when asked to listen to songs from eighty-six different societies, could easily identify the differences between different types of music—lullabies, love songs, dance music—even after only hearing a few seconds of a performance. The study "is based on all kinds of presumptions," one music professor complained to the *New York Times*. "Music is universal," rebutted another scholar in the field, "it's meaning is not." Patrick Savage, an ethnomusicologist who assisted the Harvard team, admitted that the research faced tremendous resistance because "the idea that there's anything universal in music has been looked down upon for so long" by others in his field. Savage is one of a handful of younger music scholars challenging the status quo, but they face an uphill struggle.[4]

Yet the Harvard study was only the latest in a long series of studies—almost all of them coming from scientists, not music historians—recognizing powerful cross-cultural congruencies in song. Even as ethnomusicology has resisted (in the words of music researcher Anthony Seeger) "the privileging of similarities over differences," experts in other fields have rushed in to fill the gap. We have already looked at the efforts by neuroscientists to identify physiological constants in the world's various musical cultures, but the lesser-known efforts by social scientists, whose work is essentially ignored by music historians, may have even more relevance to their discipline. Harvard professor E. J. Michael Witzel's pathbreaking work on mythology addresses the exact same questions that bedevil the field of music history, yet it remains unknown among scholars in the latter field. Witzel starts with a puzzle nearly identical to what we have found in music: many myths have close counterparts in far-flung regions of the globe—the story of the great flood, the figure of the trickster, the tale of Orpheus, and other quasi-universal stories or story components. At first glance, Witzel's proposed explanation seems almost impossible to accept: namely, that these myths all originated in our common ancestry more than sixty thousand years ago, before the "out of Africa" migrations.[5]

How can that possibly be true? It would imply that these myths were handed down for *three thousand* generations! Could stories have remained largely intact over such a long time frame, even as almost every other aspect of society and culture changed? Yet similar hypotheses about the early origins of languages and possible precursors to Indo-European and other language families are increasingly gaining adherents among linguists, and research into the genetic origins of different human populations gives credibility to their claims. Witzel boldly predicts an "all-encompassing scheme" that will "ultimately unite the 'family trees' of genetics, linguistics, mythology and archaeological cultures in one 'superpedigree.'"[6]

Other disciplines are adjusting in the face of this new paradigm, even as music scholars stand still. Fairy tales, for example, have often been dated on the basis of their first appearance in written form. More than 150 years ago, a few bold theorists speculated on a much longer lineage, notably Wilhelm Grimm—one of the brothers whose names are now inextricably connected with these popular stories—who believed they might be thousands of years old. But later experts dismissed this as a fanciful notion. An influential current in academic literary criticism interpreted such stories as book-based narratives targeted at an urban audience—in essence, a creation of the age of capitalism. Even at first glance, that just doesn't feel right. So many of these stories deal with dark and irrational themes, and the idea that they were constructed for commercial purposes seems to run counter to the whole ethos of the fairy tale. And now we are just beginning to understand how old—and universal—these stories really are. Recent research by Sara Graça da Silva and Jamshid Tehrani strongly supports Grimm's view. They studied a wide range of fairy tales and classified them into seventy-six basic types, which then could be traced in different languages and cultures. The scholars concluded that these tales originated before the Bible or Greek myths, back during the Bronze Age.[7]

Why should music be exempted from this deep lineage? Especially when one considers how often myths and folktales are sung in traditional cultures, it seems all the more peculiar that new findings in these related fields haven't been incorporated into our understanding of music. And once we integrate our study of songs into these broader currents of myth and migration, many previously inexplicable mysteries are solved. The Orpheus legend, mentioned above, provides a powerful example. As you may recall, Orpheus was renowned for the potency of his music—his skill on the lyre was so great, it even charmed Hades and Persephone, the presiding deities of the underworld, who allowed the musician to bring back his wife Eurydice from the land of the dead. Back in 1929, scholar Vittorio Macchioro shocked the community of classicists when he proclaimed, in a series of lectures at Columbia University, that Orpheus must be understood as a kind of shaman. His presence in Greek culture signifies the existence in southern Europe of an ecstatic, music-driven religion similar to those documented elsewhere by anthropologists. Scholar A. H. Gayton added fuel to the flames when, six years later, she published her study on "The Orpheus Myth in North America." "Tales of the recovery of a beloved person from the land of the dead are common in North American mythology," Gayton noted, and added that many of the specific details from the famous Greek myth, including obstacles and conditions (such as the taboo of not looking), can be found in New World variants. Gayton found evidence of this myth in more than fifty Native American tribes. Anthropologist Åke Hultkrantz would later expand on this work and document an even wider distribution of the tale. Yet the strangest aspect of this story must be the reluctance of earlier researchers to even notice the correlation. French Jesuit missionary Jean de Brébeuf had discovered an Orpheus story among the Huron as far back as 1636, yet more than two centuries would elapse before anyone recognized the resemblance to the well-known Greek myth.[8]

At the midpoint of the twentieth century, a range of researchers from different disciplines expanded on these insights. Wherever we turn, we see the same picture emerging—whether we read classicist E. R. Dodds's *The Greeks and the Irrational* (1951), anthropologist Åke Hultkrantz's *The North-American Indian Orpheus Tradition* (1957), social historian Mircea Eliade's *Shamanism: Archaic Techniques of Ecstasy* (1951), mythologist Joseph Campbell's *The Hero with a Thousand Faces* (1949), or philosopher of science Thomas Kuhn's *The Structure of Scientific Revolutions* (1962). In every direction, we encounter a new perspective emerging on the origins and connections of cultural traditions. At each juncture, the assumed division between rational Western thought and superstitious belief systems of so-called primitives, long ridiculed for their credulity and antiscientific worldviews, was questioned and found wanting. Other discoveries were adding details to the story—for example, the unearthing of the Derveni Papyrus at the same time Kuhn was publishing his influential book made clear how significant magic and mysticism were to the same Greek culture that supposedly spawned our superior scientific view of the world.

For a variety of reasons, few academics in music-related disciplines paid attention to this shift, and many worked to oppose it. Organizations such as the National Association for Music Therapy (founded in 1950) and the Society for Ethnomusicology (founded in 1955) justifiably wanted to establish the quasi-scientific rigor and academic legitimacy of their disciplines. But sometimes this led to bizarre results. When the *Journal of Music Therapy* published a huge compilation of the leading articles in the field—over nine hundred pages of scholarly and clinical work—it completely ignored all traditional therapies practiced by nonacademic populations. In the strangest entry of all, a survey of music therapy in America, the history begins with the inauguration of George Washington, and fails to mention the well-known and richly documented healing songs of Native American culture. The idea that music therapy could learn something from (or even acknowledge the existence of) 'primitive' musical traditions would have struck the compilers of this anthology as highly inappropriate, perhaps ludicrous. But even as they worked to create this divide, the cumulative impact of scholarship in other fields was toppling their complacent worldview. Music and magic and medicine and mysticism were coalescing, and perspicacious scholars in other fields were now drawing connections between these areas, not trying to ignore or erase them.[9]

If we peer ahead into the future of music studies, we can anticipate even closer connections between these different fields. At first glance, greater degrees of specialization seem to have created a fragmented discourse about music in the current day, a confusing landscape in which many musicologists remain unaware of the advances in other disciplines—cognitive psychology, evolutionary biology, neurochemistry, sociology, mythology, and other areas—that impact their field. Even so, the march of knowledge moves forward, and the reality of quasi-universal aspects of human song becomes harder to evade with each passing year. The days when we could pretend that separate musical cultures operate as incommensurable and isolated phenomena are now behind us. The turf wars between academic disciplines may slow down the emerging consensus on this convergence, but will hardly be sufficient to prevent it. Even skeptics will grasp, with increasing clarity, that the bedrock foundations of music (the pentatonic scale, the circle of fifths, triadic harmony, etc.) were not invented by musicians, but *discovered* by them—much like calculus or the theory of gravity. Just as the law of gravity applies wherever you go in the world, so do key aspects of songs. By the same token, this new wave of research will reveal how much we have in common, how much we are alike, how closely our songs bring us together, and not apart. And that shouldn't just be a matter of good research practice, but maybe even something to nurture and celebrate.

For the music historian, this convergence requires a reevaluation of the conventional accounts of previous eras, and a greater sensitivity to evidence and circumstances that the previous isolationist models of 'incommensurable' cultures failed to consider. As such, the growing body of science on musical universals may impact the past as much as it does the future. In fact, each chapter in this book should be considered as a case study in what this broader historical perspective might look like.

4

Music History as a Battle Between Magic and Mathematics

At a certain point in Western history, music became a quasi-science. Or, to be more precise, those who theorized about music managed to impose a scientific and mathematical framework that would marginalize all other approaches to the subject. We can even assign a name, a location, and a rough date to this revolution. The alleged innovator was Pythagoras of Samos, born around the year 570 BC. The impact of the Pythagorean revolution on the later course of music is still insufficiently understood and appreciated. I believe he is the most important person in the history of music—although his 'innovation' has perhaps done as much harm as good—and I will make a case for that bold claim in the pages ahead. Yet he is often treated as little more than a colorful footnote in cultural history, a charming figure who appears in anecdotes and asides, but not in the mainstream narrative of cultural history.

The very fact that Pythagoras is lumped together with other '*pre*-Socratic' thinkers is sadly revealing. He is remembered for what he *preceded,* rather than for what he actually did. In truth, we should pay far more attention to what happened before Pythagoras emerged on the scene, what I might call the *pre*-pre-Socratic era, rather than defining his contribution by what happened afterward. Greek culture before his arrival revered what we call nowadays Orphic thought (named after Orpheus, the mythical musician, but almost certainly considered a historical personage in those distant days), and believed songs possessed powerful magic. The rise of Pythagorean music theory, circa 500 BC, changed all that by conceptualizing music as a rational science of sounds that could be described in mathematical terms. Today there's a lot of talk about algorithms in music—with every aspect, from composition to curation, reduced to rules and formulas—but the very first algorithm entered Western music with this philosophical rupture that happened more than 2,500 years ago.

Pythagoras's attempt to define and constrain musical sounds by the use of numbers and ratios continues to shape how we conceptualize and perform songs in the current day, and even how we distinguish between melody and noise. Music, as it is taught in every university and conservatory in the world today, is explicitly Pythagorean in its methods and assumptions. And even when musical styles emerged from the African diaspora that challenged this paradigm, threatening to topple it with notes that didn't belong to scales and rhythms that defied conventional metric thinking, the algorithmic mindset prevailed, somehow managing to codify non-Pythagorean performance styles that would seem to resist codification. Even today, I see the Pythagorean spirit as the implicit philosophy undergirding the advances of digital music—the ultimate reduction of song to mathematics—and technologies such as synthesizers, drum machines, Auto-Tune, and the dynamic range compression of current-day recordings.

Amazing incongruities resulted from this Western convergence of music and mathematics. African music, when transplanted to the United States, defied the attempts of even the most highly trained listeners to analyze it. Musicologist Henry Edward Krehbiel was so dumbfounded by his encounter with African drummers in the Dahomey Village at the 1893 World's Columbian Exposition in Chicago that he enlisted another scholar, a specialist in Native American music, to help him notate their polyrhythms—but both gave up in dismay, realizing that these songs could not be assimilated by their schemas and systems. But fast-forward to our own times, and see how this has changed. Countless academic books on African music promise a codification of this previously elusive art, and the subject is taught dispassionately as a rule-based (or algorithmic) discipline in classrooms alongside the fugue and sonata. The music that broke the rules is now reduced to rules. By the same token, the blues emerged in the early twentieth century as a way of defying scales and standard intonation. You simply couldn't write this music down on paper. But today hundreds of method books offer to teach you the blues scale and phrasing, and are filled with musical notation to clarify each step in the process. Even stranger, the people who write these textbooks often seem unaware of how much this process of assimilation distorts the very traditions they are attempting to propagate. Even if I shudder at some of the results of this mainstreaming of non-Western music (and try to correct its excesses in the pages ahead), I must respect it. To some extent, all of us in music today are Pythagoreans.

"Pythagoras, that grave philosopher, rejected the judging of music by the senses," explains Plutarch in one of his commentaries, "affirming that the virtue of music could be appreciated only by the intellect. And therefore he did not judge music by the ear, but by the harmonical proportion." What a strange notion! Music can't be evaluated by the ear? I am reminded of Mark Twain's sarcastic remark that "Wagner's music is better than it sounds." Yet this is precisely the foundation on which Pythagoras placed Western music. Others before him had offered suggestions on how to tune string instruments—we even have fairly detailed works on the subject from ancient Mesopotamia—but Pythagoras pushed these views further than any of his known predecessors, taking what previously had been a practical craft and aiming to turn it into a scientific discipline. If theory existed previously in music, it served simply to validate practice; after Pythagoras, this relationship was flipped on its head: practice would now be validated by theory. Scholars following his example even came to accept the bizarre claim that celestial bodies created a "harmony of the spheres" permeating human affairs, yet never stopped to explain why no one could actually hear this music. The idea that it wasn't heard with the ears perhaps even heightened its allure and perceived importance. Within the Pythagorean schema, sounds were hardly worth making a noise about.[1]

And this new system has proven surprisingly resilient in the face of all sorts of challenges. By the time we get to Augustine, who wrote a treatise on music in the late fourth century AD, the reduction of music to mathematics is all but complete. He even uses the Latin word *numeri* (or "numbers") to refer to rhythm. The pulse of music is now a matter of counting, and the forward motion of a performance a type of calculation. And that's how matters remained until the African diaspora disrupted this complacent view in the twentieth century. More than two thousand years after Pythagoras, the philosopher Gottfried Wilhelm Leibniz could still define music in essentially the same way as the pre-Socratic sage: our most cherished songs, he insisted, were nothing more than "an unconscious exercise in arithmetic in which the mind does not know it is counting." To this, I note with some delight, Arthur Schopenhauer smartly responded that music was actually "an unconscious exercise in metaphysics in which the mind is unaware that it is philosophizing." Touché! But even Schopenhauer accepted that music is based on "quite definite rules expressible in numbers, from which it cannot possibly depart without entirely ceasing to be music."[2]

And in our day? Not long ago, I spoke to an academic specializing in avant-garde classical composition who told me he had recently been attacked at a conference for assessing modern works by how they *sounded*. He was told repeatedly by his peers that he should ignore such banal considerations, and focus instead on the compositional *strategies* employed. This is simply Pythagoras, plain and simple, but updated for today's progressive tastes. Even the iconoclast operating at the cutting edge of music finds it hard to break away from the rationalistic model inherited from the distant past.

We ought to remember the warning Vladimir Nabokov made in a very different context—analyzing literature—when he pointed out that arithmetic was invented to help make sense of the world, but eventually, "mathematics transcended their initial condition and became as it were a natural part of the world . . . and nobody seems to have been surprised at the queer fact of the outer network becoming an inner skeleton." In fact, this is exactly what took place in Western music at this early Pythagorean turning point (also, literally, a *tuning* point). The ratios and proportions that initially helped us grasp songs turned into the rules and constraints that defined them. The strategies and schemas were often seen as the 'authentic' music, and the actual sounds only got validation through their allegiance to what was written on the printed page (see the aesthetic theories of philosopher Nelson Goodman for an extreme example of this). The eventual result was a conceptualization of music that excluded far more than it allowed.[3]

It is fitting that Pythagoras also stands out as a seminal figure in Western philosophy and a major force in shifting the worldview of the West from magic to scientific reasoning. Today, these three spheres—science, music, and magic—appear as self-contained and unrelated disciplines, but in the context of 500 BC, the connections between them were obvious to the leading minds. Anyone who hoped to dislodge magical thinking in a traditional society and replace it with a scientific worldview was forced to address music theory, because it, too, could be conceptualized as either magic or science. Any choice between these two models would have profound implications. And not just for theory: society would be altered by how this matter was decided. Before Pythagoras, songs possessed magical potency. If Pythagoras and his followers hoped to eradicate superstition and elevate a more rational and logical worldview, they were almost forced to redefine all the parameters of musical practice.

At this juncture in our story, the historical accounts relate a charming anecdote about Pythagoras walking through the marketplace one day, where he heard the sounds of blacksmiths hammering at their anvils. He noted the various pitches produced by the blows, and started wondering about mathematical rules that might explain both the differing tones and their pleasing or displeasing qualities. Inspired by this chance encounter, Pythagoras began experimenting with the variations in tone between plucked strings of different lengths. The end result was the first systematic considerations of tuning and scales in the Western world. Pythagoras literally transformed noise—of the marketplace hammers—into music, a stunning achievement. We have already documented how weapons and the body parts of prey served as the building blocks of our musical instruments, but now we see that even the *theory* of music was constructed out of the blunt force of powerful tools. It is no exaggeration to say that music would never be the same again. Even today, every symphony orchestra demonstrates its allegiance to Pythagoras at the start of each concert by tuning its instruments and ensuring that they are all working within the same system of scales and tones. This is such an ingrained behavior that every participant—whether performer or audience member—takes it for granted.

Pythagoras's renown in Greek music tends to obscure the significance of the far more intriguing figure of Empedocles. This influential thinker, born around the year 490 BC in Sicily, had close connections with the early Pythagoreans and is usually included in their ranks. But his differences from them are crucial ones—in fact, somewhat shocking. In a tantalizingly fragmented text that deserves to be far better known, Empedocles claimed that he could teach people how to "bring from Hades the strength of a man who has died"—in other words, he could raise a corpse from the grave! This is hardly the kind of claim we expect from a philosopher, but instead aligns this seminal thinker with the shamanistic traditions we find in other parts of the world (Siberia, Africa, Australia, etc.). Indeed, this revealing assertion so disturbed classicists that they worked to hide or discredit the passage, even calling it—with no evidence other than their distaste for such superstitious views—a bogus text. I note that Empedocles played the lyre and used it in healing rituals, and was the last major philosopher in Western history to write his works in the form of poetry. I call him a philosopher because that is how later scholars have defined him, but anyone who reads the surviving fragments and biographical material would be justified in labeling him as a musical magi or sorcerer. His fame, during his lifetime, came less from his theoretical concepts than from his renown in controlling the weather and averting epidemics. It's hardly going too far to call him a "wizard for hire": he showed up with this music and magic ready for all situations, whether plague, drought, or a death in the family.[4]

Such a figure is an embarrassment to Western music history—but nothing is easier than to whisk Empedocles out of view and replace him with a sober account of the mathematical theory underpinning the Pythagorean approach to music. The classicist Bernard van Groningen insisted that such an insane passage about raising the dead must be a forgery. Empedocles's translator Hermann Diels accepted the authenticity of the text but insisted it couldn't be taken literally. In both instances, the scholars worked to purify the writings, to eliminate any reference to magic. Such things simply couldn't be allowed inside the tent of established scientific and rational Greek culture, and as a result, Empedocles is not discussed in the annals of music history.[5]

But, in real life, this discredited alternative has never disappeared completely. In the case of Western music, the subversive magical element persists in the margins of society and retains its loyal adherents, surviving into modern times. Even the Pythagorean model needed to incorporate parts of it. That's always the case when a sweeping change in worldviews is implemented: the past can't be denied completely, but instead is cleansed of its most objectionable aspects. In this instance, the new rationalist schemes still allowed a tiny scope for the potency of music. Hence the surviving stories about Pythagoras include accounts of him 'healing' the sick—although these are almost always cases of mood enhancement and character development rather than a physiological cure. We are told that Pythagoras stopped a man who planned to set fire to his mistress's home merely by exposing him to a different kind of music. In other instances, he instilled moderation and temperance via the use of certain melodies. I might even go so far as to call our esteemed philosopher the inventor of 'mood music'—clearly, he believed that emotional states were regulated through the proper scales—but he stopped well short of trips to the underworld or raising the dead. In the aftermath of the Pythagorean revolution, embarrassing rituals of this sort were excluded from the musician's toolkit.

Yet Empedocles is hardly an isolated case. The surviving writings of his likely teacher Parmenides include references to prophecies and cures, as well as an account of a trip to a dark realm that bears an uncanny resemblance to the tales of shamans visiting the underworld. Here, too, sober scholars prefer less embarrassing interpretations. A host of other early figures in Greek history—Epimenides, Hermotimus of Clazomenae, Aristeas, Abaris the Hyperborean, and others—could also be described as shamans. But don't expect to find their names in a music history textbook. Or consider the unusual case of the Derveni Papyrus, a scroll officially designated by the United Nations as the oldest book in European history. This extraordinary document, discovered in 1962, makes clear the deep respect for magic among pre-Socratic Greek thinkers, as well as their fixation on the legendary musician Orpheus. They considered Orpheus as more than just the protagonist of a pleasing myth about music; for them, he was a revered source of life-changing esoteric doctrine. Yet the Derveni Papyrus wouldn't be published for forty-four years, and even when text and photographs were finally shared, scholarly work on this crucially important document proceeded at a snail's pace. Such is the reluctant response to *superstitious beliefs*, although they might help us understand the roots of our own philosophical systems and musical practices. When confronted with Parmenides, Empedocles, and other comparable figures from this decisive moment in Western cultural history, our mindset is to label them as *thinkers*—although the poetic phrasing of their extant writings has earned begrudging respect for their artistry as well. Yet we ought to view them as the last exponents of the old regime, the hands-on practitioners of a musical magic that would soon be discredited in ancient Greece and replaced by the scientific rationalism that still dominates our day-to-day life more than 2,500 years later.

Is it just coincidence that a similar 'purification' of a subversive musical tradition was taking place in other cultures at this same moment in history? Confucius lived at the exact same time as Pythagoras and is credited with collecting the classic Chinese folk lyrics now known as the *Shijing*, or *Book of Songs*. His exact role in the compilation remains a matter of dispute, but the impact of Confucianism in imposing quasi-official status on these songs is beyond question. The 305 lyrics that make up the *Shijing* come from anonymous authors, but the obvious feminine narrative perspective on display in these texts suggests that women were responsible for many of them. Indeed, these songs sometimes display frank expressions of feminine lust and desire that must have been shocking in any context, but especially when attributed to women in a traditional society. The response of the Confucian scholars was to impose morally uplifting interpretations on the texts, outlandish distortions of their meaning that turned folk songs about love and sex into ethical treatises about good government and patriarchal wisdom. The tradition was scandalous, so theory intruded to force it into alignment with the needs of ruling elites. This is even more evident when the *Shijing* is compared with the *Chu Ci*, an alternative compilation of lyric poetry that openly incorporated shamanistic views, and never achieved the canonical status of its Confucian predecessor. Both Pythagoras and Confucius deserve credit as innovators, but they also set in motion traditions of cultural cleansing, a replacement of shameful elements in music with other, more acceptable substitutes.

A similar purification took place in the Judeo-Christian world with a reinterpretation of the biblical Song of Songs. The similarities with the Confucian *Shijing* are uncanny. A song lyric from a female perspective is revered by tradition, but it betrays disturbing expressions of sexual desire. A new interpretation is imposed on the text, and a moralizing meaning aligned with the dominant creed is attached to it, although the fit is awkward and, to many observers, unconvincing. And as with the Greek and Chinese examples, the name of a famous man is attached to the now sacred lyric. In the case of the Song of Songs, that controversial Old Testament book with its dicey content, authorship is assigned to King Solomon himself. Why Solomon would write a lyric from the point of view of a lusty woman is hard to explain, but faith has made bigger leaps over the centuries. The congregation simply accepts that the words don't mean what they seem to mean.

This is a pattern that will recur in the history of music. A heavy-handed hermeneutics, aligned with powerful interests, intrudes into cherished songs and works to obscure subversive undercurrents. Lyrics get censored or reinterpreted. Shameful songs are forced to serve as moralizing tracts. In the case of Pythagoras—whose influence on later songs would prove the greatest of any of these revisionists—a rigorous mathematical theory of music becomes normative rather than merely descriptive, while a discredited alternative view, shamanistic and magical, is ridiculed and hidden from view. Yet it can never be completely hidden.

We should not minimize the disruptive impact of this Pythagorean theory of music, or how controversial it was at the moment of its inception. Here, as at so many other stages in our history, musical experimentation was linked to calls for political reform, and those who challenged the status quo put their lives at risk. Pythagoras himself became a political exile, what nowadays we would call a dissident, and his disciples were initially viewed as a dangerous rabble. For a long period, they operated as a secret sect; today we might even call it a *cult.* Many leaders of the movement in Croton were burned to death after civic leaders set fire to the house where they were meeting. Pythagoras himself may have died in the flames, although accounts differ and details are hard to pin down. One current-day commentator describes the incident as comparable to the conflagration that killed David Koresh and his Branch Davidian cult during the course of a 1993 FBI siege on their Waco, Texas, compound. The comparison seems outrageous, but only because we have assimilated the views of this ancient counterculture. The eventual 'legitimization' of Pythagoras brought his teachings into the mainstream, and turned him into a nonthreatening figure most famous for analyzing the relationships between angles in a triangle. But that shouldn't blind us to the deeper radicalism of his worldview.

This is an important point, and needs to be stressed. This new mathematical system of music eventually became so powerful that it swept away almost every alternative approach—pushing magic and trance to the margins of accepted practice—yet even this scientific approach was initially a subversive movement that authorities attempted to suppress and destroy. Once it went mainstream, it would punish and censor in turn, so much so that almost all of our subsequent sanctioned narratives about music, both its history and theoretical underpinnings, are distorted to some degree by Pythagorean biases. In other words, *the very practice of legitimization is an act of distortion.*

The risk and danger was so marked, during this early stage, that Plato, according to scholar J. B. Kennedy, was forced to hide a secret Pythagorean code in his writings. Kennedy may be a crazy conspiracy theorist or a brilliant analyst of ancient texts, take your pick. In any event, his views, defiantly outside the mainstream of current teachings, are based on an in-depth, line-by-line analysis of the surviving documents. If you break down the twelve thousand lines of Plato's *Republic* into twelve sections of one thousand lines each, each equivalent to a note on a scale, you will find explicit references to harmony, music, pitch, and song recurring at precisely the most consonant intervals. Darker themes, relating to war and death, emerge at dissonant intervals. Kennedy believes he has identified musical structures in other Platonic dialogues, including the *Symposium* and the *Euthyphro,* and has suggested that unlocking this code gives us access to a kind of time capsule from the ancients to us. This is, of course, highly speculative, and the detected patterns may be nothing more than coincidences. Moreover, such a code must seem an extraordinarily roundabout way for Plato to make his points. Isn't the purpose of philosophy to speak unambiguously without obfuscation or secrets? Yet the *Republic* and other Platonic dialogues contain well-known passages in which Socrates defends the need for withholding information and the value of concealed meanings. And as to any apprehension Socrates might have had about putting his life in danger if he communicated too clearly . . . well, his execution by poisoning under order of the authorities suggests this might not have been an unfounded fear.[6]

Did an epistemological rupture take place in other aspects of Western society at this point in history? Certainly attitudes toward music changed, but these were probably part of a larger transition marked by a host of related shifts, all of them gradual but probably reaching a tipping point around the time of the pre-Socratics. Rational thinking began to dislodge superstition, despite attempts to punish heresy with the most severe penalties, even execution. The religion of priests displaced the magic of shamans. Songs were increasingly employed to praise famous men, rather than to adorn rituals and instigate trance states. Patriarchal institutions also became more entrenched during this period, with virile gods moving to the forefront of institutionalized belief systems; worship of fertility goddesses didn't disappear, but was gradually relegated to the discredited superstitious lore of the less educated.

The idea of a preexisting culture of feminine values underpinning Greek culture is still controversial, and the scholars who have promoted it—including J. J. Bachofen in the nineteenth century and Marija Gimbutas in the twentieth—have stirred up a hornet's nest of debate and disagreement. But the archaeological evidence relating to music certainly seems to support a shift of this sort. Before Pythagoras, women played a central role in music—especially the drumming that we have come to associate with trance states—and their activities were infused with ritualistic and mystical associations. Yet after the Pythagorean rupture with this tradition, men emerge as custodians of musical culture, which now takes on aesthetic, military, and pedagogical significance.[7]

Today we tend to think of drummers as mostly men. Certainly *Rolling Stone* believes that. When the influential magazine published its list of the "100 greatest drummers of all time" in 2016, only five women made the cut. And who can feel much surprise at how these editors made their choices? In a variety of ways, we have been preconditioned to view drumming as an expression of unrestrained masculinity. Yet if you asked the same question in the pre-Pythagorean world, you would have received the opposite answer. If we were to judge matters by the surviving images of drummers in paintings, sculptures, and other artifacts from the distant past, we would be forced to conclude that the drum is a woman's instrument—and that is true whether we turn our gaze to Egyptian, Mesopotamian, Greek, Hebrew, or other early cultures. These women are often shown playing a frame drum, a round, shallow, handheld percussion instrument that resembles a grain sieve. In fact, the word for drum in ancient Sumer (*adapa*) can also refer to a measure of grain. In our study of these societies, we see again and again that concepts of music, sexuality, and fertility (of crops and animals, and not just humans) are closely connected. This will be a recurring theme in the pages ahead, but even at this stage it is worth emphasizing that the woman's role as a drummer cannot be isolated from these other considerations. In a very real sense, her music-making was both ritualistic and functional, serving as an act of propitiation, a celebration of sexuality, a tool of propagation, and a foundation for prosperity.

Long after women relinquished their drums to men—who turned them into military instruments associated with conquest— signs of this earlier state of affairs lingered in many traditional societies, especially ones retaining shamanistic belief systems. In Siberia, where shamanism not only survived but flourished, this lineage explains otherwise puzzling elements in the local cultures. Observers often wondered why male shamans, who rely on a drum (similar in appearance to those in the ancient images) to enter a trance state, would often dress in women's attire. But this makes perfect sense if they are evoking an earlier era when females held these important roles. The word for female shaman is similar in various communities in this part of the world, while the male counterpart is called by many different names. This suggests that female practitioners are more deeply rooted in a distant past, when these languages shared a common origin. Put simply, the accumulated evidence tells us that the integration of rhythm and magic is, in its earliest manifestations, closely linked to women and feminine qualities. Only after the epistemological rupture do men come to dominate these practices, which now survive quasi-hidden on the margins of a more rationalistic world.

The best-known musical innovator of the pre-Pythagorean period is Sappho, who is often credited as the inventor of the love song and the creator of the Greek lyric. In a revealing coincidence, Sappho may have died in the same year that Pythagoras was born, and to some degree she reflects the final stages of a world in which music was deeply linked to communal needs and sexuality/fertility, while also anticipating the marked individualism and personal agency that would eventually dominate Western songs. Today her work is mostly celebrated for the latter qualities, and especially for the manner in which Sappho foreshadows the confessional nature of our own songs. But we misrepresent her significance if we don't also grasp the many ways her lyrics reflect society as it existed before the ascendancy of hard-edged Greek rationalism, a world where song was still inseparable from ritual observances, and more aligned with mysticism and concepts of the feminine. By the time of Plato and Aristotle, the Greeks had grown ambivalent, perhaps embarrassed, or even hostile, to this legacy from the past. But Sappho invites us to treat it with reverence even as she prepares us for the new order of things.

Later in this work, we will look at the remarkable shift in Western musical culture, heralded by Sappho, that allowed musicians to *sing about themselves*. We take this for granted nowadays. In fact, most of us can hardly imagine any other purpose for a song. Yet at this juncture, we need to grasp the deep significance of the other side of Sappho, her role as a quasi-priestess who invoked supernatural forces and sought to express the needs of her community. In this regard, she has no counterpart among modern singer-songwriters and reflects values and priorities that have been expunged from the music curriculum—indeed, that even the ancients tried to forget in their quest for a purified, rational science of song.

Reading the very first fragment in the standard editions of Sappho—which begins with the words "Ornate-throned immortal

Aphrodite"—we see both sides of this hybrid worldview. On the one hand, this lyric is typically viewed as a love lament expressing Sappho's broken heart; yet most of the text is devoted to the invocation of a goddess, Aphrodite. This hybrid of the personal and divine recurs again and again in her oeuvre. Sappho has two obvious concerns, and they dominate her worldview even as they expose a hidden rift in Western thought: the emotional bonds of love, and communal obligations to the gods. In the later evolution of Western music, these two approaches will veer off into their separate traditions and have little to do with each other. You could hardly imagine two music genres with less in common than love songs and religious hymns, but for Sappho these are intimately connected.[8]

The lyric will lose touch with both streams long before the rise of Christianity—we will see how the invocations of divinities become formulaic, and how the lyric turns into a platform for publicly praising military leaders and other powerful men. Strangest of all, the classical lyric will abandon even its connection to melody, becoming a text intended for recitation and reading instead of a song for musical performance. But at this early stage in the history of song, Sappho has no interest in writing *texts* or propagandizing for a state or celebrating its military victories. She even explicitly renounces this attitude in fragment 16. "Some say a host of cavalry, others of infantry, and others of ships, is the most beautiful thing on the black earth, but I say it is whatsoever a person loves." Again and again she focuses on the spiritual and emotional needs of her community—the only triumphs and failures that matter take place in the heavens and in the heart, not on a battlefield.[9]

This perspective becomes even clearer when we look at songs from the long period before Sappho. Even specialists in the lyric rarely dig back this deeply, and many are unaware that songs have survived from this period at all. Sappho is often viewed as the originator of the lyric, and the idea that there is a significant body of work prior to her birth comes as a surprise. Yet Sappho actually represents the culmination of a tradition that stretches back almost two thousand years before her arrival on the scene. Tracing this thread back to its origins brings us to the very first composer in the history of music—or at least the first whose name has survived. And what a fascinating composer she is, although she appears in few music history books, and has virtually no name recognition even among music scholars.

5

Bulls and Sex Toys

We only have the vaguest notions of what Mesopotamian music sounded like. A few scholars have tried to resurrect its sounds, drawing on evidence from surviving texts and instruments, but their efforts are mostly exercises in imaginative reconstruction. Yet I am not surprised that these restorations possess a mesmerizing, trance-like quality. Mesopotamia, during the long centuries before the fall of Babylon in 539 BC and its subsequent dominance by foreign powers, provides us with perhaps the clearest example of a flourishing ancient musical culture still under the sway of magical, ritualistic influences. We sometimes refer to the people who presided over these ancient rituals as priests or priestesses, but in many ways they are closer in spirit to the shamans who rely on music as a key component of what Mircea Eliade has called "archaic techniques of ecstasy."[1]

Even though we lack detailed information on the sound of the songs, we have learned an enormous amount about the ancient musical culture of the region since Hormuzd Rassam's 1853 discovery of the clay tablet containing the *Epic of Gilgamesh*—often described as a poetic work, but almost certainly sung to its earliest audiences. And we continue to learn more in the new millennium. Twenty new lines of *Gilgamesh* were found in 2011 on a clay tablet purchased by an Iraq museum from an unnamed individual, probably a smuggler, for $800. Just as fascinating as the texts are the musical instruments and related objects uncovered in archaeological digs, especially those found by Sir Leonard Woolley during his excavations at the Royal Cemetery of Ur, in present-day Iraq, between 1922 and 1934. We now have an abundance of evidence to draw on in describing this culture, yet these texts and objects reveal musical practices so different from our own that it is often difficult for experts to bring them into any coherent relation with current-day notions about the role of songs in a society.

There are many strange things to consider here, but let's start with the animals. In fact, you can hardly ignore them, because they are simply everywhere. Musical instruments were built to look like animals. In other instances, images of animals were added as decorations onto the surfaces of instruments. Surviving artworks also include depictions of animals *playing* musical instruments. Sumerian literary texts reveal a similar animal obsession—these creatures are the single largest source of poetic comparisons. Waves engulfing a boat are described as a devouring wolf. A bull is often employed to convey well-being and power. The roar of the bull is used to describe the speech of a ruler, the pronouncement of an oracle, or the sound of a busy temple. It's almost as if a kind of collective zoological mania prevailed among these people.

Scholars have offered a hodgepodge of theories and speculative notions in explaining the role of these animal musicians in ancient art. Confronted by representations of four-footed creatures playing instruments, esteemed musicologist Marcelle Duchesne-Guillemin surmised the existence of "a kind of profane music"—perhaps a type of wild jazz for the Mesopotamian demimonde. "Their inspiration seems less religious than facetious," she notes, and even detects the possibility of satire. But Duchesne-Guillemin doesn't rule out the opposite theory—namely, that these ancient images might be purely realistic, and the apparent animal is just a hunter in disguise, trying to capture prey. In any event, she insists that such images should not be viewed as representative of any deeply held belief system. The pioneering antiquarian musicologist Francis Galpin, in contrast, was willing to accept a religious significance, at least to the impressive bull lyres found in the Royal Cemetery of Ur, but only in a narrow sense. These instruments, he claimed, celebrate the moon deity, known as Nanna or Sin, who was patron of the city of Ur and sometimes depicted as a bull with crescent horns.[2]

Yet, as we know from our consideration of the earliest hunting communities, the relationship of animals to music-making is much older than the city of Ur—indeed, the Lascaux cave paintings predate the Sumerian city-state by more than ten thousand years. And anyone schooled in shamanism and the belief systems of traditional societies will find it impossible to accept the interpretation of these images as comic or satirical. The animal was the source of power in these communities, offering both functional support as a source of food and raw materials and magical assistance as the totemic protector and provider. In Mesopotamia, the northern area offered rich grazing lands in a region where so many other areas were barren, and cattle must have been central to economic and cultic practices. In the old burial areas, people are often found interred with tubular cylinder seals bearing images of animals, especially horned cattle, and these almost certainly were expected to provide benefits in the afterlife to the deceased. It's even possible that the courtyards facing the oldest temples of Sumer initially served as cattle enclosures, and only later evolved into the *temene*, or holy groves. In this context, we should hardly be surprised to find music associated with cattle—in fact, that is the very sign that its performance was *not* merely profane, but inextricably linked to the highest powers.

If early archaeologists were perplexed by the animals, they were even more dismayed by the sex toys. "The mounds of Nippur were fairly strewn with phallic emblems," complained John P. Peters, an archaeologist and Episcopalian minister who conducted excavations in central Iraq from 1888 to 1895. His colleague Hermann Hilprecht put together a huge collection, "commencing with the crudest representation of the male member" all the way to "conventionalized spikes and cones." But this esteemed Assyriologist soon learned that government officials did not share his enthusiasm for old phalluses. One functionary refused to include them on a list of antiquities, and the whole assortment was eventually lost or destroyed by the very officials responsible for preserving them. Peters was perhaps secretly pleased by their disappearance, but would nonetheless find a moralizing lesson in the sex obsession of the ancients, calling attention to the similarity between Sumerian myth and the biblical story of the Garden of Eden—in both cases, he explained, "it is the woman who with the serpent entices the man to the sexual act which shall make him the producer of life, like to the gods."[3]

At the very moment that the Nippur excavations were taking place, Sir James George Frazer was providing an essential conceptual framework for understanding these scandalous artifacts in his pathbreaking study *The Golden Bough*, first published in two volumes in 1890, but eventually expanded into a mammoth twelve-volume version released between 1906 and 1915. The modernist poet Ezra Pound has given us a pithy one-sentence summary of this huge body of research. Our accepted conceptions of morality, Pound explained, "go back to the opposed temperaments of those who thought copulation was good for the crops, and the opposed faction who thought it was bad for the crops." Then, Pound added: "That ought to simplify a good deal of argument."[4]

Frazer may have simplified matters, but he also created a scandal in his detailed assessment of the fertility cults of the ancient world and in his confident assertions of a link between fornication and the prosperity of the greater community. But perhaps even more shocking to Victorian readers was the implicit connection between the mythology of these rituals, with their celebration of a dying and resurrecting god responsible for the fertility of the land, and the Christian doctrine of the crucifixion and resurrection of Jesus Christ. It was hard to escape the conclusion that this latter religious tenet, accepted by believers as gospel truth, could be reinterpreted as a comparatively recent variant of a much older pagan myth found in every major ancient civilization.

Frazer's critics have often complained he was disrespectful, but have never agreed on exactly what he had insulted. For many, his unforgivable sin was reducing Christianity to the level of an anthropological ritual; for others, he went too far in imposing elaborate interpretations on pre-Christian rituals. "Frazer is much more savage than most of his 'savages,'" asserted philosopher Ludwig Wittgenstein. "His explanations of the primitive observances are much cruder than the sense of the observances themselves." In other instances, Frazer has been castigated for blaming violent and lustful human behavior on the seasonal changes, and thus committing a calumny against the natural world. One often discovers in these critiques the same kind of shame or embarrassment that has shaped so many reinterpretations of songs and lyrics over the centuries. But even as other theories of ritual have tried to go beyond Frazer, they invariably return to the constituent elements of sexuality and violence—the same driving forces that underpin so much of the flux and change in human music-making. More recent thinkers, such as René Girard, Walter Burkert, and Charles Taylor, among others, have cast light on the crucial role of ancient ritual in channeling drives for lust and vengeance that would wreak havoc if not given some sanctioned outlet. But as these rituals evolved into something resembling what we now recognize as religion, the same animating drives became embarrassments, or actual sins, offenses demanding punishment and eradication. This whole process bears many similarities with the repurposing and reinterpretation of music described in these pages. Yet this should hardly surprise us: music and ritual have always shared a closely intertwined history.[5]

For our purposes, we are concerned with the musical implications of this body of research, essential not only for our understanding of the songs of ancient Mesopotamian culture, but also for our grasp of the traditions of other societies. Perhaps our own, too. Indeed, the fertility songs and rituals of five thousand years ago bear an uncanny resemblance to the content of many pop-music YouTube videos. Researcher Sierra Helm has gone so far as to juxtapose photos of contemporary female superstars with ancient depictions of Sumerian goddesses to point out similarities between "the devotional practices directed towards the goddess Inanna in ancient Mesopotamia and towards celebrities in present-day America." Sometimes the connection with ritualistic worship is made explicit, as when starry-eyed fans refer to a sexy starlet as a goddess, or when a pop singer decides to go by the name Madonna and juxtapose her semi-naked body with religious iconography. But even when the language and settings are purely secular, the cult of the modern celebrity evokes ancient practices in many particulars.[6]

In ancient Mesopotamia, as Assyriologist Gwendolyn Leick points out, "nude male figures or phallic symbols are comparatively rarer than naked females and depictions of the vulva." I have called this same phenomenon in modern popular music the *Bob Fosse meme*, acknowledging the influence of this celebrated choreographer in designing dance routines juxtaposing a well-dressed man (usually in formal attire or a uniform) and a mostly naked woman. This combination has served as a recurring fantasy in music videos and films, from "Whatever Lola Wants" to "Blurred Lines" and beyond. The same recipe predominated—in even more explicit form—in ancient Mesopotamian imagery. The woman's sexual persona is the center of attraction. The man's sexual prowess is acknowledged, but typically in the context of its fertilizing properties. In discussing core myths filled with explicit couplings, Leick adds that "the male protagonists, typically young, vigorous gods, achieve impregnation with each orgasm." Here this predictable male potency is less celebrated than female fertility, and the music reflects this as much as the visual art.[7]

But in other ways, this ancient music is very different from our own sexualized hit songs. Eroticism in these old hymns is, again and again, linked with vegetation and the natural world. In a description of the sexual union of King Dumuzi with Inanna, the goddess of love and fertility, her naked body is repeatedly compared to a field that needs plowing. She refers to her "uncultivated land. . . . My high field, which is well-watered. My own nakedness, a well-watered, a rising mound." Then asks:

I, the maiden—who will plow it?
My nakedness, the wet and well-watered ground—
I, the young lady—who will station there an ox?

To which her lover responds:

Young lady, may the king plow it for you.
May Dumuzi, the king, plow it for you.

As the song reaches its culminating point, Inanna exclaims: "The lord of all things, fill my holy churn!"[8]

Very little gets censored on the radio today, but I suspect a song titled "Plow My Vulva" might get a shock jock fired from the station even in our current 'anything goes' society. But the ancients didn't worry about warning labels for their hymns. Sexual union was a cause for celebration, not shame. Put simply, what Brian Wilson did for surfing in his tunes, Mesopotamians did for genitalia. Even so, these songs weren't designed to titillate, or at least that wasn't their primary function. They had a higher purpose: the prosperity of the community was at stake, perhaps even the legitimacy of the king's rule. This was especially evident in the sacred marriage ritual, which scholars often call by its Greek name, *hieros gamos*. In the Sumerian version, the king was expected to have sex with a goddess on a special recurring occasion, probably held in conjunction with celebrations for the New Year. The role of the goddess was played by the High Priestess of Inanna, and the songs associated with the ritual sung from her perspective.

Scholars debate whether the couple really had sex or merely enacted a symbolic union, perhaps something akin to the simulated bed scenes in a Hollywood movie. I suspect that the coupling was real—the importance of this coming together was so great, and the surviving details of the ritual so specific, that it's hard to imagine its climax as being anything short of . . . well, actual climax. But the mechanics of their union is less important, for our purposes, than the songs that accompanied it. And those leave very little to the imagination. "At the king's lap stood the rising cedar," a religious hymn proclaims. "Plow my vulva, man of my heart," Inanna demands.[9]

Darwin never knew about such songs. He came up with his thesis about the sexual origins of music long before Frazer's research or Woolley's excavations. But Darwin clearly would have considered these rituals, and their songs, as confirmation of his theory that music originated as an evolutionary mechanism to ensure propagation. Of course, he believed that human songs led to the birth of more *babies*, not an increase in cattle or crops, but his general idea of music as a survival tool is compatible with these subsequent findings. In fact, the accumulated evidence of the 150 years since he wrote *The Descent of Man* makes it hard to comprehend the evolution of song without constant reference to magic, sex, fertility, and ritual.

This is the precise context in which the singer-songwriter first appears on the scene. Enheduanna, the oldest songwriter known to us by name whose works have survived, was a high priestess of the Sumerian city-state of Ur in the third millennium BC. She composed more than forty hymns, but these aren't your typical songs of worship, and this may explain why the "Mother of Song" doesn't appear in school textbooks. In fact, if you showed her saucy lyrics to modern-day ministers, they would be horrified by the *dirty* songs of Enheduanna. Perhaps many ancient Sumerians also objected to this music—at least if we judge by the defaced alabaster disk that contains her image, excavated by Sir Leonard Woolley in 1927. Woolley believed that the damage to the disk was deliberate, although perhaps not due to the priestess's explicit lyrics. There were many reasons to dislike, or simply fear, Enheduanna. First and foremost, she was the daughter of King Sargon of Akkad, a man famous for both shedding blood and committing sacrilege, who may have served as the inspiration for the biblical Nimrod, mastermind behind the Tower of Babel. But we must also consider whether this deliberately damaged disk isn't simply one more example of the recurring pattern, found in so many other cultures, of powerful men attempting to erase, marginalize, or reinterpret the songs of women—as documented by the disappearance of most of Sappho's oeuvre or the masculinized exegeses of the *Shijing*, the Song of Songs, and other traditional expressions of female desire.

Already by the time of Homer, a different purpose of song can be detected, one that will grow in importance over the next several hundred years. When the singer Demodocus is summoned to entertain at a banquet in the eighth book of the *Odyssey*, he is expected to sing "the famous deeds of fighting heroes." After the Pythagorean revolution, this theme becomes the primary purpose of the most respectable songs. The lyric becomes less about erotic longings and personal emotions, and more about celebrating the strong and the powerful. Sappho may be the most famous singer of ancient lyric poetry today, but the Greeks esteemed her successor Pindar far more highly, prizing his works because they celebrated the glories of his age and the worthiest of men. Few of us nowadays may care to hear a song about the wealthy tyrant Hieron, best known for introducing the secret police into Western life, or the boxer Diagoras of Rhodes (whom Pindar insists is descended from the god Zeus), famous for pummeling other men in the Olympic competitions. But this was how you made the *Billboard* charts, or whatever their ancient Greek equivalent might be, starting in the fifth century BC and continuing for many long centuries afterward.[10]

Why should we care about this today? Well, for a start, we can hardly understand our own music if we don't comprehend the persisting opposition between these two very different functions of song. Let me label, for the sake of simplicity, the tradition that emphasizes fertility, ecstasy, and magic as the *feminine* tradition in music. The contrasting approach, celebrating discipline, social order, powerful men, and group conformity, we'll call the *masculine* alternative. Take, for example, the historical role of drumming, and see how it can serve either of these functions. Historian Johan Huizinga once made the brilliant observation that the age of knights and chivalry ended when drums were introduced into military campaigns. The drum instilled uniformity and solidarity into the troops, but at the expense of the individual personalities that loom so large in war narratives of an earlier day. Huizinga's chronology can be questioned—images from the seventeenth and eighteenth Egyptian dynasties depict Nubian military drummers long before the medieval era—but he is correct to grasp the power of percussion as a tool of social control. Yet drums have also been a key source in instigating ecstatic trance states and breaking down demands for social conformity. The latter kind of drumming took place in Swing Era ballrooms, and at Woodstock, and was originally associated with women, as made clear in *The Bacchae* by Euripides and other ancient texts and images. There's extensive scientific literature to back up both of these functions of drumming—our brains respond to external rhythm both as a source of discipline and as a gateway to transcendence. These sharply defined alternatives are, in other words, guideposts not just to music history, but also to current practice. Show me how you play a snare drum, and I can tell you which lineage you claim.[11]

Let's return to ancient society. Unless we understand the magnitude of this rupture in music history, we can hardly make sense of the various commentaries on songs in the surviving literature. Plato, for example, seems to express contradictory attitudes toward music, at some points expressing apprehension and calling for prohibitions, at others insisting on the importance of song and dance in education. Yet a closer scrutiny shows that he praises music that upholds civic virtues and leads to orderly behavior, but wants to eliminate songs that inflame undesirable emotions and incite improper actions. Plato is especially hostile to musical lamentations. This may seem like a small matter, but it is very revealing. The lament for the dying god was a key part of fertility rituals, and even when sexuality was removed from the equation, these sorts of songs were considered one of the specialties of women, who relied on them to channel feelings that might otherwise remain repressed. Repeatedly, for almost fifteen hundred years after the time of Plato, the lament would get attacked as a dangerous song genre, and restrictions on it were imposed by powerful men. Condemnation of the lament was a recurring theme, for example, in medieval Christian pronouncements on 'sinful' music. Until the rise of the troubadours at the dawn of the twelfth century, dwelling excessively on overwhelming personal emotions, particularly in song, was considered a sign of moral weakness; even more to the point, it was deemed womanish. The rhetorician Quintilian summed up this contrast at the dawn of the Roman Empire, when he attacked "the lascivious melodies of our effeminate stage"—music that he claimed was "unfit even for the use of a modest girl"—and looked back with nostalgia on a better age, when music was employed "to sing praises of brave men." In a similar vein, Cato and Cicero expressed their admiration for these ideologically charged *carmina conuiualia* of early Rome. This term is sometimes translated as "ancestral songs" and refers to music performed by dinner guests in praise of heroes from the past.[12]

Here again, we need to consider funeral rituals to grasp the full impact of this shift in priorities. The ancient and medieval authorities are surprisingly consistent in their distaste for musical lamentations and tried to prevent women from singing them for more than a thousand years. The enemies of this music had little success in eradicating songs of grief and mourning, at least judging by the persistence with which they needed to repeat their attacks. But the ancients had recourse to a substitute that they elevated to a position of preeminence and strived to preserve for posterity: the laudatory song praising the deeds of the dead. Bards were enlisted to perform these uplifting alternatives to weepy-eyed lamentations. The occasion of death now became what we might call a "teachable moment"—a chance to instill 'manly' virtues, by means of suitable music, in the hearts and minds of the onlookers.

We have flip-flopped these priorities today. We now expect songs to express personal feelings, especially the most intimate kind. Songs of boasting and praise aren't unknown to modern listeners—they flourish in hip-hop (which reflects a surprising number of similarities with the ancient songs of praise by Pindar and others), as well as in calypso and a few other genres—but, except for this handful of exceptions, such exercises in braggadocious bardic behavior thrive only on the periphery of popular music. And any song that celebrates a politician or a military campaign makes us uneasy, entering a sphere that, at worst, resembles propaganda, or at best ought to be the domain of historians and social scientists. Judging by hit recordings and YouTube views, we have returned to the much older paradigm that sees music as an expression of sexuality, especially female sexuality, and deeply felt emotions. In a strange way, we have returned to the priorities of our Mesopotamian predecessors.

6

The Storyteller

We have now identified a battle line in music history. And this battle line will reappear, with surprising persistence, over the centuries. On the one hand, we encounter the music of order and discipline, aspiring to the perfection of mathematics and aligned with institutional prerogatives. On the other, we find music of intense feelings, frequently associated with magic or trance states, and resistant to control from above. This second kind of music often survives merely in hints and fragments or in some otherwise impaired condition. That tells you how cultural elites viewed it—or perhaps *feared it* would be a more accurate descriptor.

We have been taught to view the battle lines differently. The most familiar way of distinguishing music is as a competition between highbrow and lowbrow. The choice, we are told, is between the sophisticated music of the symphony hall and the populist tunes of the masses. But as we have already seen, this way of viewing the conflict misses the most essential elements, and unless we grasp the real issues at stake we will never comprehend the reasons why songs possess such power to disrupt social norms, or why the conflicts recur again and again over the course of centuries.

But here's the peculiar twist to the story: the institutional power brokers in music can't exist without periodic infusions of energy from the disreputable songs they want to exclude. This is the engine room of music history. The intense songs of outsiders and various marginalized groups possess power, and that power can't be ignored. It's like handling some dangerous radioactive substance that might provide energy for the entire city . . . or blow it up if things go wrong. That's a good way of conceptualizing music: you want it and need it, but it comes with a hazard warning.

The Greeks learned this firsthand when they tried to turn the lyric into a type of propaganda for elites and institutions. Pindar was held up for admiration as the greatest of the lyric poets, and his works were memorized by students and performed at banquets and other stately occasions, yet it remains an open question how much influence these songs exerted on the populace. Not long after Pindar's death, in the second half of the fifth century BC when ancient Greek civilization was at the height of its glory, the comic writer Eupolis already had to admit that the esteemed poet's works were seldom heard because the masses didn't care for them. The Greeks wanted to create a safe, respectable kind of song, and over time, even the music was removed from the lyric, to ensure that everything would be neat and orderly. Song got turned into mere text, drained of melody. But as the lyric gained respectability, it lost emotional intensity and much of its power to influence and inspire.

Even with Pindar, we aren't sure what role he played in the performance of his works, or whether they were intended for chorus or solo singer, and, if the latter, whether Pindar himself was the vocalist. Perhaps he was a behind-the-scenes presence, like Irving Berlin, Cole Porter, and other Tin Pan Alley tunesmiths in modern times, crafting songs for others to perform. Or maybe he trained and directed the performance, akin to a symphony conductor. We simply can't say with any assurance. But we know with absolute certainty that his lyrics upheld the prestige of the leaders and ruling institutions and were used as pedagogical tools.

As lyrics and other songs became more embedded as teachable moments, they gradually evolved into something you wrote and spoke, no longer a vibrant performance integrated into music and dance. By the time we arrive at the lyric poet Horace—perhaps the closest equivalent to Pindar in Roman society—these texts are clearly the work of writers, not singers. The authors may still adopt the pose of a musical performer. We find the phrase "I sing" in the opening line of the *Aeneid* and many other classical poems that no one expects to be sung. In Horace's biography, we find only one instance when he took part in an actual musical performance of his poetry, and that was by order of Emperor Augustus himself. This is the only situation in which we can be certain that the most famous lyricist in Latin literature actually composed what we nowadays call a lyric, namely, the words to a song.

Storytelling songs could teach lessons much better than the lyric, which had always relied more on emotional resonance than narrative clarity for its effects, and thus proved especially well suited for institutional and hierarchical needs. Storytelling songs preserved historical knowledge and religious dogma. They propagated treasured myths, cultural beliefs, and core learnings from generation to generation with extraordinary precision—you could call them the cloud storage of antiquity. And if the goal was to *praise worthy men*, as often was the case in these societies, the story song was unsurpassed. The most famous type, the epic, was built on the allure and excitement of heroic deeds. Best of all, the story song achieved all this while serving as diversion and entertainment. For this very reason, it could support power structures and elite privileges with listeners hardly aware that these purposes were served.

If you doubt the efficacy of songs as a data storage medium, consider the case of Maori children, who retain rich memories of their early childhood—in fact, they have the greatest recall of any culture measured. The average date of the first memory for members of their communities is 2.5 years of age. But when these individuals are questioned about the details of their oldest memories, they tend to describe them in different ways from people of other cultures. Maori are far more likely to connect these recollections to family stories, and less likely to refer to photographs and memorabilia. Mothers often tell children their 'birth story,' in which the arrival of a new member of the family is turned into a narrative. In this way, even an individual's sense of personal identity is grounded in storytelling. Other prominent incidents, such as trips or outings, are also preserved in this way—not as images in a scrapbook, but as part of the established lore of the family unit. Long after visual memories fade, the aural memories of a heard (or sung) tale remain.[1]

It is hard to escape the conclusion that storytelling shapes our brains in ways that even powerful images, such as home movies and family portraits, cannot match. Fieldwork in surviving hunter-gatherer societies tells us that storytelling skills are among the most prized talents in these communities. When anthropologist Andrea Migliano surveyed three hundred members of the Agta, a group of hunter-gatherers in the Philippines, she asked each individual to pick five members of their society that they would most want to live with. She expected that they would prefer those most skilled in hunting, or with the greatest physical strength, or perhaps with the most detailed medical knowledge. In fact, she learned that the Agta valued storytelling above all other skills. She concluded that these stories were more than just entertaining tales, but were key contributors to the survival and functional capabilities of the group. An old adage tells us that a picture is worth a thousand words, yet in terms of our personal development, the words seem to have the more lasting impact—but only if they are embedded in a tale.

The ability of tribal elders to remember long stories has been widely documented, but their skill in preserving scientific knowledge is just as impressive, if less well known. When members of the Navajo tribe collaborated with zoologists in classifying the insects in their native territories, they drew on their songs and folklore in providing descriptions of over 700 species. The Hanunóo tribe on the island of Mindoro in the Philippines proved far more skilled at identifying plants than the trained botanists who collaborated with them—they eventually classified 1,625 plants and provided in-depth information on their medicinal properties and suitability as food. The Matsés, who reside in the Amazonian rainforest on the frontier between Brazil and Peru, recently decided they should document their collective memories of traditional medicine in print—a process that resulted in a 500-page encyclopedia.[2]

Although these communities are separated by thousands of miles, they rely on a surprisingly similar set of cultural tools to preserve their accumulated knowledge. Songs are a key part of this process. "An Aboriginal elder might know a thousand songs," notes researcher Lynne Kelly. "Songs must encode every landscape feature and every resource, not just the plants and animals. Elders need to know where to find flint and obsidian, salt and ochre, while the ability to navigate across terrain with no roads, that often appears the same in all directions, is critical to collecting these resources and to trading them." The leading experts on memory dating back to ancient times have noted the power of connecting facts to physical locations, whether real or imagined—a technique that worked back in the sixteenth century for Jesuit missionary Matteo Ricci, whom many considered a wizard because of his ability to recall lengthy texts and word lists (which he could also recite in reverse order, if requested) via his "memory palace" technique. This method is still the foundational mnemonic trick for eight-time world memory champion Dominic O'Brien in the current day. "All modern memory champions use the same method," Kelly notes, "as no more effective method has been found."[3]

The combination of songs and physical milestones is especially powerful in storing information—but mystifying to outsiders unaware of the power of this technique. Sue Churchill, a wildlife ecologist, discovered its efficacy firsthand when working with tribal elders whose expertise with the Australian songlines guided her research into the habitats of cave-dwelling bats. She was traveling without maps in an old Land Cruiser in search of caves the elders had not visited in years. At one point, they needed to cross one hundred kilometers through sand dunes "to a cave that couldn't be seen if you stood more than three meters from its small vertical entrance," Churchill wrote. "The old men who guided us were navigating by the shape of the sand dunes. They would stop every now and then and sing a long song to help them remember the landmarks of the journey." These were songs they had learned as young men, but they continued to serve as guideposts decades later.[4]

Other cultures have relied on handmade objects to fill this same role. In Siberia, the Evenki managed to 'store' seven hundred songs on a notched stick. In Native American communities, beaded belts could serve a similar function. For the Luba Empire in precolonial Central Africa, important information was retained with the help of the *lukasa*, a kind of memory board or memory stick—even this casual description summons up mental images of semiconductors and USB devices—decorated with carved reliefs or embedded beads and shells to expand its storage capacity.

Lynne Kelly now believes that Stonehenge, and other formations like it, served as a way of preserving tribal memories for groups that had shifted from nomadic, hunting lifestyles to stable farming lives in one location. Fearing they would lose valuable information, they constructed more compact landmarks that could be used as mnemonic placeholders. In this way, the stones were large-scale equivalents of the traditional memory sticks. Modern-day researchers lament that the people who created Stonehenge were nonliterate, and thus left behind no documents. But in this instance, the surviving stones may be the very reason why such texts do not exist. Under this hypothesis, we simply lack the songs and knowledge that the stones were built to preserve.

I dwell on these matters to make clear how much we underestimate the power of song, which we are taught to view as a mere tool of entertainment. And when we find a particular kind of song that possesses a special potency, whether because it stores information or shapes behavior or exerts some other impact on the community, we need to look for the ways in which power brokers fought to control its scope and influence. Storytelling may seem like merely another form of entertainment, but these songs could be a matter of life or death, inspiring wars and romantic escapades and a hundred other momentous events. If you found a way to control these songs, you could shape the behavior of entire communities and protect your own position of status or authority.

Even literate societies learned that stories and cultural lore become more resilient when preserved in the form of songs. And the ultimate proof of this fact is the very survival of these stories in the current day. Much of what we know about the ancient Greeks comes from those great sung epics the *Iliad* and the *Odyssey*. The 1853 discovery of the *Epic of Gilgamesh*, often considered the oldest surviving major literary work, is the most significant breakthrough in the history of Assyriology. It's unclear whether the Hindu epics the *Mahabharata* and the *Ramayana* originated as recitations or musical performances, but I tend to believe that the comment by the Greek orator Dio Chrysostom (born circa AD 40), that "Homer's poetry is sung even in India, where they have translated it into their own speech and tongue," actually refers to these Sanskrit works. In these and many other instances, sung stories have survived for thousands of years, and now serve as foundational texts in the study of myth, literature, history, and—how peculiar that this last ingredient is rarely noted—music.[5]

That last fact would seem obvious, yet if you track down the ten or twenty most influential academic works on epics, you will find that not one was written by a music scholar. Indeed, we rarely rely on songs to tell stories nowadays, and thus minimize how closely integrated these traditions once were. Instead, we expect songs to convey vignettes of intense personal emotion. These most frequently relate to love—the inspiration behind around 90 percent of our most cherished melodies. But in a pinch, another powerful feeling can suffice. For a punk rocker, it might be anger, for a rapper it could be defiance, for a country singer it may be that lonesome feeling you get when you drive a pickup truck off into the sunset. But a song in the current day needs a powerful emotion, and without that you won't find an audience, and you don't have a hit.

But if music specialists have forgotten about the epic, literary scholars have been forced to consider the importance of music. In fact, the single biggest breakthrough in our scholarly understanding of epic poetry and oral transmission took place during musical entertainments at a coffeehouse. No, I am not exaggerating. In the mid-1930s, Harvard classicist Milman Parry and his student Albert Lord changed our understanding of Homer and the origin of traditional epics by leaving the libraries and archives behind and seeking out the last living performing bards in the actual settings where they made music. Even at this late stage in the shift from oral cultures to literate culture, these venerable singers of tales could still be found, but only in locales relatively untouched by modern entertainment—most notably, out-of-the-way coffee bars.

"The best method of finding singers was to visit a Turkish coffee house, and make inquiries there," Albert Lord later explained. That hadn't been the original plan. Lord's teacher Parry had first hoped to undertake fieldwork in the Soviet Union, but he couldn't secure the necessary permissions and travel documents. He then decided that the Serbo-Croatian epic tradition in the Balkans might provide a source, but only if he could find musicians still capable of performing the old songs. Equipped with a custom-made transcription machine that incorporated two turntables with a toggle switch—thus enabling Parry to make continuous recordings of long songs—the Harvard scholars embarked on a fifteen-month collecting expedition that permanently changed our conceptions of the epic and the origins of Western culture. Their biggest breakthrough came with an introduction to the extraordinary person they later dubbed "our Yugoslav Homer." A Turk in the coffeehouse said he knew many singers, but the best was Avdo Meðedović, an illiterate peasant farmer who performed elaborate songs while accompanying himself on the *gusle*, a one-string instrument with surprising similarities to the diddley bow used by so many Mississippi blues musicians.[6]

One of the main goals of this book, as noted at the outset, is to show how 'respectable' musical traditions now associated with cultural elites actually come from outsiders—slaves, bohemians, rebels, peasants, and others on the margins of society. Here we find a striking example of this principle at work: not only did an untutored peasant reveal the essence of epic poetry to our esteemed

Harvard scholars, and change the course of modern scholarship, but this farmer actually represents the closest modern counterpart we have to Homer and the literary masters who created the foundational works of Western culture.

This is hardly an isolated instance. At almost the very same moment that Milman Parry encountered Avdo Međedović, the great American song collector John Lomax met an amazing performer he would later describe as a "black Homer." This remarkable individual, who went by the name of James "Iron Head" Baker, was an African American serving a ninety-nine-year sentence at Huntsville Penitentiary in Texas. Like Međedović, Iron Head was in his sixties, apparently past his peak years, and a member of that last generation of songsters born before the invention of the phonograph. The careful student of cultural history finds other such individuals, usually mentioned in the margins of surviving documents—for example, the herder Beatrice Bernardi, who dazzled the famous art critic John Ruskin with her ability to sing lengthy tales by memory. Or the illiterate epic singer Vasily Shchegolenok, who amazed Leo Tolstoy with his storytelling, so much so that the famous novelist even emulated aspects of the peasant's style of delivery in his own writing. In fact, at the very start of the history of our own English language we encounter the mysterious figure of Caedmon, another herder, who so impressed the Venerable Bede with his song that the latter preserved "Caedmon's Hymn" in his early eighth-century ecclesiastical history. It is the oldest surviving poetic work in English.

When I studied literature as an English major in college, I was taught almost nothing about the oral tradition and how it shaped landmark works in our cultural heritage. We studied Chaucer, but never learned about the influence of performative storytelling on his work—even though the framing plot of *The Canterbury Tales* revolves around precisely this kind of tradition. More recently, scholar Christopher Cannon has asked whether Chaucer really was a writer at all, and suggests that he might have recited all eight thousand lines of his *Troilus and Criseyde* from memory. Cannon notes that a famous portrait of the author owned by the library of

Corpus Christi College, Cambridge, is often described as "Chaucer reading from a book," but there is no book shown in the image. "This Chaucer," he concludes, "is not a writer but a declaimer or reciter." An even more persuasive case can be made for John Milton, that other great epic poet of the English language, as a performer/reciter. We know with certainty that the blind poet dictated *Paradise Lost* to his daughters. By his account, the lines came to him during the night, and he was ready to share them for transcription with the coming of dawn. The third canonic poet of the English language, Shakespeare, was also clearly a performer, on the stage if not elsewhere, and music played a key role in his plays—his works include or refer to around one hundred songs. Shakespeare apparently had little interest in turning his performances into printed books: the first publication of his plays, in quarto format, almost certainly occurred without his participation, relying perhaps on audience members or actors drawing on their recollection of lines spoken onstage. Add *Beowulf*, the anonymous oral epic that is the first great work of English literature, into the mix, and you get a surprising result. The four writers who defined the greatness of English poetry during its first thousand years after "Caedmon's Hymn"—Chaucer, Shakespeare, Milton, and the author of *Beowulf*—were not really writers in any conventional sense. They were performers and reciters, more akin to traditional bards than modern authors, and each relied on extraordinary skills of memorization.[7]

Lord and Parry found a marked resistance to relying on written texts in their field research. In fact, they claimed that every one of the great singers of tales they encountered was illiterate. The scholars concluded that this was a more consistent trait than blindness, often associated with great bards (even Homer himself, according to legend). In other words, the ability to see played a marginal role in a singer's success, but the ability to read would almost certainly hinder the development of the prodigious capacity for memory these musicians demonstrated. In the most striking demonstration of this gift, Međedović recounted a song over the course of seven days that later filled an entire book. This work, *The Wedding of Smailagić Meho*, goes on for 12,311 lines and is roughly the same length as Homer's *Odyssey*. Indeed, Lord later noted that the tale shared many similarities with the story of Telemachus in the famous Greek epic.

Parry and Lord had now solved one of the great mysteries of classical scholarship. At the time they conducted their research, most experts believed that the Homeric epics had originated in a society that lacked writing. This theory raised the obvious question of how such complex works were preserved. Međedović and his peers made it clear that writing might actually have been a disability to those who invented sung stories. That's sobering for us to consider in our own age, when data storage is so prevalent and the memory skills of individuals are proportionately devalued by society. Are certain kinds of creativity, even today, hindered by our reliance on external storage?

But if writing was no asset to the inventors of these tales, a musical instrument proved essential. The Harvard researchers found, to their dismay, that some singers could not remember the words to their songs unless they had their *gusle* in their hands. One performer explained that "he could repeat a song that he had heard only once, *provided that he heard it to the gusle.*" As soon as the musical element was removed, the stories fell apart. Singers who dictated texts to a transcriber got muddled over the number of syllables in a line, sometimes lapsing into prose. "Such cases are instructive," Lord concluded, "because they indicate that a dictated text, even when done under the best of circumstances and by the best of scribes, is never entirely, from the point of view of the line structure, the same as a sung text. . . . The singer is struggling with traditional patterns under unusual circumstances."[8]

A similar warning should be given, however, to readers: the traditional epics, despite centuries of precedent in treating them as literary texts, do not reveal their true essence on the printed page. They are, first and foremost, embedded in our musical heritage, and would neither have emerged from human history nor lasted until the present day without the support of rhythm and melody. If you track down the films made of Avdo Međedović in performance, you will sense this immediately. The mesmerizing quality of the music, both for the performer and the audience, jumps out at you even in the grainy footage and poorly recorded audio of 1930s portable technology.

When I first encountered these performances, back in my early twenties, I was struck by the similarities with jazz. Lord and Parry found that the only way epic singers could deliver such complex stories was by relying on improvisation and the manipulation of a wide range of verbal formulas and patterns. Certain phrases were used again and again, because their syllabic length and meter made them useful in a range of contexts. At the same time that I was reading Lord's research, I was studying transcriptions of jazz solos by saxophonist Charlie Parker and other bebop improvisers, and I saw the exact same thing in these musical performances. Parker relied on certain trademark phrases, and demonstrated an extraordinary mastery in fitting them into different contexts. The notes and accents might stay the same, and even the overall phrase length—sometimes only a couple of beats and rarely more than one or two measures—would almost never change. But Parker would exercise endless ingenuity in using these melodic building blocks in different harmonic contexts, or he would start them on different beats, or insert them at unexpected places in a phrase. Studying such strategies in the context of jazz was a revelation to me: I saw that what might sound, to an untrained ear, like a completely spontaneous improvisation often involved a fair amount of repetition and clever juxtaposition of formulas. And then I learned from Lord and Parry that the repetitions in Homer's epics—for example, the recurring references to "rosy-fingered dawn" or "swift-footed Achilles"—arose from similar methodologies. The singer of tales, just like a jazz soloist, turns to these set phrases in order to meet the demands of improvising creatively in the heat of live performance. After achieving this insight, I could never read Homer (or other epic writers) in the same way again.

One last finding from Parry and Lord is worth highlighting, and it has less to do with the performer than the audience. Epic song, the scholars learned, "forms at the present time [the mid-1930s], or until very recently, the chief entertainment of the adult male population in the villages and small towns." Here again the elite status of these works is called into question, and the traditional epic starts to look more like the blockbuster movies, TV shows, and video games of our own day. In the coffeehouses of the Balkans, our scholars saw firsthand how a work such as the *Iliad* or *Beowulf* or the *Chanson de Roland*, could have served as mass entertainment when presented as a musical narrative. The listeners might very well be illiterate peasants—no different from the performers, as we have seen—but that proved no obstacle to their enjoyment of these 'literary' classics. Here again, our conventional distinctions between highbrow and lowbrow music mislead us, keeping us from grasping the reality at hand.[9]

But if we label these works as entertainment, we should hesitate before describing them as *escapist*. Nowadays those two words often go together. Entertainment is escapism in contemporary society. But matters were far different in the traditional societies that gave birth to these epics. As we have already noted, songs serve as repositories of knowledge and wisdom for these societies. An epic such as the *Iliad* helped prepare young males for the life of a soldier. Homer describes the deaths of 201 Trojans and 54 Greeks during the course of that epic—and this involves the use of a range of weapons, including spears (responsible for 100 of these fatalities), swords, arrows, and rocks. If you saw that kind of carnage in a movie nowadays, you would assume it was put on the screen to add to the excitement. But in ancient Greece, members of the audience were learning about situations they might very well encounter in real life. You may need to kill someone with a spear, or with a sword, or—lacking such tools—with a big rock. Even if you didn't want to participate in such doings, the Persians, or perhaps even your fellow Greeks in Sparta, might force your hand.

But even in ancient times, the entertainment value of these story songs made them susceptible to potential use as propaganda tools and supports for the ruling class. Although a new way of singing might originate as the expression of a peasant, an outsider, a bohemian, or a rebel, the established powers will seek ways of channeling its force into a socially acceptable direction. This process is so ingrained in human history—from the *Shijing* to Elvis—that we do well to look for it, even in cases where firsthand accounts and direct evidence are lacking.

These recurring patterns allow us to construct a plausible hypothesis about the nature of the sung epic. Homer and other singing bards were probably not born into nobility, but more likely achieved their influence through their remarkable mental capabilities, much like Avdo Međedović, Beatrice Bernardi, Caedmon, or James "Iron Head" Baker. Whether a single individual or a group was responsible for the finished epic is open to debate, but what we have learned from these modern bards is that a person of genius is perfectly capable of creating, memorizing, and performing epic works with minimal input from collaborators. The resulting song proves its power in actual performance and finds an enthusiastic audience, although these first hearers may well share the same lowly origins as the singer of tales. But the ruling class eventually discovers the value of narratives that have such inherent appeal, and seeks out ways of turning these songs to their own advantage. The epic is now celebrated for its value in stirring up patriotism, inspiring the courage of solders in battle, creating group cohesion, and justifying various political initiatives. At this stage, the epic is preserved as a revered text, and its origins as the creative work of a herder or a peasant are forgotten. The result—and this endpoint our scholars well know, because it is the starting point for their research—is that the poem survives in great detail, while the biography of the poet is virtually a blank page.

The available evidence on the preservation of the Homeric epics tends to support this theory. The zeal to preserve and propagate these texts can be traced back to a key turning point in the sixth century BC, when the Athenian tyrant Peisistratus, according to legend, issued a decree that the Homeric epics would be recited in their entirety at a midsummer festival. Many see this era as the juncture when these sung poems got enshrined as revered texts, and it can hardly be a coincidence that a dictator seeking legitimacy and popular support would align himself with Homer and the heroic epic tradition. Another story from the sixth century BC tells of the Athenians and Megarians involved in a dispute over control of Salamis, with each side citing a passage from the *Iliad* for support. Whatever the origins of these sung narratives, their destiny was to serve as political tools.

7

The Invention of the Singer

oday we take for granted the connection between singer and song. It's a kind of cause-and-effect. The singer creates the song, and the music is an expression of the emotions and inner life that went into its making. We are so fascinated by this process that the performer gets more attention than the music. I'll even wager that more people can identify world-famous singers from photographs than from recordings. In the parlance of modern commerce, the artist's image is a kind of brand or embodied logo for the music.

We can hardly imagine a world in which the opposite was true. Yet for most of human history, the song was more powerful than the singer—performers and composers were so unimportant that their names weren't preserved. This anonymity of the singer went beyond hiding a work's origins. The songs themselves did *not* express personal emotions. From a sociocultural standpoint, we might say the composer didn't exist. The music articulated communal priorities and demands, and if we want to find a source for these works we do well to forget about our mythos of the individual artist and focus instead on the power structures of society.

Even in those explicitly sexual songs attributed to the Sumerian high priestess Enheduanna, her inner life is strangely absent from the proceedings—despite the apparent intimacy of the lyrics. We never forget that her actions are embedded in ritual and driven by higher priorities than her own desires. She is playing a role, and self-expression is not part of the script.

Musical practices eventually changed, and song turned into a platform for the inner life, almost a kind of musical autobiography. Songs might actually deserve credit as the point of origin for psychology, a door into the psyche for societies that didn't have access to Freud or Jung or pay-by-the-hour therapists. Music not only expressed the inner life, but legitimized it as something worthy of expression and consideration. In the context of civilizations that lacked democratic ideals and protections of individual rights, the importance of this shift in the nature of art should not be minimized. Song could now serve not only the deities and rulers, but also the lowly performer, who even begins to achieve a kind of glamorous allure in the process.

Sappho, the Greek poet of Lesbos, is often given credit for inventing the lyric, the song form that serves as the main conduit for this music of emotional expression—although even here the ritualistic quality of her surviving texts is as pronounced as the confessional aspects. We need to dig back even earlier, however, to find that magical moment when singers first stood out as individuals against the institutional and social framework and began to express their souls in song. More than five hundred years before Sappho, we discover the first stirrings of this more personal approach in the surviving songs of the Egyptian New Kingdom, which date back to the thirteenth century BC. If we want to trace the history of the modern concept of the singer-songwriter, the creative spirit who turns private emotions into music, this is our proper starting point, the birthplace for much of what we cherish in songs today.

This is an unlikely setting for the singer to emerge as an individual. Egyptian culture saw artists as anonymous, interchangeable figures. We don't know the name of a single ancient Egyptian writer who can be linked with certainty to a body of literary work. No painter is identified with a painting, and few sculptors are known by name. Even when a sage is mentioned, such as the esteemed polymath Imhotep, no book of writings survives to document the personal expressions of the supposed genius. And songs are never connected by name with their performers or composers.

Yet a marked change can be detected in Egyptian attitudes toward music around the same time the first love lyrics appear. Surviving art shows Egyptian musicians performing in many contexts, ranging from temple rituals to military endeavors, but the most frequently depicted setting is now the banquet. Here we find string and wind instruments, percussion and singers, as well as people clapping and dancing. During the course of the New Kingdom, which extended from the sixteenth to the eleventh centuries BC, a markedly sensual quality becomes more prominent in these scenes. We see flowers, jewelry, and other evidences of luxury. An image from the tomb of Kynebu in Thebes, for example, shows female performers wearing flimsy, transparent gowns, and two of them are engaged in a provocative dance. This is obviously no ritualized funeral banquet, but a festive occasion for carnality and self-indulgence.

This kind of eroticism takes on even more prominence in images of musicians found in the Turin Papyrus, which dates from approximately 1150 BC. Some have even labeled this artifact as ancient pornography, or, in the words of one pundit, the "world's first men's mag." This striking collection of images shows attractive women trying to play musical instruments and perform sex acts at the same time. The men are balding and overweight, hardly candidates for the pantheon of gods, so it's clear we are witnessing something very different from the ritualized sexuality of the fertility cults. Indeed, it's hard to describe the scene as depicting anything less than a full-scale orgy.[1]

Is it mere coincidence that this scandalous papyrus was found in Deir el-Medina, the same locale that gave us the most extraordinary love songs of antiquity? I don't think so. These are the same lyrics scholar Peter Dronke called in as evidence when seeking to prove that the different musical traditions of the world testified to universal human attributes.

> *Her name is that which lifts me up. . . .*
> *When I see her I am well again,*
> *When she opens her eyes, my body is young again,*
> *When she speaks, I grow strong again,*
> *When I embrace her, she banishes evil from me.*[2]

This song, and others like it, did not come from the pharaohs or nobles of the New Kingdom, but instead from the artisans who played a key role in the construction of their tombs in the Valley of the Kings on the West Bank of the Nile opposite Thebes. When these extraordinary documents first came to light, some described them as songs of the common people and the poor lower classes of ancient Egypt. But that's hardly an accurate description of the inhabitants of Deir el-Medina, where these workers lived with their families. By the standards of the day, they were well paid. They enjoyed leisure time, and owned cattle and other valuable property. They were also more highly educated than the typical Egyptian. A large percentage of the inhabitants of Deir el-Medina could read and write, perhaps even a majority of them. By contrast, literacy among the wider population was rare—probably less than 10 percent. If your work involved inscribing hieroglyphs on a tomb wall, or keeping administrative records, or following plans on a complex construction project, literacy was a great asset, and often a necessity. No, these weren't the poor, but neither were they rulers and elites. Here, for the first time in human history, we get a clear sense of how songs could express the inner lives of individuals who weren't at the top of the institutional power structure.

If you were writing a history of personal autonomy and human rights, this small village would demand your attention. A labor dispute during the reign of Ramesses III, ignited by a reduction in grain distributions to the workers, may have been the first recorded strike in human history. The disgruntled workers even staged what we would now call a 'sit-in' at a temple site, and 'management' eventually met their demands. Again, this can hardly be a coincidence—we see here, as elsewhere, that innovations in the music of personal expression are linked to an expansion in human rights. This same village also gave us many of the best-known literary works of ancient Egypt, including satire and narrative fiction. This conjunction of circumstances offers invaluable insights into the kinds of societies that foster creative expression.

Perhaps we need to reevaluate how we define a *political* song. When most people hear that term, they conjure up images of anti-war chants at student protests, or defiant workers singing "The Internationale." Most music fans know that these protest songs exist, but don't pay much attention to them, assuming they represent only the tiniest portion of our cultural soundscapes. The idea that traditional love songs might serve as radical political statements is a strange one, almost a paradoxical one. The lyrical expression of intimate emotion is the *exact opposite* of the political song, according to conventional wisdom. Yet the history of music tells a very different story. Few things are more threatening to power brokers than the signs of individualism and self-directed behavior embedded in a new kind of love song, whether in ancient Egypt or during our own lifetimes.

Just ask the protesters who took part in the Stonewall uprising in 1969. Stonewall sounds like the name of a battlefield fortification or a Civil War general, and might even seem out of place as the identity of a dance hall—in this case, a nightclub on Christopher Street in Manhattan that allowed gay couples to dance in the face of constant harassment from cops. But those overtones of combat were fulfilled when club patrons and their allies decided to confront the police, and after a series of defiant and sometimes violent responses forced authorities to back down. These six days of protests and resistance are today recognized as "the motivating force in the transformation of the gay political movement," according to historian David Carter. In the aftermath, gay rights organizations sprang up in New York and other cities, mobilizing support and political intervention. There's now a monument at the site of the Stonewall riots, and those who lived through the turmoil know from firsthand experience how threatening romantic music can be to the ruling elite.[3]

Yet the same thing had happened five years earlier with the British Invasion—here we find a war metaphor deliberately used to describe the introduction of a new kind of love song into American life. When the Beatles performed for seventy-three million television viewers on *The Ed Sullivan Show* on February 9, 1964, every number they performed was a love song, yet that persistent focus on romance only alarmed parents and other authority figures all the more. And the same thing happened with Elvis in the 1950s, Sinatra in the 1940s, swing in the 1930s, jazz and blues in the 1920s, and on and on, all the way to the troubadours, or even further to Sappho, or the Eighteenth Dynasty in Egypt. They were all just singing love songs, but they were also, in their own way, protest songs, because they aimed to change society and its norms. When dealing with music, the personal *is* the political, and always has been.

Deir el-Medina offers us still other clues to how musical innovations take place. I have argued elsewhere that new approaches to art spread like diseases—indeed, the use of the term *viral* to describe this process could hardly be more apt. Even today, the mathematical formulas applied by businesses to forecast the dissemination of a new product or technology are drawn from the medical field. This entire field of analysis originated in the attempt to predict the course of plagues and contagions. The arts are no different, and the same conditions that help spread a disease also lead to artistic revolutions. The most significant causal factor, in both instances, is the close intermingling of people who come from previously separated population groups. This is why port cities and melting pots—New York, New Orleans, Liverpool, Venice, Havana, and others—exert so much influence on music history, and why some of the unhealthiest places on earth change the course of cultural history. The high point of ancient Greek tragedy coincides with the Great Athenian Plague of 430 BC. The Black Death killed much of Florence's population in 1348, but the birth of the Renaissance is dated, by many scholars, to that same city in 1350. Shakespeare's artistic achievements took place amidst recurring deadly plagues in England. New Orleans gave birth to jazz at a time when it was also the most unhealthy major city in the United States, with an average lifespan for an African American resident a mere thirty-six years. The very factors that made these communities cosmopolitan and open-minded, by the standards of their day, turned them into sources of virality from both an artistic and epidemiological standpoint.[4]

The same must have been true at Deir el-Medina. Although it was a small community, more than thirty different foreign names have been found in the materials unearthed by archaeologists— an extraordinary diversity in the context of the time. Skilled artisans must have come from great distances to live there. This was the melting pot of ancient Egypt, and the findings there testify to the connection between multiculturalism and artistic innovation. When so many diverse people bring conflicting practices and attitudes to a new locale, a creative flux results that challenges old-fashioned ways and creates new ones. Yet here, too, we see signs of the associated public health issues that are characteristic of these same creative communities. Stanford archaeologist Anne Austin has even suggested that the birth of public health policy originated in this same Egyptian village. As infection and other medical problems spread among the inhabitants, overseers responded by implementing 'state-subsidized' policies and programs. We will see this connection between musical innovation, diversity, and disease at many junctures in the pages ahead.[5]

The appearance of this new kind of song is a milestone moment in the history of music, yet we can merely guess at how it was disseminated from Egypt—or perhaps the love lyric wasn't disseminated, but sprang up independently in different places, spurred on by some quasi-universal drive toward self-expression and personal autonomy. Could the lyric have traveled from Egypt to Greece, where it later flourished under the influence of the most famous ancient singer of intimate songs, Sappho? Hundreds of years and kilometers separate the two settings. Yet I note that even today the island of Lesbos, home to Sappho, is the most frequent entry point for refugees from the Middle East seeking a new home in Europe. At the height of the Syrian crisis in 2016, new arrivals would show up on Lesbos almost every day, making their treacherous journey on small boats, rafts, and inflatable crafts. Even as I write, thousands of refugees still reside on this island. Certainly Lesbos must have served as a meeting point between cultures even in ancient times. We can state with some confidence, from observing comparable situations in other parts of the world, that songs are the possessions most likely to survive long journeys, remaining the property of the newcomer even when everything else has been taken away. We can't prove that the confessional song of love arrived in the Western world by this path of transmission, but it stands out as a persuasive hypothesis.

We have even better reason to believe that the love lyrics of Egypt influenced the Song of Songs, that strange and powerful work of Judeo-Christian scripture that mixes religious belief and eroticism in a poetic text unlike anything else in the Bible. Commentators have long struggled to reconcile this overt sensuality with the expectations we bring to holy scripture, and have resorted to elaborate symbolic interpretations—viewing the invitations to sexual intimacy in the Song of Songs as references to the relationship between God and the people of Israel, or between Christ and his bride, the Church. Many mystics have been drawn to this text, finding in its poetic passages a call to passionate union with the divine. Martin Luther constructed a political interpretation of the text—reading it as Solomon's words of thanks and praise for God's confirmation of his kingship. More recently, feminist theologians have been drawn to this section of the Bible, which seems to express a woman's sentiments, embracing it as a platform for defusing the patriarchal ethos of the Old Testament.

Yet those familiar with the sacred marriage ritual of ancient Mesopotamia and the love songs unearthed in Deir el-Medina cannot help but see the Song of Songs as an extension of these earlier traditions. The apparent paradoxes in the text merely reflect the clash of different musical paradigms. The prevailing tension in the work is the same one that recurs again and again in ancient music, namely, the unresolved question of whether song should serve the religious sphere, the political sphere, or the personal sphere. All three vie for control of the scriptural text. As a result, we have three corresponding ways of defining the narrative voice of the poem: it can be interpreted as the song of a king, or a prophet, or a lover. To the modern mind, those are three different stances, but in the sacred marriage ritual they coexisted.

Solomon, by tradition the author of the Song of Songs, can be described in all three ways. But even his ability to take on each of these roles leaves much unexplained. A female voice also emerges almost at the very beginning of the work: "Let him kiss me with the kisses of his mouth: for thy love is better than wine. . . . The king hath brought me into his chambers. . . . I am black, but comely, O ye daughters of Jerusalem." If we take the text at face value, this is not the voice of Solomon, but of his black lover. Needless to say, there is firm resistance to the surface meanings here.

Rabbi and scholar Michael V. Fox believes that "Egyptian love poetry was sung in Palestine." The sacred text thus must be seen as "a late offshoot of an ancient and continuous literary tradition." But such obviously secular—and sensual—lyrics seem mismatched with the context. How did they end up in the Bible? The idea that ancient Israelites couldn't tell the difference between love songs and religious songs simply defies belief. The same is true of those who think the inclusion of the Song of Songs in scripture was some sort of mistake. In fact, a surviving account tells of Rabbi Aqiba complaining, almost two thousand years ago, about people singing this sacred text in taverns for entertainment. Religious authorities were well aware of the potential misuse of the Song of Songs; nonetheless, they must have felt they needed this particular song. Why? First of all, we don't need to embrace implausible theories based on grand misunderstandings of a fairly straightforward text. We can find a far more likely explanation by looking at other examples from music history—when, for example, St. Francis borrowed from the techniques of the troubadours for his religious canticle, or when the Vatican tried to take over the opera and turn its scandalous music into the service of the pope, as happened in Rome during the 1630s, or when Elvis Presley was invited to the White House by Richard Nixon. The dynamic is easy to understand: power brokers want to take advantage of the allure of sinful, sensual music, so they attempt an odd balancing act: borrowing it and trying to put it to the service of the prevailing institutions. The result is often awkward—go look at a photo of Ronald Reagan's meeting with Michael Jackson, if you doubt it—but both parties gain from the transaction. King Solomon was no different. Even ancient prophets knew they could strengthen their divinely inspired messages if they mixed them up with popular lyrics. The apparent difficulty of deciphering the Song of Songs disappears when approached from this perspective.[6]

We also know how this story ends. The authorities try to control these passionate songs, but music resists this kind of imposed respectability and subservience to ruling institutions. Over the long run, songs defy the ruling class and create an expanded space for individual freedom and personal autonomy. Commentators may try to pretend that the women expressing their sexual desire in the songs of the "Airs of the States" from the *Shijing* were actually offering Confucian precepts on government, but the surviving texts do more to celebrate private life than to promote public virtue. Sappho's intimate expressions were supplanted by Pindar's praise of worthy men, but nowadays, Sappho speaks to us more profoundly, even in fragmented form, than those successors of hers who courted official favor. As a matter of fact, you don't even need to read any of these texts to figure out which paradigm prevailed in the long run: instead, just turn on the radio or watch the latest hit music videos. Songs of personal expression are everywhere, while hymns expressing official dogmas are nowhere to be found, except in those rare dictatorships that force people to sing the officially sanctioned lyrics of the powers-that-be. In North Korea, you can hear pop songs entitled "We Shall Hold Bayonets More Firmly," "The Joy of Bumper Harvest Overflows Amidst the Song of Mechanization," "Potato Pride," and "I Also Raise Chickens." But inside these authoritarian settings, songs of personal autonomy and self-assertion no doubt flourish in hiding, despite the hostility of authorities. And even North Korean propagandists try to borrow from elements of K-pop from across the border, craving its mass-market appeal. Ancient rulers would have recognized this gambit, because they practiced it themselves.

We ought to keep this latter example in mind as we study the different epochs of music history. The past was, in comparison with our own times, more like North Korea, and less like a hyperindividualist capitalist economy. In many instances, the songs that have survived aren't the ones that had the most significance in their time, and on those rare occasions when the music of the masses was preserved, it probably had to be purified and co-opted by institutional forces before gaining sufficient respectability to get set down on papyrus or parchment, or embedded in stone or on cuneiform tablets. This process continues in our day: consider the process of 'purification' a rap song undergoes before showing up on network television—the jarring, disruptive words that almost define the ethos of hip-hop are the first ones to get bleeped out by censors, or voluntarily removed by the performers themselves, who know they can't be too edgy on mass media. If this kind of winnowing and window-dressing goes on in our tolerant times, in societies that promise musicians the full protections of freedom of expression, imagine how much more often they happened under the authoritarian rulers of the past. So don't be surprised if a woman's erotic love song gets turned into a scriptural utterance by a king. That's how the history of music unfolds, especially for anything innovative or transgressive.

8

The Shame of Music

After the Pythagorean revolution, the rupture in Western music comes out into the open. Perhaps it was always there, that divide between the sacred and the vulgar, or, put differently, the insider and the outsider. But I'm not entirely convinced of that. Historians should always beware of seeking a Garden of Eden in their discipline, a distant era of holistic life without the antagonisms of social structures as we now know them. Even so, I still hold onto the possibility that our forebears, in those distant days of hunting and herding and primitive agriculture, knew only songs that everyone shared. Music possessed power—it was their technology and made things happen in the universe—but it was a communal resource. Everyone relied on it for the good of all, collectively and individually. Yet if that Edenic era ever existed, it had disappeared by 500 BC, the dawn of the era known as the Golden Age of Greece.

We now increasingly encounter a divide in the musical lives of nations, communities, even households. The politically sanctioned music, approved by elites, is celebrated, taught, propagated. But that can't hide the existence of a different sphere of music, far less dignified—although few details about it have been preserved for posterity. We know it existed, if only because of the vehement attacks against it. The ruling powers, alas, did little to document these scorned performances for our inspection. This is the single biggest reason why our accounts of music history are so one-sided, emphasizing the respectability of song while downplaying its capacity for subversion. In the context of ancient Greek music, this manifests itself as a deep fixation on tuning systems—a subject that has received enormous attention from scholars, more than any other aspect of the ancient music ecosystem, and with far less scrutiny applied to the discords and dangerous sounds such systems were designed to exclude. The culture was obsessed with removing 'noise' from its musical life, but that was only the beginning of its program to regulate song. In many ways, the zeal for tuning musical instruments must be viewed as a metaphor for a much more ambitious quest to instill harmony in society at large.

In Plato, we repeatedly encounter these two different kinds of music. One type is essential to a well-ordered society; the other is risky and must be dealt with cautiously, or perhaps even prohibited. Plato would have understood quite well the concept of subversive music—he constantly warns against it. "Beware of changing to a new form of music, since it threatens the whole system," he proclaims in the *Republic*. This passage is probably the source of Allen Ginsberg's spurious quote from Plato: "When the mode of the music changes, the walls of the city shake." The philosopher never said it in such stark words, but he no doubt feared that songs could undermine the social order. Yet Plato also argued that music, used prudently, could form character and even shape the soul—in fact, the term *soul music,* for all its Motown connotations, might be the most apt way of describing the supreme Platonic conception of song.[1]

Even before we can be educated and influenced by language, Plato reminds us, we are impacted by music. From the moment of birth, infants use sound as a tool of intervention with their surroundings—more so than other newborn animals. The human baby is the most vocal of all creatures, and the absence of linguistic tools limits neither the volume nor the persistence of the child's cries, as all parents can testify from sleep-depriving experience. Yet the world, in turn, can placate the child with sound and rhythm, via rocking and lullabies. The key fact, for Plato, is that song, even at this first stage of life, can correct an imbalance in the soul, restoring calm to an infant who, only a moment before, was unsettled and clamoring. Two types of sound meet head-on: the disordered cry of the baby and the soul-soothing lullaby of the mother. The soul music prevails.

These two models of music stand out in stark contrast in the *Phaedo*, Plato's account of the death of Socrates. Here Socrates differentiates between "popular music" (*dēmōdēs mousikē*) and the "greatest music" (*megistē mousikē*). The former is poetic and mythic, while the latter is aligned with philosophy. As he faces death, Socrates explains that he has devoted his life to the latter. The lower forms of music, in contrast, he has repeatedly attacked in his teachings. We see this in the *Symposium*, when Socrates rudely dismisses a young woman who plays the *aulos*, a reed instrument typically described as a flute in translations (we will follow that convention, although the fit isn't precise—this double-reed instrument probably sounded more like an oboe or even bagpipes), noting that such music is suitable only for women to hear. His dislike of this so-called flute is even more pronounced in the *Republic*, where he warns that it dissipates the spirit and cuts out the very sinews of the soul. Aulos music is for drunkards, he explains, yet even the music itself can intoxicate, without the alcohol. He is horrified that responsible individuals sometimes open their ears to this pernicious sound. "The result is that such people become quick-tempered, prone to anger, and filled with discontent."[2]

A musical instrument can do all that? Yet Aristotle shared this same horror of the aulos. "The flute is not an instrument which is expressive of moral character," he warns in the *Politics*. "It is too exciting." He then offers a strange supporting argument: namely, that a musician can't play the flute and use language at the same time, and so the potential for this music to serve as a tool of education is limited. String instruments are superior, in his mind, because they can accompany morally uplifting, sung messages. This shallow argument shows up repeatedly in diatribes aimed at the aulos, and sometimes the grimace on the face of a musician blowing into the instrument is offered as additional support. *Just look at the face of that aulos player! How disgusting!* Aristotle also held strong convictions about melodies and rhythms; some contribute to virtue, he explains, but others are dangerous and intoxicating. Indeed, every aspect of music requires *political* consideration and guidance. If rulers choose poorly, listeners might enter into a religious frenzy—and here the philosopher's words summon up images of Bacchic rites and practices that we would nowadays call shamanistic.[3]

How odd that the two foundational works of Western political philosophy, Plato's *Republic* and Aristotle's *Politics*, should devote so much attention to a specific wind instrument, or to any kind of music. Yet these are hardly exceptions. One can trace an opposition between the lyre and flute throughout the course of Western philosophy all the way down to Arthur Schopenhauer (who played the flute as part of a daily routine), his disciple Friedrich Nietzsche (who championed the flute, although he composed music primarily for piano and voice), and beyond. Nietzsche saw the lyre and flute as emblematic of the opposed Apollonian and Dionysian tendencies in ancient culture—the former emphasizing rule-making and restraint, the latter embracing rule-breaking and irrationality. The lyre, as a well-tuned string instrument, promotes the harmony and order of society, while the flute draws on human breath for its soul-shaking sounds, and thus serves as a dangerous instigator of passion and ecstatic states. Many readers see this opposition as symbolic, but for the leading Greek thinkers, some musical instruments were not just *emblems* for disorder but actually contributing *causes*, and as such needed to be regulated.

We may think we have left such debates behind in modern times, but anyone who has read cautionary statements on music from the modern heirs of Plato—for example, Allan Bloom in his book *The Closing of the American Mind*—will find similar arguments, although with the electric guitar replacing the flute as the source of moral contagion. Bloom is labeled as a conservative intellectual, but his views echo with surprising congruence those advocated on the Left by the modern Marxist philosopher Theodor Adorno, who also feared the negative impact of popular music. In fact, these seemingly old-fashioned ideas show up with surprising frequency in the works of many progressive modern thinkers. In Jean-Paul Sartre's novel *Nausea*, for example, the reader encounters a surprising resolution to the story when the protagonist Roquentin cures his existential angst by listening to a vocal recording—in an incident that inevitably reminds us of Plato's description, cited above, of a woman's singing bringing balance back to a troubled soul. No matter what political structure one advocates, the wrong music can apparently send it toppling. Perhaps the strangest aspect of this evolution is its reversal of the ancients' philosophical dichotomy. The guitar, a kind of modern lyre, is now the dangerous source of disorder, while the flute is seen as a prim, subdued instrument evoking respectability and orderliness. This is one of the most striking examples of the dialectic at play in music history in which *things turn into their opposites.*

This is not mere happenstance. The guitar shook things up in the twentieth century because it was the focal point for the African diaspora's attack on the Pythagorean paradigm that had dominated Western music since 500 BC. As blues guitar techniques entered the mainstream, they validated the use of bent notes and introduced sounds outside conventional scales. This assault on Pythagorean notions of playing in tune—which for centuries had required musicians to keep within the boundaries of carefully delineated scales and maintain a *proper* tone—threatened to overturn all the hierarchies of established music, both social and aural. We asked above what the Greeks were trying to eliminate by their obsession with tuning, and although the answer isn't specifically *the blues*, it was no doubt something along the same lines. They feared those dangerous manifestations of music that operate outside the rulebook of both scales and social control.

The distinctive bending of notes that first emerged in the blues, and later spread to jazz, R&B, rock, and other performance styles, was achieved at first with knives and parts of broken bottles, and later with a host of plugged-in technologies. Once again, weapons enter the sphere of music-making, as was the case with the first stirrings of human song, and it almost seems as if the radical practitioners of these bent guitar notes want to do physical violence to the very instruments that had been sanctioned by the established orders, those tuned strings so beloved by ancient philosophers. When the early blues guitarists put a knife to their guitar strings, they weren't really trying to kill Pythagoras and his philosophy of the well-tuned soul—but it sure looks like it. And, in a way, they were doing just that, albeit on a conceptual and symbolic level. This African counter-paradigm represented the most forceful attack in more than two millennia on the codification of music into a system of discrete notes. The knife could bend a guitar note in a way that a hand or finger could not. With a weapon in hand, the subversive performer could rediscover music's origins in unconstrained sound. As such, the modern guitar represents the exact danger that Plato had perceived in the flute more than two millennia before: an untuning of the universe.

Here's the oddest part of the story: When Plato was on his deathbed, instead of summoning a family member or friend to comfort him, the great philosopher wanted to listen to a Thracian maiden play the aulos, the same instrument he had vehemently opposed throughout his life. The comfort he now desired could not be provided by the well-tuned lyre, but required the dangerous flute. The type of music that upholds a political system was no longer suitable as he faced that most personal of all transitions, when life ends and the soul moves beyond the sway of rulers and laws. This is an extraordinary moment in the history of Western music, but one that is rarely even noticed. Plato embraced the very untuning of the universe he had worked so hard to prevent.

This deathbed conversion is testimony to the fluidity with which forbidden music can become legitimized. Yet it also reminds us of the allure of prohibited songs. Even their most vocal critics cannot resist their charms. Adorno, despite his hostility to rock music, learned the guitar as a youth, and later recalled the state of intoxication inspired by the dissonance of its sounds. Even Allan Bloom, so hostile to the electric guitar, recognized the power of music—perhaps far more than his critics did. "Music is the medium of the human soul in its most ecstatic condition of wonder and terror," he asserted. How many current-day record producers possess even half of Bloom's confidence in the enchantment of song?[4]

In our own time, we tend to see political science and music as completely different disciplines. If you tune into CNN on election night, you don't expect to encounter discussions about songs. Nor do you anticipate a digression on the relative merits of the flute and the guitar in a civics class at school. But this was no digression for Plato and Aristotle—or Allan Bloom, for that matter. They were afraid of music, and grasped with great clarity its subversive potential.

In this context, we arrive at the pioneering work of Aristoxenus, Aristotle's pupil, who has been called the father of musicology. Aristoxenus's surviving text *Elements of Harmony* is our first specialized study of the structure of music, but the most interesting parts of it deal with the author's irritation at other approaches to the subject, especially those rebellious practices that threatened to undermine his new science of sound. On the one hand, Aristoxenus wanted to distance himself from the extreme Pythagoreans, who believed that music was a matter of pure mathematics. Yet he was even fiercer in denouncing a group he called the *harmonikoi*—the harmonicists—performers he bitterly attacked for their ignorance and pretensions. His account is vague and sometimes contradicts itself, but many of the details he provides remind me of early twentieth-century denunciations of jazz and blues musicians. Aristoxenus was irritated by how the harmonicists found music in their instruments instead of recognizing the superiority of elaborate theoretical schema; he disliked the simple diagrams they used, which, like a jazz player's fake books, left out the richer details; and he scorned their desire to court the favor of amateurs. Another attack against the *harmonikoi* appears in a papyrus discovered at Hibeh in Egypt in 1902, but here, too, details are scant, although we get a clear sense that the writer abhorred this group's rule-breaking practices, viewing them as a kind of moral laxness. These diatribes provide no adequate summary of the songs of the *harmonikoi,* and scholars are still undecided on the scope and specifics of their activities. As is so often the case in the history of music, we are left to reconstruct songs that subvert the system merely from surviving accusations and reproofs. Yet the very intensity of these denunciations indicates that the rise of a rational and systematic approach to musicology did not happen without opposition. A cadre of dissidents emerged virtually at the outset, and they earned condemnation and marginalization for their resistance. In this instance, the *harmonikoi* were effectively silenced, or at least prevented from sharing their perspectives in the surviving texts cherished by posterity.

For the ancients, the hostility and suspicion directed at music was more than just a matter for philosophizing. By the time of Plato, political leaders such as Alcibiades were expressing their contempt for the aulos and denouncing its coarse associations. A phrase referring to the aulos player's vulgarity became a proverb among the Greeks, and even the greatest performers on this instrument found themselves subject to scorn and ridicule. Many stories survive about Ismenias, a Theban aulos player who flourished around 400 BC and was famous both for his virtuosity and for the healing properties he claimed for his music. But when the philosopher Antisthenes heard praise of this artist's ability, he quipped that Ismenias couldn't be such a skilled aulos performer unless he had a bad character.

This growing concern over the political ramifications of music helps us understand otherwise puzzling circumstances. We now can grasp why Sappho, who had been honored in an earlier day as the greatest practitioner of lyric song, was turned into a comic figure two centuries later. Surviving sources tell us that Sappho was the title character in comedic works by Ameipsias, Amphis, Antiphanes, Diphilus, Ephippus, and Timocles. Our information on Greek Middle Comedy, which flourished in Athens from around 400 to 320 BC, is almost entirely secondhand, but we know that these dramatists relied on the ridicule of stock figures. In this context, the recurring appearance of Sappho serves as disturbing testimony to a marked shift in attitudes toward music in the post-Pythagorean

Greek world. The conflicting stories surrounding her that have survived can also be explained, at least in part, by the growing divide between those who embraced music as a channel for individual emotions and those who wanted it to serve the needs of religion and political elites. On the one hand, we find evidence of a dignified Sappho who mentors and inspires the young women in her circle. On the other hand, we see the stirrings of a different view of Sappho, dangerous and libidinous. The confusion this dichotomy caused was so great that the rhetorician Aelian eventually decided that two different women named Sappho must have resided on Lesbos, one a poet, the other a whore. More likely, only one Sappho existed, but two warring camps battled over her legacy.[5]

This divide also helps us understand why the Greek historian Ephorus of Cyme (circa 400–330 BC), who lived during the same period when dramatists lampooned Sappho, insisted that music only served to promote "deceit and quackery." The phrase suggests that shamanistic practices involving the use of music in occult healing rituals persisted even after the Pythagorean rupture—a hypothesis supported by our earlier consideration of Ismenias's musical cures, Parmenides's trip to the underworld, and Empedocles's extraordinary assertion that he could raise a soul from the dead. We can't say with any certainty how many musical healers continued to practice these disreputable arts after the Pythagorean rupture, but those who dared to do so were increasingly treated as charlatans, scorned by cultural elites the same way storefront psychics and astrologists are derided in the current day. In more recent years, the musical healers of antiquity would also become a source of shame for university classicists, who found the notion of raising the dead and journeying to the underworld subjects best restricted to fairy tales and folklore, and incompatible with the dignity of their academic discipline.[6]

We also encounter here a more prominent linkage between music and slavery—a recurring theme in the pages ahead. This debasement of the performer could hardly be more opposed to our current-day expectations, when the vocation of musician is highly coveted, and those who reach the pinnacle of this profession are treated as elite members of society. The Greeks certainly treated *some* musicians in this way—for example, the lyric poets who sang (if in fact they did sing, and not merely recite) of glorious deeds, or the winners of sanctioned music competitions. But many spheres of music were simply off limits to decent people. Aristotle expresses horror, in Book 8 of his *Politics*, that a chorus leader in Sparta would play the flute in performance, or that anyone other than a slave would learn this instrument. Yet aulos players were in great demand—to set the pace for rowers, to perform at sacrifices and symposia, to accompany marching, and in other settings. In these instances, slaves were enlisted, and if free individuals participated, they were tainted by the shame associated with this degraded form of music-making. Many of these slave musicians appear to have come from the east. Phrygians and Lydians are often mentioned— even today these terms are used to denote musical modes, but in antiquity they were no doubt associated with the slave performers who hailed from these parts of current-day Turkey.

It may seem strange that the technical terms for different melodic modes would originate with slavery, but such connections reveal important truths about the role of outsiders in musical inno- vation. This thorny issue will be dealt with in greater detail later in this book, but it's worth noting at this point that the scale that exerted the greatest impact on music in the twentieth century, the blues scale, also originated among slaves and the descendants of slaves. In Greece, the new attitudes toward music described here coincided with a significant increase in slaveholding. Not just the wealthy, but most Athenian households, probably owned at least one slave. In this setting, as in the Antebellum American South, the slave population gained recognition as a major source of musical talent and entertainment. It's sobering to consider that, even today, when music students learn about the Lydian and Phrygian modes, they are being taught a terminology that initially referred to dif- ferent groups of captive populations associated with these sounds.

What an unlikely turn of events! The ancient Greeks created one of the most xenophobic societies in Western history—the very word *xenophobia* comes from the Greek word *xenos*, signifying "stranger" or "foreigner." By the same token, our word *barbarian* was initially a Greek word referring to any group that didn't speak Greek. For the ancients, it became a catch-all label for Egyptians, Persians, Phrygians, and members of a host of other societies. Yet for all their scorn of the outsider, the Greeks found themselves drawn to these cultures for a kind of antidote to the excesses of Greek rationalism. The immense popularity of foreign cults during the late fifth century BC, especially those of an intense, orgiastic nature, testifies both to the allure of such non-rational practices and to widespread belief among the Greeks that the most powerful sects came from outside their own borders. This zeal for something more magical led these staid ancients to turn to a wide range of imported rituals, including, according to classicist E. R. Dodds, "the worship of the Phrygian 'Mountain Mother,' Cybele, and that of her Thracian counterpart, Bendis; the mysteries of the Thraco-Phrygian Sabazius, a sort of savage un-Hellenized Dionysus; and the rites of the Asiatic 'dying gods,' Attis and Adonis." We can safely assume that music played a key role in all these practices and contributed further to the pervasive notion that exciting, controversial songs were associated with 'barbarian' influences.[7]

This marked stratification in music is our most lasting legacy from the Greeks. From this juncture onward, we seek in vain for a unified musical culture in the Western world. Some musicians gain status through connections with cultural elites, while others are disdained, marginalized, censored, or punished for their corrupting influence. Music can be virtuous or sinful, praised or ridiculed, dignified or degraded, celebrated or forbidden. Even stranger, the same musician and songs can move from one extreme to the other depending on a host of circumstances, many of them barely mentioned in the surviving records.

In other words, from this stage onward, any attempt to grasp sudden shifts and apparent innovations in the sphere of music must start with the same question criminal investigators ask: *Cui bono,* or, in simple translation, *Who benefits*? Why did this kind of music flourish at this particular moment, and what forces supported or opposed its ascendancy in the hotly contested social soundspace?

Moreover, when we witness the celebration of certain types of songs—approved by those in a position to grant approval—we ought to ask what other types of music did not meet their litmus tests. And, most important of all, when we find this history presented as if songs are mere songs, value neutral and lacking these charged associations, we ought to suspect that the most important part of the story has been left out.

9

Unmanly Music

The rupture in ancient music increasingly takes on the form of a debate over manliness. Even in Plato's time, we can see the outline of this new way of defining what constitutes an appropriate song. In *The Laws*, he explains the need for distinguishing "the songs fitting for females from those fitting for males," adding that "it's necessary to legislate at least the outlines of these matters." He goes on to suggest that manly music would include "whatever inclines to courage," while the songs of women should be "determined by the very way they differ in nature," and thus encompass "whatever leans rather toward the orderly and the moderate."[1]

There's a disturbing hypocrisy in this proclamation. The Greeks were aware that women's songs were anything but moderate—almost every famous narrative of dangerous music in their cultural heritage assigned the blame on women. We see this in the account of the beguiling Siren songs of Homer, which lure men to their deaths, and in the violent Dionysian cults, depicted by Euripides in the *Bacchae*, whose female participants kill blindly while in an ecstatic trance. Almost any kind of song that contained excessive feeling—whether a passionate love lyric or the wailing lament of a mourner at a funeral—was associated with the emotional susceptibility of women. For the Greeks, this element of passion was typically a defect, not a virtue. In *The Laws*, Plato was describing the songs women *ought* to sing, not the ones they were often associated with.

This fear of unmanly music would only grow stronger with the passing centuries. With the Romans it would evolve into an obsessive concern over the effeminacy of their musical culture. Christianity raised the ante even more, striving to control the wicked songs of women through every tool at its disposal—papal denunciations, church council rulings, fire-and-brimstone pronouncements from the pulpit, and whispered exhortations in the confessional. We find the same fixation in the Muslim world, where the songs of *mukhannathun*—perhaps best translated as *effeminate men*, a group that might also have included eunuchs, homosexuals, and others—were both popular and intensely controversial. In China, as we saw in Chapter 4, scholars employed elaborate schemes to reinterpret women's songs in terms of Confucian teachings, with the extraordinary result of making the women disappear from their own lyrics and turning these songs into political tenets for the male-dominated ruling class. We find a similar tension in Japanese society, as depicted in *The Tale of Genji*, where the musical skills of women are recognized as a key part of social relationships, but they often perform while hidden from view, because of the moral danger associated with this music. No matter where we turn our view in ancient and medieval times, songs are connected to gender roles, and praised, dismissed, or reinterpreted on that basis. Perhaps we retain some of Plato's hypocrisy in the current day when we celebrate female pop singers as alluring sirens even while questioning the marked objectification inherent in this kind of fame and acclaim.

In the discourse *De Musica*, of unknown authorship but initially attributed to Plutarch, we find an irritated complaint about the debased state of current music, especially its unmanly qualities—an oft-expressed concern that the Romans inherited from their Greek predecessors. "In the cultivation of music the ancients respected its dignity, as they did in all other pursuits," the author explains, "while the moderns have rejected its graver parts, and instead of the music of former days, strong, inspired and dear to the gods, introduce into the theaters an *effeminate twittering*." The treatise goes on to criticize the Lydian mode, because it is "high-pitched" and "appropriate to lamentation"—here we are again reminded that the lament, for ancient and medieval authorities, is connected to female weakness and susceptibility to overpowering emotions. Then the author praises the Dorian mode, in contrast, for its "grandeur and dignity." Its sound, the text claims, is "proper for warlike and temperate men." I note that the Dorian mode was one the Greeks named after themselves, in contrast to the less praiseworthy modes named after foreigners.[2]

By the same token, Greek culture strived to transform the shameful music of sexuality into something more respectable. Both tragedy and comedy must have arisen from fertility rites. The etymology of tragedy brings together the words *tragos* (goat) and *aeidein* (to sing)—it is literally the song of a goat, the sacrificial victim. But in the transformation to dramatic spectacle, the human protagonist becomes the sacrifice. Comedy comes from the priapic festivals, and is the counterweight to the death of the victim. So here are both sides of the resurrecting god, the tragedy evoking the death, the comedy celebrating the rebirth. Yet these lust-ridden and ritualistic origins must have been considered an embarrassment at some stage, and a more purely aesthetic perspective was applied to these performances. The Romans inherited this purified ideal, and we have taken it on from the Romans. The sexualized origins of stage plays and musicals, in contrast, are hidden in the mists of time.

Eminent Romans repeated these grave warnings about the emasculating dangers of music again and again. Seneca the Elder fretted that the "revolting pursuits of singing and dancing" corrupted the youth, and before you knew it they were "braiding their hair and thinning their voices to a feminine lilt." Quintilian grumbled that music had been "emasculated by the lascivious melodies of our effeminate stage." Pliny the Younger explicitly compared the "unmanly elocution" of the debased orators of his time to the songs of stage performers. Indeed, the negative connotations of song were so pronounced that orators would criticize their opponents by accusing them of 'singing'—a charge that brought with it associations of weakness and womanliness. A similar view is embedded in the English term *sing-song*, which is often used to ridicule the voice of a speaker whose effete, melodious proclamations lack power and firmness.[3]

How shameful was music-making during this period? The Roman historian Livy tells us that early actors in Roman theater did not sing their own songs—they merely made onstage gestures while others did the actual vocal work. Many scholars have dismissed this account as implausible. "It is difficult to believe that tragedy and comedy were performed this way," writes classicist H. D. Jocelyn. Scholar Sander Goldberg agrees, suggesting that Livy may have confused drama with pantomime—quite an extraordinary accusation, akin to claiming that the historian was unaware of the most basic elements of his own culture. Others have presented evidence that actors merely wanted to save their voices for the strenuous demands of reciting the dialogue, and thus assigned the singing to a slave—although one wonders why no concern was ever expressed over the slaves preserving their voices for subsequent performances, especially given the greater demands of singing over recitation. Were missed vocal notes more acceptable to audiences than hoarse spoken lines? Even if the explanation of the strained voice is true, the decision to let a slave handle the singing is revealing. This was clearly the less dignified aspect of the public performance, and thus a task best suited for a slave.[4]

A plantation owner from the Antebellum South in the United States would have had no trouble believing Livy's claim. This society was fascinated with the songs of its enslaved black workers, and only travelers from afar were puzzled by how frequently African performers were featured at elite social gatherings. Within this society, the assigned role of the slave populace in musical performances was merely taken for granted. The breach in music described in the previous chapter, that aimed to divide sanctioned songs from vulgar ones, has always been mirrored in a similar distinction between musicians. Some songs simply could not be performed with dignity. That would have been just as true during the early Abbasid era in the Islamic world as during the peak period of the Roman Empire, or in the Deep South during most of the nineteenth century, or Brazil during its period of slave labor. In fact, the capoeira performances in Brazil, which combine Afro-Brazilian music and dance with elements of acrobatics and martial arts, were viewed with such distrust that they remained illegal long after slavery was abolished—a prohibition that continued until the 1920s. Put simply, songs face a caste system just as severe as those applied to people. That has been an ingrained part of our musical lives for more than 2,500 years. Alas, what the ruling class has learned repeatedly, typically with shock and dismay, is that the forbidden or despised songs are often the ones people most want to hear.

This tells us how we should understand the famous anecdote about Emperor Nero fiddling while Rome burned. The scandal here, it's worth emphasizing, is not the fire—a force often beyond human control—but the music. Again the charge of unmanliness is brought into the mix. Roman historian Dio Cassius attributes to the Celtic queen Boudicca these words ridiculing Nero for his effeminacy: "While he may have the name of 'man', he is in fact a woman, and the evidence for this is that he sings and plays the lyre and prettifies himself."[5]

Nero probably didn't play the fiddle during the great fire of AD 64, which destroyed 70 percent of the city of Rome. The fiddle didn't exist in antiquity, although its predecessors did. The kithara is a far more likely candidate—so we would be on a firmer footing if we said the emperor jammed on a guitar during the conflagration, a kind of "Smoke on the Water" moment for the toga crowd. Tacitus, our best source for this story, doesn't mention any instrument; he relates that Nero was singing about the destruction of Troy, but labels this as a rumor, not substantiated fact. Yet the specifics here are less important than the larger truth, namely, that the most famous musical performance in the history of the Roman

Empire was a focal point of scurrilous hearsay and derision, served up as an emblem of both authoritarian callousness and the general shame of music-making. Here, too, we have preserved this attitude in the English language—even today, the term *fiddling* carries a meaning of wasting time, of engaging in worthless pursuits while ignoring more pressing matters.

If the Romans were ashamed of the unmanly music of popular entertainments, they attempted to compensate by institutionalizing the manly music of warfare. They did not invent the practice of military music, although they had great zeal for it, both for ritualistic and utilitarian purposes. Far earlier, among the Egyptians, we find a schema that would last for thousands of years, with drums used to enliven and impose order on the soldiers, and horns employed for signaling. The Greeks had odder ideas about military music, ignoring the drum—perhaps a sign of a culture more devoted to individualism than to orderliness—and instead bringing choral singers into battle. Classicist John Winkler has even suggested that the chorus in a Greek tragedy was modeled on military lines, perhaps involving young men training for battle, and that their movements in performance imitated the orderly procession of troops. It's a peculiar notion, and not universally accepted, but the theory gains credence from the many other examples, presented in these pages, of hidden-beneath-the-surface linkages between entertainment and carnage.[6]

In any event, these motions, whether on stage or the battlefield, probably did not resemble the movements we typically associate with marching troops. Athenian soldiers did not march, at least not in the conventional manner of modern armies, although the Spartans may have. The latter aligned their movements to the sound of the aulos—despised in other settings for the strong emotions it evoked, but passionate feelings have their value on the battlefield. The Cretans used the lyre for the same purpose. The Etruscans, a closer role model for Rome, were acknowledged among the ancients as inventors of the military *tuba*—a long tube ending in a bell shape, very different in appearance from our modern tuba and more akin to a trumpet—which was a key part of their arsenal. We are told that this horn not only issued signals, but also instilled fear in adversaries. The instrument was so closely associated with Etruscan pirate raids that the term "robber-trumpeters" appears in ancient texts. In fact, almost every violent or forceful act in Etruscan life had its musical accompaniment: hunting, fighting, boxing, even punishing slaves. The skills of the Etruscans in metallurgy enabled them to invent proper instruments for each of these functions, leading us to the disturbing conclusion that advances in horns were due to the need to shed blood. From these varied sources, the Romans constructed their own distinctive and 'manly' approach to military music, which accompanied every aspect of a soldier's life, from training before battle to the glorious triumph after victory.

The Romans also ignored the drum in military music, but they made extensive use of wind instruments. They borrowed the Etruscan tuba, for instance, and used it to order advances and retreats. The *cornu*, a long G-shaped horn, was blown to transmit the general's orders in the midst of battle, or to accompany the planting of colors. This was a huge horn—a complete instrument recovered in Pompeii is more than ten feet in length. The similar but C-shaped *buccina* had other uses: it might announce the night watch, meals, and wake-up times, or solemnize the execution of a soldier. The players of each type of instrument had their special names, set numbers, and assigned locations in the midst of battle. The music itself was as definitive as a commander's orders, and had to be obeyed without hesitation. In a society that worried about degraded, effeminate music-making, these were melodies that retained authority and demanded respect.

Yet all the pomp and ritual could not hide the fact that official Roman music was often hollow at the core. Recall that this society had taken the most powerful forms of Greek song—the epic and lyric—and removed their music, even as these literary forms retained a pretense that a bard was singing. In the opening line of the great Roman epic the *Aeneid*, Virgil declares that he *sings* of war and the man of battle—two appropriate subjects for song, from the standpoint of Roman authorities—but this was all sham and

posturing. Epic poets no longer sang their works in the age of Caesar Augustus. When a dignified song from the past was retained,
it often bordered on play-acting. The Salian Hymn, respected by
the Romans as one of their most venerable songs, was performed
with great dignity, but the words were so obscure that, by the first
century AD, even learned Cicero was unable to comprehend the
entire chant. The same was true of the songs of the Arval brethren,
a priesthood whose history was traced back to the origins of Rome,
but whose rituals and music were largely incomprehensible to the
Romans of the Augustan Age. Consider it the equivalent of modern revelers singing "Auld Lang Syne" to hail in a new year, yet without any clear notion what those words mean. The Romans revered
what they could not understand—so much so that the name of
Caesar Augustus was inserted into the words of the Salian Hymn by
decree of the Roman Senate. They still believed in the magical efficacy of the music, even if the words were baffling, and they wanted
its ritualistic protection to continue long after they had forgotten
the song's original purpose.

   This was old magic indeed. Recent excavations of objects resembling Salian shields at Italian archaeological sites dating back to the
ninth or tenth century BC suggest that the ritual was far older than
Rome itself. The Salian priesthood would employ these shields as
percussion instruments, clanging on them as part of a ceremony
with marked military overtones. The performers were dressed as
warriors, carrying swords, and their dance to a three-beat rhythm,
the *tripudium*, could be described as a kind of holy leaping. The
word would eventually get applied by Latin writers to a wide range
of ritualized movements related to combat, exultation, or other
activities requiring great effort. Seneca refers to the *tripudium* as a
virile dance—"the manly style that was the normal practice of those
men of old when they used to dance in times of entertainment
and festivals without incurring any risk of losing dignity, even if
they were being watched by their own enemies." When Petronius,
in his *Satyricon*, describes four slaves dancing a *tripudium* before
removing the lid from a cooking pot, the absurdity is enhanced
by these nobler associations. The dance may have survived into

the Middle Ages, or at least was referred to when church authorities attacked pagan traditions. As late as the thirteenth century,
St. Francis was said to have performed songs and dances with
groups of *tripudianti*.[7]

But those seeking the real popular music of the Roman world
must look beyond sanctioned rituals of manliness and formidable
displays of military horns. The centers of mass entertainment were
the theaters, spread out all over the empire, and these left behind
a more lasting impact on musical culture than did soldiers or officials. In Italy and Sicily alone, we know of at least 175 theaters,
and even more in the provinces from Lisbon to Cappadocia. More
than 50 theaters have been identified in just a single North African
province, Africa Proconsularis—a territory that included parts of
present-day Tunisia, Algeria, and Libya.

And what kind of musical entertainment did audiences expect
at these theaters? "If a friend invited you to visit a Roman theater
in the imperial period to see a well-known star perform you would
have little doubt about the sort of performance you would see,"
explains scholar John Jory. "It would not be a comedy or a tragedy
but a dance performance and the artist would be a pantomime."
In these settings, a masked dancer would enact a story through
gestures, movements, and athletic displays to a musical accompaniment. These dances, however, weren't restricted to theaters, and we
hear of them taking place in private homes and even on the street.
At one point in the controversial history of this genre, Roman sena-
tors were forbidden to go to the houses of pantomimes, and knights
prohibited from participating in their processions—injunctions
hardly necessary if these gatherings were simply a matter of light
entertainment for the masses. Here again, elites crave the music
of the rabble, although they court shame by this very attachment.[8]

In a strange but recurring phenomenon in music history, the
performances that had the most widespread impact on the public
are often those least well documented by posterity. Scholars have
devoted far less attention to pantomime than to ancient tragedy and
comedy. They are perhaps excused by the sketchy surviving information about pantomime. Not a single libretto of clear authenticity

has survived. Even descriptions from eyewitnesses leave many questions unanswered, and what we are told is sometimes contradictory. For example, we are assured that pantomimes were "effete, limp and feckless," but accounts also emphasize the athleticism of the performers, demonstrated by leaps, spins, bends, and boundless energy. Then again, the Romans seemed to fear the taint of feminine weakness in many types of musical performance, their inheritance from the Greeks, and may have simply been projecting onto the entertainer the dreaded moral impact on the spectators.[9]

Large crowds could be unruly at these events. The "pantomime riots" of AD 14 and 15 must have been tumultuous—no fewer than six historians refer to the incidents. It was a kind of Altamont moment in antiquity, when the powerful feelings aroused by entertainment turned ugly. The canceled appearance of a star performer in a dispute over pay may have instigated the outburst, but many causes of discontent probably contributed to the unrest. Accounts leave us in little doubt about the frenzy of pantomime attendees. In AD 23, Tiberius even banished the pantomimes and their fiercest advocates, claiming they were "frequently the fomenters of sedition against the state and of debauchery in private houses." It almost sounds like what critics said about hippies and their music back in the 1960s. But in ancient times as in the Vietnam era, such measures had little long-term impact. The pantomimes eventually returned to Rome, and their fame spread throughout the empire. They would continue to figure in popular entertainment until the end of the sixth century.[10]

We can merely speculate on the sound of the music that accompanied these performances, but the use of percussion instruments is repeatedly mentioned in surviving accounts. The most characteristic instrument in pantomime was the *scabellum*, a wooden clapper played by the musician's foot that provided a metronomic pulse to the dance. But we hear of a range of other percussion instruments that might show up in a performance, including drums, cymbals, and castanets. Wind and string instruments are also mentioned, including the much-despised aulos. But it's worth noting that the ancients frequently employed this so-called flute to accentuate the beat, whether they were synchronizing the rhythm of rowers or the steps of dancers. So we should perhaps consider the music of these pantomime performances primarily as a source of passion and intensity—probably producing the kind of rhythm-driven entrainment, or alignment of brain waves with external rhythms, studied by neuroscientists in our own day—rather than as mere background accompaniment. Against this mesmerizing beat, the chorus would sing the libretto, but the story would have been a familiar one drawn from well-known myths and legends. The audience's focus was less on the unfolding plot than on its artistic—and emotionally charged—enactment.

Participants at these events must have craved the noise. Accounts frequently stress the loudness of the pantomime, and we know from our own experiences with live music how the power of its sound can have as much impact as the actual notes played. The zeal for decibels among pantomime attendees, however, is made most clear by accounts mentioning the use of the water organ (or *hydraulis*), a technical innovation that, in the words of Virgil, drew on the power of "water and of air, which is forcibly agitated, and like a trumpet it emits long, booming notes." This instrument, it's worth noting, also accompanied gladiator fights. Whether bloodshed or dance was on the bill, it probably served the same purpose: to provide a visceral boost to both spectators and participants by its very loud sounds.[11]

Given all this, can we be surprised that the shame of music so pervaded the attitudes of Roman elites that they willingly allowed outsiders and slaves to dominate this field? In the words of the classicist John Landels, the Romans came to accept that "foreigners (especially Greeks) were 'better at that sort of thing than we are'. By way of compensation for this admission of inferiority, they cherished the thought that foreign musicians were all effeminate, 'camp' and generally disreputable."[12]

This may be our most noticeable musical legacy from the Roman Empire—a psychological one, rather than any marked innovations in theory or technique. We have inherited, to some degree, this sense of embarrassment over the emotional power of music.

I encountered such attitudes firsthand while researching my book on the history of the love song. My first indicator was the surprising reluctance of scholars to write about the subject. No complete survey of the love song had ever been published—a remarkable omission given the fact that love has been the most popular topic of songs for at least the past one thousand years. I began mulling over critic Dave Hickey's unanswered question: "I wondered why ninety percent of the pop songs ever written were love songs, while ninety percent of rock criticism was written about the other ten percent." I eventually discovered that this phenomenon wasn't restricted to rock writing, but was symptomatic of the broader field of music history. When I discussed my research with other scholars, I could detect an uneasiness bordering on embarrassment when I started to talk to them about love songs. They wouldn't have used the same words as the Romans—dismissing them as effeminate and debased—but their visceral reaction to this music wasn't so different from Seneca's or Juvenal's. The sentimental love song was somehow undignified and associated with shame.[13]

Here again, we need to consult the dominant philosophical doctrines in order to grasp the ideological forces that distorted musical culture. And in the case of ancient Rome, we find ethical and political considerations again intruding on aesthetics. The most powerful philosophy in Roman imperial times was stoicism. In fact, before the spread of Christianity, stoicism was the most revered and practical worldview available to the European mind. Its teachings rested on a bedrock foundation: namely, the realization that the more we limit our emotions and desires, the less likely we are to be frustrated in life. If sorrow arises from not getting what we want, the solution is to stop wanting. That may be painful advice, but its logic is incontestable.

This antagonism to 'feelings' gives us the context to understand the derisive attitude toward the lyric in a famous putdown shared by Seneca: "Cicero declared that if the number of his days were doubled, he should not have time to read the lyric poets." This isn't a literary judgment on Cicero's part, but a moral condemnation. "The lyric poets are avowedly frivolous," Seneca goes on to explain.

The lyric was degraded by this stage, its early roots in song all but forgotten. It still retained its role as a channel for emotional expression, but this brought with it dangers—and not just social or moral ones. You could even get physically sick, the Romans believed, from the lyric. In one of the strangest chapters in medical history, the ancients invented a disease, *leptosune*, that manifested the weakness of the literary and musical culture in the human body. The *leptoi* became stock figures in comedy—and served as a forerunner of the 'sissy' in pre–World War II Hollywood films.[14]

It's striking how little musical innovation we encounter in this survey of the Roman world. So much of Roman music was borrowed or adapted, mostly from Greece, but also from other conquered territories. The allure that foreign practices held for the Romans is probably seen most clearly in the rise of the so-called mystery cults, one of the few areas in which old rituals still inspired zeal among practitioners. Although we know little about the proceedings or the specifics of the music involved, it's evident that participants sought something more than dry dogma and formalities. The most favored adherents might even be granted an ecstatic experience or access to an altered form of consciousness, especially with the accompaniment of the right kind of music. But for these kinds of experiences, the Romans craved exoticism. The cult members put their faith not so much in homegrown deities as in foreign gods: Mithras from Persia, Isis from Egypt, Cybele from Phrygia, or Sabazios from Thrace. Yet here, as well, the cultural elites scorned the passionate practices of the masses. The musicologist Aristides Quintilianus, writing in the third century AD, dismissed the cults as fodder for "less educated people" who hoped that their "depressive anxiety" could be reduced through melodies and dance. In a society whose self-image relied far too much on decorum, discipline, and manly virtues, even spiritual transcendence—and its musical sources—were viewed with suspicion.[15]

This is the divide bequeathed to us by Roman imperialism, whose military successes allowed these ancient conquerors to lay the groundwork for Western music culture, even though they themselves had little confidence in their own musicality, and often felt ashamed over its most popular manifestations. They inherited this painful split between sanctioned and vulgar music from the Greeks, but the chasm grew all the wider under the dominion of Rome. The contrast between the raucous and sometimes prohibited entertainments of the pantomime and the manly music of the military could hardly be more pronounced. But just as striking is the difference in vitality between the musical entertainments enjoyed by the masses and the increasingly hollow formalities of Roman sacred and ritual music—much of it destined to disappear with the rise of Christianity. Above all, we witness the growing realization among the Romans that the most intense musical experiences must be sought from outsiders—slaves or foreigners—rather than from their own ruling class. These are the defining characteristics of Roman musical life, yet they rarely rise to the surface of the surviving texts from antiquity, which celebrate the manly forms of music that were central to how Roman elites saw themselves, and provide only the most tantalizing hints of the real soundtrack of everyday life, usually in the form of critique, denunciation, and satire.

We see here, in microcosm, how different this subversive history of music is from mainstream accounts. Prevailing narratives of Roman culture start by enshrining Virgil, the epic poet, and Horace, the lyric poet, but for us these are peculiar, troubling innovators who, for all their demonstrable merits as *authors*, severed the vital ties between music and text. Their close affiliation to the emperor, viewed by others as validation of their merit, is for us an emblem of the growing stratification of a culture in which political power increasingly determined what was praised and preserved—or, conversely, panned and prohibited.

We must look beyond the surviving texts and strive to comprehend why, for example, so many tragedies by Seneca were handed down to posterity, while entire genres of mass entertainment, genres that played a much larger role in day-to-day life than the now enshrined *classics* of ancient times, are known to us merely by hearsay. We must aim to recover the real music from the official and sanctioned music, and should be most curious about the songs that excited controversy and opposition, knowing that these are recurring flashpoints for innovation and catalysts for change in societies. And finally, we need to see, after correcting for these distortions, an entirely different music culture, shame-based yet craving the ecstatic release provided only by song. With this broader view of ancient music, we can construct a more accurate, if perhaps less dignified, music history—one that tells us important truths not just about Rome, but also about later societies, our own not excluded.

10

The Devil's Songs

We haven't encountered the concept of *sin* yet, but that will now change. The ancients had many worries about music, but these tended to focus on practical matters relating to its impact on character and society. The notion that the gods might have strong opinions on musical entertainment rarely entered into their thinking. The deities, of course, had their own music, embedded in ritual observances, and this needed to be handled with proper decorum, but the objections to secular music so frequently raised by cultural elites focused on the here-and-now, not the hereafter. Zeus really didn't care what songs you heard in your spare time.

This same practical approach to music, which needed no concept of an afterlife or sin to enforce the most severe strictures on performance styles, can also be found beyond the boundaries of Greco-Roman influence. In fact, it reaches its highest pitch in the extraordinary diatribe *Against Music* by the Chinese thinker Mozi, who lived around the same time as Socrates and taught a philosophy of austerity and restraint. *Against Music* is the most hostile manifesto on the subject that has survived from ancient times, and few in the succeeding centuries have even come close to matching its bitter protestations. Where other theoreticians distinguished between permitted and forbidden songs, making fine discriminations among instruments, modes, and styles, Mozi offers a sweeping claim: "Making music is wrong!" He allows for no exceptions, insisting that if rulers want to "promote what is beneficial to the world and eliminate what is harmful, they must prohibit and put a stop to this thing called music!" And yet the concept of impiety or sin never enters into his thinking; nor does he make any references to notions of the sacred or profane. Mozi bases his objection to music entirely on practical concerns. He wants the time and money spent on music directed to more useful projects.[1]

Music does nothing to feed the hungry or clothe the poor, he points out. Music does not contribute to social order, or reduce the ever-present chaos of day-to-day life. Hence its allure must be resisted by both high and low, the powerful and the weak. If rulers allocate resources to music, they are taking them away from more pressing needs. Farmers who listen to music will neglect the crops. Women who pay attention to music will forget to spin and weave. In a well-ordered society, such dereliction of duty cannot be allowed.

The severity of this position is striking, but its obsession with utilitarian factors is very much in keeping with prevailing concerns about music in ancient times. Confucius held quite different opinions, but also adopted a hardheaded practical outlook, emphasizing music's central role in education and ritual. He well understood the sensual pleasure involved—a famous story tells of his rapture, lasting three months, spurred by hearing the *shao*, a kind of pantomime accompanied by music attributed to the legendary Emperor Shun (another powerful authority who gets credit for musical innovation). But the appeal of this music was linked to its beneficial impact on morals and character. Confucian thinking would eventually focus on the practical value of song almost to an absurd degree. Even the most innocuous folk song was twisted and turned, dissected and reinterpreted, so that teachable moments could be extracted from its lyrics. The notion that good, well-ordered songs contributed to a good, well-ordered society was the foundation of Chinese music theory.

For example, the song "In the Bushlands a Creeper Grows" seems to have an obvious meaning.

> *There was a man so lovely,*
> *Clear brow well rounded.*
> *By chance I came across him,*
> *And he let me have my will.*[2]

In this lyric from the *Shijing*, two lovers meet in a secluded spot. Or do they? Later commentators showed enormous ingenuity in finding other ways of interpreting this simple heartfelt song. They tell us that the people meeting are not a romantic couple but two worthy men, or else that this kind of thinking about "random encounters" was a consequence of bad governance—taking place because the "lord's favor did not flow down to the people [who were] exhausted by military uprisings." Once they discarded the surface meaning of a lyric, there was no limit to how far they could push the moralizing interpretation. In "Guan Ju" (or "The Ospreys Cry"), the words clearly reference the pain of unrequited love:

> *Shy was his noble lady;*
> *Day and night he sought her.*
> *Sought her and could not get her;*
> *Day and night he grieved.*

But this lyric got turned into a political commentary, a moral lesson, even a celebration of virginity and chastity. As a result of such interpretive liberties, the essential qualities we seek in lyric, namely, the expression of heartfelt feeling and personal agency, were shuffled offstage as inconvenient barriers to the edifying potential of sanctioned texts.[3]

But it's worth stressing that this expedient, for all its violence to the surface meanings, was still driven by pragmatic considerations. With the rise of Christianity in the Western world, in contrast, romantic lyrics were scrutinized not for their teachable lessons, but in order to eradicate their metaphysical danger to the souls of believers. At this junction, the notion of sin moved to the forefront of musicology, and would stay there for a thousand years and beyond. Every aspect of music was now scrutinized for signs of profanity and impiety—not just the lyrics, but also the instruments, the time and place of performance, the character and sex of the performer, and the emotions stirred by its melodies and rhythms. Priests fulminated against the evils of music from the pulpit, church councils issued rulings on its use, theologians disputed its nature, even the pope intervened on occasion, clarifying and condemning as the situation warranted. All this was handled with the most deadly seriousness: after all, salvation or damnation in the next life hung in the balance.

Perhaps the most surprising aspect of this massive intervention into music criticism was how little impact it had on the practices of believers. During the first one thousand years of Christianity, the same musical abuses were identified again and again, countermeasures were implemented, penalties and penances imposed, yet these sinful songs never seemed to go away. The impieties continued unabated, and each generation held onto the evil songs of the previous one or invented new ones of its own. And when secular music finally emerged from this barrage of invective and censorship, with the rise of the troubadours in the twelfth century, the 'new' style of song entering the mainstream of elite culture revealed the same obsession with carnality and lustfulness that the clerics had been battling for the previous millennium.

Christianity was not hostile to all kinds of music. From the start, music was integrated into the daily practices of adherents. In the Epistle to the Ephesians, Paul urges believers to abandon drunkenness and instead turn to "psalms and hymns and spiritual songs, singing and making melody in your heart to the Lord." The mention of music as an alternative to intoxication suggests that the early Christians well understood the ecstatic properties of song, its ability to induce trance and altered states of consciousness. Paul refers to music again in the Epistle to the Colossians, but here focuses on its use as a pedagogical tool: "Let the message of Christ dwell among you richly as you teach and admonish one another with all wisdom through psalms, hymns, and songs from the Spirit, singing to God with gratitude in your hearts." But these are two very different views of music—songs as a pathway into euphoric trance and as a source of teachable moments—and often in conflict with one another. The resulting tension has never been adequately resolved by Christianity. Over the course of centuries, its leading authorities have tended to favor the pedagogical paradigm, but rank-and-file believers still seek ecstasy and transcendence—and no religion can entirely dispense with those ingredients, despite the danger and unpredictability they bring in their wake.[4]

"Christians in the succeeding era often designated liturgical song as their sacrifice, thus distinguishing it from pagan sacrifice," explains scholar Johannes Quasten. This concept of religious songs as sacrifice may seem straightforward and uncontroversial to us nowadays. Even two thousand years after the rise of Christianity, believers often speak of church services as a sacrificial rite without thinking much about the full implications of that concept. Yet in this subversive history, so attuned to the hidden linkages between music and violence, we need to look at the actual history of sacrificial music, and consider what it tells us about both the past and present. In many ways, this seldom discussed topic in the annals of musicology can even help us grasp the significance of contemporary performances, fully secular in tone and without any religious affiliations, that draw capacity crowds to concert halls and stadiums.[5]

This is a side of music history many would prefer to ignore. Plutarch, for example, makes the extraordinary claim that music in the Carthaginian sacrifices was not meant to solemnify the ritual or even to enhance the mood, but to drown out the cries and wails as parents offered up their children to Baal Hammon. We find a similar connection in the Hebrew scriptures, where child sacrifices by the ancient Canaanites are harshly condemned. These sacrifices took place at Topheth in Jerusalem, and that name is derived from the Hebrew word *toph*, or drum—a linkage emphasizing the prominence of drums to mask the sounds of the slaughter. This is the troubling origin of sacrificial music, harkening back to a violent era when the offering of blood and flesh took place without any soothing transubstantiation into bread and wine.

Is this irrelevant to our modern musical practices, a savage anachronism that has no bearing on our more refined, peaceful, and peace-promoting rituals? Social theorist Jacques Attali in his provocative book *Noise* asserts otherwise. In fact, he argues that throughout history, and even today, "the musician is an integral part of the sacrificial process, a channeler of violence." Such a claim may seem bizarre at first blush . . . until you start to consider the actual performance rituals of heavy metal, punk rock, and hip-hop artists—to cite only the most obvious genres—with their stirring of the most potent emotions in closely packed settings, where inhibitions are often further reduced by alcohol or other intoxicants. Attali draws here on the theorizing of critic René Girard, who devoted decades to studying the linkages between ancient sacrificial rites and contemporary cultural institutions. This body of work is almost entirely beyond the purview of music writers, but is essential for grasping how violence and conflict can be sublimated in performance rituals. In other words, the sacrificial rite is alive today, and church services represent only a tiny portion of it. Go to the annual gathering Burning Man in the desert of northwestern Nevada—even the name reveals the linkage to sacrifice—for a full taste of one version of this ongoing tradition. The high point of the event is the fiery death of a large human effigy that takes place on the Sabbath. The more things change, the more they stay the same.[6]

This is the context in which we should view the rise of Christian 'sacrificial' music. The believers wanted to channel the energy of pagan sacrifice, but they also needed to purify it. This point is made explicitly in the *Oracula Sibyllina*, one of the oldest surviving texts on Christian music. This anonymous work in Greek hexameters was already cited by early church authorities back in the second century AD, and it is clear that they understood both the ritual's connection with human sacrifice and the need to cleanse it of these associations. "We may not pollute ourselves with burning fat from flesh-consuming pyres or with the horrible smells of the ether," the author asserts. "But rejoicing in holy speech, with a happy heart, with the rich gift of love and generous hands, with psalms and hymns worthy of our God, we are encouraged to sing your praise, O eternal and unerring one." Along with this elimination of blood sacrifice, a change in music was absolutely required. Under the new approach, "no kettle drum is heard, no cymbal, no many-holed flute, instruments full of senseless sounds, not the tone of the shepherd's pipe, which is like the curled snake, nor the trumpet, with its wild clamor." All these musical traditions were, according to this revered text, tainted by their violent associations.[7]

As far as church authorities were concerned, only one musical instrument was above reproach, namely, the human voice. Instrumental music was considered dangerous, both for its pagan history and the pernicious influence it supposedly exerted on moral temperament—although it's ironic how often this contagion was described in language revealing the influence of the pagans themselves, notably Plato. Putting aside their drums and cymbals, converts to the Christian faith were encouraged to sing hymns and psalms, giving praise with their voices. St. Pambo, one of the early desert fathers, even discouraged hand-clapping and foot-tapping because, he insisted, they carried heretical associations—and this controversy continues to the present day in many Christian ministries. You might even divide all current-day congregations into two categories, clappers and non-clappers, and probably would find that this distinction is closely correlated with a host of other attitudes and practices. But in the early centuries of Christian ascendancy, few disputed the superiority of psalms and hymns to all previous forms of ritual music, and the results of this shift would prove far reaching.

Singing became entrenched as the dominant musical practice in Europe, and it remained so until the seventeenth century. This preference for vocal music can be measured in many ways, but perhaps the simplest is to examine the career paths of the leading Western composers in the period before Bach. Consider, for example, the lives and times of Pérotin, Guillaume de Machaut,

Guillaume Dufay, Josquin des Prez, Hildegard von Bingen, Johannes Ockeghem, Giovanni Pierluigi da Palestrina, Thomas Tallis, and most of their leading contemporaries. They either sang in choirs, supervised choirs, or composed their leading works for choirs. In some instances, they also demonstrated skill on musical instruments, but this was a small part of their legacy when compared to their vocal music. After Bach, this not only changed, but reversed entirely—the keyboard and violin, not the voice, began to serve as the calling cards of composers in the Western world. That's still true today, when an aspiring composer is expected to study the keyboard but hardly need consider joining a choir. Yet the 1,500-year elevation of the human voice to a position of unassailable pre-eminence in Western music must rank among the most influential cultural interventions in the history of Christianity.

Vocal music, for the early churchgoers, not only uplifted their earthly worship, but even gave them a taste of the Paradise to come. Aurelian of Réôme, author of the oldest surviving work of medieval music theory, *Musica Disciplina*, explained that it was possible for a select few to hear the singing of angels, and told of a pious priest of Auxerre who was treated to a celestial rendition of the 148th Psalm. Another anecdote describes a hymn that a monk of the monastery of St. Victor learned from a choir of angels during a vigil—he later taught it to clerics in Rome, where it was sung by the entire congregation. "The very world and heaven above us," he announced, "circulate with a harmonious sound."[8]

Yet there's something peculiar about this shift. Singing (or chanting) the Psalms became central to church life, yet the Psalms themselves celebrate instrumental music, and do so repeatedly. Musical instruments figure prominently in at least sixteen different Psalms, and typically in a tone of exhortation. "Praise the Lord with harp: sing unto him with the psaltery and an instrument of ten strings," announces Psalm 33. In Psalm 149, we find this admonition: "Let them praise his name in the dance: let them sing praises unto him with the timbrel and harp." And in Psalm 68 we even encounter that much-feared representative of paganism, the female tambourine player: "The singers went before, the players on instruments followed after; among them were the damsels play-ing with timbrels." This connection is so prominent that David, the attributed composer of the Psalms, is frequently depicted with harp in hand. This recurring image, a staple of religious iconography, also serves as a reminder of merited rewards in the afterlife, where the harp figures prominently—not just in cartoons, jokes, and pop-ular culture, but in Christian texts and images going back to the Book of Revelation.[9]

The elimination of musical instruments, especially percussion, from ritual had the unfortunate effect of removing those very ingredients most closely associated with ecstasy and trance. We now understand how much influence rhythm exerts on brain activity, and the key role drumming plays in this process, whether measured in a clinical study by a scientist or in actual trance-producing set-tings out in the real world. Perhaps the leaders of early Christianity were instinctively aware of this, and made a deliberate decision to construct a ritual structure conducive to conformity while avoiding the intensely individualistic experiences that come in a trance state. But that's a hard policy to enforce: songs have a dual power. They can produce both disciplined group cohesion and an uncontrolled throwing off of all discipline and restraint. As social movements evolve from their early charismatic stage to more bureaucratic and codified practices, any extreme kind of ritual ecstasy becomes, at best, an embarrassment, and at worst a threat to the hierarchy. At that juncture, it's best to put the drums away and sing cohesion-producing anthems instead. Church leaders may have been con-scious of this, or perhaps merely grasped it through trial and error.

In any event, the church solved one problem and caused another. Religions require trance as much as they do dogma, per-haps even more. I suspect that the later emergence and institution-alization of intense chanting in medieval Christianity, which would eventually become the core element in monastic life, drew on this need for transcendence, and the discovery that rhythmic chanting was the best way of achieving it within the constraints imposed by the church's prohibition of drumming, hand-clapping, and other more straightforward paths to neural entrainment. But there's a catch: a drum can change your state of consciousness in around ten minutes, but with chanting, a much longer period of time is necessary. Ritual and dogma must adjust to this biological necessity.

A surprising confirmation of this necessity took place in the late 1960s, when the iconoclastic music therapist Alfred Tomatis intervened in a crisis at the Abbaye d'En-Calcat in the south of France. Here the monks were afflicted by collective exhaustion and widespread depression. In Tomatis's words, they "were slumping in their cells like wet dishrags." Other medical practitioners had failed in their remedies, but Tomatis immediately grasped that the listless monks were suffering from recent restrictions on their chanting imposed by the monastery in the aftermath of the Vatican II reforms. He convinced the head abbot to reinstate the traditional chants. "By November, almost all of them had gone back to their normal activities," Tomatis would later boast, "that is their prayer, their few hours of sleep, and the legendary Benedictine work schedule." When allowed to chant, the monks could get by on just four hours of sleep and still have ample energy for hours of chanting as well as all the chores of monastic life. Without the chant, no amount of sleep could compensate for the disruption in their psychic energy.[10]

The life of a medieval monk was steeped in music. The rise of the monasteries in Western Europe marked a reaction against the worldly entanglements of the church and offered a simpler mode of devotion focused on prayer, manual work, and discipline. As the practices of these groups became more codified, the late-night vigils and daily interludes of prayer were replaced with the prescribed chanting of the Psalms. St. Benedict (480–547) established the *Rule*, the most influential guide to monastic life in the history of Christianity, and one that still inspires followers more than 1,500 years later. The prominence this work gives to the performance of the Psalms can perhaps best be measured by comparing the eight chapters Benedict devotes to faults and punishments with the twelve chapters on the Divine Office. Here Benedict specifies in detail how Psalms should be chanted over the course of the hours and days and seasons of monastic life. With vehement insistence, he tells his followers that they must "sing the psalms that mind and voice may be in harmony," remembering always that they are "in the presence of God and his angels."[11]

But one could easily be misled by this celebration of vocal music. The same religious authorities who fostered singing when it was under their control also worked zealously to eliminate all its other manifestations. No force in the history of the Western world has ever matched the early Christians in their determination to police, prohibit, and punish singing among the populace. The intrusive music criticism of the clerics, which reached even into homes and bedchambers to enforce its dictates, prevailed with remarkable consistency for a period of almost one thousand years. At first glance, the priests' success in this project seems stunning, at least when we consider that virtually no secular songs in the vernacular European languages have survived from the long centuries preceding the rise of the troubadours. Yet we know these songs existed. There were probably tens of thousands of them, but almost all were excluded from the texts preserved for posterity. Occasionally a few stray lines appear, furtively copied in a religious document, perhaps by chance, or maybe in perverse defiance by a rebellious scribe. But these were rare exceptions.

How can we be certain these songs flourished? Our best evidence is the frequency and intensity with which they were condemned. Hundreds of attacks on these songs have survived, yet scholars have paid surprisingly little attention to these intriguing documents from the history of music criticism. "To my knowledge, no single study has been devoted to these many condemnations," remarks medievalist John Haines, yet he also notes their relevance to modern discussions about the role of music in society. When Haines first began studying the subject, it brought up vivid memories of his upbringing among fundamentalist Christians, and in particular a fierce denunciation of rock 'n' roll he had heard from a visiting preacher, who "told harrowing tales of Alice Cooper consorting with demons, of Linda Ronstadt seducing men of God and of John Lennon claiming he was bigger than Jesus Christ." Thirty years later, immersed in his studies of a forgotten branch of medieval life, Haines was surprised how little had changed in the tone of the attacks on popular music. "All the themes of his sermon, implicit and explicit were there: middle-aged apprehension of youthful energy; adolescent desire for rhythm and beauty; the devil and his drums; voluptuous women and effeminate men dancing to Satan's beat and singing diabolical songs; and the power of song to seduce and damn to hell."[12]

Yet I'm not sure which is more surprising: the eerie echoing of medieval polemics in modern society, or the almost complete lack of interest by researchers in this strange chapter in the history of song. The amount of scholarship devoted to church music in the medieval period would fill a library, but the music the church didn't want you to hear stirs up very little curiosity. The conventional history, as Haines accurately summarizes it, presents the evolution of this music as "a progression of great or greater men whose innovative achievements move the reader towards the perfection of late medieval polyphony." The foundation of this process is the Gregorian chant, named after the most powerful man in Christendom during the late sixth century, Pope Gregory the Great, who is celebrated in almost all of our source documents as a towering musical innovator—not just a reformer of ritual, but the preeminent composer of his day. We should perhaps be suspicious that temporal power again coincides so perfectly with attributions of artistic vision. By now we have seen this same overlap many times— in the assignment of musical innovations to King David, King Solomon, Emperor Shun, Confucius, and others. Skepticism is the only proper response when those who hold the reins of power turn into music superstars in the surviving accounts, but we ought to be even more concerned over what such texts omit. Imagine what the history of modern song would look like if we eliminated from consideration the music denounced by religious (and other) authorities?[13]

In Christian Europe, these denunciations were frequently directed at songs performed on religious feasts or in holy places. "Do not allow women's song and ring-dances and playful games and songs in the church and churchyard," declared Pope Eutychius in the third century. St. Augustine, in the early fifth century, complained about blasphemous performances at the resting place of St. Cyprian: "All night long in that place abominations have been sung and danced to with songs." A century later, Caesarius of Arles was still lamenting people "who come to the feasts of saints only to get drunk, dance, sing songs with lewd words, lead ring-dances and twirl like the devil." These and other complaints by clerics might seem to suggest that the populace harbored a taste for blasphemy and waited for religious holidays to vent their diabolical urges. Perhaps that was true, and medieval equivalents of Ozzy Osbourne and Alice Cooper showed up in the churchyard to wreak havoc. But I believe we get closer to the reality of these musical performances if we simply consider them as typical of the festive life of the people. Their vernacular songs came to the forefront during holy days for the simple reason that these were the times set aside for celebration and revelry.[14]

Who sang these sinful secular songs? Again and again, religious authorities call attention to the pernicious role of women in spreading musical contamination through Christian society. When church leaders gathered at Auxerre in the late sixth century to consider how to extirpate the superstitions and pagan practices of Teutonic and Gallic converts, they issued a prohibition on *puellarum cantica*, or "girls' songs," in church. None of these songs have survived, so we can't say with any certainty what naughty subjects the girls might have addressed in their music. But around this same time, Bishop Caesarius complained about the many women "who know by heart and recite out loud the Devil's songs, erotic and obscene." In the middle of the next century, the Council of Chalons condemned "obscene and shameful songs . . . with choruses of women." Further details were provided at the Council of Rome in 853, where women were accused of using *verba turpia* (dirty words) in their songs, as well as dancing and forming pagan choruses.[15]

Only on the rarest occasions were these songs specifically attributed to prostitutes. For example, Bishop Haymo in the early ninth century referred to the "whorish wantonness" of the "songs of prostitutes." Lawgivers sometimes joined in this crusade, implementing statutes restricting the singing solicitations of women in the streets at night—prohibitions that remind us that, until very recently, singing has been considered, in almost every part of the world, a valuable skill in the sex trade. But overt solicitations were only the smallest part of the contagion of female vocalizing feared by the medieval mind. No woman was exempt, whether virgin or housewife, from church oversight of her musical choices. Even nuns, we learn, required close supervision, as demonstrated by Charlemagne's instruction to abbesses in 789 on the dangers of *winileodas* (songs for a friend)—"On no account let them dare to write *winileodas*, or send them from the convent." How friendly were these songs for a friend? We will never know. These forbidden lyrics were not preserved. Yet from the frequently repeated prohibitions and attacks we know that women continued singing licentious songs throughout the first thousand years of Christendom.[16]

What is striking from all this is how closely Christian authorities maintained the same priorities as their pagan predecessors. Their theoretical observations and metaphysics were completely different, hence the clerics' obsession with sin and blasphemy, but the real-life applications of their music criticism are almost identical with those favored by the elites of ancient Greece and Rome. The dangers of music, in both instances, were associated with feminine qualities, especially with regard to sensuality and emotional excess. The Christian councils even adopted the ancient condemnation of musical laments, a form of song invariably associated with women. The medieval church leaders could hardly have known that the lament, in its earliest days, was inextricably connected with sexuality, where mourning for the dying god was combined with the explicit imagery of fertility rites, and probably, in many instances, actual fornication. But church authorities hardly needed such information to denounce the lament: the strong emotions these songs aroused in women were sufficient reason to prohibit their use.

Here, too, we encounter an unexpected correlation with musical matters in our contemporary world. It's worth noting that the Chinese government, in the present day, is trying to eradicate the practice of hiring strippers to perform with musical accompaniment as part of funeral rites. This tradition is especially popular in rural areas—a puzzling and disrespectful custom in the minds of twenty-first-century authorities, but very much aligned with the ancient connection between the music of death and songs of eroticism. Here all three ingredients recur: laments for the departed, music as an enticement to fornication, and repression by the authorities. Once again, the more things change, the more they stay the same.

In both pagan and Christian teachings, men were the unsuspecting victims of the alluring songs of women, who might, for their part, be Sirens, witches, whores, or just a chaste peasant girl singing on a saint's feast day. No matter what the role or intention of the performer, such music required intervention and, wherever possible, replacement with the sanctioned songs of the entrenched institutions.

Yet even the dominant institutions are more complex than we may realize. A recurring theme of this book is the significance of outsiders and renegades in launching musical innovations that are later adopted—and legitimized—by the leaders of mainstream culture. We shall see in the next chapter how the same women incessantly attacked by the church for their filthy songs about love and sex anticipated the biggest shift in the history of Western music, marked by the rise of the troubadours and the legitimization of secular songs about personal emotions. But even our understanding of music *inside* the Catholic hierarchy is enhanced by grasping the rebel streak in its leading music innovators. Many of the key aspects of Christian musical life came from controversial reformers. This is just as true with St. Benedict, who placed chant at the center of monastic life in the sixth century, as it is with St. Francis, who composed the first song in vernacular Italian in direct imitation of the sinful troubadours of the thirteenth century. Yet after the Benedictines became established, battles over music still raged within its ranks and innovators were punished. Hucbald, the leading Benedictine music theorist of the late ninth and early tenth centuries, was forced out of the order and had to seek the protection of the bishop. Guido of Arezzo, who joined the Benedictines a few decades later, is lauded today as the inventor of musical notation, but he was also evicted from the monastery because of his disruptive musical practices. In a surviving letter, he bewails "the conspiring of the Philistines" who caused him to be "banished from pleasant domains"—and goes on to complain that "the jealousy of the artisan made him unwilling to teach anyone his secret."[17]

What in the world is he talking about? Nowadays it's hard to imagine anyone getting angry about musical notation, but in the medieval era that simple expedient posed a threat to singing masters and choir leaders. Before the arrival of written music, you needed to go to those power brokers to get taught songs, but with Guido's notation you could learn the melodies on your own. Guido of Arezzo is, for us, an esteemed innovator, but in his day he was a nuisance and a threat.

The same is true of Benedict himself, now a revered saint but in his own time a radical who incurred the wrath of powerful adversaries inside the church. We are told that Benedict survived two attempts at poisoning by angry clerics and faced many obstacles and persecutions because of his obstinate attempts to reform religious life. Benedict is now considered one of the great spiritual visionaries in Western history, but no one thought the details of his life worth preserving until several decades after his death. Can you guess who finally decided to research and preserve Benedict's life story? Pope Gregory, nowadays honored as the father of Christian chanting, is the source of almost everything we know about St. Benedict. Gregory based his account on discussions with four of Benedict's disciples, and left us a detailed narrative relating the great deeds and miracles of the reformer who, in his own day, left Rome in disgust at the decadence he saw there.

We can look at this process as a straightforward case of Pope Gregory expressing belated approval of St. Benedict's reforms, but it's just as true, and perhaps even more revealing, that Gregory legitimized his own activities, musical and otherwise, by linking himself with this once controversial predecessor. Roughly half a century elapsed between the death of Benedict in the year 543 and the papacy of Gregory in 590—approximately the same length of time between Bob Dylan shaking up the establishment with his protest songs and his later acceptance of a Nobel Prize. That's a typical duration for this process of musical mainstreaming, whether we are talking about rockers or chanters. The rebellion is institutionalized, but it's a messy process that happens slowly, confronting many obstacles along the way. History books retain the official account, downplaying details of the earlier friction, and the most revealing evidence is often destroyed.

As such examples show, many of the most transgressive musical movements of the medieval era sprang from the heart of the Catholic faith, often to the dismay of church leaders. Among these, none is more intriguing and deserving of attention than the music of the renegade clerics known as the Goliards. If Christian society during this period could be said to have a counterculture, the Goliards operated at the heart of it, and though few of them achieved positions of rank and influence, they played a decisive role in secularizing European music. Many of the Goliards had abandoned their religious orders for a less disciplined life, surviving on the fringes of society. They often traveled from town to town, and for that reason were sometimes referred to as *vagantes*, or "wandering students." They were most noticeable in university towns, where they lingered either to study, to teach, or merely to enjoy the bustling activity of such settings. In an age when literacy was rare and erudition even rarer, the Goliards stood out wherever they traveled due to their learning, although their worldly wealth was modest. They made their way in society by relying on their wits, their education, and—most important for our history—their skills as performers or entertainers.

Even though religious vows represented a lifelong commitment during the Middle Ages—Pope Innocent III claimed that even he had no authority to rescind this holy obligation—clerics had long sought ways of escaping from their orders, some literally climbing over the wall, others merely walking out the door. As far back as the early fifth century, St. John Cassian had noted that monks, like slaves, might try to sneak away under cover of darkness, and St. Benedict in his *Rule* was forced to make provisions for monks who left the community and wished to return. The label "Goliard" would not emerge until the twelfth century, but we have good reason to believe that these renegade clerics had an impact on European music and entertainment long before their songs were documented in manuscripts.

As with so many other secular songs, we first learn about those of the disobedient clerics from attacks made against them. The Council at Auxerre, in the sixth century, prohibited priests from singing and dancing at feasts—clearly an extension of the concerns mentioned above over the pagan overtones of these celebrations. But the specific reference to members of religious orders tells us that even at the dawn of the Middle Ages, priests and monks had aspirations to entertain. Complaints and prohibitions about the secular leanings of wandering clerics and those who aspired to a religious life date back even further. As early as 370, the Roman emperors Valens and Valentinian ordered the arrest of "devotees of idleness" who, abandoning their civic responsibilities, "under the pretext of religion have joined with bands of hermit monks." In 451, the Council of Chalcedon issued harsh restrictions on the movements of clerics—prohibiting them from changing dioceses, serving in multiple churches, or officiating in new locations without the permission of their bishop. A host of later councils and authorities imposed similar rules, with increasing reference to the unseemly behavior and performances of these feral monks and priests. For example, an Irish canon from the seventh century denounces clerics who "jested with foul words" and "sang at banquets, not building the faith but gratifying the ears."[18]

The Goliards' repertoire included something to upset almost everyone: satires, drinking songs, parodies of liturgy and religious music, bawdy lyrics, criticisms of powerful people (including the pope), love songs, gambling songs, and other idle entertainments. For example, this lyric from the *Carmina Burana*, the most famous collection of Goliard texts, describes a long visit to a bordello:

For three months, I suppose, I lingered there with her,
and as long as my purse was full I lived as a man of
distinction.

*But now on leaving Venus, I have been relieved of
money and clothing,
and so I am a pauper.*

But the author takes a moralizing stance at the end of his story: "Young men, let this story which you hear deter you."[19] We find such disavowals again and again in these lyrics, but they possess about as much conviction as a tobacco company's warning label on a pack of cigarettes—what the Goliard advises against he also tries to sell. As, for example, in this song in praise of Decius, the god of dice, which both warns against deceit and exalts in its benefits:

*The gambler's god
Is simply fraud;
The pang of losses
One counts a joke
When double-crosses
Win him a cloak.*[20]

In another lyric the charge of homosexuality is raised, but quickly rebutted: "Why does my mistress hold me in suspicion? . . . I am content with natural love and have learned to take the active, not the passive role."[21] But not every Goliard sin comes with a disclaimer or denial. "No finer song in praise of drinking has ever been written," the scholar George Whicher declared in praise of the Archpoet's *Estuans intrinsecus*, sometimes called "The Confession of Golias":

*My intention is to die
In the tavern drinking;
Wine must be at hand, for I
Want it when I'm sinking.*[22]

The noble sentiments of courtly love, which would soon infiltrate poetry and song throughout Europe, are occasionally found in the Goliards' lyrics, some of which predate the earliest troubadour works. But these coexist alongside coarser descriptions that have not lost their ability to shock. *Grates ago Veneri*, attributed to Peter of Blois, starts out describing a romantic encounter; but soon it turns into a disturbing description of a sexual assault:

> *With overboldness I use force . . .*
> *She coils herself and entwines her knees to prevent the*
> *door of her maidenhead from being unbarred . . .*
> *I pin her arms, I implant hard kisses. In this way*
> *Venus' palace is unbarred.*[23]

Here the original text is in Latin, and this would have limited the audience for such lyrics. Yet we can't help but conclude that similarly offensive works must have circulated in the vernacular languages of Europe—part of that vast body of secular lyrics never preserved for posterity.

Some scholars believe that the word *Goliard* is drawn, in part, from the name of the medieval theologian Pierre Abélard (1079–1142), whose calamitous personal story serves as a fitting case study to close this chapter. Abélard would be esteemed today for his contributions to scholastic philosophy, if he wasn't more famous for his scandalous affair with Héloïse d'Argenteuil. Their renown as lovers was all the more remarkable when one considers how seldom the doings of private individuals became widespread news in those days. Abélard was a brilliant young man from a noble Breton family. He studied at the cathedral school of Notre-Dame de Paris and established himself as an eminent teacher while still in his early twenties. His mistress, Héloïse, was a formidable scholar in her own right—her knowledge of Latin, Greek, and Hebrew and skill in writing would have been rare in any individual of the time, but especially for a woman from outside the nobility. Abélard was her instructor before becoming her lover.

"With our lessons as pretext, we abandoned ourselves entirely to love," Abélard later wrote in his account of their affair. "In short our desires left no stage of love-making untried, and if love could devise something new, we welcomed it." Héloïse became pregnant and gave birth to a son. The couple were married secretly, but her uncle still bore a grievance for his niece's dishonor and sought revenge, his anger aggravated by Abélard's unwillingness to admit publicly that Héloïse was his wife. A servant was bribed to allow assailants entry to Abélard's sleeping quarters, and there they "took cruel vengeance on me of such appalling barbarity as to shock the whole world; they cut off the parts of my body whereby I had committed the wrong of which they complained." The denouement finds Héloïse taking vows as a nun and eventually rising to the rank of abbess, while Abélard retreats to the life of a monk and occasionally a hermit. He continued to teach and write, but faced repeated charges of heresy that followed him until his death. This is not the ending Hollywood would have chosen for a love story, but one suitable for the purposes of those upholding public order and morality.[24]

Yet the student of music history will be especially intrigued by a revealing admission in Abélard's account of the affair. "Now the more I was taken up with these pleasures," he relates in regard to his passion for Héloïse, "the less time I could give to philosophy . . . and when inspiration did come to me, it was for writing love-songs, not the secrets of philosophy." Given the paucity of surviving secular songs from this time and place, the revelation is worthy of note, but even more fascinating is the philosopher's next comment. "A lot of these songs, as you know, are still popular and sung in many places, particularly by those who enjoyed the kind of life I led." Lest anyone ascribe the fame of these songs to Abélard's vanity, Héloïse validates his claim in a surviving letter of her own. She writes to her former lover:

> You left many love-songs and verses which won wide popularity for the charm of their words and tunes and kept your name continually on everyone's lips. The beauty of the airs ensured that even the unlettered did not forget you. . . . And as most of these songs told of our love, they soon made me widely known and roused the envy of many women against me.[25]

The fact that Abélard's famous (in their day) songs have not survived, at least not with any clear attribution to him, is extraordinary, especially when we consider that this scholar's preserved texts amount to around one million words and could fill a library shelf. Was there no room in all these manuscripts for a few love lyrics—especially songs that were so popular that today we would describe them as hits? But we learn an important lesson from this fact: namely, that the real history of music, as it flourished among the "unlettered" (to borrow Héloïse's term), is often hidden from view, and the perspicacious researcher must often go beyond the sanctioned texts and reconstruct past events—almost like a detective at the scene of a crime—from stray clues and dropped hints. That will become especially evident as we try to unlock the origins of the great revolution in Western song unleashed during Abélard's own lifetime, by the troubadours in the south of France.[26]

11

Oppression and Musical Innovation

We are familiar with musical innovations coming out of Africa. For more than a century, that's been the main plot in the narrative of popular music, with contributions from the descendants of African slaves rewriting the rules of commercial songs in every decade. From ragtime to hip-hop and beyond, with all the stopping points in between, African American musicians have played the role of creative disruptors, outsiders who shock and outrage parents but delight youngsters and set the standards for hits and hit-makers. Along the way, black innovators have established the soundtrack for each new generation, and sometimes have lived long enough to see their controversial songs enter the mainstream of global culture. This has been the story of my musical life as a listener, and probably yours as well.

But few realize that a similar process has taken place in the past, and with the same disruptive impact on the conventions of Western song. Even in the least likely setting—among the nobles of France in the late medieval period—a musical revolution took place that drew on the scandalous songs of slaves who came into Europe from North Africa and the Middle East. Here we see the recurring pattern of musical innovation in the starkest terms: the despised outsider creates a bold new way of singing, and then the powerful insider steps in to take control of this provocative performance style. And often to take credit for it as well. Then comes the inevitable cover-up, with the official historical accounts denying that this cultural transaction ever happened.

In this instance, fame and glory accrue to the troubadours, those nobles of southern France who are given credit for the invention of secular song in the vernacular language, a moment of liberation for Western music when the chains of clerical interference were thrown off and music was finally allowed to express the most intimate thoughts and feelings. The hero of this story, according to conventional accounts, is William IX, Duke of Aquitaine, acclaimed as the first troubadour. He is the innovator who set the tone for the next thousand years of Western song, which even today bears the unmistakable stamp of this musical revolution. The very word *troubadour*, still used to describe a singer-songwriter, translates as a "finder" or "discoverer"—implying that these visionaries created a whole new way of singing marked by a more individualistic tone and a deeper sensitivity to the inner life.

In the current day, we simply take it for granted that songs are vehicles of personal expression, not tools for achieving institutional objectives. We look into the song and expect to find the singer, and the more confessional and intimate the revelations, the more we are pleased. Yet how odd that a powerful duke, one of the wealthiest men in Europe, was the catalyst who made this happen. Are members of the nobility more in touch with their feelings than commoners? Do they experience stronger emotions and suffer more from the pangs of love? Yet if we believe C. S. Lewis, who analyzed this cultural turning point in his seminal book *The Allegory of Love*, William IX and his followers exerted an impact that went far beyond music, even defining the concept of romance as it persists today. "They effected a change which has left no corner of our ethics, our imagination, or our daily life untouched,"

Lewis exclaims. "Compared with this revolution the Renaissance is a mere ripple on the surface of literature."[1]

As we saw in the previous chapter, peasant women in Europe were singing scandalous songs about love in the vernacular for centuries before the troubadours. If the lyrics of these songs had survived, we could judge how much the nobility borrowed from these predecessors. But even on the evidence presented so far, we would be wise to consider the troubadour revolution as a process of legitimization rather than innovation, as the decisive moment when ways of singing previously censored and marginalized found powerful champions who could not be silenced by the authorities. Indeed, the singers now *were* the authorities.

No, the troubadours did not invent new ways of singing about emotions and the interior life—we have already seen how the Egyptian artisans of Deir el-Medina were doing that two thousand years before the nobles of Provence. Nor did they invent the concept of romance, which even the ancients knew and feared: their anxiety can be measured in the fact that they turned Cupid into an armed assailant whose arrows could subdue even the greatest warrior. But we still must give these singing nobles credit for transforming the musical culture of the Western world, for they set a beguiling example that still charms us in the present day. I suspect that our own notions of romance are still haunted by the attitudes of courtly love that permeate the troubadour lyrics. So even if William IX, known in his time as a warrior and seducer, did not invent the love song, he did impart an elegance and glamour to it that no peasant or slave could have conveyed. That may not seem fair to us today, given our modern egalitarian principles, but are we really so much different? The romances of celebrities—even of princes and princesses, where they still survive—do not fail to attract intense interest in our own time. We may never be royals, as the words of a familiar pop song tell us, but apparently we still fantasize about it.

But these lusty nobles had role models to follow, and not just from the Christian world. Traditional accounts of the troubadours ignore the most important precedent for their secularization and sensualization of song. Female slave singers from the Arab world set the example for Europe hundreds of years before the birth of William IX of Aquitaine. Although Baghdad served as the epicenter of this style of singing, it spread through North Africa and into Europe after the Muslim conquest of the Iberian Peninsula in the early eighth century. These enslaved singers, known as *qiyan*, are the least well-known innovators in the history of music. No performers of the entire medieval period were more daring, or anticipated the later shifts in musical culture with greater prescience. Yet their contributions have been hidden from view, even in specialized scholarly works on the origins of troubadour music.

Once we grasp the significance of slaves in shaping our music, many mysteries are solved. For example, why do our romantic lyrics so often rely on images of bondage and servitude? How did our notions of courtship and romance ever get connected with ropes and chains and *Fifty Shades of Grey* imagery? This is bizarre and even a little creepy. Yet those with no taste for fetishism nonetheless sing that they are slaves to love, seemingly oblivious to the painful and debased history behind this concept. And it was even stranger when the nobles of France declared that they were slaves to their beloved. How could a duke be a slave? How can a duke even *pretend* to be a slave? But this ridiculous playacting makes perfect sense when we grasp that the people who invented this way of singing were actually enslaved. Today the slavery of love is a metaphor; back then it was reality.

We have encountered slaves as innovators before in this book, and will do so again in the pages ahead. So perhaps this is a good time to ask why slaves have exerted so much influence on our music. Is it just happenstance that the Greeks named their most disruptive modes after their Phrygian and Lydian slaves? Is it mere coincidence that the Romans brought slaves onstage to deliver the crowd-pleasing songs in their theatrical performances? Is it an accident of fate that, two thousand years later, southern plantation owners did the same thing, relying on the creativity and artistry of an oppressed underclass for their musical entertainment? By what

strange series of events do the most vulnerable and exploited people in a society emerge as a musical elite?

The slave has only one advantage in these settings, but it is a
huge advantage, at least from the standpoint of creativity and artistic innovation. The slave is the outsider, and for this simple reason
has no allegiance to the conventions and values of the surrounding
society. Breakthroughs in song always require a willingness to disrupt the status quo, and the rich and powerful are the least likely
people to do this—which is why we should always be suspicious
when historical accounts give credit to a political or religious leader
(King Solomon, Pope Gregory, Confucius, Duke William IX) for
paradigm-changing musical works. The outsider is almost always
the catalyst, the carrier of new genes in the musical DNA. In most
cases, slaves also bring specific musical skills and knowledge from
remote lands, different ways of performance that will enrich the
culture that holds them in bondage. Finally, the slaves are granted
one freedom not allowed to the rulers: they are expected to sin, to
deviate from the intrusive moral rules that role models must obey,
especially in sexual matters. In the case of the *qiyan* of the early
Abbasid era, who date back at least to the eighth century AD, these
female slaves were allowed to move about in public without covering their faces; they could wear colorful clothing instead of the
loose-fitting dark garments prescribed for 'respectable' women;
they could engage in flirtatious banter with men and have affairs.
These freedoms came at a heavy price. In other matters, the *qiyan*
had no rights; they could be sold to the highest bidder or forced
into prostitution. But their position outside the prevailing norms
gave them artistic license, ensuring that their songs would have a
freshness and audacity that no cultural insider could match. Eventually the freeborn learned to imitate these songs, but only after
the slave showed the way.

Anyone who hopes to comprehend the revolution that took
place in Western music in the late medieval period must grasp this
dynamic. The loosening of the institutional strictures that turned song
into a platform of personal expression will otherwise be completely

misunderstood. A mighty duke did not grant that freedom of romantic (and sexual) expression; he merely recognized its already-existing artistic power and gave it official sanction, if only because he wanted a taste of it himself. By the same token, this conceptual leap—a leap that allows us to see slaves and outsiders as catalysts for musical revolution—testifies to the pressing need for a *subversive* history of song. We celebrate outsiders in these pages not to be edgy or to adopt a fashionable revisionist pose, but for the simple reason that these individuals are, again and again, the people who cause the major shifts in our shared musical lives to take place. They are the ones who make our old songs new again. We ought to be grateful and, at a minimum, give them proper credit for the freedoms they have granted us—an acknowledgment always tinged with tragic irony, given how little freedom they enjoyed themselves.

The tradition of slave singers in the Arab world predates the rise of Islam. The slave population, even in this earlier period, was a multicultural mix that included Persians, Ethiopians, Egyptians, and Byzantines, among others. The clash of musical perspectives produced by such multicultural settings has often served as a foundation for new ways of singing. The biblical myth of the Tower of Babel warns us that the intermingling of our planet's varied languages leads to conflict and confusion—and many perhaps still believe this today, even in an age of instantaneous digital translation—but our historical knowledge of these melting-pot societies teaches us the opposite lesson when it comes to music. When different races and ethnic groups coexist in close proximity, the music flourishes. Just make a list of the music genres that came to prominence in port cities and border communities, whether we are talking about New Orleans, Liverpool, Kingston, Havana, Venice, or, in the current instance, the domain of William IX of Aquitaine, whose territories extended to the boundary of current-day Spain, where, in those days, Muslim musical practices and female singers of secular songs flourished.

With the spread of Islam and its military victories, both the number and diversity of slave musicians expanded in the Arab world. We even have the surviving text of an auction catalog that distinguishes the pros and cons of a dozen different geographical sources of female slaves, praising Berbers for their "fidelity and energy," warning about the "self indulgence and delicacy" of Nubians, and condemning Abyssinians as "useless for singing and dancing." As these descriptions make clear, musical skills were important, but hardly the only traits sought after by owners of human chattel. Most slaves, as in all times and places, worked as servants or laborers, often in abusive settings or degrading occupations. Yet a few slave women in the early Abbasid period parlayed their skills into positions of comfort or even influence. Singing and versifying were valued talents, as were wit and conversational ability, and those who possessed these desirable attributes might secure privileges otherwise unobtainable. Yet we would be led astray if we didn't also recognize the importance of beauty and sensuality in the special position these women held in Islamic society. The appeal of a musician, then and now, was sometimes discerned by the eye rather than the ear. In any event, by the ninth century a true salon culture built around female slaves had developed. Although Baghdad in modern-day Iraq served as its epicenter, its cultural influence would be felt throughout the Muslim world and into the Iberian Peninsula.[2]

When men participated in this cultural shift, they were often branded as effeminate in both the Christian and Muslim worlds—just as they had been in the pagan cultures of Greece and Rome. In the Arabic world, we frequently find important singers described in surviving texts as *mukhannathun,* a group we looked at briefly back in Chapter 9, and who helped lay the groundwork for the later troubadour revolution. As noted there, *mukhannathun* is a catch-all term, often translated as "effeminate men," and in specific contexts it might encompass anyone who did not conform to prevailing notions of masculinity. These individuals often faced discrimination, punishment, and exile. The stigma of the label can be gauged by a ninth-century stricture noting that a false accusation claiming someone was a *mukhannath* should be disciplined with twenty lashes—the same penalty listed for homosexual intercourse or, for that matter, spreading the slander that a true believer was a Jew. Yet not only were these *mukhannathun* admired in the field of music, but there is considerable evidence that the feminine image of these performers enhanced their popularity.

The story is told of the singer Hakim, who was denounced by his son for switching to the singing style of the *mukhannathun* in his old age. "Be quiet, ignorant boy!" Hakim responded, noting that he had performed in a more manly style "for sixty years, and never made more than my daily bread," but after embracing the more popular style he "made more money than you'd ever seen before." Another revealing text concludes its praise of the singer al-Dalāl with these enthusiastic words: "And there is something yet greater than that! . . . Anyone who hears this will know that it is by a *mukhannath* in truth!" A music fan today can't help but be reminded of the cult of authenticity that permeates the followers of various genres. Just as blues singers are more celebrated if they hail from Mississippi instead of Iowa, or hip-hoppers lose their street cred when they grow up in suburbia and not the inner city, so did Muslim musicians of the eighth century get a boost from their perceived effeminacy.[3]

The complex and contradictory role of the *mukhannath* performer comes to the forefront in the life story of Tuways, who is often celebrated as the first great musical innovator of the Islamic world. Tuways was the earliest renowned *mukhannath* singer, but many feared him as a jinx, a man of ill-omen. It's worth noting that his name appears in two proverbs that have nothing to do with music. A person cursed by destiny was sometimes described as "more unlucky than Tuways," while a similar saying would brand a man with delicate manners as "more effeminate than Tuways." These associations seem to have done little to hurt his popularity as a singer, although a marked generational divide could be seen in his reputation. The older ruling class disapproved of his performances, while young men were drawn to this new way of singing—a divide that most of us know from firsthand experience. Perhaps we aren't surprised to see this conflict between old and young showing up in early Islamic society, but the connection of musical innovation with sexuality and the open flaunting of an 'alternative' lifestyle give us a sense of just how large the gap is between historical reality and prevailing assumptions about the attitudes of traditional societies toward music.[4]

This gap is also evident in the authorized narrative about Abū Nuwās, the great master of wine songs in classical Arabic literature. His historical importance cannot be dismissed, but the Egyptian Ministry of Culture burned six thousand copies of his poetry in 2001 because of its homoerotic themes, while other works of this musical innovator were blocked from publication—apparently too hot to handle twelve centuries after his death. The *Global Arabic Encyclopedia*, an authoritative thirty-volume reference funded by the Saudi Arabian government, offers a highly sanitized account of his life. Authorities can't ignore him, but neither can they accept him on his own terms. These interventions offer powerful testimony to how much subversive protagonists in music can still shock listeners more than a millennium later, but they also give us a glimpse into the ways history is reinterpreted to accommodate their legitimization. Centuries may have passed, but the disinformation campaign continues unabated—often unwittingly assisted by those who put their trust in the sanctioned accounts.

I mentioned above that slaves and *mukhannathun* enjoyed a strange kind of freedom as outsiders to sing of subjects that might otherwise be taboo. But even they had to be careful to avoid political themes or satires aimed at the ruling class. Insults and ridicule directed at other entertainers were allowed, perhaps even encouraged, but the established institutions, and especially slavery itself, could not be attacked. In the face of such strictures, the personal always becomes a substitute for the political. Those studying the songs of slaves and other oppressed groups have learned to tease out coded meanings. Henry Louis Gates introduced the term *signifying* to encompass this practice and identified a number of common ingredients of coded communication within African American culture, but it's surprising how many of the same features are found in the songs, poems, and anecdotes of the Islamic *qiyan*. Here we encounter the mischievous attitudes of the trickster, the stylized use of invective and loaded meanings, a brash irreverence, a desire to goad and provoke, a flaunting of community standards, and sometimes shocking profanity. Take, for example, the response of the slave singer 'Inan, who responded with the following song after a long bout of wine drinking and unsatisfying lovemaking:

> *There is no pleasure in a lover that is unattainable.*
> *O host of lovers, how execrable is love*
> *if there is flabbiness in the lover's prick.*

The power dynamic hinted at here raises such sentiments above shallow vulgarity. The woman whose views have no influence in other settings takes advantage of the one sphere, the lovers' bed, where her judgments are solicited and even feared. Intimate expression serves as surrogate for prohibited modes of complaint.[5]

Scholars long ignored or minimized the influence of Islamic songs on European performers, but the mounting evidence no longer allows us to reject a path of dissemination through North Africa and via the Iberian Peninsula into France. Ezra Pound anticipated this hypothesis back in 1923 via a perspicacious line from his *Canto VIII*, where he asserted that William of Aquitaine "brought the song up out of Spain / with the singers and viels." Pound had focused on the troubadours during his graduate work at the University of Pennsylvania, and the poet's father submitted his book on the subject, *The Spirit of Romance*, to the chair of the Department of English, in hopes it would fulfill the dissertation requirement and secure a PhD for his son. The department chair, Felix Schelling, an expert in the Elizabethan lyric, dismissed the request out of hand—a poor move, in retrospect. But even Pound had no way of anticipating the extraordinary discovery made in 1948 by an Oxford student, Samuel Stern, who found that apparently incoherent lines in eleventh-century Hebrew and Arabic lyrics were actually in a vernacular Romance language. Just a few years earlier, Spanish musicologist Felipe Pedrell had declared that "our music has absorbed no influence from the Arabs," but now dozens of lyrics, newly reinterpreted, revealed a multicultural mingling of influences. Even more striking, the lyrics Stern translated emphasized intense personal feelings at a time when vernacular songs of this sort went unrecorded in the Christian world. The most likely interpretation was that the Arabic texts drew on popular lyrics that were circulating in the Iberian Peninsula—probably similar to the very ones the church leaders had repeatedly attacked over the centuries.[6]

Then, in the 1960s, a fragmentary document came to light from Ahmad al-Tifashi, a thirteenth-century Arabic poet who dealt with homoerotic themes. Al-Tifashi credits the Andalusian Arabic scholar Avempace, who lived during the first stirrings of the troubadour movement, with having "combined the songs of the Christians with those of the East, thereby inventing a style found only in Andalus, toward which the temperament of its people inclined, so that they rejected all others." The conclusion is inescapable: this 'fusion' music that celebrated intense personal emotions not only existed, but represented the most popular songs in the most intensely multicultural society in the Western world. This is the platform on which the troubadour revolution took place.[7]

We know that William VIII, the father of the first troubadour, brought hundreds of Islamic prisoners back from his Spanish campaigns. These captives must have carried their music with them— they always do, songs and folklore are the only inviolable properties of those in bondage—and it is likely that the future 'inventor' of the troubadour lyric heard similar songs during his childhood performed by *qiyan* trained in the flourishing styles of the Arabic world. He may even have learned Arabic. In recent years, scholars have gone so far as to suggest that several lines in a surviving version of one of his lyrics, *Farai un vers*, are in that language. In any event, the nobility soon made the leap from listening to performing secular songs of this sort. In this regard, they followed the example of the Abbasid elite who had imitated the language of slave singers long before the troubadour era. The caliph Harun al-Rashid, who reigned during the time of Charlemagne, is even attributed as author of a lyric celebrating his 'bondage' to three especially favored slave women. "The whole of mankind obey me, while I am ruled by them and they submit not to me," he declared, concluding: "It can only be the sovereignty of love." This is the essence of courtly love, but expressed three hundred years before the rise of the troubadours.[8]

All of this took place in the context of a larger dissemination of musical influences from Africa to Europe in matters both small and large. Consider, for example, the origins of the lute, seen by many as the quintessential Western musical instrument during the late medieval era and Renaissance. This instrument was brought to Europe via Spain by the Moors, and is essentially an *oud* from the Islamic world, but with the addition of frets—the frets were required to eliminate all those microtonal bends, essential to African music but incompatible with the Pythagorean paradigm and its insistence on pure, scalar notes. In fact, the non-European origin of the lute is reflected in its name, likely derived from the Arabic *al'ud*, signifying "made of wood," and also the source of the word *oud* itself. In the *Cantigas de Santa Maria*, perhaps the most influential collection of songs from the late medieval period, we find an intriguing illustration of two lute players, one dark skinned and the other white, with the African clearly positioned in a place of preeminence while his Christian accompanist appears to be looking on and imitating his companion.

But we hardly need such illustrations to prove that outsiders were the leading music teachers in southern Europe during this era. The center of music education at this juncture was Córdoba, which had the largest population of any European city in the year 1000, with around half a million residents—more than ten times as many inhabitants as Paris or London at that juncture. The most famous medieval music teacher in Spain was Ziryab—a name that translates as *blackbird*, and indicates the skin color of this celebrated polymath, who was probably either of African or mixed Arabic and African descent. Ziryab might have spent his entire career in Baghdad if a bitter rivalry with his teacher Ishaq al-Mawsili hadn't forced his departure. He worked in present-day Syria and Tunisia before settling in Córdoba, where he established a music school that was the Juilliard of its day. His songs and lute-playing exerted a long-lasting influence, but his innovations extended into other areas as well. His influence on food, fashion, hair styling, and personal grooming testifies to the superstar status he enjoyed. Historians of music would do well to pay more attention to this seminal figure. His merging of African and European traditions anticipates many later developments in music and other spheres.

My focus in this chapter has been almost exclusively on the Islamic world, but now, as we turn our attention to Europe, we will see the same themes and trends emerging with striking clarity in the context of Western culture. In particular, the ethos of servitude embedded in the *qiyan* songs of this era will get a new name in Europe. We now know it under the label of "courtly love"—a very elegant title for the submissive groveling of a slave before an idealized beloved. The troubadours didn't come up with that name—the phrase "courtly love" doesn't appear until the nineteenth century. But it aptly describes the graceful and stylized attitudes of their lyrics. Even so, the trappings of servitude are still apparent at every turn. "The lover is always abject," C. S. Lewis notes in his survey of this influential poetic style and manner of courtship. "Obedience to his lady's lightest wish, however whimsical, and silent acquiescence in her rebukes, however unjust, are the only virtues he dares to claim." Servitude, in this new guise, becomes romantic, even glamorous.[9]

Is there a more powerful meme in the history of Western culture? How many songs celebrate the courtship of the lover and deference to the beloved? There are too many to count. The same is true of novels, short stories, plays, movies, poems, soap operas, musicals, comic books, and every other form of narrative. Even if the troubadours didn't invent the vernacular love lyric, they achieved something perhaps even more impressive. As we shall see in the next chapter, they took the emotion-filled sentiments of peasants, Goliards, slaves, and other despised groups and transformed them into a playfully romantic game of knights and lovely ladies. They turned love into a spectacle of picturesque and chivalrous behavior. In short, they created the concept of courtship, and all its stylized attitudes. In doing so, they defined our fantasy life for the next one thousand years. Indeed, much of our erotic imagination remains immersed in medieval trappings, more than we care to admit. A Google search for the term "knight in shining armor" comes back with ten million hits—most of them seemingly describing longings for the future rather than our characterization of the past. At some deep level of our collective psyches, we remain both the serving vassal and the put-on-a-pedestal beloved.

12

Not All Wizards Carry Wands

S uch a powerful idea was destined to go viral, as we would describe it in contemporary terms. Even today we embrace the musical attitudes the troubadours brought to their performances, starting in southern France during the late eleventh century. Nowadays we simply assume that songs express personal emotions, especially feelings about love, and that they are intertwined with the biography and worldview of the singer. But before the rise of the troubadours, such notions only existed on the fringes and in the shadows of musical life in Europe, facing censorship and backlash whenever they became too prominent. This now would change, first for a small number of performers, many of them nobles, but eventually for almost everyone else. We should count ourselves among these beneficiaries.

The rapid spread of this new approach to song can perhaps be gauged by the name of one of the earliest troubadours, Cercamon, whose pseudonym literally translates as "circle-the-world." We can connect him to the oldest troubadour, William IX, Duke of Aquitaine—one of Cercamon's surviving works is a *planh*, or funeral lament, for the duke's son, William X—but his travels may have brought him to many other locales, perhaps even on the Second Crusade as a follower of Louis VII. Marcabru, another prominent early troubadour, was probably a student of Cercamon's, and he, too, took his craft on the road, perhaps at first as a *joglar*, a performer of songs created by others, and later as composer of his own works. We hear of him at the court of King Alfonso VII of León and Castile, and the spread of his work is testified by frequent references to him by later writers.

If the surviving accounts of these singers indicate the geographical reach of the troubadour art, they also make clear its even more impressive leap across barriers of class and privilege. Marcabru is said to have been a foundling of illegitimate birth, yet this didn't prevent him from unloading scathing attacks on the nobility. The lowborn now had a platform for denouncing their rulers, if only via song. Bernart de Ventadorn, the most distinguished of the next generation of troubadours, was the son of a servant—not even a baker, we are told, but merely the person who gathered the wood and heated the oven where the bread was baked. Yet he was bold enough to sing love songs to the wife of the Viscount of Ventadorn, and perhaps even share her bed. The viscount himself allegedly thought so: he eventually put his wife under the watchful eye of a guard and forced the amorous troubadour to leave his court.

But Bernart, described as a handsome man in a surviving text, found the favor of an even more exalted lady, Eleanor of Aquitaine, who possessed the rare distinction of serving as queen of both England and France. Our lowborn troubadour may even have been on hand in Westminster Abbey at the coronation of Eleanor and her husband Henry II in 1154. That a career of this magnitude could be built on love songs—and no troubadour sang about love with more devotion and passion than Bernart de Ventadorn—tells us not only how much these songs were valued during this period, but also how profoundly the world had changed since the time of Charlemagne, who had Gregorian chant taught in his palace, and when he was seeking musicians, had them supplied by the pope.

The nobles set the tone, and everyone followed their example. "Now these days everyone—Christian, Jew, or Saracen, emperor, prince, king, duke, count, viscount, vavasseur, cleric, bourgeois, peasant—simply everyone great or small, is putting his whole heart into singing and composing," complained Raimon Vidal, a Catalan troubadour of the early thirteenth century. "You could hardly find yourself in so private or solitary a place, with so few or so many persons, that you would not hear someone or other, or all together, singing; for even the most rustic shepherds of the mountains find their greatest solace in song." And these songs, more than ever before, were about the singers themselves—for high and low, music now served as a channel for emotion-driven autobiography.[1]

The new rules of music not only fostered self-expression, but also created an unprecedented degree of fame for those who excelled at it. This marks a major change in the musical culture of Europe. A significant portion of the art, writing, and music of the medieval period was produced anonymously, and though the silence surrounding the people who created these works was by no means absolute—composers such as Hildegard von Bingen, Léonin, and Pérotin are known to us by name—nothing prepares us for the hero worship directed at the troubadours. Some five hundred of them are identified in the surviving literature. We can hardly avoid the conclusion that some aspect or essence of this music struck its listeners as inseparable from the personalities of those who created it. When music served God—as was the case with almost every song preserved from the early medieval period—the humans who created it were obscured by the higher purpose of their craft. Now that music celebrated love and glory, the singer emerged as the focal point of the lyrics, the real subject of every song. At this juncture, the cult of personality entered the DNA of Western music, where it remains to this day, the dominant gene passed on to each new generation of singers, surviving all other changes of style and genre.

How did the church respond to this? A few priests continued to rail against the erotic tone of these popular songs, but their prohibitions no longer had much impact on the musical tastes of the day. On the other extreme, some Christians adopted the troubadour's craft for their own purposes. The most prominent example is St. Francis of Assisi, whose *Canticle of the Sun*, the oldest surviving lyric in vernacular Italian, clearly imitates the troubadour lyrics he heard during his youth. Francis even referred to his friars as "jongleurs of the Lord"—adopting the same word, *jongleur* (or minstrel), used to describe performers of secular songs. But most responses fell between these two extremes, and an uneasy truce emerged between Christianity and the new music.

I believe that the rules of this truce explain otherwise paradoxical attitudes toward sexuality embedded in these lyrics. Again and again in these songs, we find the most heated expressions of sexual desire placed side by side with calls to chastity. Troubadours sing about their libidinous passions, and then deny they want to act on them. What's going on here? Most readers nowadays will view this as little more than hypocrisy. The seductive songs we know about inevitably aim at seduction, so it's hard for us to comprehend any other end in mind. We assume the troubadours were celebrating actual sexual union with the beloved—otherwise, what's the point? But this attitude reflects a basic misunderstanding of the rules of the game—not just the dictates of courtly love, but also the implicit compromise between secular and religious forces that allowed this music to come out into the open.

The troubadour revolution was built on the view that, in the words of troubadour Guilhem de Montanhagol, "from love chastity comes forth, for if a man aspires entirely to love he cannot then act badly." Not every singer lived up to this ideal, and a few troubadours were perhaps chronic offenders. But such lapses could be viewed as a result of human weakness, and thus did not topple the prevailing theology. Indeed, the troubadour's art could not have flourished if it hadn't accepted a measure of restraint and rule-based ordering of sexual desire. It's worth noting that some of the lustiest of the surviving lyrics were dedicated to noble ladies or the wives of powerful men. We deceive ourselves if we view these songs as calls to adultery. On the contrary, the very unattainability of these women made them the perfect subjects for such songs.[2]

But let's be honest. Over the long run, this attempt to turn lusty lyrics into a vehicle for moralizing was doomed to failure. Sexy songs are poor platforms for imposing ethical guidelines—although authoritarian regimes, even in our own day, haven't stopped trying. Even as I write, the Communist Youth League in China continues to release videos by the attractive boy band TFBoys, whose songs celebrate the joys of romance while encouraging deference to the party line. North Korea strives to create K-Pop equivalents—for example, relying on the attractive Hyon Song-wol to sing uplifting songs, such as "I Love Pyongyang," "She Is a Discharged Soldier," or "We Are Troops of the Party." Nonetheless, hardline regimes still haven't figured out how to balance demand for erotic music with the strictures of prevailing dogma. In 2015, Ugandan singer Jemimah Kansiime found herself in jail for rubbing soapsuds over her body in a music video, and in 2017, an Egyptian vocalist, Shyma, was arrested after eating a banana while performing her song "I Have Issues." In most instances, authoritarian regimes have learned, it's best to bend in the face of musical trends, and find ways to coexist with a little give and take on both sides. At least that was the compromise that allowed secular songs of personal expression to come out of hiding in the Western world during the late medieval period. Even if the truce couldn't survive, the impact on music was irreversible. From this point onward, musicians would continue to sing about their love lives, no matter what the dictators dictated.

What role did women play in this cultural shift? At a minimum, they laid the groundwork for the new way of singing. The prohibitions on secular songs in earlier periods had repeatedly targeted women, perpetuating the ancient mythology of the female 'siren' song as the epitome of risky music. And even when these songs were given scope for expression in the Islamic world, women were acknowledged as preeminent in the music of longing and desire. The rise of so-called courtly love, from this perspective, ought to be seen as the long overdue legitimization of a feminine approach to song. Certainly the songs themselves are built on an idealization of the feminine, as well as an implicit acceptance that women are the judges and arbiters in all matters relating to emotions and intimate relationships—an extraordinary claim in a culture that gave so little real power to females. The very words these lyrics used to describe a man's intercession to a woman—a "suit" offered by a "suitor"—are the ones we still apply when making a legal appeal to a judge. Yet the woman's authority apparently ended when she wanted credit for her own songs. Women account for just 5 percent of the singers we know by name from this era, and only around two dozen songs by female troubadours, known as *trobairitz*, have survived—in comparison with around 2,600 by men.

Most *trobairitz* are known for only a single song, while just two, Castelloza and the Comtessa de Diá, have left us several lyrics. Very little biographical information survives, and in most instances the details emphasize the women's noble families or the powerful men they knew and loved. Many male troubadours came from humble origins, but a *trobairitz* needed influential connections for her songs to be preserved for posterity.

Yet we must pay close attention to this small body of work if we hope to understand the true dimensions of the troubadour revolution. Lyrics by women from this era reveal a different approach to singing about love. They devote less energy to wordplay, and offer more realistic depictions of romantic affairs. The situations described are less stylized but more plausible. Note, for example, the direct, conversational tone Castelloza adopts in this heartfelt lyric:

Handsome friend, as a lover true
I loved you, for you pleased me,
but now I see I was a fool,
for I've barely seen you since.
I never tried to trick you,
yet you returned me bad for good;
I love you so, without regret,
but love has stung me with such force
I think no good can possibly
be mine unless you say you love me.[3]

Compare this with the over-the-top protestations of Bernart de Ventadorn, who jumps from metaphor to metaphor as he seeks out the most extravagant ways to describe his frustrations as a lover:

Like some great trout that dashes to the bait
Until he feels love's hook, all hot and blindly,
I rushed toward too much love, too rash to wait,
Careless, till ringed in by love's flames I find me
Seared as by furnace fires upon a grate
Yet not one hand's breadth can I move, so strait
And narrow does this love enchain and bind me.[4]

We must give Bernart credit for anticipating the most fashionable tone in European love lyrics during the centuries ahead, when countless chansons, Petrarchan sonnets, frottolas, and madrigals would enumerate the sufferings of lovers with a quasi-sadistic relish, but dressed up with the most ostentatious poetic conceits. Even so, Castelloza is more attuned to the raw confessional tone of our own day. But even beyond that, her approach is far more credible.

The surviving texts of the women troubadours are important for another reason. I believe they give us a reasonable approximation of the forbidden vernacular songs during those long centuries when church authorities tried to prevent women from singing about their lives (and failed), while working to eliminate all written record of this music (and, alas, succeeded). If we hope to penetrate behind the veil imposed by censorship, and grasp what the songs of day-to-day life might have expressed, the *trobairitz* offer our best entry point. For the first time in a thousand years, a group of women in the Christian world were given the opportunity to express their inner life in nonreligious music, and their lyrics—at least, a few of them—were preserved for posterity. We do well to take such songs seriously.

Men certainly participated in this prohibited music-making before the rise of the troubadours, but if we can judge by church proclamations and denunciations, they were far less likely to sing these kinds of passionate songs than women—at least until the nobles of southern France made clear that a man's masculinity wasn't in doubt if he sang about a broken heart. When men finally embraced this style of performance, they gained renown as the innovators, so much so that women who sang about emotions during the era remained mostly in the shadows. But men changed the idiom even while serving as powerful advocates for it. They developed a far more stylized manner of singing about their feelings, still infused with passion, but consciously aspiring to a more embellished, and often poetically indirect, mode of expression. I can't help but be reminded of the lyric poets of the ancient world, who also took a tradition of singing closely linked with a female innovator—namely, Sappho—and turned it into a literary genre. In the case of the male troubadours, fervent singing became a highly self-conscious art marked by textual niceties and subtleties. The fact that we typically treat troubadour lyrics nowadays as written poetry is, of course, largely due to the absence of surviving musical notation, but the lyrics themselves facilitated this transition to the printed page.

By now we have gathered enough evidence to highlight the many incongruities and paradoxes in the history of women's music. There's something deeply disturbing in the fact that the two groups of women most closely associated with singing during the medieval period were nuns and prostitutes. There were, of course, many other women singing songs, including the *trobairitz*, but they hardly captured the medieval imagination the way these two groups did. Yet this stereotyping testifies to the fear and anxieties stirred up by female voices raised in song. Such music was sanctioned only in the safety of the nunnery, while in other settings it tended to licentiousness and sin—with very little room for anything in between. Despite these apprehensions, women managed to provide the creative impulse behind several categories of secular song, especially the three L's: the lament, the lullaby, and the love song. By this same token, these were three genres that rarely got preserved for posterity.

We have already seen how the love song and the lament were condemned for channeling dangerous emotions, but why was the humble lullaby marginalized? Thousands of lullabies must have been sung daily by medieval women, yet as scholar John Haines points out, "no titles, no composers and no dated or notated specimens survive." Even stranger is the continuation of that marginalization in our own time. We have hardly progressed beyond the closed worldview of the medieval authorities, for whom this whole category of music remained, in Haines's words, "anonymous, common, childish, and lacking written codification." We have seen how love songs got accepted as legitimate and artistic only after the nobility started singing them. May I hazard a guess that the lullaby would have gained similar prestige if dukes and lords had specialized in them? That never happened, so the whole genre still awaits its acceptance as art music.[5]

I have proposed elsewhere that a special group of songs exists that I call *performatives*, drawing on the terminology of philosopher J. L. Austin. Back in the 1950s, Austin pointed out in lectures at Oxford and Harvard that certain words have the power, when spoken, to *change the world*. They are only uttered on special occasions, and after they are said, human events are noticeably altered. One example took place on my wedding day, when I said: "I take you, Tara, to be my wife." Not only my spouse, but legal and tax authorities, treated me differently after I made that statement. The same thing happens when I tell a friend: "I promise to pay you back the money on Friday." Breaking that vow may have fewer consequences than violating a marriage vow—unless my friend is a loan shark with a penchant for vengeance—but saying these words still changes my external environment in a meaningful way. Other examples of performatives include "I'm naming our new dog Aristotle"; "I dub thee Sir Galahad"; "I say to thee, thou art Peter"; and "I'll give you a six-point spread on the Lakers-Celtics game." When J. L. Austin wrote a book about performative statements, he titled it *How to Do Things with Words*—a fitting name for a work that celebrated the efficacy of language in altering the world when spoken in certain contexts and settings.[6]

I raise this matter because I believe we need to undertake a similar expansion in our notions about music. Some songs are also performatives—they actually change human affairs rather than simply express emotions and moods. No scholar, to my knowledge, has noticed that women always seem to play a central role in these specifically performative genres of music. We have already seen how the magical music of the shamans is associated with femininity, even to the point that male shamans sometimes dress in women's attire. The same is true of the music of witches, sirens, courtesans, even mothers and lovers. In each of those cases, the woman's song is a performative, by Austin's rigorous standards. The lullaby, by definition, is a song that aims to put the child to sleep, and its success is judged not by artistic standards, but by its power to change behavior. Recall that both the love song and the lament, those two maligned specialties of medieval women, originated in the fertility rites of antiquity, where they aimed to resurrect a dying god. That's a powerful song! Indeed, women's music would not have been feared so much if it hadn't been associated with this performative ability to alter the external environment.

Only on the rarest of occasions did the mainstream culture encourage the intervention of these efficacious songs. In those instances, the powers of feminine songs were channeled in an acceptable or desirable direction—for example, in healing, in courtship, or in the sanctioned activities of a nunnery. Even as love songs were viewed with misgivings and sometimes prohibited outright, many communities refused to recognize the legality of a marriage ceremony that lacked music—a stricture that persisted in parts of Europe until the late Renaissance. Because songs possessed genuine power, they simply couldn't be discarded; yet relying on them always was a dangerous proposition.

Once we understand this dynamic, we can see that the rise of the troubadours wasn't merely a case of men discovering and legitimizing the love song. These celebrated singers also imposed different aesthetic standards on the genre that subtly altered its performative qualities. Seduction songs were no longer intended to seduce, at least not as their primary function. Love songs often had no function in a real courtship; they merely extolled and praised the powerful, just as Pindar and his imitators had done centuries before. Rather than aiming for efficacy, these songs, in their new masculine guise, now aimed for artistry, often in an intentionally stylized and exaggerated manner.

This is perhaps the most significant aspect of this whole interlude in Western music, but it is a mixed blessing. The secular song in the vernacular was turned into art, but the performative capabilities of the music, so closely connected to the women who had laid the groundwork for this shift, were weakened in the process. From this moment on in Western music, songs were rarely expected to do much beyond signifying meanings, expressing feelings, and—in ideal cases—giving the musician a way to earn a living.

Of course, the magic of music couldn't be dismissed so easily. Performative songs still exist, even in the current day. Our fashionable theories of musical aesthetics don't have much place for songs that try to do things, but that hasn't stopped people from keeping these traditions alive. Shamanism and other forms of healing music still have their practitioners in a modern age, and can even draw upon a growing body of scientific evidence to support their use. When this evidence shows up in a sufficient number of peer-reviewed academic journals, these practices get relabeled as *music therapy*, a term that can now be applied in therapeutic situations by certified professionals in white coats. Courtesans are no longer expected to sing their alluring siren songs (although this was still a valuable job skill for them until only a few decades ago); but lovers and seducers continue to rely on music at every stage of a relationship, whether long-term courtship or short-term fling. In fact, there's not a single hour of the day or night when performative music isn't on the agenda. Recent surveys indicate that 70 percent of people believe music makes them more productive, and 62 percent rely on it to help them sleep. On the other extreme, music is used by organizations and institutions for a range of manipulative or unsavory performative tasks: assisting in enhanced interrogations (perhaps we should call it "musical torture"), dispersing loiterers and the homeless, encouraging shoppers to purchase specific items in retail environments, and so on. We may live in a culture that views music as mere diversion and entertainment, but it's surprising how often the music of our day-to-day lives resists this pigeonholing and aims instead to alter the world around us.[7]

We rarely use the word "magic" in such settings. The troubadours legitimized secular songs as art, and not as incantation; and the whole official pedagogy of music, even a thousand years later, hasn't deviated a whit from that ingrained approach. Both as performers and audience, we are taught to view music as an aesthetic experience, not a source of enchantment. I find people get anxious when I talk about music as a magical force, so I have learned to use different words: I call music a *change agent* in human life, or a *catalyst*. But it's still magic, even under a fancier name. Not all wizards carry wands and wear pointed hats. Some show up at work with a saxophone or guitar in hand. And we still crave their life-changing interventions, even if that aspect of their craft remains mostly unacknowledged.

13

The Invention of the Audience

When I was a youngster in elementary school, some teachers still called it the "Dark Ages." That long interlude from the fall of ancient civilizations to the start of the Renaissance was treated like the cultural equivalent of the power grid going down. Your lights will come back on, folks, but you may need to wait a while—up to a thousand years, give or take a century or two.

But the period is not considered quite so dark anymore. During the course of the twentieth century, the number of university teaching positions in medieval studies increased by a thousandfold, and these academics fought against the second-class status of their field, which had so often been treated as a less talented warm-up act for the stars of the Renaissance. Scholars as diverse as Johan Huizinga, C. S. Lewis, Marc Bloch, Jacques Le Goff, Étienne Gilson, and Dorothy Sayers contributed to a gradual rebranding (if I may borrow the appropriate Madison Avenue term) of the age. And the new positioning turned the old one on its head. In Sayers's words, the Middle Ages were now a "new-washed world of clear sun and glittering color"—no more darkness here—although, in a spirit of full disclosure, she admits that it was a period "full of blood and grief and death and naked brutality."[1]

Despite this recalibration, for the most part well justified, much of the music that is the focus of this book remains clouded in darkness. Even as we piece together a more accurate picture of the musical life of the Western world, large parts of it are lost to us, probably never to be recovered. Finally, with the dissemination of the troubadours' craft more than a thousand years after the rise of Christianity, a far wider range of musical activities emerged into the light, and it was suddenly being discussed and documented and sometimes even treated as worthy of respect. Changes that first appeared in southern France moved on to Europe at large, transforming the musical culture in each and every place they touched. But it's still not entirely clear whether the documented changes represent a substantial shift in how people sang: perhaps Europe only saw a rise in the status of vernacular styles already in circulation but previously despised and marginalized. It's likely that, in many instances, it wasn't the meme that spread, merely the light.

Traditional accounts continue to give credit to the nobility, not just for the innovations in the songs, but also their dissemination. We are told that Eleanor of Aquitaine, granddaughter of our first troubadour, William IX, brought this music with her, almost as a kind of cultural dowry, to her marriage to Louis VII, ruler of France, in 1137. In the aftermath of this union, the songs of the *trouvères*, as these singers were known in the north, came out into the open, finding their way into manuscripts and anecdotal accounts. (By the way, the only surviving art object linked to the queen is her wedding gift to her husband, a rock crystal vase currently in the Louvre inherited from her troubadour grandfather, who had received it, in turn, from the Islamic ruler of Zaragoza—a tangible physical symbol of artistic transmission from the Muslim world to Provence.) Even after the annulment of this marriage, a few weeks before Eleanor became wife of Henry Plantagenet, future king of England, her daughters Marie and Alix continued as patrons of secular music and champions of the ethos of courtly love.

A similar story is told of Princess Beatrice of Burgundy, who married Frederick I, Holy Roman Emperor, around this same time. Beatrice is credited with bringing the love songs of France into Germany. We know, for example, that her retinue included a trouvère, Guiot de Provins. This French singer may even have introduced the story of Parsifal, knight of the Round Table, into Germany, setting the stage for its transformation into a national epic under the auspices of Wolfram von Eschenbach and Richard Wagner. Other royals and nobles are credited with similar roles in legitimizing and disseminating these exciting and sensual songs. Even King Richard the Lionheart of England, son of Henry II and Eleanor of Aquitaine, shows up in the annals of history as a champion of new performance styles, both via his own songs and through his alleged patronage of the minstrel Blondel de Nesle.

How should we treat these colorful stories? Could it be true that the hereditary rulers of Europe were also the driving force behind musical innovation during this intensely creative period in the history of song? As we shall see below, other, less exalted personages were actively spreading the music without the assistance of a royal pedigree. Even so, we need to take the prerogatives of these nobles seriously in assessing the tectonic shifts underway in Western music, especially as performers freed themselves from the constraints of Christian authorities. It's no coincidence that the first troubadour, William IX, was excommunicated twice by the church, or that the great period of musical innovation in the south of France ended with the Albigensian Crusade—that unprecedented moment when the pope launched a holy war on European soil against French Christians suspected of holding heretical views. The whole history of Pope Innocent III's attempt to eradicate the dangerous Catharist theology from Christendom is beyond the scope of this study; suffice it to say that the zealots who pushed this campaign (and laid the groundwork for the Inquisition, which was established to combat any lingering effects of the heresy) could hardly have been pleased to see Islamic-influenced musical traditions flourishing in France.

Greil Marcus, in his seminal work *Lipstick Traces*, speculates on possible connections between the Catharist heresy and the later rise of punk rock—with the Paris-based Letterist International movement of the 1950s, a kind of more radicalized European equivalent of the Beat Generation, serving as a linchpin. At first glance, this theory may seem extraordinary, but my research reveals the paths by which this alternative mode of Christianity not only reversed the musical hierarchies of its own time, but may have set the stage for future upheavals and rebellions. In southern France, religious heresies were full-fledged anti-authoritarian movements, rejecting the taxation and earthly dominion of church officials. "In the long history of heresy in Occitania from the thirteenth to the seventeenth century," writes Emmanuel Le Roy Ladurie in his study of the medieval Catharist village Montaillou, "the conflict over tithes is always underlying and recurrent." Disputes over dogma, in contrast, are "often absent, or important on only a few fascinating but isolated points." Yes, the Cathars were proto-punks, if we are willing to define that term broadly enough. The rejection of conventional morality in their midst was aided by the sect's replacement of Catholic baptism with a very different ritual, the *Consolamentum*, which absolved sins for most believers right before they died. This practice allowed for a degree of licentious behavior among the hale and hearty that almost certainly influenced Cathar musical culture, assisting in the emergence of more overtly sexualized lyrical expression.[2]

But the heretics apparently had help from Africa in making their blasphemous music. The main danger of the heresy, from the perspective of Rome, may have been its dogmas, but music was a symptom, and like any diseased organ, must be treated or lopped off like a necrotic limb at its root—and that root was growing out of the Muslim world. We lack the documentation to study the impact on music of these larger battles in sufficient detail. The burning of heretical Catharist texts (and sometimes the burning of the Cathars themselves) limits our access to dissenting views and other empirical evidence that would help us understand the role songs played in this conflict. I suspect that surprising archival material may still emerge someday, and will show how much these larger rivalries influenced matters we now would categorize as "popular culture." For example, women played a key role in the Catharist movement, and they appear to have outnumbered men among the ranks of believers. Can it be pure coincidence that a feminization of music occurred at this same time, and that passionate secular songs—previously associated with sinful women—rose in esteem and gained new adherents? Alas, so much is still hidden from view during this period; we are mostly limited to speculation on the basis of fragmentary evidence. Yet the larger picture remains fairly clear, providing ample evidence of the boldness with which excommunicated nobles and like-minded allies freed music from its ecclesiastical restraints.

But royals don't get *all* the credit. Songs went viral in other ways. Traveling entertainers date back to ancient times, and they persisted after the rise of Christianity despite hostility from church and political authorities. As far back as the fourth century, entertainers were denied Christian sacraments, although the church rarely did more than harass these performers, never quite managing to eradicate them. To some extent, religious leaders were on the defensive, fearing that sinful songs would contaminate not just the attitudes of churchgoers but also the holy life of the clergy. In the eighth century, the Council of Cloveshoe forbade Benedictines from allowing "poets, harpers, musicians, and buffoons" into their monasteries, and a priest was strictly forbidden from "playing the gleeman with himself or others." Such rules were frequently violated: traveling musicians sometimes even participated in the divine music-making of holy services. Visitors to St. Mary's Church in Beverley, East Yorkshire, can still see a striking column, known as the minstrel's pillar, depicting a group of singers dressed in secular garb. In Paris, a chapel was dedicated to "St. Julian of the Minstrels," and in London St. Bartholomew's Hospital was constructed on a site originally established as a "minstrel's priory" by Henry I in 1102. These monuments testify to the coexistence of humble street entertainers and the established institutions of medieval Europe.[3]

Yet traveling musicians frequently encountered slander, banishment, legal restrictions, and even physical assault. In Siena, statutes

allowed citizens to attack a minstrel without suffering legal consequences. The *Sachsenspiegel*, a legal code of the Holy Roman Empire
written in German in the early thirteenth century, declares that
"hired fighters and their children, minstrels, and all those illegiti-
mately born are all without rights." In essence, the musician was no
different from a bastard or a thug.[4]

Medieval musicians were frequently accused of sorcery. Some
people even believed that the devil took on the form of a minstrel
and in that guise enticed Christians to perdition with beguiling
songs and dances. The story of the Pied Piper, which dates back
to 1300, captures both the fear and awe these itinerant performers inspired in the villages they visited. According to the tale, a
piper is hired by the town of Hamelin to use his magical music
to lure the rats infesting the city into the Weser River, where they
drown—but when the mayor refuses to pay him for his work, he
does the same with the children of the town. Today we consider
this a fairy tale, but to the medieval mind such musical witchcraft
represented a genuine threat. Surviving records from Hamelin
show that residents in the late medieval period saw this account
as factual history rather than symbolic myth. Even in the current
day, we instruct our children to beware of strangers. Just add to
that a social milieu in which many of the most mysterious newcomers to a community are entertainers of various sorts, and mix in a
heavy dose of superstition and credulity, and it's easy to see how
a musician could become demonized. Even in the twentieth century, wandering blues musicians in the United States were accused
of making deals with the devil, and some of the performers themselves may have felt that playing this sinful music represented an
implicit contract with demonic forces. Half a century later, during
my teenage years, heavy metal rockers were accused of satanic
worship—in fact, they often promoted these dark affiliations
themselves as a kind of marketing angle. Have we really evolved
that far beyond the medieval mindset?

Despite these obstacles, traveling musicians persisted, even
thrived. Many in the community must have welcomed their presence, not just for the songs and skits, but also for the news they

brought from afar, especially in an age of widespread illiteracy when individuals, not documents, were disseminators of the leading 'stories' of the day. News and music were closely intertwined in this period—even the town crier or herald came equipped with drum or hunting horn or gong or bell. But villagers must have been especially pleased when the stranger in town was a skilled performer who could combine information with entertainment. Even if some civic and religious authorities might have preferred an environment in which these outsiders never disturbed the self-sufficient isolation of day-to-day life, the services provided by itinerant musicians were too valuable to allow their absolute prohibition. Councilors and clerics also needed status reports from afar, and the risk of blocking these links to the outside world, however disruptive in some circumstances, was a chance few were willing to take.

In the pages ahead, we will find ourselves increasingly concerned with the impact of the audience on music, and this juncture in the late medieval period represents the tipping point when the prerogatives of the listener came to the forefront in European life. The audience certainly existed before, but it got legitimized as an arbiter of cultural tastes only after the intercession of the troubadours. We have already seen how the Roman elites scorned the crowd-pleasing antics of pantomime and other popular entertainments. The satirist Juvenal captured this disdain in one of the most quoted Latin phrases, *panem et circenses*—"bread and circuses." These were all the masses wanted, he suggested, cheap food and crass entertainment. The ancient Romans most admired for their artistry, such as Virgil and Horace, made their works for the empire and its powerful leaders, not for a popular audience. Indeed, the concept of *pop culture* would have seemed an oxymoron to these ancients, as well as to the Christian authorities who followed in their wake. Music that aimed to please the *populus* was, by definition, a degraded art. Other goals and higher considerations—instilling virtue, advancing civic or community interests, serving God, or appeasing the powerful—were deemed more important.

And yet, as the innovations of the troubadours spread, they helped raise the status of this previously despised audience. A symbiotic relationship now emerged between the performer and listeners, with the renown and reputation of the former inextricably linked to the response of the latter. Even the church came to recognize this shift within its own sacred precincts. It's hardly a coincidence that composers of Christian music were finally recognized by name and achieved unprecedented status only after this mainstreaming of the vernacular lyric. More than a thousand years elapsed after Emperor Constantine converted to Christianity, in AD 312, before a sung mass gained renown for its composer. But we shouldn't be surprised to learn that the musician behind this work, Guillaume de Machaut, was already acclaimed for his songs and poems about courtly love. As in so many other instances in music history, a powerful institution recognized a shift in *popular* music and aimed to tap into it for its own organizational purposes—hence Machaut, a singer of fleshly love, gets transformed into a celebrant of divine love as embodied in church liturgy.

Before Machaut's mass, compilations such as the *Ivrea Codex* and the *Apt Codex* pulled together a range of anonymous settings, and priests could mix and match Kyries and Glorias and so on without any concern over presenting a unified statement from a single composer. In other instances, manuscripts might contain an individual mass setting, as in the *Tournai Mass*, the *Barcelona Mass*, the *Sorbonne Mass*, and the *Toulouse Mass*—but even here the music was anonymous, and scholars today believe that different composers were responsible for various parts of these works. In very rare instances, the name of a composer of religious music (although not an entire mass) survives from the period before Machaut. For example, Hildegard von Bingen left us an impressive body of work from the twelfth century—the most emotionally powerful music of the period, in my opinion. But even in this case, her music would probably never have been documented with such care if she had not served as head of a monastery and could thus directly supervise the preparation of manuscripts. For the most part, sacred composers gained distinction in the Western world only after secular performers had stepped out from the margins of society and gained some degree of acclaim from their listeners.

At this point in history, hundreds of performers emerged as stars of the music world, and there were scribes to document not just their songs but also the details of their lives. Even singers who were not born nobles could now achieve renown, and the rules of royal patronage were subtly altered as a result. Powerful elites, who found that their status was linked to the fame of the musicians attracted to their courts, soon realized that their own reputations might be enhanced if they received praise in the lyric of an esteemed singer. The most prominent singers, in turn, gained confidence from the growing proof that they were no longer dependent on the good favor of an earthly lord, because they could always travel elsewhere and find others to support their artistry. The surviving biographies of singers from this era are filled with gaps and dubious facts, yet frequently include triumphant declarations about the extent of the journeys made by these wandering performers—boasts that imply that, even back then, success in taking the show on the road served as an indicator of artistic merit. This new phenomenon carried with it the first stirrings of a dangerous idea, radical at the time and unprecedented in the history of Western music: namely, that the *audience*, defined broadly, is not just a legitimate arbiter of artistic excellence, but perhaps the highest, most trustworthy judge of musical achievement.

To understand how momentous this shift is, we must recalibrate our own notions about audiences. This term, derived from the Latin *audientia* (referring to the act of hearing or listening), may be the most misunderstood concept in all of music. I've heard serious theorists go so far as to assert that *every* piece of music is created with an audience in mind. They not only dismiss, but actually ridicule, any suggestion that music exists outside of this reciprocal relationship between entertainer and audience. I would argue the exact opposite. Based on the available evidence, I am forced to conclude that most music during the course of human history has flourished without requiring any audience to legitimize it. Indeed, in many cases, no meaningful distinctions between performer and audience can be drawn. When prehistoric hunters communicated back and forth via musical phrases while stalking prey, who was the audience? The notion is meaningless, because these hunters were all participants in the same holistic process. When traditional communities joined together in festive singing, who was the audience then? Once again, any line we might attempt to draw between participant and performer would be arbitrary, if not actually misleading. After all, when everybody sings, there's no one left to play the role of passive listener. Who was the audience when monks gathered together in the predawn hours to chant in medieval times, or when the members of church congregations join their voices in song even in the current day? You might postulate that God is the audience, but that would be a misleading, reductionist model; it fails to grasp all the subtle dynamics of group bonding and personal ecstasy that define these situations. When prisoners in work gangs sang during forced labor, who was their audience? If you say they were singing to entertain the prison guards and overseers, the only 'audience' present at these performances, you simply show how little you understand the situation. Who was the audience for the sea shanties of sailors? The fish, perhaps? No, I don't think so. And who was the audience, during my own schooldays, when we all joined together to sing the National Anthem at an assembly? The flag? No, that doesn't make sense. What about when you sing in the shower, or along with the radio in your car? I could add dozens of other examples, but the point should already be clear. In most of human history, music has been so deeply woven into the fabric of our lives that the concept of audience is an unnecessary addition, and sometimes a narrow-minded distortion.

That's why the emergence of the audience as the judge of aesthetic merit during the late medieval period and Renaissance represents such an extraordinary moment in cultural history. Instead of singing for God and country, for the sanctity of the ritual, or for some other 'higher' purpose, entertainers now performed for the enjoyment of listeners—in fact, were now *expected* to please their audience—and the music changed dramatically in this new symbiotic relationship. "Development proceeded by trial and error," explains medievalist H. J. Chaytor, "the audience being the means of experiment." These face-to-face encounters served as sources of artistic judgment, particularly since "medieval literature produced little formal criticism in our sense of the term. If an author wished to know whether his work was good or bad, he tried it on an audience; if it was approved, he was soon followed by imitators." This seems like simple common sense to us, but in a hierarchical society that had long deferred to religious authorities and accepted the divine right of kings, this was a disruptive change. Taken to an extreme—and that would inevitably happen—it turned the untutored crowd, the despised rabble, into the sanctioned adjudicator of aesthetic matters. This was the subversive moment when pop culture got its pop. We still live with the consequences of this shift today.[5]

As the innovations of southern France spread elsewhere, the impact of this change became more obvious. In Arras, one hundred miles north of Paris near the present-day border with Belgium, an unprecedented blossoming of secular song took place, spurred primarily by the rising middle class. In this city, enriched by its wool industry, a surprisingly wide range of people turned to singing songs about courtly love, intimate feelings, the pleasures of life, and occasionally religious subjects. Around half of the surviving trouvère lyrics come from this single community, where merchants, clerks, priests, soldiers, and other citizens helped create the most vibrant center of music-making in France during the late thirteenth century. At a time when only around twenty thousand people lived in Arras, the city may have served as home for some two hundred professional and amateur singers. In this hothouse of amatory song, nobles continued to participate in the musical life of the community, but they were now clearly outnumbered by the bourgeoisie.

In some ways, the songs stayed the same even after the musical culture became more inclusive. The exploits and concerns of nobility would remain central to Western popular music for centuries to come. I once undertook a statistical study of the folk ballads collected by Francis James Child during the late nineteenth century, and was amazed to find that 55 percent of them focus on the nobility—a remarkable fact when one considers that these songs are treated as textbook examples of the music of the common people. These folk ballads are filled, in a peculiar anachronism, with knights and princesses and the sentiments of courtly love. But the groundwork for this obsession was laid in the late medieval period and Renaissance, when the lower classes gained renown for their music but still adopted the ethos of the ruling class in their lyrics. Perhaps this practice helped cement the emerging view that the craft of the singer was inherently noble, conferring on its leading practitioners an elite status. In part, it must have also been a kind of pleasing posture, delighting audiences and elevating the dignity of performers who, only a short while before, had been despised as lowly jongleurs and minstrels.

But in other ways, the music changed, and these changes demonstrate how songs were adapting to the dictates of audience-driven aesthetics. We have already seen how slave singers and other musicians outside the power structure of society have frequently employed coded language in their songs, a practice called *signifying* by scholar Henry Louis Gates. The early troubadours, despite their more secure links to the nobility, often did the same—so much so that we sometimes get the impression they were singing for other knowledgeable insiders, rather than for a broader audience. In some instances, the vagueness of the signifiers approaches a kind of avant-garde impenetrability rarely found in song lyrics. Given this, I'm hardly surprised that the troubadour Arnaut Daniel (1150–1210) was later championed by Ezra Pound and other modernist poets known for their difficult texts. These more recondite troubadour songs, like Pound's *Cantos,* aim to conceal as much as reveal. Scholars nowadays call this medieval style of expression *trobar clus,* a closed form marked by deliberate complexity and obscurity that kept out the riff-raff while pleasing discerning insiders. But when this style of singing spread to the trouvères in the north and the *Minnesingers* of Germany, they rejected this foreboding hauteur in favor of clearer and more direct forms of expression. In other words, they were *playing to the audience.* In this and other ways, the shift in song styles reflected a change in the power structure along with a growing realization that pleasing the crowd could be as important as institutional affiliations in securing a musician's next meal.

These same singers also embraced storytelling as part of their repertoires, and it's hardly a stretch to see innovations from this period laying the groundwork for the mass entertainments of more recent times. A number of popular song genres from this period—lai, chanson de toile, pastourelle, and so on—drew on the same narrative techniques that show up in movies and television shows today. Here, too, the need to hold the attention of an audience came to the forefront, shaping the performer's art. Entertainers could shift from music-making to storytelling with surprising ease, and their leaps of imagination sometimes had far-reaching consequences. It's hardly a coincidence that the most influential storyteller of the period, Chrétien de Troyes, was a trained trouvère. This French musician's colorful tales of brave knights and highborn ladies would leave a lasting mark on Western European culture, so much so that he claims the unique distinction of inspiring the defining British national stories—tales of King Arthur—as well as the famous German stories about Parzival. I would go further: we can draw a direct line from Chrétien's work to the blockbuster adventure film franchises of our own day, which build on the same combination of heroic deeds and passionate romance that never seems to go out of style. It's not a huge leap from Arthur, Lancelot, and Guinevere to Luke Skywalker, Hans Solo, and Princess Leia. But a trouvère came up with the recipe long before George Lucas got into the act. In fact, Lucas even features the Holy Grail, an icon that first appears in Chrétien's tale *Perceval, le Conte du Graal* (circa 1190), in his Indiana Jones films. In both medieval and modern instances, the formula serves as a type of wish-fulfillment for a mass audience, who demand that heroic protagonists go through their paces for the stimulation of their private fantasies. Only the special effects have gotten better.

You could call this enjoyment-driven aesthetics, and one of its main premises is that music's purpose is to create the greatest amount of pleasure for the greatest number of people. That's the essence of popular culture, but you would seek in vain for this view in Plato, Aristotle, Seneca, Boethius, Confucius, Augustine, or any of the other revered sources of opinion about music in the long centuries leading up to the late medieval era. Augustine even went so far as to explicitly reject any pleasure-driven method of evaluating a performance: "As often as the song pleases me more than the sense of what is sung, just so often do I confess to having sinned grievously." In other words, the more you enjoy it, the worse it is. For all its reversal of our own value system, Augustine's view was typical of those in positions of authority over a period of more than a thousand years. Many of them probably tolerated such songs for the same reason that Augustine defended prostitution and brothels—in one of the most surprising proclamations from the history of Christian theology—namely, because they served as a kind of sewage drain for society, siphoning off sinful energy that might be put to even worse use if this outlet were prohibited.[6]

By the same token, we have very little information from these esteemed thinkers on the importance of music for dancing, which gained unprecedented visibility during the late medieval period and Renaissance. We know that physical movement and music have always gone together, even back in the days of hunter-gathering societies, but this was hardly acknowledged by theorists and elites, who sought a higher purpose from music than just swaying bodies and tapping feet. The same clerics who attacked the sinful songs of their parishioners were invariably hostile to the dances that often accompanied them. Little effort was made to document popular dances, and for the same reasons we have already encountered. Such performances were considered too undignified or vulgar to deserve preservation. This is why no detailed dance manuals appeared until the fifteenth century. Yet long before these "how-to" books showed up, a shift in the social status of rustic and folk dances can be detected. With the acknowledgment of pleasure as an artistic standard and the growing influence of the crowd, dance music steps out of the shadows in European history.

Many of the song forms favored by the most popular performers were explicitly connected to dances. These origins are often preserved in the musical terminology we use today. The *rondo* is now treated as a specifically musical form with a recurring refrain, but the term likely derives from the circular dance that accompanied the *rondeau* of the wandering musicians of the late medieval era. Today we use the word *carol* to describe a Christmas song, but it comes from a very popular dance of that period, the *carole*. A host of other terms, from *minuet* to *waltz*, are now used to describe concert hall music, but originated among dancers. I doubt we will ever grasp the full impact of dancing on musical style, which shows up even where we least expect to find it. Charles Rosen, in his seminal study *The Classical Style*, marvels over the process by which the four-bar phrase gained a "stranglehold on rhythmic structure" in classical music, and is forced to conclude that "the periodic phrase is related to the dance, with its need for a phrase pattern that corresponds to steps and to groupings." In other words, even the elitist masterworks of Mozart and Beethoven move to the beat of the peasants' feet.[7]

In dance music we see the same leveling of social barriers and emulation of feared outsiders that marks the musical culture of the time. "The carole, in particular, was performed by all classes of society—kings and nobles, shepherds and servant girls," explains music scholar Robert Mullally, who has done exceptional work rescuing the details of this dance from the scattered texts and images that have survived to our time. "It is described as taking place both indoor and outdoors," he notes, and is mentioned in a surprising range of literary works, not only "fictional texts, but also in historical (or quasi-historical) writings, in moral treatises and even in a work of astronomy." We may never know how this dance originated. As Mullally points out, scholars have typically focused more attention on the etymology of the word *carole* than on the actual dance. But it seems likely that secular dances often came from the same non-European sources that anticipated the musical innovations of this era. The circular dances that gained ascendancy in Europe at this time reveal similarities to the ring shout, the most persistent and far-traveling ritual of the African diaspora. And in the Morris dance, so revered as a homegrown British tradition, we find a specific reference to "Moorish" antecedents in its very name. Given the paucity of source materials, we can hardly go beyond idle speculation on these matters. But of the big picture there is no room for doubt: the previously sinful and marginalized dances of the populace are now forgiven and gain legitimacy as art. The subversive enters the mainstream. Even better, this is art that can be enjoyed by peasants and the illiterate just as easily as by knights and highborn ladies.[8]

In aggregate, these are stunning changes in the musical life of the West. But they also challenge our traditional demarcations of cultural history. These daring medieval singers and dancers already anticipate most of the innovations typically assigned to the Renaissance. This is an embarrassment to our schemas and systems. The musical culture seems to rush ahead of the visual arts and philosophical systems, and establishes, almost as a kind of military beachhead, the humanistic ethos of the future. Long before the rest of society catches up with them, the musicians have already asserted the legitimacy of secular culture, the leveling of social hierarchies, the idolization of the artist, the workings of a marketplace and patronage system, and, most important of all, the confident assertion of the individual's creative freedom in the face of institutional demands.

Yet I am hardly surprised by all of this. I'm convinced that songs are a kind of cultural equivalent of what economists call "leading indicators." Those practitioners of the dismal science have learned that certain statistics—building permits, help-wanted ads, housing starts, and the like—can be relied on as predictors of future economic trends. In contrast, other sources of information—for example, corporate profits—serve as lagging indicators, helping to clarify what happened in the recent past. In the sphere of social history, music is the most powerful leading indicator of them all. Just look at how the lyrics of 1920s blues songs anticipated the later sexual revolution (forty years in advance!), or how the lifestyle habits of jazz-obsessed beatniks, embraced by a tiny subculture in the 1950s, set the tone for the youth movement of the late 1960s and 1970s. This sensitivity to new ways of behaving is embedded into the musical arts, and for the simple reason that this is what we expect from our singers. We want them to be hypersensitive, attuned to subtle emotional currents, a kind of central nervous system for the social body. Long before treatises and editorials pick up on the coming changes, they have already been set to music.

14

Musicians Behaving Badly

The Renaissance, which makes its official appearance in the second half of the fourteenth century, according to our conventional timelines, serves merely to amplify the prestige and power now enjoyed by the once despised musician. This is most noticeable in the awestruck deference, almost a cult of personality, inspired by leading artists, musical or otherwise. We have already tasted this in the breathless tales of the exploits of troubadours, trouvères, Minnesingers, and other performers. But for their Renaissance successors, this gossipy fixation on musicians and their private lives grows into something approaching celebrity worship.

Great artists were now allowed to ignore laws and conventions that others had to obey. Indeed, they were expected to do so. Many readers turn to the autobiography of Benvenuto Cellini—our single best source of what the life of a Renaissance artist was like—for its details on his work as goldsmith, sculptor, musician, and poet. But we can also learn from the insights it provides into crime and punishment, especially its author's skill in committing the former while evading the latter. By my count, Cellini confesses to fourteen different violent crimes in the course of his autobiography—as well as a host of lesser infractions, including extortion and vandalism. But *none* of these transgressions were punished by the authorities. Cellini was incarcerated twice, but only as a result of his disagreements with powerful patrons. Murder and aggravated assault, in contrast, were tolerated from an individual with his rare gifts. My favorite passage from Cellini's memoir describes the pope's reaction when an adviser suggests that the artist ought to be punished for committing a murder. "You don't understand the matter as well as I do," the pontiff responds. "You should know that men like Benvenuto, unique in their profession, need not be subject to the law."[1]

In this history, I have dwelt on the recurring linkage between music and violence. But in most cases, musicians have been victims or bystanders. Yet after their rise in social status in the late medieval era, performers frequently turn into perpetrators. As we have seen, Jacques Attali has suggested that the observances of the concert hall can serve as a kind of ritualized substitute for sacrificial violence, and that observation may help us understand the cultural significance of the music of this earlier age. But the student of Renaissance music hardly needs to look for hidden symbols of violence in artists' compositions. In a number of cases, they committed actual assaults and murders. Bartolomeo Tromboncino was one of the leading musicians of his day, famous for his frottolas, gentle popular songs that anticipated the later rise of the madrigal. But Tromboncino's notoriety was only enhanced when he murdered his wife in a jealous rage. Music lovers may even have found his love songs all the more authentic when they learned that his romantic attachments came packaged with such violent passions. His guilt seems never to have been in doubt, but Tromboncino went unpunished for the crime. Carlo Gesualdo, one of the finest composers of madrigals, went even further than Tromboncino, murdering both his wife and her noble lover, the Duke of Andria, and mutilating their bodies. Witnesses saw him enter the apartment exclaiming, "Kill that scoundrel, along with his harlot! Shall Gesualdo be made a cuckold?" and leave a short while later with blood dripping from his hands. Then he muttered,

"I do not believe they are dead," and went in the apartment a second time, to inflict more wounds on his victims. In other instances, Gesualdo burnished this hard-earned reputation for brutality, and some commentators have not hesitated to label him a sadist or a psychopath. "Say what you will about Gesualdo," notes the music critic Alex Ross. "He was irrefutably badass." Yet he was never punished for his crimes, and probably found his allure as a composer got a boost from his violence as a lover.[2]

But Renaissance artists didn't need to murder a duke to prove that, under the new rules of the game, they no longer kowtowed to nobility. As the example of Cellini makes clear, an artist could skillfully outmaneuver even pontiffs and kings, playing patrons against each other, and moving on to a new benefactor whenever the current one grew too demanding or parsimonious. In this regard, the fragmentation of political control in a patchwork of Renaissance city-states, kingdoms, and ecclesiastical territories helped tilt the balance in favor of the artist, who could easily shift allegiances—and avoid legal consequences for crimes committed—by moving to another jurisdiction. Yet even in this ongoing battle between patron and artist, the audience played a crucial part. When Cellini was engaged in various disputes with Cosimo de' Medici over the artist's most ambitious work, the now-famous *Perseus with the Head of Medusa*, still visible in Florence's Piazza della Signoria, both paid the closest attention to comments from onlookers and passersby. Cosimo even hid behind a window in the plaza to hear the verdict of the crowd before venturing his own opinion. Such was the importance of the 'general public' (as we would call it today) that even powerful rulers deferred to its whims and preferences.

Amidst this widespread fascination with passionate and crowd-pleasing artists, we encounter the first superstar of Western music. The composer Josquin des Prez, born around the year 1450, attracted hero worship to a degree previously unknown in Christian music, and his renown mounted even higher in the years following his death. The Tuscan diplomat Cosimo Bartoli (1503–1572) compared Josquin to Michelangelo—an extraordinary admission for a

Florentine patriot—and Swiss humanist Heinrich Glarean (1488–1563) viewed the esteemed composer as the equal of Virgil. After Josquin's death, younger composers penned dirges in his honor filled with lofty praise, and Jean Richafort wrote an entire requiem mass for his deceased master. Before two decades had elapsed, his preeminence was asserted by no less an authority than Martin Luther, who claimed that other composers must serve the musical notes, but only Josquin could force them to do as he willed. No previous composer, even the most celebrated, such as Guillaume Dufay and Johannes Ockeghem, had gained such acclaim. Yet the most striking measure of Josquin's impact may be the sheer number of works falsely attributed to him—publisher George Forster later joked that Josquin had the unique skill of composing more music after he died than while alive. So powerful was his authority that the name Josquin became a kind of brand name or stamp of excellence rather than a proper attribution of a work's origins.

Here we see the same process of legitimization and mainstreaming that is a recurring theme in this book. During his lifetime, Josquin was criticized for his difficult, prickly behavior, and admiration for his music was tempered by irritation at his rebellious ways. Glarean, who drew on the testimony of those who knew Josquin personally, balances his praise with the admission that the composer did not "soberly repress the violent impulses of his unbridled temperament." He goes on to admit that "an immoderate love of novelty" sometimes marred the composer's works, as well as "an excessive eagerness to win a little glory for being unusual." One of the few surviving descriptions of Josquin's personality from his own time shows up in a letter to Duke Ercole I of Ferrara. It warns the duke, an ambitious patron of the arts, against hiring such a cantankerous, demanding individual. In this revealing text, singer Gian de Artiganova suggests that Heinrich Isaac would be a better choice, even though he was the inferior talent. Isaac was deemed "more good-natured and companionable," according to this observer, "and he will compose new works more often. It is true that Josquin composes better, but he composes when he wants to, and not when one wants him to, and he is asking 200 ducats in salary while Isaac will come for 120—but Your Lordship will decide." The duke did decide, in favor of Josquin, and the incident testifies both to how rebellious musical superstars could be under the new rules and to how much patrons were willing to tolerate in order to engage their services.[3]

A tension now comes to the forefront in music that will continue for the rest of our history. Even when musicians become insiders, they are expected to act like outsiders. This invariably creates friction, and sometimes open discord. But over the long run, the artistic visionary almost always prevails—other powers must retreat in the face of creative prerogatives—and is often admired all the more for the disruptions and conflicts caused along the way.

The new ascendancy of public tastes also resulted in the first stirrings of what we would now call a *standard repertoire* of popular songs. "A curious thing happened in the third quarter of the fifteenth century," explains Renaissance music scholar Allan W. Atlas. "About a dozen or so chansons were written that gained such 'hit' status with other composers (and presumably with audiences) during their own and the next two generations that they generated about three hundred new compositions. . . . While some of the derivative works were Mass settings, the overwhelming majority were secular." Hosts of new works were built on the foundations of "De tous biens plaine," a song about a lover's beautiful mistress attributed to Hayne van Ghizeghem, which various composers incorporated into more than fifty new pieces, including sacred music honoring the Virgin Mary. Johannes Ockeghem's "Fors seulement," the lament of a heartbroken narrator awaiting death, found its way into at least five masses and more than thirty secular songs. "L'homme armé," a song of unclear origins that warns listeners against a dangerous "armed man," shows up in more than forty sung masses, including two by Josquin. If, as I have suggested earlier, the process of legitimization reaches its peak when the unclean origins of a song are obscured, or even forgotten, after its appropriation by ruling institutions, these transformed songs of love and violence present almost textbook examples of what this cleansing process looks like in practice. Sometimes these lust-born melodies were so carefully integrated into their new sacred contexts that their scandalous origins all but disappeared from view. The purified versions would serve as role models in their own right, and today enjoy a cherished position in the annals of Western culture as paragons of religious music.[4]

In the mid-fourteenth century, musicians started appearing on the payrolls of European cities with greater frequency. These performers might have played in both secular and sacred contexts, but urbanization had shifted the balance of power away from church authorities and created new opportunities for musicians. By 1300, many major cities in Europe boasted one hundred thousand or more inhabitants, but dozens of other communities had populations in the tens of thousands. The city councils in these locales now emerged as significant employers of musicians, relying on them for practical services as well as pomp and ceremony. Take, for example, the city of Montpellier in southern France, where city records from the period frequently refer to "our five minstrels," musicians who received regular payments and formal uniforms for their services, and occasionally new instruments. The livery of these performers included fancy trappings, such as fur linings or the city's coat of arms embroidered on their sleeves, and was designed to impress the populace. The minstrels accompanied the city council in processions and performed on important occasions. Indeed, a remarkable number of events required their presence— including the reception of royalty, the mounting of a bell in a tower, a competition among crossbowmen, or the display of a holy relic. Many of the occasions were religious in nature, especially feast days or Christmas processions, but the musicians served to assert the importance of civic officials (as well as their own—just consider their dazzling attire), even above that of the local church functionaries. At times we can even detect a competition between bishops and city leaders in their attempts to gain prestige from their musical entourages.

Other factors contributed as well to the growing bargaining power of musicians in a market economy. In France music guilds began to form: in Paris in 1321, in Montpellier in 1353, in Amiens in 1461, in Rouen in 1484, and in Toulouse in 1492. The musicians of London gained a royal charter for their guild in 1472 from Edward IV, and other communities in Britain soon imitated this structure, which both provided security for local performers and limited the incursions of wandering minstrels. The Meistersingers in Germany created a similar organizational structure for performers during this period. Although these singers liked to make grand claims for their ancient origins—tracing their history back to long-dead bards or even the times of the Old Testament prophets—it's clear that their formation and influence were actually linked to the growing economic power of cities during the fourteenth and fifteenth centuries.

This new group cohesion among previously isolated performers sometimes came at a heavy price. The Meistersingers, for example, often acted more like a bureaucracy than an artistic cooperative. Their *Tabulatur* (or law-book) was filled with arcane rules controlling every aspect of their craft: the rhyming of words, the number of syllables allowed in a line, the places where a singer could take a breath, a performer's fidelity to approved biblical texts, and other such matters. As a result, the famous singing contests of the Meistersingers tended to reward the avoidance of mistakes rather than skill in artistic expression. The justifications for these rules often seem arbitrary: a surviving *Tabulatur* from Nuremberg goes so far as to explain that the proper length of a line was connected to the duration of a day. As might be imagined, audiences were often indifferent to this rigid institutionalization of music, as well as to the moralizing tone of the songs of the Meistersingers. Records from the guilds include numerous complaints about the lack of interest among the public, which is usually blamed on deteriorating morals and bad manners. Under pressure to reform, the Meistersingers eventually embraced new melodies and secular subjects, and here, too, we see the growing power of the audience in musical matters. By the sixteenth century, however, the Meistersingers were in decline: they were too slow to change, and too many performers clung to the old rules. In such cases, we see the dangers when artistry loses its subversive edge and grows too comfortable in its role as prop to ruling institutions. Yet during their period of ascendancy, these organizations enjoyed a power and prestige that testifies to the growing stability and influence of performers, who, in an earlier day, led insecure, wandering lives.

By this stage, we might be tempted to declare that the 'Dark Ages' of music history were over. With such a wide range of performing styles now documented, notated, and legitimized—even those previously sinful tunes embraced by the vulgar, untutored, and illiterate—I am perhaps best advised to conclude my book at this juncture. How can a historian explore the music hidden in the margins of society, those despised songs excluded from serious consideration, if all styles of performance are granted equal status and dignity? Is there any room left for a subversive history of music?

Ah, but this apparent democratization of music is an illusion. Even after the dawn of the Renaissance illuminated the artistry of famous performers, most of the music-making in Europe still remained in the dark. Daily life was immersed in musical sounds now lost to us. Countless songs escaped documentation because they were considered insufficiently refined or dignified: work songs, lullabies, folk music, melodies for games and pedagogy, and the like. In other instances, entire categories of music were seldom discussed, because they were considered too sinful or blasphemous for preservation. These would include the beguiling songs of prostitutes, the musical incantations of so-called witches and superstitious believers in dark arts, and other profane melodies.

On occasion, a scandal would grow so large that it demanded documentation, and these rare incidents offer some of the most fascinating chapters in cultural history—although even these dramatic cases are rarely considered from a musical perspective. For example, the outbreaks of *tarantism* in Italy during the sixteenth and seventeenth centuries are generally dealt with as examples of mass hysteria. Whole communities were overcome by a mania for dancing, with participants believing that their compulsive movements resulted from a spider bite—the dance known as the *tarantella* is said to have originated from this delusion. Because of the medical associations of this musical frenzy, sober researchers such as Athanasius Kircher and Francesco Cancellieri felt justified in writing about the phenomenon. But many other unconventional musical practices must have flourished during these centuries without anyone documenting their peculiarities. The same is true of the Loudun possessions of this same era, which found a convent of French nuns engaging in the most scandalous performances, ostensibly under the influence of demons. This, too, might have passed unnoticed by official chroniclers, except that thousands of onlookers gathered to watch the sexualized gyrations of the bedeviled sisters, as well as the attempts of priests to exorcise the dark spirits responsible for their antics. Here, as in so many other performance settings of the time, the responses of the audience dictated who got noticed and celebrated. One wonders how many other people, unremarked by history, engaged in 'performances' of this sort and later blamed them on the devil.

Yet even the most inoffensive and pervasive music of day-to-day life was doomed for oblivion, disappearing with hardly a trace left behind. Anyone strolling through the marketplaces of a city or town during this same period would have heard vendors singing the praises of their merchandise. Composers often found inspiration in these tuneful solicitations, the forerunners of our modern advertising jingles. An anonymous motet from the thirteenth-century *Montpellier Codex* incorporates a tenor part calling out "Fresh strawberries! Wild blackberries!" Around this same time, poet Guillaume de Villeneuve compiled a collection of Parisian cries, and in the fourteenth century Florentine composer Francesco Landini wrote a work that drew upon these same humble themes. In perhaps the most famous example of this legitimizing process, Clément Janequin incorporated dozens of these melodies into his four-part vocal work "Voulez ouyr les cris de Paris." But how many street songs found their way into the classical music canon without leaving any trace of their lineage? We know that Handel once admitted that he borrowed musical ideas from street singers, and many other composers must have done the same, even if only unconsciously.

Yet these stylized adaptations give us little idea of the vitality or pervasiveness of this source of music-making, which survived until very recent times. As late as 1938, the Federal Writers' Project documented a wide array of improvised market songs found among the several thousand street vendors of New York City, and called attention to an especially rich soundscape on the "sidewalks of Harlem." This neighborhood featured, according to researcher Terry Roth, "sprightlier music than is heard on the East or West side of the city, for carefree street vendors employ amusing jingles and syncopated rhythms in offering their wares." Yet this document provides only a few lyrics, and no actual recordings were made. Over a period of decades, I have tried to collect the surviving field recordings of this now extinct mode of commerce, but—alas!—have found very few examples. Singing vendors flourished until the middle decades of the twentieth century, and yet precise information about this practice is all but lost to scholars of the current day. And how much more obscure to us are the street cries of five hundred years ago, once an essential part of the musical fabric of day-to-day life, but silenced forever even for the most dedicated researcher.[5]

By the same token, we know almost as little about the melodies of the musicians hired by civil authorities throughout Europe. Numerous documents tell us that trumpeters or other horn players were hired to "sound the watch" from central towers, and apparently they used a range of signals for their announcements. Their music gave notice to the opening or closing of city gates, the approach of an enemy, danger from a fire, or just the passing hours, and perhaps many other incidents and contingencies now unknown to us. In some instances, these signals must have hardly deserved the title of a performance—we hear, for example, of guards untrained in music using horns that were little more than noisemakers, a kind of primitive *vuvuzela* prized for loudness rather than artistry—yet in other instances, highly skilled instrumentalists took on these responsibilities. We are curious to know exactly how they exercised their creativity in crafting these melodies, so familiar to the citizens of those distant days, but this will forever remain a matter of conjecture for us.

Consider, for example, the intriguing case of John Blanke, one of the first Africans to find employment in England. Blanke served as trumpeter for King Henry VII in the early 1500s. We have no idea what kind of music he played in his official capacity (or in unofficial settings, for that matter), but can safely assume that his services were highly prized. When King Henry VIII came to the throne, Blanke was rewarded with a wage increase, and a later document indicates that the trumpeter received a lavish wedding gift from the monarch. We hear of other black trumpeters and drummers in Europe during this period, but the surviving documents offer few details. Yet the case of John Blanke is especially frustrating—even though he thrived in the court of the most famous ruler of the late Renaissance, his songs and life story are literally a *blank*.

Just as much uncertainty surrounds that most awe-inspiring music of day-to-day life, the ever-present sound of bells. This was the most persistent soundtrack of European life for a thousand years. But how well do we really understand the bells? Even the Latin word frequently translated as bell, *signum*, more precisely refers to a signal or sign. We hear of people called to prayer or work by a *signum*, but can we assume this summons came from a bell? Some commentators seem convinced that any signal delivered from a tower must have been a *ringtone* (to use the contemporary parlance). Yes, we still regulate our lives even today with such terminology. But as we have just seen, musicians often performed on trumpets and other instruments from a place we would now describe as a belfry. So we can merely guess at what was happening in those loftiest of performance spaces, just a step below heaven itself.

Even so, we cannot doubt the enormous prestige attached to bells during this long period of European history. The desire to have bigger bells than neighboring communities prompted tremendous investments of time and energy in metal-casting technology at a time when innovation was rarely a high priority. With the development of the carillon, a set of tuned bells played by a kind of keyboard first introduced in Flanders in 1510, more elaborate melodies resounded from the towers, and both the range of expression and the artistic ambitions of the bell ringers took another leap forward. How many bells rang in Europe on a typical day during the

Renaissance? The historian Jules Michelet once boasted that Joan of Arc had been honored with the ringing of the *five hundred bells* of Rouen—a claim that is hard to believe. Yet the larger truth is indisputable: if you lived at that time, you were seldom out of range of a bell or went long without hearing its resounding call.

But it is far easier to imagine the sounds of bells than to comprehend the mixed emotions they must have elicited—a strange combination of fear, loathing, reverence, superstition, and civic pride. The bells imposed a harsh discipline, forcing you to rise from your slumbers, summoning you to work or prayer, demanding obedience at every turn. In fact, no other instrument has figured more prominently in the long history of musical sounds as repositories of political authority and social control than the humble bell, not even the drum or trumpet. Yet, strange to say, bells hardly warrant even a passing mention in most music history books. Records from the fourteenth century show that not only priests and city councils, but also businesses relied on bells to impose order on the populace. The community of Aire-sur-la-Lys in northern France gained permission in 1355 to build a belfry to regulate the comings and goings of textile workers, and similar applications of bells existed in Amiens and Ghent during this period. Even the bosses now found themselves in servitude to the tocsin, with cities imposing fines on councilors and aldermen who were late in responding to the call of the bell. Bells increasingly emerged as contentious points in worker disputes, with varying results. In Commines, a sizable penalty of sixty Parisian pounds was imposed on any unauthorized person who seized the bell to summon a popular assembly, and execution was mandated if the bell were used to call for rebellion against the king. But at Thérouanne in 1367, workers managed to extract a promise to silence "forever the workers' bell," and in Ghent in 1349 the aldermen resolved a work stoppage by allowing weavers to choose their own work hours instead of regulating their lives by the bell. In confrontations of this sort we see in the clearest form the relationship between musical sounds and power, a connection often hidden (albeit implicit) in so many other contexts.

Even today we talk of someone getting "saved by the bell"—a revealing acknowledgment of the quasi-magical power possessed by these regulating sounds.[6]

In this charged environment, control of a belfry was a coveted symbol of authority, and it often seemed as if battles were fought over the bells themselves. The abduction of a city's bells was humiliating, and victors in battle proudly displayed these as the ultimate sign of military triumph. When Florence defeated the imposing fortress at Montale in 1303, the only part of the edifice spared from destruction was the bell, which was later mounted in the campanile of the Palazzo of the Podestà as a symbol of conquest. In the battles between Christian and Muslim forces over control of the Iberian Peninsula, bells served as powerful emblems of opposed religious practices—the contrast between the muezzin's call to prayer and the tolling from the belfry standing out as a musical representation of the larger conflict. Christian narratives describe how the bells of Santiago de Compostela were used as lamps for the Great Mosque of Córdoba. More than two centuries later, the supposed affront was still viewed as a public disgrace, so much so that after Córdoba was captured in 1236, the lamps were returned home by order of Ferdinand III of Castile. These ringtone conflicts were still stirring up powerful feelings half a millennium later. In his unique study *Village Bells*, historian Alain Corbin recounts numerous occasions when the clash of values surrounding the French Revolution focused on incidents involving bells. Even at this late juncture, the bells not only defined civic identity, religious practice, and the milestones of daily life, but could represent the very core beliefs for which combatants might fight and die.[7]

During the intervening period, bells were often assigned personal identities and attributed with supernatural powers. Historian Johan Huizinga tells of bells called Big Jacqueline and Bell Roland, and in many other instances they were inscribed with the names of saints or the Virgin Mary. Miracles and superstitions were often associated with these quasi-religious icons: perhaps the most dangerous and persistent was the belief that hail, hurricanes, thunderstorms, and other tempests could be halted by ringing church bells. This widely held notion bedeviled the life of a bell ringer, who was forced to ascend to the highest point in the community in the midst of the fiercest lightning storms. As late as the eighteenth century, the French Academy of Sciences felt it necessary to warn against the practice, and various legal decrees were implemented to prohibit it. Yet the bell ringers continued to risk their lives in this manner even into the nineteenth century. As late as 1899, a bell ringer of the Dawlish parish in Devon, a seaside resort in southwestern England, worked furiously during a thunderstorm in order to "overcome the Spirit of Lightning."[8]

In the face of this litany of poorly documented and now lost musical practices—from singing prostitutes to daredevil bell-tollers—we can hardly hope to comprehend more than the smallest part of the rich aural lives of typical village and city dwellers during these long centuries. We can stuff our history books full of stories of superstar composers invited to play for a pope or king, but this provides no true account of the imposing soundscapes that dominated European life for many generations. And our aesthetic theories of music hardly do justice to their inextricable connections to violence, sex, magic, power, and money.

In this regard, European music learned how to imitate European society. A reverence for hierarchy permeated both, with a tiny number of elites gaining most of the attention, while the activity of the great masses disappeared from view with hardly a trace. Music at this stage became more stratified than ever before. By the same token, it was far less participative. In other parts of the globe—for example, in Africa, or throughout the New World, then experiencing the first attempts at colonization—traditional communities still tended to treat everyone as a contributor to shared musical experiences. But European culture had erected its musical superstructures on a different model. This stratified approach would create amazing masterpieces: grand symphonies, intricate fugues, elaborate operas, and other luminous spectacles of sound. But for this to happen, the vast majority of the population had to accept extreme constraints on how they accessed music. They were neither creators nor collaborators, but rather, an *audience*. They were expected to revere elite musicians, who now exercised a degree of freedom and egotism hitherto unknown, and cover all the costs for these badly behaving stars.

Yet even in this humble guise, the audience would exert tremendous impact, eventually insisting that this intensely hierarchical culture act as a *popular* culture. That's the formula we still embrace today, and it's so familiar that we hardly recognize its paradoxical tensions and contradictions. But a paradox it remains. The audience is often manipulated, sometimes despised and ridiculed, and invariably excluded from creative input. Yet it still pulls most of the strings—and even haughty superstars must court its favor, or face the consequences.

15

The Origins of the Music Business

ost of the grand turning points in cultural history are illusory. What appears in the rearview mirror as a sudden disjunction, a leap from the old to the new, could hardly have happened without a long series of smaller shifts and alterations making it possible. The role of the chronicler is to bring this trail of events to life, revealing the gradual, organic processes behind the apparently spontaneous arising of the new. Put differently, there are no on/off switches in history. Even the sudden moments of illumination require a long vigil to prepare us for the coming dawn.

Even so, there is something remarkable about the year 1600. I'm hardly surprised that Michel Foucault focused on this juncture as the moment when a great rift emerged in the order of things, leaving behind the categories of the classical world and opening the way for new modes of representation. Foucault pays little attention to performance styles from this period—music was outside of his purview—but we could hardly find a more important date in music history than 1600. The oldest surviving opera, *Euridice* by Jacopo Peri, had its premiere in Florence on October 6 of that year.

Emilio de' Cavalieri's *Rappresentatione di Anima, et di Corpo,* often considered the first oratorio, made its debut in Rome a few months earlier, in February. The madrigal was also flourishing in 1600, with Claudio Monteverdi working on many of the defining masterpieces of that genre. The basso continuo emerged as an important musical technique around this same time—seemingly a small matter, until one realizes its significance in tilting the balance away from group-oriented polyphony and toward individualistic works built on melody and accompaniment. This same shift could be seen in the increasing use of the term *sonata* to describe instrumental works for a soloist or small group of musicians. Each of these shifts had different causes and ramifications, but the overall trend was an accentuation of the personality-driven ethos in music.[1]

Not everyone greeted these changes with enthusiasm. In that same momentous year, music theorist Giovanni Artusi admitted that though "it pleases me, at my age, to see a new method of composing," he was dismayed by newcomers who seemed determined to "corrupt, spoil and ruin the good traditional rules handed down in former times by so many theorists and most excellent musicians." This refrain should be familiar by now: the hostility and resistance brought out by musical innovation. Artusi had the greatest composer of his day, Claudio Monteverdi, in his crosshairs, and now stirred up one of the most heated controversies in the history of music. Yet here we also encounter, a few years later, the same process of legitimization documented again and again in this book. In 1633, Monteverdi went so far as to claim that his hostile critic had embraced the new modern sounds before his death. "Not only did he [Artusi] stop overruling me—turning his pen in my praise—but he began to like and admire me." This is the way musical revolutions almost always end: the acrimony is washed away, and connections between former combatants are emphasized. The details differ from century to century, but the motivation is almost always the same: the loser in a culture war decides to join the winning side.[2]

It was the dawn of a new age. In the past, the musicians had been asked to serve a higher power—which didn't always mean God. More often earthly potentates, and their sometimes hidebound institutions, called the shots. They still aimed to do so in the age of Monteverdi, and even after, but their weakening control over musical matters was increasingly apparent. The number of options in the marketplace for musicians to earn a living as freelancers expanded rapidly in the early decades of the seventeenth century. True, many musicians had made money on a transaction-by-transaction basis before this—even Pythagoras and his followers hired out their services, back when Western music was first codifying its practices—but never had they faced such a rich array of profitable ventures. At the close of the Renaissance we encounter true music *businesses.* (In fact, one of them is still operating today: Zildjian, a leading supplier of cymbals and drum accessories, with its headquarters in Massachusetts, was founded in Istanbul in 1623 by the family that still runs it.) Music publishing gained traction in the early 1600s and set practices in motion that the entertainment industry still follows today. Opera emerged as a privileged spectacle for the wealthy, then gradually turned into commercial entertainment for the general public. Other income streams, from concertizing in public to teaching in private, expanded with the growth in the market economies of Europe.

Despite these opportunities, few of the leading composers supported themselves solely by freelancing. Elite musicians still sought the security and prestige of an official appointment in a church or court. But almost all the major figures from the Baroque period, as this era came to be known, doubled as entrepreneurs, seeking out attractive commercial engagements in the marketplace. It's worth noting, in passing, that critics initially applied the term *baroque* as an insult, deriding the fussy intricacy and extravagant individualism of the aesthetic vision and contrasting it with the holistic elegance of the Renaissance. This label, too, like many of the musicians under discussion here, was later legitimized, and became a term of praise. But there is something unsettling and eccentric about the new order of things, with everything still in flux and the stars of the era fluttering from opportunity to opportunity. In an odd yet fitting way, the newfound freedom and flexibility in seventeenth-century music is matched by composers themselves in their career paths, which were just as baroque as the music of the era. We must puzzle over Monteverdi, so skilled at imparting an "aroused eroticism" (in the words of musicologist Gary Tomlinson) to his famous songs of love, taking orders as a Catholic priest. By this time, the composer had already been married and had fathered three children. Or take the even more unusual résumé of Jean-Baptiste Lully, who not only composed ballet music but danced to it—with Louis XIV as a dancing partner!—and at various points in his career played guitar, performed as a street entertainer (dressed as a harlequin), collaborated with the playwright Molière, invented the French overture, helped establish opera in France, experimented with unconventional and 'exotic' instruments, from castanets to bagpipes, and, of course, like all his peers, wrote music for Catholic religious services. With our current mindset of genre specialization, we can hardly imagine careers that move so effortlessly from idiom to idiom, but such was increasingly the norm in that age of redefinition and excess.[3]

These revered figures, who seem like the definitive 'establishment' composers of their day, were far more prickly and independent than we might guess from their institutional affiliations. Musicologist Richard Taruskin has suggested that Monteverdi's surviving letters are the earliest examples on record "of artistic alienation" in Western classical music, and calls particular attention to "a hair-raisingly sarcastic reply . . . the most famous letter by a composer before the eighteenth century." Here the composer goes on for page after page lambasting his Mantuan patrons, denouncing their lack of respect and tardy payments, bragging about his renown, his superior salary and freelance income in Venice, the better musicians now available to him, etc. He ends by asserting that the Gonzaga family, the target of this abuse, should give him some landed property that he could pass on to his children, because it would accrue to their "everlasting honor."[4]

In the case of Lully, the causes of conflict were different, and controversies stemmed from many sources—for example, a scandalous poem about his patroness, and various love affairs with young men (concurrent with a marriage that produced ten children).

Lully even lost the favor of the king after the composer seduced a young page, Brunet, who was training for service in the royal court. Lully was fifty-three years old at the time, and he was able to escape prosecution because of his renown and connections. Brunet, for his part, was sent off to a monastery for roughshod rehabilitation. In the cases of Lully and Monteverdi, as for so many others in the pantheon of classical music, we need to look past their institutional affiliations, which are almost always fraught with tension and provide a misleading aura of respectability to their biographies, to grasp how often they battled with the norms and expectations of their times. History paints them as the consummate insiders, but the details of their day-to-day lives tell a different story.

In the Monteverdi letter mentioned above, the composer brags about his ability to earn money from sideline activities, in addition to his salary as maestro di cappella at the Basilica San Marco in Venice. Venice was the perfect place for a freelance musician at this time. The city stood out as the most vibrant center of music publishing in the world, and was the incubator where opera evolved from a patron's self-indulgent spectacle into true popular entertainment. Here again, a port city that served as a gateway to other cultures emerges as a center of musical innovation, much as Lesbos did in ancient Greece, or New Orleans in twentieth-century America. Despite these advantages, Monteverdi could only count on freelancing for around one-third of his income. Intellectual property rights for composers were primitive, mostly limited to the simplest work-for-hire terms without any of the residual or royalty income we are familiar with nowadays. If composers wanted to make a real business out of publishing, they needed to set up as publishers themselves. And a surprising number of them took this step, typically as part of their relationship with a powerful patron.

Queen Elizabeth granted William Byrd and Thomas Tallis a patent on the printing and publishing of music in England for a period of twenty-one years. This right extended to blank music staff paper other composers used to write their works—even before a single note was written, Byrd and Tallis got their cut. Similar arrangements took place elsewhere in Europe and influenced the dissemination of music for more than two centuries. In 1521, Bartolomeo Tromboncino received a fifteen-year exclusive privilege from the Venetian Senate for printing music, although he may have never taken advantage of it—indeed, this favor may have been intended more as a copyright than an actual incentive to enter the publishing business. But a patent awarded to organist Marco Antonio Cavazzoni in 1523 clearly aimed to provide him with a monopoly over a new technology, apparently an innovative form of music tablature; we can merely guess at its scope, because the only works published by the holder employ conventional notation. Half a century later, composer Orlando di Lasso secured a printing privilege covering his works in France, and later sought similar rights in present-day Germany from Rudolf II, Holy Roman Emperor. Lully was elevated almost to the level of a cultural czar around this time, and even controlled all opera performances in France—a perk that allowed him to leave behind an estate of 800,000 livres, more than what many powerful government ministers of the time accumulated during entire careers. These pay-for-play privileges continued into the eighteenth century. As late as 1724, composer Joseph Bodin de Boismortier received a royal license on music engraving, and thus turned a second-class talent into substantial wealth. He allegedly responded to criticisms of his undistinguished music with boasts about how much money he was earning.

At first glance, this might seem a wonderful turn of events: musicians were given control of the latest technology in their field, and could use it for the betterment of the art form. Sad to say, the reality was far different. Musicians often proved just as domineering as the patrons of old, or driven by envy and spite. (Are you surprised?) They frequently relied on their patents and privileges to hinder the dissemination of music by others. When the original patent granted to Byrd and Tallis expired in 1596, a brief interlude of creative ferment ensued as their rivals were finally allowed to publish their works—"making 1597 a high point in the history of English music publishing," according to musicologist Graham Freeman. In other words, music flourished when the musicians *lost* control. The patent holders may also have used their authority to control the kinds of music that circulated in England. I note, for example, the absence of published lute music during the period of the initial patent, and wonder whether Byrd's lack of interest in the instrument may have played a role in this neglect. We find other instances in which these privileges served to constrain rather than advance musical arts, and are left with the displeasing notion (to me, at least) that musicians themselves may not be the best custodians of new technologies in their field.[5]

The music ecosystem seemed better served when patents went to printers, not composers. Ottaviano Petrucci used his patent on music publishing in Venice to advance the technology with his application of triple impression printing. This process demanded great care, with words, staves, and notes applied in separate steps, but represented a major improvement in the field. Petrucci published more than sixty volumes of music, and did more than almost anyone of his day to transform music into a true business, a field where entrepreneurs could prosper without playing an instrument or composing a note. Even so, this leap forward hardly allowed for true mass production, or for 'best sellers' as we would define them today. A typical print run for a musical work was a few hundred copies. Other printers in Europe, most notably Pierre Attaingnant in Paris, adopted a cheaper printing technology, using a single impression, that was better suited for high-volume production. Still, Attaingnant's press runs were probably only around one thousand copies. As a result, composers often had to reach into their own pockets to subsidize the printing of their works, although their intellectual property rights in the finished product were limited. How amusing, yet sadly revealing, to consider the first copyright warning on a published work of music, found attached to a collection of motets by Salamone Rossi issued in Venice in 1623: it involved no legal threats, merely a curse on anyone infringing on the composer's rights. Anyone who dared reprint the works without permission would get bitten by a serpent—and this threat, readers were told, was authorized by angels. Given these various constraints, no musician in these early days could envision getting rich from publishing music, or even consider it a primary source of income. But it did serve as a powerful source of legitimization for a composer, established a canon of 'classic' works, and laid the groundwork for true mass consumption of printed music at a later stage in history.

In fact, the rise of opera did more to help the economic prospects of musicians during this period than the expansion in music publishing. Yet, strangely enough, composers weren't the main beneficiaries. Singers were the true stars, and were also the ones who could demand the most money. Soprano Giulia Massotti incited bidding wars, and in 1666 she could demand more than four times as much money as the composers whose works she performed; before the end of the decade, she was getting paid six times as much. The cost of singers could take up more than 40 percent of the total budget for producing an opera, and the other participants fought over the rest. Composer Pietro Ziani complained to impresario Marco Faustini that singers were receiving ten times or more what he had made for *Annibale in Capua* (1660), even though this was his fifth opera for the promoter. As opera gained in popularity and more theaters were built, the competition to secure vocal talent only grew more intense, and even a famous composer needed to take a back seat to the diva onstage. More than half a century later, soprano Francesca Cuzzoni was still earning more for singing Handel's music than Handel made from composing it.

Other perks confirmed the status of the *prima donna* (or "first lady"), as these singers were now called. These privileges went far beyond private boxes and special allowances, extending into artistic control over the music and libretto. A star singer could decide whether songs were added, cut, transposed, or edited, and in some instances dictate the creation of an entirely new role. But even this was not enough to please some fickle performers, who brought their favorite songs with them from other operas, insisting on their inclusion in a new production. The term *diva*, which would eventually be applied to these singers, is revealing of their high status: in Italian, the word means *goddess*, a veritable female deity. The challenges in pleasing such celestial beings are so extreme that the label of diva is sometimes used nowadays on a lesser talent, or even someone who doesn't sing, provided their demands are sufficiently outrageous and their assertion of special privileges beyond the pale. This all started with the switch from opera as a private spectacle for a patron to a profit-driven entertainment business.

Yet what an amazing change this represents in the social status of female vocalists! Consider the fact that, until the late sixteenth century, the two types of female workers most closely associated with singing in the Western world were, as noted in Chapter 12, prostitutes and nuns. In other words, the songs of females were either sinful seductions . . . or else kept under lock and key in the cloister, where they could be heard by God, and not lust-ridden men. A significant turning point occurred in the 1570s and 1580s, when Alfonso II d'Este, Duke of Ferrara, began enlisting female singers as permanent members of his court. At first, these women performed in ensemble with men, but eventually formed a segregated single-sex unit known as the *concerto delle donne* (the consort of ladies). Other nobles were quick to emulate this new concept. It's hard for us today to grasp how fresh and exciting this approach was at the time, although many must have been scandalized as well. Some observers were convinced that these women were really courtesans who gave out sexual favors as part of their job descriptions. The available evidence tells a different story. It shows that many of these women not only avoided scandal, but secured desirable marriage matches and gained great social prestige via their vocal skills. In any event, the music world shifted permanently at this turning point, with singing women finally securing a career path outside of a brothel or nunnery.

Yet even the patrons who hired these singers may have had mixed ideas about the skills and requirements for this new kind of performer. Note, for example, the disturbing case of Caterina Martinelli, who was forced to undergo a medical test to certify her virginity at the age of thirteen before Duke Vincenzo I of Mantua would hire her. Perhaps he was only trying to avoid scurrilous rumor and ensure that the female performers at his court were above suspicion; or maybe he wanted to make clear that he was not involved in what we would today call sex trafficking. But the request reminds us how much musical and sexual matters have always over-lapped in Western culture. So who can be surprised that audiences allowed entrée to these unprecedented performances might also speculate—or perhaps fantasize—on matters of erotic intrigue.

The cult of the opera prima donna, which represents in some ways the next step in this evolution of the professional female singer, was also shaped by these sexual rumors and musings. For the next three centuries, opera retained a reputation that bordered on dis-honorable and sinful, and sometimes crossed far beyond the bor-der. In Paris at the close of the seventeenth century, eminent men tried to arrange private meetings with opera singers, or invited them into their private boxes. Many of these performers eventually opted to live under the 'protection' of a noble. One might even conclude that the most prosperous career path went directly from the stage to the bedroom. A commentator of the period joked that the Academy of Music, a Parisian opera house, ought to be renamed the "Academy of Love." Yet these venues didn't need to serve as pickup spots to upset the primmer members of the com-munity. The activities presented onstage were sufficiently shock-ing to stir up protests. How many of the most popular operas deal with prostitutes, mistresses, adulterers, and other 'fallen' women? The aura of legitimacy attached today to works such as *La Traviata* (which translates, in effect, as "fallen woman"), *Carmen, Madame Butterfly, Don Giovanni,* and other canonic operas shouldn't blind us to the fact that they were the edgiest entertainment of their day.[6]

Yet male musicians also found themselves subject to erotic gazes during the same period. I suspect that the sexual resonance on display was linked to the rising popularity of music featuring a solo singer backed by instrumental accompaniment, an important part of popular European culture since before the days of the trouba-dours, but now gaining greater momentum as a form of artistic expression. I hope scholars someday undertake a detailed statistical analysis of the use of first-person grammatical constructions in the songs of the Western world during the sixteenth and seventeenth centuries, but even a cursory examination of the lyrics shows the growing tension between meaning and delivery in this music. The madrigal composers might be writing elaborate works requiring several singers, yet they still felt compelled to use the first-person singular "I" in their texts. The romantic themes, so popular among listeners, demanded this contradiction. Yet consider the incongruity of Monteverdi composing a song declaring "Ardo, avvampo, mi struggo, ardo: acorrete" (I burn, I catch fire, I'm consumed, I burn: run), but setting it for performance by eight singers. Is this the setup for an intimate romance, or incitement for an orgy? Form and content were out of alignment, and something would need to change to restore the lost equilibrium.[7]

It can hardly be a coincidence that solo singing with lute accompaniment was so popular during this same period. The lute captured the public's imagination as the instrument of seducers—check out the various appearances of the instrument in Shakespeare's plays to gauge the range of its erotic associations. By the same token, portraits of men playing the lute, a sexualized subject popular with European visual artists since the early days of the Renaissance, frequently evoked a marked lasciviousness. The lutenists who appear in paintings by Giovanni Cariani, Bernardo Strozzi, Valentin de Boulogne, Hendrick ter Brugghen, and others are presented as romantic protagonists, men who, while gratifying the ears, also threatened the chastity of their listeners. As we have seen, no lute music was published during the period when the ardent (but secret) Catholic William Byrd controlled the patent on music publishing in England. That may have been a matter of chance or musical taste, but I suspect certain moral qualms might have entered into the equation as well. Even so, the moralists were bound to lose this battle. The public wanted seductive music, and this meant that sacred polyphony by Byrd (and others) would inevitably be forced to compete in the marketplace with the passionate songs of opera divas and doe-eyed lutenists.

A cultural shift in matters of love and sex was also taking place around the year 1600—a final rejection of feudal sentiments that had lingered far beyond their expiration date and turned into embarrassing anachronisms—and this move inevitably fed into the profound changes taking place in Western music. It's hard to overstate the stagnancy of the love lyric at this juncture. As the example from Monteverdi shows, songs often repeated the same clichés of the suffering lover that Petrarch had brought into the forefront of Italian poetry more than two centuries before. And Petrarch himself was holding onto many of the clichés of the courtly love ethos that were two centuries old when *he* was born. The world had changed, and the constraints of feudalism had disappeared in the real world, yet in the fields of storytelling and popular songs, the notion of fawning, masochistic service to an idealized lady still permeated European culture at every turn.

If we fail to grasp that incongruity, we can hardly understand why *Don Quixote*, published in two volumes by Miguel de Cervantes in 1605 and 1615, had such a profound effect. This story not only ridiculed the notion of knightly servitude to a perfect lady, but specifically targeted the popular culture works that celebrated it. The protagonist literally loses his mind from consuming too many popular romances, and ends up pursuing ridiculous adventures in service to a lady who doesn't exist. Cervantes was not a songwriter, but his work signaled that these old-style love lyrics needed to be replaced with something more vibrant, more realistic, and more attuned to the new world of the seventeenth century. At that same point in history, Shakespeare was ridiculing knightly pretensions in the guise of Sir John Falstaff, perhaps his most popular character—he appears in three of the Bard's plays (and is referenced in two others), the final time in *The Merry Wives of Windsor*, coinciding with Cervantes's work on his famous novel. Shakespeare's lost play *The History of Cardenio*, performed in 1613, was apparently based on an episode in *Don Quixote*. Consider the significance of the two greatest writers of the time—and indeed, of their respective nations—working almost in tandem to undermine the outdated romantic notions of their day. Composers of songs would inevitably follow along the same path.

This is the very moment when Monteverdi, the greatest madrigal composer, embraces opera, the idiom that will redefine how human relations are presented in musical settings over the next three hundred years. Monteverdi couldn't abandon the older form entirely—his audience demanded new madrigals, and his talents were perfectly suited to the form—but, like Shakespeare and Cervantes, he must have understood that the old recipes were losing their aesthetic force.

At this moment, a chasm enters into Western song. Two opposing visions contend for dominance. Those who followed the models of the past still wanted songs that drew audiences to something larger than reality, into a realm of purified Platonic ideals where spirituality, well-regulated human relations, and harmonious behavior triumphed over all obstacles, stepping out from the chaos of everyday life with glimmering perfection. The emotions celebrated here often collapsed into stylized sentimentality or a reverent and decorous devotion demarcated by poetic clichés. But now there was an alternative, a kind of song that evoked something closer to real life, perhaps even exaggerated the messiness and passionate disorder in how people deal with each other.

In an earlier day, powerful leaders or religious authorities might have dictated which of these two models most deserved emulation. But in the new era of audience-driven art, raw emotions offered a more compelling spectacle and would inevitably triumph over Platonic ideals. Songs of entropic messiness were destined to displace anthems of perfection—at least if the promoters hoped to sell tickets and fill the house. By necessity, this process would play out slowly, with many bumps and temporary reversals along the way. But who could doubt the endpoint? By any reasonable measure, we are still living in it now.

16

Culture Wars

apologize for paying so little attention to religion (and its earthly representatives) in the preceding discussion of socio-economic shifts in the music landscape. I perhaps have given the impression that this new audience-driven music easily overcame the moralizing objections of church leaders, and that a tolerant humanism now presided over the cultural life of Europe.

Nothing could be further from the truth. More extreme religious authorities worked to halt the advance of almost every innovation in music, mustering a hodgepodge of arguments against any substantive change to the status quo. They were ardent polemicists who drew sharp battle lines "between plainchant and vainchant," in the colorful words of music historian Rob Wegman. But the fervor of their pronouncements could not hide the fact that these priests lacked the power of their ecclesiastical predecessors. They stirred up countless debates and conflicts, but over the long run lost every one of them. The church no longer possessed the clout to prohibit new modes of musical expression, and had to settle for merely censoring the most blatant violations of public decency. Yet the upholders of religious scruples never acquiesced willingly in this lesser role, and made—in fact, continue to make—constant incursions into musical matters of all sorts. Sometimes they hatched plans to halt unwelcome change in its tracks. Failing that, they aimed to influence and co-opt. And, failing that, they settled for wailing and gnashing of teeth among themselves. Truth to tell, there has been much wailing and gnashing of teeth.[1]

Vocal polyphony is today considered a high point of Catholic musical culture, but even this innovation encountered a maniacal degree of resistance. The Dominicans issued a prohibition of vocal polyphony as far back as 1242. The Carthusians did the same in 1324, and we find similar measures among Benedictines, Cistercians, and other religious orders. The pope himself intervened, issuing the first papal decree dealing solely with music. In *Docta sanctorum partum* (1324/1325), Pope John XXII railed against "disciples of the new school, concerned with dividing the beat," who "fabricate new notes which they prefer to sing more than the old ones." Their music "is choked with notes. They dismember melodies with hockets and sing lubricious discants, frequently inserting second and third voices in the vernacular. . . . They know not upon what they build." The pope stopped short of prohibiting polyphony, but wanted to see it limited, and tried to steer composers toward his preferred intervals: the octave, the fourth, and the fifth. (In a curious irony of history, the church would not elect another Pope John for more than six centuries, but that pontiff, John XXIII, instigator of the Second Vatican Council, not only failed to uphold his predecessor's traditionalism but set in motion the most ardent embrace of musical modernism in the history of Catholicism.)[2]

Why did these clerics dislike polyphony? The short answer is that they saw it as an incitement to sin. In a fourteenth-century work, the English theologian John Wycliffe denounced the "vain tricks" of polyphony "which stir vain men to dancing." The mystic and theologian Denis the Carthusian (1402–1471) identified "pride and a certain lasciviousness in music of this kind." The Dominican Giovanni Caroli turned to the familiar calumny, already seen many times in the preceding pages, that assigned moral weakness in music to its feminine qualities. "Those polyphonies are both new and unheard of," he declared. "Indeed I rather hate and detest those things, since they most truly seem to pertain more to the levity of women than to the dignity of leading men." The inevitable process by which this feminine music gets attacked and later legitimized should no longer surprise us. But we can hardly ignore the peculiarity that when the same songs are praised by later generations, the commentators no longer call attention to the womanly nature of the music. Femininity in music is only worth mentioning, it seems, in the context of an attack.[3]

This battle continued to simmer within the church until the Council of Trent (1545–1563), where a proposal to ban polyphony made it into the preliminary draft recommendations, although not the decrees. An oft-told anecdote claims that a performance of a mass by Palestrina changed the critics' minds. The notion of this great composer of liturgical music single-handedly saving polyphony makes for an inspiring tale, but the evidence for any such heroic intervention is weak. In any event, opponents of this progressive music backed down—although by then church polyphony was hardly new, and more tangible threats to the Church of Rome's influence in musical matters loomed everywhere. The council settled for a formulaic denunciation of popular music and dance songs intruding into church rituals, and an insistence on the clarity of the words used during services.

Too much is made, perhaps, of these proclamations. By this time, religious leaders had found more creative ways of influencing the musical culture. Clumsy tools such as excommunication and council decrees had failed to halt musical transgressions even during the period of the church's greatest power. By the time of the Council of Trent, they served as little more than symbolic gestures or opportunities to vent. A more promising path was to co-opt the innovation, assimilate rather than prohibit, and channel its power into the service of God. I saw this process firsthand during my childhood, when the same churches that denounced guitar-driven popular music eventually launched guitar religious services with hopes of attracting teens. At first these were fairly tame Kumba-yah-ish events, but in the late 1970s Christian heavy metal music made its debut, followed in the mid-1980s by the first recordings of Christian hip-hop, each a half-hearted attempt to make a deal with the devil—but embraced only after harsher methods of containment had failed. This path of co-option is never the first resort, but is always the last, or next-to-last. The final stage, of course, is frequently the moment when even co-opting has failed and religious leaders retreat from the battlefield, bloodied from a culture war they were destined to lose from the start.

We have already seen St. Francis borrow the idiom of the troubadours in his "Canticle of the Sun," and we can hardly grasp the power of the cult of the Virgin Mary, spreading throughout Europe during this same period, without understanding how closely its homage to an idealized lady resembled the romantic yearnings found in popular songs and stories. Yet this process of co-option was hardly restricted to Christian Europe. In China around this same time, Confucian scholars continued to impose moralistic interpretations on the folk songs of the *Shijing*, collected more than 1,500 year earlier. Philosopher Zhu Xi (1130–1200) stirred up an intense controversy with the seemingly bland assessment that some of these songs "came from streets and alleys as folk songs. Youth, male and female, sang to each other, expressing their love and feelings." Yet this sensible, straightforward view implied that revered works of Chinese culture were, in the words of Sinologist Kuang Yu Chen, "composed by licentious or promiscuous young women. Even in the most liberal society, which ancient China was unlikely to be, it is hard to imagine that so many songs made by licentious women would enter the official collection and become an orthodox scholarly text." This battle continues in the twenty-first century, with some scholars still striving to turn these same folk songs into something less shameful and more attuned to institutionally sanctioned moral values.[4]

Yet a far more extraordinary example of moralistic co-option appeared in India at this same juncture. The *Gita Govinda*, a lyrical epic by the twelfth-century Sanskrit poet and composer Jayadeva, is a masterpiece of erotic spirituality celebrating the passionate desire of the milkmaid Radha for the Hindu deity Krishna. Up until this point, Radha had played a modest role in Hindu spirituality, but as with the cult of the Madonna in Europe, she now took on a far more prominent position, and a host of later poets, singers, and dancers drew on this same love story as the basis for their own channeling of sensual impulse into spiritual expression. Of course, such an erotic tale required a purifying interpretation—just as Judeo-Christian institutions imposed a spiritual gloss on the Song of Songs, and the Confucian scholars cleansed the *Shijing*. For devout readers of the *Gita Govinda*, lust is transmuted into holy love, and sexual union serves as a symbol for humanity's embrace of the divine.

The subject of erotic spirituality has many ramifications beyond music, and a full account of it would delve into tantric practices, the Kabbalah, and many other areas beyond our purview. An in-depth survey would make clear that this hybrid of religious devotion and carnal desire often manifests itself in clumsy and calculated ways, but can also produce cultural works of the highest order. One need look no further than the poetry of Dante to see how the mixture of theology with elements of popular culture and the formulas of romance can reconcile seeming opposites into an epoch-defining masterpiece. Consider for a moment the oddity of an author who turns his real-life beloved (Beatrice Portinari) into the object of his passionate love lyrics in one work (*La Vita Nuova*), and then installs her as a tour guide to heaven in another (*The Divine Comedy*). Yet somehow Dante's ploy works—indeed, is all the more pleasing because of its confident assertion that physical desire can serve as a conduit for the sacred. From a purely musical perspective, this quest to merge sensuality and transcendence is a much more powerful force than is usually acknowledged. It has exerted a constant pull on composers, as demonstrated by diverse works spanning the range from the hymns of Enheduanna in ancient Mesopotamia to John Coltrane's *A Love Supreme*. In a few instances, entire movements have embraced new ways of musical expression built on a virtuosic balancing of the carnal and the holy.

We see this, for example, in the Bauls of Bengal, spiritual minstrels of South Asia whose musical mysticism has led to accusations that they are mad or hedonistic; yet they have also served as role models for centuries, and their worldview has shown surprising resilience in crossing cultural and generational divides. A century ago, Rabindranath Tagore drew on their inspiration to propel a cross-disciplinary renaissance in Bengali culture, and as a result earned the Nobel Prize in Literature—the first person outside Europe and North America to receive that honor. (By the way, those who grumbled when Bob Dylan—who once described himself as an "American Baul"—won the Nobel Prize, claiming that songwriters weren't supposed to be considered for the award, should note that Tagore wrote more than two thousand songs and composed the national anthem for two different countries.) A half century later, the Bauls found new followers among the Western counterculture via exponents such as Dylan and beat poet Allen Ginsberg. It's easy to deride these cultural stars for their embrace of fashionable mysticism suitable for coverage in the mass media; yet this crossover could hardly have happened if its merging of the sensual and spiritual didn't answer a deep-seated hunger left unsatisfied by the prevailing ideologies of commercial entertainment. The recurrence of this hybrid in the future, in musical formats impossible to predict, is likely, perhaps even inevitable, and paradoxically ensured by the very dominance of a pop culture hegemony seemingly immunized against such metaphysical ventures.[5]

But the most powerful example of the merging of the sacred and the sensual comes from the Islamic world. The Persian figure Jalal al-Din Rumi brings together almost all the themes mentioned above. Like Dante, Rumi was a poet who celebrated a transcendent sensuality. Like St. Francis, he propelled a religious movement and gained authority as a source of spiritual wisdom. Like the Bauls of Bengal, he has been adopted in modern times by pop culture and New Age audiences, who channel his influence in ingenious and sometimes awkward ways. A quick search on Amazon for Rumi-oriented merchandise comes back with an amazing range of offerings: Rumi coffee mugs, Rumi cellphone cases, Rumi wall calendars, Rumi apps, Rumi baby clothes, and other items for home, office, and travel. Finding the real historical figure behind all this is a daunting task, and I admire the approach of scholar Franklin Lewis, the most authoritative guide to Rumi in English, who provides separate discussions in his seven-hundred-page study of the "mythological" Rumi and the "biographical" Rumi. Lewis grasps that facts are important, but also knows that myth is sometimes even more effective in propagating a movement or inspiring posterity.[6]

It would be easy to lose sight of Rumi's influence on music in all this (and he rarely appears in music history books). Yet by establishing the *Sama* ritual—a Sufi ceremony integrating music, dance, poetry, meditation, and prayer—he created what is perhaps the most powerful model within the world's major creeds for integrating the human aesthetic and spiritual impulses into a codified practice of ecstasy. This was a bold endeavor, an attempt to bridge a gulf that many still see as unbridgeable. For critics, it represented an unacceptable merger of the sacred and profane. Music and dancing, as Franklin Lewis notes, "were associated with royal courts, slave girls, wine drinking and debauchery." They weren't always prohibited within Islamic society, but any attempt to include such suspect activities in religious rituals was fraught with danger. And the controversy has hardly ended today, more than 750 years later. The United Nations may have designated the *Sama* ceremony of Turkey a "masterpiece" of our shared human cultural heritage, but the practice was banned after the establishment of the Turkish Republic in 1923. In 1956, restrictions were loosened and the Mevlevi Order, which traces its origins back to Rumi, was granted some limited freedom. But these performances of the "Whirling Dervishes," as the practitioners are often called, have been encouraged more as tourist attractions than as religious ceremonies—hence the peculiar insistence that the ritual be performed in public, not private. Practitioners in Iran continue to face government harassment, and accusations of immorality and sacrilege against dervishes repeat familiar charges against subversive musical traditions. But there is an odd twist here: the attacks aren't directed at advocates of secularism or popular musical entertainers, but at a religious practice that simply brings music and dance within its purview.[7]

The institutions of religious life perhaps have good reason to fear these intruders in their midst. Music and dance offer the surest path to ecstatic trance within the framework of organized faiths—perhaps with the exception of those marginalized cults that consume magical mushrooms or other mind-altering substances as part of their 'devotional' practice. But ecstasy is risky business, especially for those institutions and bureaucracies of faith that put the 'organization' into organized religion. I'm not even sure that parishioners in the pews want more than a tiny taste of it. Ecstasy is disruptive. Too much of it, and you have *disorganized* religion.

Social scientists have often asked a troubling question: What's the difference between a religion and a cult? Some will suggest that membership numbers alone make the difference. When practitioners turn into a suitably large voting bloc or consumer group, they rise from dangerous cult-hood to respectable creed-holders. Yet the most significant difference between a cult and a religion might simply be the contrasting attitudes toward ecstasy. The cult promises an alternative experience beyond the normal. Established religions are fearful of such practices, and this always influences their attitudes toward music.

Yet we must marvel at the uncanny compatibility between secular—and even allegedly sinful—music and religious dogma. We have already followed the strange path by which slaves influenced the evolution of popular song, inserting notions of servitude and bondage into the music of the ruling class. This may be the most subversive act in a long history of subversive music. Yet consider, for one moment, how suitable these concepts are for both romantic *and* religious music. The same images, the same language, the same metaphors figure prominently in both genres, moving seamlessly from one to another. The notions of subjugation and devotion are pervasive in *all* spheres of our musical culture. Audiences laugh when Whoopi Goldberg, playing the part of a lounge singer hiding out from the mob in the film *Sister Act*, teaches the nuns to sing the Motown hit single "My Guy," but modified into "My God." The boundaries between sacred and profane should not be so easily breached. Yet they are, and again and again. No matter our place in the social hierarchy—pauper or king, pop star or minister, rapper or diva—when we sing, we sing from the bottom looking up. We adore our ideal, which might be a deity or a romantic partner, and maybe sometimes even we are confused which of these is the target of our devotional song. Should we be surprised, then, when we find musical and religious innovations coming so often from those operating outside the power structures of society? Something in the nature of both, or in the constructs we have built around them, makes us predisposed to look for that new path to ecstasy, musical or otherwise, residing across the tracks in the dodgy side of town.

So we should never be surprised when we find religious institutions boldly borrowing from the same song styles they previously denounced as vulgar. Even so, we have now arrived at what may be the most bizarre merging of religious impulse and popular music in the history of Western culture. The Church of Rome confronted the growing popularity of opera and decided that *castrating male singers* might be an appropriate response. Here, too, the practice spanned both secular and sacred music. Even within the church, castrated boys had long been viewed as valuable additions to religious choirs. Their voices were considered angelic, a taste of what the saints might hear in heaven. Since these choirs prevented women and girls from membership, the only way to savor those celestial high notes without crossing the great divide was via young boys, before their voices broke, or castrati. Many of the latter sang both on the opera stage and in church, as did others who never went under the surgeon's knife. Venetian records from the late seventeenth and early eighteenth centuries show that around forty members of St. Mark's choir also worked in opera—here, again, the dividing line between saintly and secular song is contravened with ease. Yet the castrati seemed to have enjoyed a special appeal in the world of entertainment. The most favored could demand astronomical sums, more than celebrated composers, and in addition to their contracted fees received generous gifts from admirers. The castrato Caffarelli made so much money from his music that he eventually bought a dukedom and built a palace on his Italian estate.

Yet even as the castrati emerged as superstars, a pervasive aura of shame surrounded the practices that gave rise to their illustrious careers. When music historian Charles Burney (1726–1814) tried to learn more about the surgery, he was stonewalled at every turn. "I enquired throughout Italy where boys were chiefly qualified for singing by castration, but could get no certain intelligence," he griped. "I was told at Milan that it was at Venice; at Venice it was at Bologna; but at Bologna the fact was denied, and I was referred to Florence; from Florence to Rome, and from Rome I was sent to Naples. The operation most certainly is against the law in all these places, as well as against nature; and all the Italians are so much ashamed of it, that in every province they transfer it to some other." The Vatican never officially approved the procedure, and sometimes even threatened surgeons who practiced it with excommunication. Yet the results were not only tolerated but encouraged, both for the alleged sublimity of the castrato's voice and the church's stated desire to remove women, those dangerous temptresses, from performance situations where they might inspire impure thoughts.[8]

The termination of this tradition is as hard to track in the archives as its origins. As late as 1913, the castrato Alessandro Moreschi sang in the Sistine Chapel—he is the only castrato to make solo recordings, and he was actually recorded at the Vatican. But some have speculated that soprano Domenico Mancini, who performed in the papal choir until 1959, was also a castrato, although there is little evidence to back this up besides his skill in the falsetto register. Who knows what information still sits unreleased in the Vatican archives? In 2001, the Italian newspaper *Corriere della Sera* urged the pope to make a formal apology to the castrati who were the victims of this practice, but our knowledge of its full extent and the parties complicit in its maintenance is still mostly a matter of conjecture. In many instances, contemporary accounts avoided the matter by serving up vague anecdotes about accidents—a kick in the groin, an attack from an animal, a fall from a horse—as suitably plausible explanations for the credulous.

In all fairness, the Vatican cannot assume total responsibility for this lamentable tradition. Audience demand and economic interests may have played an even greater role, and we see that these factors continued to hold sway even after female opera singers were widely accepted. Yet the Church of Rome had other ways of influencing the evolution of opera that were uniquely its own, and far less aligned with popular tastes. In some instances, the church tried to ban operas or at least impose a moratorium on performances during Lent. But ingenious fans found ways around the prohibition—for example, they attended "open rehearsals" of operas that didn't count as actual performances. When Pope Clement XI imposed stricter controls, and managed to halt opera productions in Rome from 1703 to 1709, oratorios served as stealth operas, presenting passionate love stories in the guise of edifying allegories. Even earlier, the Vatican had tried to encourage operas about the lives of saints, resulting in Roman productions of *Il Sant' Alessio* (1632), *Santi Didimo e Teodora* (1635), *San Bonifatio* (1638), and *Sant'Eustachio* (1643). Many within the church, and especially among the Jesuit order, had high hopes for musical and theatrical productions as a tool in propagating the faith, and we even hear of opera performances in monasteries.

The selection of Giulio Rospigliosi as Pope Clement IX in 1667 seemed to signal a new age of harmony between the spiritual aspirations of the church and the aesthetic evolution of opera. As a young man, the future pontiff had written the libretti for the sacred operas mentioned above, and had even helped invent the comic opera with his contributions to *Chi soffre, speri* (1637). Rospigliosi had ambitious schemes for turning the Church of Rome into a champion of musical theater. After his election as pope, he authorized the construction of the first opera house in Rome, and hatched plans to employ the Sistine Chapel Choir as a platform for his religious theatrical concepts. But Clement IX died in 1669, after serving for less than a year and a half. His successors had different views of opera, less sympathetic and sometimes overtly

hostile. The dream of opera as a source of edifying Christian doctrine would probably have failed even under the most favorable
circumstances—unless, perhaps, a composer of genius had arisen
to soften its didactic edges, the way a Milton or Dante could do in
the medium of poetry. After Clement's death, even the dimmest
hopes of such a rapprochement faded away.

The epicenter of the culture wars had already shifted northward
by this point. The Reformation, initiated with the promulgation of
Martin Luther's Ninety-Five Theses in 1517, spurred actual military wars as well—the conflicts didn't subside until the conclusion
of the Peace of Westphalia in 1648. At least five million people died
in the course of these battles over competing Christian worldviews,
and some experts would put the number at more than twice that
level. But military engagements could hardly resolve the incompatible visions of creed, conduct, and culture at stake. Conflicting attitudes toward art and music may not have been the dominant causes
of this rupture, but they contributed to the disagreements and
served to define important attitudinal differences, both between
Protestantism and Catholicism and within the different branches
of the reform movement. The Church of Rome had succumbed to
the allure of art, its critics proclaimed, and encouraged the faithful
to offer their devotion to the graven image of God, the painted vis-
age of a saint, and elaborate musical phrases that hid the meaning
of the sacred word. Within Protestantism, religious leaders held
differing views on the degree of purification necessary to counter
these excesses, but all agreed that the old practices required scrutiny and, in some instances, violent eradication.

Almost every issue of musical controversy from the preceding
two thousand years was resurrected as part of this reform. Readers who have traveled with me this far will perhaps be dismayed to
learn that virtually none of these past disputes had been resolved.
All the same concerns that had aroused the suspicions of Plato,
Seneca, Augustine, and other sober elders now returned in the
context of the Reformation. Did the pleasure of music weaken our
moral fiber? Were edifying words besmirched by getting attached
to vulgar dance songs? Could listeners even understand the words

when sacred texts were married to elaborate melodies? Did certain instruments pose a special risk—or perhaps *all* instruments? Under the best case, didn't music represent an unnecessary waste of time and money? Even the old accusations linking music to dangerous effeminacy got recycled by the reformers. In his attack on Catholic practices, Zurich reformer Ulrich Zwingli asked how an Old Testament prophet would react "in our times, if he saw so many different kinds of music in the temples, and heard so many different rhythms . . . while the effeminate canons went to the altar in their silk surplices? Truly, he would cry out so that the whole world could not endure his word."[9]

Zwingli was an extreme case. Under his influence, church organs were sold, damaged, or destroyed. In the fervor for reform, the organ got dubbed as "the Devil's bagpipe"—or "the pope's bagpipe"—and sometimes the organist was vilified as a seducer of the flock. A story has survived about the organist of the Grossmünster, the Zurich cathedral originally commissioned by Charlemagne, who "stood by, helpless and weeping," after witnessing the destruction of one of the great instruments of its day. Things got so bad that, in 1525, *all* church music was eliminated in Zurich. An austere ritual replaced the mass, with paintings and colorful vestments put aside, and congregants told to focus instead on the edifying words of the sermon.[10]

Yet Zwingli himself was an exceptionally gifted musician, with more demonstrated skill in this field than any of the other major reformers. One of his contemporaries, Bernhard Wyss, claimed that Zwingli could play more than ten instruments, "and anything else that would be invented." Zwingli, who worked so vigilantly to eradicate music from the spiritual lives of the faithful, also was a talented composer. Shortly before his death, he even wrote the music for the first modern performance of a Greek comedy in the original language. At first glance, these two facets of the Swiss reformer seem irreconcilable, yet we have seen other comparable instances. Abélard, the composer of popular love songs, rejected all acclaim for this achievement later in life and aspired to a dour religiosity. By the same token, a traditional (and perhaps unreliable) account of

Folquet de Marselha, acclaimed as a troubadour in his youth, tells of him seducing the noblewomen celebrated in his songs, but later, as bishop of Toulouse, he earned even greater fame for shedding the blood of heretics and championing the Inquisition in the south of France. Such examples remind us that, even when religion falls short in its ambitions to reform song, it still often manages to enlist the support of some unlikely allies along the way, including the same musicians who had mastered these sinful styles in their youth.[11]

Even in modern times these turnabouts take place. A surprising number of the leading blues performers of the early twentieth century later renounced the music of their youth. In 1963, when blues researcher Gayle Dean Wardlow tracked down Reverend Ishmon Bracey, who had recorded lusty blues songs in the 1920s, the preacher expressed "terrible guilt about the blues and the blues life. He was almost paranoid about it." When a possible recording contract was dangled as a lure, Bracey insisted that he would only perform religious music—thus torpedoing a potentially lucrative comeback. Around this same time, Reverend Robert Wilkins resurrected a blues career he had left behind back in 1936, but he cleaned up his repertoire to make it more godly before returning to the stage. In contrast, Son House, who had served as mentor to the legendary blues guitarist Robert Johnson back in the 1930s, agreed to play the old blues again some thirty years later, but demonstrated genuine anguish about it, often lapsing into passionate sermonizing during his nightclub and coffeehouse performances. And what about Johnson himself, who filled his now iconic songs with spiritual anxieties of the same sort—who knows what he would have done if he had lived longer? Still other performers, such as Blind Willie Johnson and Reverend Gary Davis, championed the techniques of the blues, but channeled them into saving souls. Perhaps the most amazing turnabout of them all found Tom Dorsey evolving from renowned singer of dirty blues to the inventor of modern gospel music.[12]

If we are seeking reasons for these flip-flops, perhaps the simplest one offers the most convincing explanation. Musicians understand better than anyone the power of song—they experience it firsthand in the act of performance, where they witness the mesmerizing effect they have on an audience. It makes sense that any sort of conversion experience or shift in ideology would make them more zealous than others in extirpating dangerous elements in the prevailing musical culture. The situation isn't much different from reformed drinkers who become the most vocal advocates of abstinence. Or I think of my father, whose addiction to tobacco shortened his life, and imagine how he would have responded to almost any infraction by me with forgiveness except smoking cigarettes. He would have wept to see a child of his with a pack of Marlboros. Those who know any practice most intimately are often the most vigilant in combating it.

Martin Luther was also a musician and composer, and though he rejected the more repressive measures of the extreme reformers, he, too, grasped the deep power of song on weak human nature. Catholic music historian Felice Rainoldi has gone so far as to proclaim Luther "the greatest writer on music in the Western church since Augustine himself." Luther confidently proclaimed that "faith comes from hearing"—a tenet drawn from Paul's Epistle to the Romans—and that "miracles for the eyes are far inferior to those for the ears." For the most part, Luther advocated tolerance in an environment where his more meddlesome contemporaries would have destroyed most of the existing music ecosystem. He was a skilled singer and composed his own hymns, while encouraging others to do so as well. Luther also welcomed the adaptation of popular melodies and Catholic works, updated with new texts congruent with the reformed theology. Traditions others viewed with suspicion, including polyphony and even the use of Latin texts, continued under his guidance. His influence on the practices of his time is obvious, yet we also do well to ask how his actions may have influenced the later evolution of Western music. During the three centuries following his death, Germany dominated the musical culture of the Western world and set a standard of excellence that many believe has never been surpassed. This could hardly have happened if a more severe reformer had set the rules for German musical life in the early sixteenth century. Shouldn't we give Martin

Luther a little more credit for the later creative resurgence that produced Bach, Beethoven, Brahms, and so many other revered masters of concert hall music?[13]

By the same token, we should perhaps be grateful to King Henry VIII and his daughters for the mildness with which they introduced musical reforms after Britain broke with Rome and established the Church of England. Henry VIII composed songs himself, including the famous "Pastyme with Good Companye," with its raucous lyrics celebrating festivities and merry-making. Henry VIII's seizure of monasteries and other church properties sometimes resulted in the destruction of important musical manuscripts, but choirs continued to perform at cathedrals, at various colleges, and in royal settings, including Windsor Castle. Many leading composers began writing sacred music in English, but Latin also survived in some situations. Catholic liturgical and musical practices were revived after the 1553 coronation of Mary I, the only surviving child of Henry's first marriage. Even complex polyphony came back into vogue. After Mary's death five years later, her half sister, Queen Elizabeth I, reestablished the authority of the Church of England. For the most part, Elizabeth took a moderate stance on musical reform, restraining those seeking more extreme measures in the culture wars. Like her father, Queen Elizabeth took pride in her own musical efforts. Her favorite instrument was—so appropriate!—the *virginal*, a relative of the harpsichord (yes, its name arose because it was played by innocent young women), and an anecdote has survived relating her delight in surpassing Mary, Queen of Scots, as a performer on the keyboard. In the Elizabethan *Injunctions* from 1559, she defended the use of hymns and other songs beyond the austere psalms favored by more fanatical reformers, explicitly mentioning their legitimacy in the "comforting of such as delight in music." The admission that church music should contribute to the listening pleasure of parishioners may seem like a small matter, but within the context of the larger battles over music raging through Europe during the course of the sixteenth century, this declaration from the queen was a significant victory for the forces of tolerance.[14]

These culture wars were eventually reconciled in the gentlest way imaginable—requiring neither the destruction of instruments nor cruel and unusual punishments. The Protestant churches throughout northern Europe and Britain eventually became the largest employers of musicians in the marketplace. Instead of burning organs, they hired organists. Instead of banning polyphony, they paid for it and hired choirs to perform it. Lutherans and other denominations gradually discovered what the Catholics had already learned: that the safest way to control music was to keep the leading composers on the payroll. I am reminded of that famous line from *The Godfather*, the bit of advice Don Corleone gives his son: "Keep your friends close, but keep your enemies closer." But perhaps that isn't fair. Church leaders gradually forgot they had ever been opposed to music—at least not sacred music. Yet culture wars over secular music will continue to loom large in the pages ahead, and probably the years ahead as well. I doubt that we will ever get beyond fighting over music. We may be hardwired to do so: research shows striking correlations in nervous system activity (heart rate, respiration, body temperature, pulse, etc.) between listening to pleasurable music and fight-or-flight responses to danger. Those two options, ecstasy and conflict, have always lived in close quarters, and probably always will. Yet the glory of music is that, paradoxically, songs are also the strongest team-building and coalition-building forces in human culture. Music may set off the culture war, but it also provides the tools to end it.[15]

As we look forward beyond the age of Reformation, we see just such a period of peaceful coexistence between musicians and the institutions of church and state throughout the Western world. Or so it seems, at first glance. Virtually every leading composer of the period would have financial ties to church and nobility, and in many instances entire careers and livelihoods depended on this seemingly harmonious relationship. Yet below the surface, conflict still raged. A paycheck may buy compliance, but not always contentment. And great musicians, perhaps even more than others who work for hire, detest servility to ruling powers. Even amidst the truce, they believed they were rulers themselves, albeit in a different domain, but perhaps with just as much a connection to the sacred, maybe even a direct line of communication with the divine. In their hearts, and sometimes with their words and actions, they nurtured a faith in a different hierarchy, one in which they were not servants, but masters. Given this conflict in worldviews, the culture wars couldn't really come to a peaceful conclusion. They merely went underground for a time.

17

Subversives in Wigs

You can hardly find a more sanctioned and orthodox insider than J. S. Bach, at least as he is typically presented. He is commemorated as the sober, bewigged Lutheran who labored for church authorities and nobility, offering up hundreds of cantatas, fugues, orchestral works, and other compositions for the glory of God. Yet the real-life Bach was very different from this cardboard figure. In fact, he provides a striking case study in how prickly dissidents in the history of classical music get transformed into conformist establishment figures by posterity.

"Suppose instead we start to view him as an unlikely rebel," suggests conductor John Eliot Gardiner in his revisionist study *Bach: Music in the Castle of Heaven*. Musicologist Laurence Dreyfus, in a spirited 2011 lecture, even goes so far as to label our stolid church composer "Bach the Subversive." Yet there is tremendous pushback to those who dare taint the atmosphere of respectability and propriety attached to this towering figure, a cultural icon who remains, even today, the poster boy for "serious music." Amidst the celebrations linked to the 250th anniversary of the composer's death in 2000, Bach scholar Robert L. Marshall sounded a cautionary tone when admitting that the availability of new information demands a reinterpretation of the composer's life and works, but he and his fellow experts were "avoiding this challenge and we knew it." As Dreyfus has pointed out, much of the current writing on Bach comes across as if it were "modeled on the lives of saints."[1]

I've talked to people who feel they know Bach very well, but they aren't aware of the time he was imprisoned for a month. They never learned about Bach pulling a knife on a fellow musician during a street fight. They never heard about his drinking exploits—on one two-week trip Bach billed his church for beer, and the amount he demanded was enough to purchase eight *gallons*—or that his contract with the Duke of Saxony included a provision for tax-free beer from the castle brewery; or that he was accused of consorting with an unknown, unmarried woman in the organ loft; or about his reputation for ignoring assigned duties without explanation or apology. They don't know about Bach's sex life, at best a matter of speculation, but what should we conclude from his twenty known children, more than any other significant composer in history (a procreative career that has led some to joke with a knowing wink that "Bach's organ had no stops"), or his second marriage to a twenty-year-old singer, Anna Magdalena Wilcke, when he was in his late thirties? They don't know about the constant disciplinary problems Bach caused, or his insolence toward students, or the many other ways he found to flout authority. This is the Bach branded as "incorrigible" by the councilors in Leipzig, who grimly documented offense after offense committed by their stubborn and irascible employee.

But you hardly need to study these incidents in Bach's life to gauge his subversive tendencies. Just listen to his music, which must have disturbed many austere Lutherans, and even fellow musicians, with its ostentatious display of technique and bold architectonic structures. Not much music criticism of his performances has survived, but the few surviving reactions of his contemporaries leave no doubt about Bach's disdain for the rules by which others played. We hear a complaint about him improvising for too long during church services. We read an angry denunciation from fellow composer

Johann Adolph Scheibe about Bach's "bombastic" and "confused" music-making. Bach was even forced to provide a memorandum to the city council in 1730 explaining why it was necessary to embrace "the present musical taste" and "master the new kinds of music." Here he insists that "the former style of music no longer seems to please our ears," and demands the freedom to follow the most progressive trends of his day. But perhaps the most revealing commentary comes from Scheibe's diatribe, where he complains that Bach's music was "darkened by an excess of art" and marred by an "unending mass of metaphors and figures." In other words, the very signs of Bach's greatness for later generations were the elements that made him suspect during his own time.[2]

These reservations continued after Bach's death. Some have suggested that Bach's work was forgotten until Felix Mendelssohn helped focus attention on it in the late 1820s. That's not entirely true. Bach's music retained a following in those intervening years, but primarily for pedagogical purposes. There was simply too much to learn from this composer to allow his artistry to disappear. But that didn't absolve Bach of all his transgressions. Johann Abraham Peter Schulz, a composer who came of age in the generation following Bach's death, complained that his predecessor's chorales set a dangerous precedent for those who "would rather display their learnedness . . . and multiply dissonant progressions—which often render the melody quite unrecognizable—than to respect that simplicity which in this genre is so necessary for the understanding of the common people." As late as 1800, Abbé Georg Joseph Vogler felt compelled to make Bach's chorales more acceptable by simplifying complex passages.[3]

When the mythos of Bach's genius finally emerged, it coincided with a rising sense of German nationalism and a religious revival, movements that hoped to use this now long-dead composer to advance their own agendas. It's not even clear that Bach self-identified as a German—rather than as a Saxon or a Thuringian. Yet by 1802, a biographer, Johann Nikolaus Forkel, proudly proclaimed, "This man, the greatest musical poet and the greatest music orator that ever existed, and probably ever will exist, was a German. Let his country be proud of him." This is the familiar recurring cycle in the history of subversive music, revealed repeatedly in the pages ahead in very different circumstances (with blues guitarist Robert Johnson or ragtime composer Scott Joplin, for example). These artists are scandals in their own time, but legends at a to-be-determined later date when their legacies are appropriated by powerful institutions and reinterpreted to support sanctioned narratives. The role of the music historian is to bring this rehabilitative process into the open, but for some it is all too tempting—perhaps even irresistible—to participate in turning the life story of a troublemaking provocateur into a monument to the new status quo.[4]

Dreyfus specifies six different aspects of Bach's subversive practices, a veritable manifesto of resistance. According to his schema, Bach subverted conventional notions of musical pleasure—take, for example, the Fugue in B minor in Book I of *The Well-Tempered Clavier*, whose theme employs all twelve notes of the chromatic sequence, defying traditional notions of what constituted a beautiful melody. He subverted religious conventions that made liturgical music subservient to *logos*, the divine word. He subverted prevalent notions of musical propriety, which demanded that expressive style adapt itself to the specific functions and purposes of the occasion. He subverted the dogma that art was a mirror to nature, and must adhere to natural forms of expression rather than impose its own self-referential value system onto artistic works. He subverted the traditional metrics of musical invention, those time-honored techniques by which melodic ideas were introduced and developed. Finally, he subverted the expectations of musical piety, which demanded that a work of art should express its devotion in reverent and orderly subservience to the grandeur of God, and not the glory of the composition or its composer. A hagiographer who wants to maintain Bach's reputation as a paragon of respectability and poster boy for the establishment could bicker about one or more of these claims, yet it is impossible to dismiss the gestalt that emerges from a broad-based and open-minded survey of this seminal figure, his life story, and his body of work. At a very deep level, Bach distrusted officials and power brokers, demonstrating his independence whenever the occasion arose—and sometimes forced the occasion when his muse so demanded. If he eventually became symbolic of the status quo, it was only because the status quo came to adapt to his prerogatives, not the other way around.

Conventional accounts of music history during the century following Bach's death in 1750 focus on a dazzling expansion of techniques put to use in symphonies, string quartets, concertos, sonatas, and other rapidly evolving platforms for creative expression. It's worth noting that none of these formal structures have much to do with religious practices—a peculiar state of affairs when one considers how much churches were covering the cost of European music during this same period. Even Bach, the great exponent of Lutheran music, is best remembered nowadays for his secular works—just check out his current-day 'best sellers' on the charts if you doubt it. His keyboard music gets more clicks than his cantatas. His Passions and the Mass in B minor are masterworks of sacred music, but are they heard more often than the *Brandenburg Concertos*, which, though little known during Bach's lifetime, are played over and over on "drive-time radio," or his cello suites, now practice-room staples for string players? After Bach's death, the secularization of musical culture became even more pronounced. Charles Rosen, in the revised edition of his seminal study *The Classical Style*, notes the hostility from his critics for his scant attention to the church music of the era. But how could Rosen do otherwise? It is, he explains, "unhistorical to pretend that the setting of religious texts did not present very radical stylistic problems in the last quarter of the eighteenth century, and ideological problems as well. . . . [T]hat style was stone dead when Haydn wrote most of his masses." The oddity here isn't the shift in musical styles. That was inevitable in an age of loosening church ties and thriving secular music. The real disjunction comes when we consider how all this happened during a period when virtually every major composer found some way to extract money from religious institutions.[5]

Composers learned to lead double lives during the eighteenth century, adopting very different postures to secure church favors and marketplace success. Vivaldi was ordained as a priest, but only administered the sacraments for around one year. He found other ways of supporting himself in teaching, composing, and publishing. His most famous work, *The Four Seasons*, is more pagan than Christian, evocative of the fertility music of antiquity—which, you will recall, celebrated a deity dying in winter and rising in spring. Handel started out his music career as a church organist, but soon moved on to the more lucrative and exciting field of opera. When he returned to religious music late in life with the *Messiah*, it was designed for performance in theaters, not churches. Handel may have written *Soli Deo Gloria* (To God alone the glory) at the end of his score, but his actions reflect a greater trust in the marketplace to put a proper value on his work.

The overall trend is clear. The great composers of this period increasingly looked for ways to prosper outside the jurisdictions of religion, even though most musicians still started their careers inside churches. Consider the example of Joseph Haydn, who enjoyed his first taste of acclaim as a choirboy in Vienna. The future composer could have pursued a singing career, and might have agreed to the castration required to maintain his youthful voice, but his father vetoed the plan. Soon after, Haydn was forced to leave the cathedral choir and found a place in a rented attic, where he diligently studied music theory and practiced the keyboard sonatas of Carl Philipp Emanuel Bach—a son of J. S. Bach—whose work served as a role model as he developed his own skills as a composer. Haydn's job title with the Esterházy family might have been *Kapellmeister*, but we would be wrong to translate that as "chapel master"—he was more a musical director than a church functionary. In truth, Haydn never abandoned religious music, and despite Rosen's reservations, he was even capable of creating a masterpiece of biblical interpretation in *The Creation*. But like Handel, Haydn wrote this oratorio for paying audiences in concert settings, not devout parishioners at church. Religious music, in aggregate, represents only a small portion of his oeuvre. And even when he embraced it, he did it as much for Mammon as for God.

By the close of the eighteenth century, the marketplace had emerged as the leading arbiter of success in the field of music, but until that time composers relied primarily on two options for career advancement: religious institutions or private patronage. Yet the dividing line between these two alternatives was often blurred. Sometimes a church functionary was also a wealthy noble—for example, Mozart's patron Hieronymus Colloredo, whose title was Prince-Archbishop of Salzburg. In other instances, a composer might be hired by nobility but requested to write music for sacred purposes. Many of Bach's finest cantatas were composed while he was working for Duke Wilhelm Ernst. On the other hand, when Bach served Leopold, Prince of Anhalt-Köthen, he could devote most of his time to secular music. In Leipzig, Bach focused on sacred works, but his employer was the city council. The specific circumstances varied, but almost every one of these career options was based on an increasingly antiquated notion that the musician was a servant to those higher up in the social hierarchy.

This was an awkward state of affairs. Antoine Lilti, in his study *The Invention of Celebrity*, tells us that the concept of celebrity "appeared during the eighteenth century" at the very time when these composers were still operating in this semifeudal arrangement. Of course, other kinds of fame had been celebrated in earlier eras, but these primitive types of notoriety were based, in Lilti's useful schema, on either *glory* (at amazing deeds—feats of bravery or heroism and the like) or *renown* (for extraordinary achievements, including works of art or literature). Celebrity was something different, a kind of fame that took on a life of its own, going far beyond sober appraisals of works and deeds and generating an obsessive public fascination with even the trivial private activities of the 'star' personage. We tend to think of celebrity culture as a defining aspect of our own times, but the word *celebrity* actually achieved its peak usage in written texts, both in English and French, around the year 1800. Not only did the word get used more frequently, but its meaning shifted dramatically during this period. In the first half of the eighteenth century, the term had often carried negative connotations, referring to a kind of shameless self-promotion that a more dignified person would avoid. But around 1760 or 1770, the word started taking on a different resonance, and was now attached to those rare individuals who somehow inspired the passion and curiosity of the wider public.[6]

This is the same moment when Joseph Haydn got hired as a servant of the Esterházy family. The composer's contract, dated May 1, 1761, was kept in the family archives, so we can gauge the full degree of Haydn's servility. He was required to dress in a uniform, much like other attendants and lackeys. He wasn't allowed to eat or drink with his employers, but was expected to dine with other servants. He needed to avoid familiarity or casual intercourse with the family, and had to appear before "His Highness" twice each day to take orders. As if these requirements weren't sufficiently humiliating, Prince Esterházy would decide what music Haydn wrote and own the rights to his compositions. To close off any loopholes, the contract also prohibited Haydn from composing music for anyone else without the prince's explicit permission. By our standards, these terms are punitive, perhaps even unconscionable. Yet this was one of the most desirable positions in European music at the time.

These feudal trappings of artistic patronage could hardly survive the changes taking place in the wider world. Even within Haydn's lifetime, the balance would shift. When composer Carl Ditters von Dittersdorf received a private audience with Joseph I in 1789, he found himself interrogated by the ruler of the Holy Roman Empire about the comparative merits of Haydn and Mozart. In an amazing revelation, this powerful ruler admitted that he had written an essay assessing the virtues of the two composers, and was anxious to show it to his visitor. Rulers were now fans themselves, their own curiosity piqued by the new breed of musical celebrities.

Some enterprising scholar should conduct a detailed study of the changing language composers used with patrons over the course of the eighteenth century. Here in compact form we can trace the same liberation from formal constraints writ large in the composers' musical scores. Back in 1709, Antonio Vivaldi felt compelled to offer this dedication to King Frederick IV of Denmark and Norway: "It gives me great confidence to offer you my abasement which in real consideration of my nothingness could not in any way be more diminished." To Venetian nobleman Vettor

Delfino, the great composer gushed: "Your good taste in [music] has reached such a perfection that there is no artist who would not wish for the glory of having you as a master." To Count Gombara of Venice, Vivaldi effused: "I will not lose myself in the vast expanse of the glories of your most noble and excellent family, for I would not find my way out again, since they are so immense in greatness and number." At the far end of that same century, we find Beethoven offering similarly servile language in his dedication of three sonatas to the Prince Elector of Cologne, modestly daring "to put my first youthful works at the foot of Your throne." It's possible that these words were actually written by Beethoven's father or his teacher; in any event, the composer was only twelve years old when he wrote those works, and he would never again adopt such a self-abasing tone in future dedications. In between these two extremes, we find Haydn, whose attitude toward his patrons changed markedly over the course of his career. He, too, could play the role of the obsequious flunky, particularly in his early years with Prince Esterházy. In a letter to his patron from 1766, Haydn offered "to kiss the hem of your robe for graciously presenting us with new winter clothes." But these protestations eventually disappeared from his correspondence with the Esterházy clan; he replaced them with boasts of his popularity and complaints about the demands on his time: "My arrival caused a great sensation," he wrote to the new prince, Anton Esterházy, from England, in 1791, "and forced me to move on the very same evening to larger quarters. I am so burdened with visitors that I will hardly be able to reciprocate within six weeks." He closed the letter with a bland promise to "dutifully report" again when he found time, but not for at least another month, and in a postscript he sent kisses to his boss's "charming wife," an attractive twenty-two-year-old woman who was thirty-six years younger than the composer.[7]

It would be interesting to know more about Haydn's relations with women—not out of salacious curiosity, but to gauge how much the new obsession with celebrities impacted the real day-to-day lives of musicians during the period. How closely did their intimate moments resemble those of current-day concert hall stars? Do we find here further evidence to support linkages, high-lighted back in Chapter 1, between musical skill and advantages in sexual selection? Haydn's last will and testament was filled with bequests to women who were not related to him by blood. Per-haps this merely reflected his generous, charitable nature—but we might also detect the emergence of what we today would refer to as *groupies*, ardent fans who marked their devotion to musicians via a short-lived sexual dalliance. Yet we know so little about these relationships in past eras, and are forced to read between the lines as best we can. Even so, there can be no doubt that Haydn experi-enced celebrity mania firsthand—a 1785 British newspaper article even encouraged his enthusiastic fans ("aspiring youths") to kid-nap the esteemed composer in order to liberate him from "the court of a miserable German Prince."[8]

The same unanswered questions loom even larger in the case of Mozart's private life. We do know that he created the most famous work of highbrow culture about hook-ups and one-night stands, the opera *Don Giovanni*, composed with the assistance of librettist Lorenzo Da Ponte, a real-life philanderer who learned seduction skills firsthand from his close friend (and notorious lover) Giacomo Casanova. But what can we say with any certainty about Mozart's own romantic relationships? True, he left behind ample docu-mentation of his private life, especially in his voluminous surviving correspondence, which he wrote with a crudity that has alarmed many prim admirers of classical music. But these missives are some-times more mystifying than explanatory, and even after they were finally presented to the public in uncensored form (a rarity until the twentieth century), they left much open to speculation. A kind of coded eroticism is displayed here, and Mozart's frequent indi-rect expressions add to the confusion. Consider, for example, the phrase *spuni cuni fait* (which no scholar is quite sure how to trans-late); or his hints to Baroness Martha Elisabeth von Waldstätten that he must hide some aspects of their communications from his wife; or his declaration to his cousin, switching into French for this remark, that he will kiss her hands, her face, her knees, and, in fact, "everything you will allow me to kiss." The editors left this last word untranslated in the English edition of Mozart's letters—and perhaps with good reason, because *baiser* doesn't merely signify kissing but can serve as an equivalent to the English term *screwing*. Mozart himself admitted to his father that he felt the sex drive more acutely than most men, reinforcing the image of him as a passionate lover much like his stage creation Don Giovanni.[9]

Some commentators have built on such clues to construct a biography of the composer marked by affairs with servants, singers, and other females in his path during his travels around Europe. Yet Mozart also had strong religious scruples and made protestations to his father that he avoided casual affairs out of a sense of honor. I'm not sure whether we can believe the latter claim, but even if it's true, Mozart's need to assert it demonstrates that eminent musicians, at this stage in history, had opportunities to parlay their celebrity into bedroom escapades.

We are on more solid ground when trying to determine the subversive political messages in the works of the great composers of the era. Director Peter Sellars has labeled Mozart "one of the most intensely political artists in history," pointing out that "every single opera is a radical gesture of equality between the ruling class and the working class." Take, for example, Mozart's first opera with Da Ponte, *The Marriage of Figaro*, now considered by many as the epitome of respectable highbrow entertainment for the affluent. Yet when they decided to write this opera, the Pierre Beaumarchais play that serves as its basis had recently been banned in Vienna on the explicit order of Emperor Joseph II. Even earlier, Louis XVI had tried to prohibit its staging in Paris, and when it did make its debut, a riot ensued, with three fatalities. The French Revolution was only three years in the future when *The Marriage of Figaro* returned to the stage as an opera, and it isn't hard to connect the harsh critiques of nobility presented here, even in Da Ponte's more circumspect rendition, with those that would soon take over the streets in Paris.[10]

Was Mozart a revolutionary? I don't think we can go that far. Sellars tries to explain the absence of explicitly seditious comments in Mozart's letters as subterfuge: "You have to remember that censorship was so intense, anyone who expressed revolutionary ideas or those that led to the French Revolution would be likely to be interrogated by the secret police." But I think historian Paul Johnson comes closer to the truth when he declares that Mozart's "politics, though by no means revolutionary, were discreetly but emphatically subversive." This, he believes, explains why Mozart received so little patronage from the ruling class despite his renown. "Mozart was left high and dry in Vienna because of his politics."[11]

Consider as well Mozart's membership in the Freemasons, which he joined in 1784. His involvement in the organization is sometimes seen as a quaint sideline, or as a source of the symbolism in *The Magic Flute*. But secret societies were feared by rulers during this period. In 1785, just a year after Mozart's enlistment, Emperor Joseph II restricted the number of Masonic lodges and demanded that magistrates receive updated membership rosters and meeting times. Scholars still debate whether Freemasonry played a role in spurring the French Revolution four years later, but there can be little doubt that nonmembers with more traditional leanings distrusted the organization. By the same token, although the significant role the Masons played in the classical music of the eighteenth century is not proof positive of revolutionary intent, the attraction this secret society held for Haydn and Mozart provides insights into the personalities of the new cadre of celebrity composers of which they were a part. Composers increasingly viewed themselves as outsiders even as they drew on their connections to insiders for career advancement.

In fact, Mozart sometimes explicitly came down on the side of monarchy rather than revolution. During the course of the American Revolution, he declared, in a letter to his father that exulted in the British victories over the French in that conflict, "I am an out-and-out Englishman." But even here we must recall that England, for many in Vienna at the time, represented a land of independence and personal liberty. There's no room to doubt Mozart's views on *those* matters—his life exemplified them—but his attitudes here might be as much a matter of personality as ideology. Certainly Mozart had little patience for the domineering and hidebound ways of the cultural elites of his day, and this attitude comes across with equal clarity in his character and his compositions.[12]

Relations between patrons and composers had changed dramatically in the two decades since Haydn had offered to kiss the hem of his patron's robe. The story is told of composer Luigi Boccherini, ordered by his royal Spanish patron to change a passage in one of his works, responding by making it twice as long. During this same period, Carl Philipp Emanuel Bach wrote an autobiography—an extraordinary undertaking for a composer during this period, when musicians' memoirs were all but unknown—and used this platform to express irritation at those who dared criticize him. Mozart was a freelancer out of necessity for most of his career, but even when he enjoyed the support of a patron he grumbled about it. In a letter to his father from 1781 filled with complaints about his position with the Archbishop of Salzburg, Mozart exclaimed: "What distinction, pray, does he confer upon me?" He scorned the archbishop's treatment of him as a servant, and told his father that this position served only to hide his talent—a reversal of the traditional view that association with a wealthy patron raised a musician's status. Perhaps Haydn felt the same way around this time, but he probably did a better job of hiding his irritation from his employer. Mozart was not so cautious, and must have caused quite a scene. When he was finally dismissed, the archbishop's steward threw the great composer out of the palace with a literal kick in the ass. Mozart's reaction: he declared his intention of returning the kick, even if took twenty years to find an opportunity. Such were the relations between Europe's greatest composer and his most important patron in the years leading up to the French Revolution.[13]

But we can't attribute this testiness merely to seditious political beliefs. Mozart could afford his arrogance because of the enormous expansion of freelancing opportunities available to musicians in the closing years of the eighteenth century. As his own boss, Mozart had five significant sources of income. First, he made money from giving lessons, no different from musicians today. We don't know the full extent of his pedagogical work, but a letter from 1782 finds him boasting to his father about the income from three of his students. Second, he performed at public concerts, and sometimes even organized these events—taking charge of selling tickets and covering the rental of the hall. Third, he gave private concerts for members of the nobility and other wealthy music lovers. Publishing provided a fourth source of income, and though this endeavor didn't bring in as much money as it would with today's copyright laws, opportunities were constantly expanding with the spread of pianos into middle-class homes and the rising demand for printed music. Finally, Mozart could count on commissions for works, especially operas—but here, too, payments were onetime work-for-hire arrangements without the ongoing royalty income composers enjoy nowadays.

Despite these limitations, Mozart still made a considerable amount of money. You will sometimes hear allegations that he lived and died in poverty, but nothing could be further from the truth. Mozart enjoyed an upper-middle-class lifestyle by the standards of the time. He had a desirable apartment in the center of the city, dressed in style, hired a coach when needed, and dined in restaurants. He paid for a barber to visit him daily for dressing and powdering his hair. Visitors to his home would be surprised to see a billiard table, a possession rarely associated with the households of the impoverished. True, Mozart had problems with his debts, but that reflected his spendthrift ways, not a lack of earning opportunities. And it is likely that, had he lived longer, Mozart would have enjoyed considerable affluence. The success of his widow, Constanze Weber, in monetizing his artistry, even without the benefit of new works to sell, shows how much economic value even a dead composer possessed in the marketplace after the dawn of the nineteenth century.

But if we are looking for a symbolic turning point, a moment in music history when composers abandoned servility and turned into celebrities who lived by their own rules, I would call attention to an easy-to-ignore incident that took place around this time. Even when the changes are gradual, sometimes a single shift in the ecosystem reflects a reality previously hidden from view. Such was the moment in 1790 when a stranger knocked on Haydn's door, without an appointment or advance notice, and declared to the bewildered court composer: "I am Salomon of London and have come to fetch you. Tomorrow we will arrange an accord." This German-born impresario, Johann Peter Salomon, could see what Haydn had not yet realized: the degree of acclaim and income that awaited the composer in London. Unlike Mozart, who was fluent in English, Haydn lacked even a rudimentary knowledge of that language. But music and money speak eloquently without much need for words, and Haydn was more than conversant with the latter and an acknowledged master of the former. In London, Haydn found that he could earn twenty times as much as he had with the Esterházy family. He now performed for adulatory audiences and with the benefit of large, well-trained orchestras. And when Haydn wasn't concertizing, he was feted by the Prince of Wales and other members of the royal family, and awarded an honorary doctorate at Oxford. In these circumstances, he was inspired as never before. For this initial visit and his second London stint in 1794–1795, Haydn created many of his most celebrated works, enjoying a creative peak in his late fifties and early sixties seldom matched in the history of music.[14]

Have I dwelt too much on socioeconomic factors here? I think not. Extraordinary changes were taking place in musical forms during the final decades of the eighteenth century, but we can't adequately account for them without taking full measure of these shifts in the social position and renown of Europe's leading composers. Celebrity status was blurring the line between a composer's biography and art, and the structural underpinnings of musical works had to adapt to this new state of things. Musical compositions were taking on a narrative form, even when they were works of 'pure' music without an explicit text to guide the listener. "The symphony was forced to become a dramatic performance," explains Charles Rosen, "and it accordingly developed not only something like a plot, with a climax and a dénouement, but a unity of tone, character and action it had only partially reached before." Works were increasingly named after events in the lives of the composers who wrote them. Haydn's "Oxford Symphony," as it is called today, wasn't really composed for his Oxford visit—it had actually been commissioned by a French count and performed previously in Paris—but audiences preferred to see such works as autobiographical statements inspired by momentous personal events and perhaps inner emotional turmoil. Even if Mozart's Requiem wasn't really composed for his own death, many of his admirers preferred to view it as such.[15]

But for music to bear this weight, every aspect of it needed to change. The poised, extended flow of Baroque music was hardly suitable for conveying extreme dramatic effects; it had to be replaced by a varied rhythmic landscape marked by expressive shifts, pauses, peaks, and valleys of sound. Dynamic changes needed to become more forceful. The flow of energy during a piece required constant management, even micromanagement, to produce contrasts of sublime distinction. Devices that had seemed too outrageous before—irregular phrases, disjunctive shifts of key, unexpected silences, even comic effects—were now cultivated by composers and celebrated by audiences. They were just a different slice of the eccentricities and quirks expected from the demigods of classical music.

These two trends will propel music forward at a dizzying pace from this point onward. First, music becomes inextricably tied up with biography and character, to such an extent that pure musicology, any definition of song or style by the notes alone, turns into a fool's gambit, a willful refusal to read the personal memoirs inscribed in the staff lines. Sometimes this personal stamp is obvious, as with the evolution of the concerto—which reaches a new level of artistry around this time under the impetus of Mozart's perfection of the form—with its growing emphasis on the soloist as protagonist in a quasi-narrative structure. But even symphony and tone poem, or, in an extreme example, liturgical music that ostensibly aims to celebrate the Creator with a capital *C*, end up manifesting the composer-creator with a small *c*. The second tendency, linked to the first, finds audiences demanding not just autobiography from their leading composers, but radical, explosive self-representations that proclaim the composer's greatness and exemption from all the everyday rules of ordinary people. And then there's the unspoken third factor that lingers hidden in the listener's fantasy life: namely, the implication that they are enjoying this same freedom by extension, a kind of surrogacy of outrage. As fans, they, too, can enjoy the snubbing of authorities and the breaking of rules.

This is the recipe, a kind of packaged subversion ready for sale in the marketplace, and it still fits the bill in the present day. Henceforth audiences will demand music that acts as a kind of social irritant and platform for the prickly personalities who make it. Of course, all this promises revolution, or, more accurately, revolutions, ongoing ones without cease that will drive music forward with unrelenting momentum, and neither endpoint nor resting spot. Songs, from now on, might be good or bad, happy or sad, fast or slow, just as they were in the past, but they will increasingly disrupt and provoke as well—and sometimes spur their listeners to do the same.

18

You Say You Want a Revolution?

This leads us, by necessity, to the subject of Beethoven. All these tendencies reach their culmination in him. Music is now the declaration of the human spirit, and not just an ordinary human spirit. The audience demands a towering figure, larger than life. If subversion and outrageous behavior were previously hidden from view by musicians, kept to private moments when a patron wasn't around to observe, they are now cultivated and put on display. Even stranger, musicians are now expected to have *opinions*, views on all sorts of matters, from the personal to the political. The music itself is transformed into a kind of sociopolitical manifesto, a statement on the world as well as a harbinger of changes to come.

No one really cared much about deciphering Bach's political views, certainly not during his lifetime, and hardly at all even after he became enshrined as a canonic composer. But with Beethoven, everything gets viewed through a prism of revolution, upheaval, and clashing value systems. For the first time in music history, political factions battle over musical scores, fighting for them as if they were territory at stake in a war.

Do you still have an image of Beethoven as the ultimate classical music insider, the bedrock of the symphonic tradition, and symbol of the establishment? When Chuck Berry wanted to announce the triumph of rock 'n' roll in 1956, he declared "Roll Over, Beethoven," in a hit song that kept returning to the charts in various cover versions over the next quarter century. And every sock-hopper, hot-rodder, and rebel-with-or-without-a-cause knew exactly why the esteemed German composer was singled out for abuse. He was *the Man*, the whole annoying tradition of fuddy-duddy respectable music summed up in a single oppressive figure. Six years after Berry's record took over the airwaves, Anthony Burgess published his novel *A Clockwork Orange*, featuring a young thug who is trained via aversion therapy to get nauseous every time he hears Beethoven's Ninth Symphony. The System is out to destroy you, mates, and the "Ode to Joy" is its tool of domination.

Don't believe a word of it. These are defining examples of the dialectic explored repeatedly in these pages, that remarkable flip-flop that transforms musical radicals into upholders of the status quo. Old musical revolutionaries never die, they just get assimilated into mainstream institutions. If you only see the institutional figure, you are missing the real action. You have been given Beethoven as brand franchise, a construct used to serve various interests, almost certainly financial or ideological in nature, and usually both.

And no figure in the history of Western music has been co-opted and distorted with more vehemence than Ludwig van Beethoven. His "Ode to Joy" has been embraced, over the years, by the leaders of both Nazi Germany and the Soviet Union, Mao's Cultural Revolution (at a point when almost all Western music was forbidden in China), the Peruvian Shining Path terrorist Abimael Guzman, and the Apartheid regime in South Africa. Beethoven's Ninth Symphony was performed to commemorate the fall of the Berlin Wall, but the very regime toppled had previously claimed the great composer as one of its own. How can a single work carry so much symbolic resonance for such disparate—and opposed—ideologies? (Oddly enough, this symphony has also figured in technology battles: when Sony and Philips collaborated on the development of the compact disk, they bickered endlessly over the necessary running time for the new format. According to legend, they finally agreed that a CD should have sufficient storage space to accommodate the full duration of Beethoven's Ninth.)

And the battles over this single work in Beethoven's oeuvre continue in the current day. The "Ode to Joy" from this symphony was selected as the official anthem of the European Union in 1985. Beethoven's Ninth thus emerged as a protest song when Britain voted to exit the European Union. At a concert in the Royal Albert Hall in July 2017, ushers even intervened to stop audience members from waving EU flags during a performance of the Ninth Symphony. When Donald Trump and Vladimir Putin showed up in Hamburg for the G-20 conference that same month, German chancellor Angela Merkel made sure this same Beethoven work was part of the entertainment. This was a pointed political statement, and seen as such by onlookers. Yet Putin himself has announced his allegiance to Beethoven, naming the German composer as one of his favorites, and in the very same week as the G-20 gathering, Trump told an audience in Warsaw that his own policies were like a symphony—a comment that some observers perceived as a kind of Beethoven impersonation by the visiting president. Chuck Berry clearly missed the mark. Beethoven is alive and well, and apparently a supporter of every party and regime.

This debate has been going on since the birth of Beethoven scholarship. After Beethoven's death, his secretary and early biographer Anton Schindler presented the great composer as an outspoken radical and supporter of revolution. But composer Vincent d'Indy, who published a biography of Beethoven in 1911, denounced this claim. "Jacobinism," he declared, "could be only repugnant to his honest heart." Beethoven's most famous biographer, Alexander Wheelock Thayer (1817–1897), aimed to take a middle ground in his meticulous accounting of Beethoven's day-to-day life—"I fight for no theories," he proudly proclaimed—but that hardly stopped the debate from raging on into modern times. In recent years, scholar Steven Rumph has confidently asserted that conservative values eventually dominated Beethoven's worldview.

Biographer Maynard Solomon, in contrast, celebrates Beethoven as a utopian visionary. And, according to a Potsdam conference held before the end of communist rule, Beethoven "reached the threshold of Marx's teachings" and viewed his music as a "revolutionary, practical-critical deed." The scholars, it seems, are just as contentious as the politicians in their turf wars over the long-dead composer.[1]

Beethoven didn't help matters with the conflicting and shifting bits of evidence he left behind. Even his most famous political gesture was marked by wavering and indecision. Beethoven wrote his Third Symphony to honor Napoleon, but then scratched out the dedication from the score. The work that was supposed to be called *Bonaparte* is now known as the *Eroica Symphony*. This repudiation is often explained by citing Beethoven's dismay when Napoleon declared himself emperor. Yet even here we will find no consistency in the composer's behavior. Did Beethoven oppose monarchical institutions? Hardly! His first two sonatas for cello were dedicated to Friedrich Wilhelm II, King of Prussia. His Septet in E-flat major, Opus 20, is dedicated to Empress Maria Theresa. In 1802 he dedicated three sonatas for violin and piano to Tsar Alexander I of Russia. In 1813, he composed *Wellington's Victory* and dedicated it to the future George IV—and even interpolated "God Save the King" into the score. His Ninth Symphony was dedicated to Frederick William III of Prussia. And the last substantial work he completed before dying, the new finale to his String Quartet No. 13 in B-flat major, given its initial public performance a month after the composer's death, was part of a piece dedicated to Russian Prince Nikolai Golitsyn, member of a powerful family that even today proclaims its impressive titles over vanished fiefdoms.

Many other examples could be cited of Beethoven's comfy relationship with royalty, spanning his entire career. By the time of the Congress of Vienna in 1814, where Beethoven provided entertainment for his generation's equivalent of a G-20 conference, the one-time admirer of Napoleon seemed to be in full Ted Nugent mode, serving up music for the forces of reaction. But should this surprise us coming from a composer whose very name—with its Dutch "van" resembling the German "von" as a sign of noble birth—misled people into thinking he was of exalted origins? Beethoven did little to clear up this false perception, yet he also saw himself as a man of the people and a supporter of the downtrodden—just watch his opera *Fidelio* for proof positive. How do we reconcile these contradictions? Perhaps the safest thing one can say about Beethoven's allegiances in the battle between haves and have-nots is that he could play either side as the occasion warranted.

Even so, I believe we can get behind these confusing facts and arrive at a reasonably clear understanding of Beethoven's core values. In fact, he is a perfect case study for the claims I've made in this book. A recurring phenomenon traced in these pages—a surprisingly consistent one, despite marked differences in epochs and cultures—finds innovations coming from disruptive outsiders who shake up the very same institutions that later lay claim to them. If these rebels live long enough, they may even participate in the mainstreaming of their previously radical pose. Elvis shows up at the White House to hobnob with Nixon. Dylan accepts a Nobel Prize. Jagger gets knighted. In other instances, the shift happens behind the scenes, undocumented by scribes and historians, although incriminating evidence gets left behind. An erotic love song from an anonymous woman is somehow turned into Old Testament scripture and attributed to King Solomon, or finds its way into the *Shijing* and adds to the glory of Confucius, or a noble troubadour imitates it, transforming it into canonic literature. The resulting synthesis can be denounced as appropriation or outright theft of intellectual property, but this process remains an ongoing engine of change in music history. It happened before; it will happen again. Even so, we must guard against the gullible acceptance of the revisionist history that almost always accompanies this assimilation. The historian of music needs to look beyond the ideological interpretations that the prevailing institutions impose after the fact—they are almost always spinning a story to justify their own agendas—and work to recover the essence of the innovation, the prickly and disruptive force from the outside that set the whole process in motion.

What do we find if we use this explanatory model to unravel the mysteries of the composer Beethoven? If we study him in his earliest manifestations, does he fit this pattern? Does his status as a slick, skilled insider disappear as soon as we trace his impact back to its roots? Let's see how a contemporary perceived Ludwig van Beethoven at an early stage of his career. Frau von Bernhard, a pianist who encountered the composer at private gatherings, left us this description: "He was short and insignificant with an ugly red face full of pockmarks. His hair was very dark and hung tousled about his face. His attire was very ordinary and not remotely of the choiceness that was customary in those days and especially in our circles. Besides, he spoke in a pronounced dialect and had a rather common way of expressing himself, indeed his entire deportment showed no signs of exterior polish; on the contrary, he was unmannerly both in demeanor and behavior. He was very proud." This could just as easily be a description of Johnny Rotten or Lou Reed, but it's Beethoven we're dealing with here. Frau von Bernhard continues with an anecdote about a countess begging Beethoven to play piano at a gathering, and even getting on her knees before him as he sat on the sofa, only to be rebuffed by the rising young music star. Composer Carl Czerny shares another extraordinary example of Beethoven's scornful attitudes. After dazzling an audience with his improvisation, bringing them to tears (some audibly sobbing), Beethoven laughed at his listeners and openly mocked them. "You are fools!" he declared. "Who can continue to live among such spoiled children?" Czerny concludes: "He declined to accept an invitation from the King of Prussia after an improvisation of this kind."[2]

We would like to believe that leaders of the music establishment overlooked the fact that Beethoven was "short and insignificant with an ugly red face," and that they grasped the rare genius behind the boorish exterior. In this case, we don't need to guess, as is so often the case with earlier composers, where little documentation exists about the first responses to their works. Music criticism was flourishing during Beethoven's formative years, so we know exactly how opinion leaders viewed his innovations. What did they say at the time? The first review of the *Eroica Symphony*—now revered as a milestone in music history and a monument to German Romanticism, that all-pervasive zeitgeist out to shape the psyches and soundscapes of European high culture—arrived on the newsstand even before the official premiere, dismissing the music as "strident and bizarre." Another journalist, covering the debut, admitted that the work had some defenders, but for the average person "the symphony was too difficult, too long and [Beethoven] himself was too impolite." This assessment was no exaggeration. Carl Czerny, who attended the concert, reported that one listener rose up in the middle of the performance and shouted: "I'll give another kreutzer if the thing will only stop!"[3]

I could fill up an entire chapter with such attacks and curt dismissals. And these critics weren't ignorant or eccentric fools, but knowledgeable representatives of the established order. They weren't outliers, but part of a movement. In fact, they clearly consulted with one another, because the same words appeared again and again in attacks on Beethoven. His music was deemed strange, peculiar, arbitrary, bizarre, mysterious, gloomy, and laborious. Even Haydn, who seemed inclined to serve as a mentor and champion for the young Beethoven, backed away from the full implications of his disciple's style. When Beethoven showed Haydn the three piano trios in his Opus 1, the older composer advised him that the final work in the group should not be published. Beethoven recognized (as has posterity) that this was the most important of these early trios, the most mature and impressive. Perhaps Haydn was jealous and resentful of the next generation, as Beethoven surmised. But our knowledge of the older composer's enthusiasm in praising Mozart makes it unlikely that he would denounce a younger talent simply because of marked signs of genius. The conclusion is inescapable: even the greatest living composer in Europe saw Beethoven as a volatile outsider whose impulses needed to be held in check, an unpredictable upstart who ought to adapt to established ways of doing things. The institutional rebranding of Beethoven was still years in the future, and driven by agendas that have little connection with the actual innovator—and in most instances, do more to mislead than clarify. For those on the scene, Beethoven was a disruptor, not a consolidator.

The key point is that almost all the apparent paradoxes and clashes over Beethoven fall away when he is seen as part of this recurring process of disruptive innovation followed, after a few years, by establishment turf battles to claim the very individuals previously attacked. Even Beethoven's political views can be deciphered with a reasonable degree of confidence, and no intellectual gymnastics required. When Beethoven explicitly inserted a core value into a musical work—as with "freedom" in *Fidelio* or "joy" in the Ninth Symphony—it is invariably done in the most straightforward, most direct possible way, without a lot of ideological baggage. *Fidelio* was part of a popular subgenre of rescue operas, not much different from the prisoner breakout movies of modern times, such as *The Great Escape, The Shawshank Redemption*, or *Rambo: First Blood Part II*. Then as now, these stories can be fitted into a wide range of historical settings, but are hardly vehicles for serious philosophical thinking on matters of human liberation. The same could be said of the "Ode to Joy" in the Ninth Symphony, the piece so frequently and easily co-opted by various movements—but for the obvious reason that it makes such vague claims. If this is a political manifesto, it's hardly a controversial one. The most dicey claim in the text Beethoven chose for this work is that all of us are linked in brotherhood, or perhaps the acknowledgment of a divine creator. The simplicity of the message is part of its essence and appeal.

To understand what Beethoven actually meant by freedom, we do well to turn to a crucial distinction that intellectual historian Isaiah Berlin made in his influential essay "Two Concepts of Liberty."[4] Berlin calls our attention to the profound divide between what he calls *positive* liberty, which often involves elaborate political agendas to achieve its goals, and *negative* liberty, which can be as simple as freedom from interference. Beethoven leans more closely toward the negative camp. Just look at the words to his 1792 song "Wer ist ein freier Mann?" (Who is a free man?):

Who is a free man?
The man to whom his own will alone,
And not any overlord's whim
Can give him the law.
That is a free man![5]

This is essentially the definition of negative liberty. The famous scene in *Fidelio* of the prisoners emerging from their cells is almost a fantasy image of that value made manifest on the stage. The captives shake off their chains and emerge into the light of day, no longer held in bondage by oppressors. The same sentiment is made manifest in the "Ode to Joy," which celebrates no party platform, but rather the inviolable human spirit. Advocates of negative liberty such as Beethoven might enter into short-term alliances with various parties, programs, and potentates—indeed, they are often forced to do so in order to maintain their own cherished independence—but shifts in these affiliations should not surprise us. From the larger perspective, Beethoven maintained extraordinary consistency in his core values, which were primarily driven by a sense of human dignity rather than institutional allegiances.

Ninety-nine percent of the disinformation and propaganda in music history comes from institutions—and, of course, the unwitting dupes who swallow their tall tales. They aim to promote their agendas, not serve as beacons to historical truth, and their claims must always be scrutinized and checked against primary sources. This is as true with Beethoven as it is with Enheduanna, the first musician known to us by name—to recall the account from Chapter 5, the very stone disk that celebrates her importance was defaced and broken into pieces by some later power broker—or any of the other innovators dealt with in these pages. The only thing that's changed: institutions tend to be subtler with their methods nowadays, and only occasionally resort to defacing stone memorials.

We need to keep this in mind as we grapple with another apparent paradox of nineteenth-century music. The cult of Romanticism coincided with the emergence of celebrity musicians and expanding economic opportunities that reduced their dependence on

ruling institutions. Almost everything about this movement celebrated the individual and rejected the institutional. The emotional
and psychological underpinnings of musical creativity were revered
as never before. Even the rudeness and overweening pride of the
music star were not only tolerated, but now cherished as the unmistakable attendants of genius. When artists, leaving vanity behind,
aspired to still greater heights of power and expression, they were
expected to turn to nature—a landscape or lonely cloud or starry
night sky—as their guiding light, not to a pope or prince. Experi-
ential and emotional truths were seen as irrefutable and, wherever
you looked, the personal trumped the political.

We can only grasp how liberating this must have felt by comparing it with the previous three thousand years of music history,
a troubled narrative of high and mighty rulers intruding at every
turn on artistic prerogatives, with even tiny gains in expressive freedom coming at a heavy cost. Finally, the roles were reversed. Percy
Bysshe Shelley was hardly exaggerating when he declared in 1821
that "poets are the unacknowledged legislators of the world"—but
he probably should have also included composers, novelists, painters, and sculptors in his imagined parliament of creative spirits.
Princes now kowtowed to leading artists, aiming to secure their
favor and bask in the reflected glow of their self-made nobility. But
here's the paradox: the whole spectacle of music during the nineteenth century is marked by political, religious, and nationalistic
factions who claim these composers and their music as their own.
These composers are constantly portrayed as representatives of this
cause or that faction. Even as their independence is celebrated as
the essence of their artistry, it gets denied again and again by people in positions of authority.[6]

Be wary of this spin—or what we would call nowadays a *refram-
ing of the narrative*. I won't deny that the great musical artists of
the nineteenth century could make gestures of accommodation to
ruling institutions, especially if they lived long enough. Franz Liszt
eventually joined a religious order, became a Franciscan, and took
on the title of *abbé*. But if we tried to view him through the prism of
church music we would arrive at a very misleading picture of Liszt's

significance. The same is true of Gioachino Rossini, who even gave up writing operas, and composed instead some fine works of sacred music—yet we would fundamentally misunderstand his artistry if we took those as the starting point of our inquiry into his oeuvre. After his rise to fame, Johannes Brahms received the Maximilian Order for Science and Art from Ludwig II of Bavaria, and Duke George of Meiningen gave him the Commander's Cross of the Order of the House of Meiningen. Was he a closet monarchist? If you want to assess Brahms's actual ideological leanings, you would probably do better to heed Antonín Dvořák's description of him: "Such a man, such a fine soul—and he believes in nothing! He believes in nothing!" Even when Brahms drew from the sacred music tradition while composing *A German Requiem*, he seemed inclined to leave out both the Christian and German elements. He told conductor Karl Reinthaler: "As far as the text is concerned, I confess that I would gladly omit even the word German and instead use Human; also with my best knowledge and will I would dispense with passages like John 3:16 ['For God so loved the world that he gave his only begotten Son']. On the other hand, I have chosen one thing or another because I am a musician, because I needed it, and because with my venerable authors I can't delete or dispute anything. But I had better stop before I say too much." Or perhaps he said just enough.[7]

And what of musicians who died so young they couldn't receive the perks of institutional acclaim? Even they get caught up in posthumous political wrangling. Take, for example, the case of Franz Schubert. You could hardly find a less likely joiner-of-causes. To his contemporaries, he was immersed in music, not factionalism and ideology, and his personality could serve as a textbook example of the stereotyped Romanticist composer as a lonely poet of haunted soundscapes. "He was silent and uncommunicative," wrote Franz Eckel, Schubert's friend since their student days, who noted that even those close to the composer had trouble breaking through this aloof exterior. "On the walks which the pupils took together, he mostly kept apart, walking pensively along with lowered eyes and with his hands behind his back, playing with his fingers (as though on keys), completely lost in his own thoughts." Louis Schlösser, who visited Schubert at his home in Vienna, was shocked at the composer's lack of interest in his surroundings. His residence lacked the usual comforts of home and hearth, and looked instead like an artisan's workshop, filled with his piano, string instruments, music stands, a few chairs, and piles of scores. "Music was the atmosphere in which he lived and breathed," Schlösser concluded, "in which his subjectivity unconsciously attained its highest development."[8]

But even if we lacked these firsthand accounts, we ought to conclude as much from Schubert's output. He had the shortest life span of any of the great composers of his era—Schubert died at age thirty-one—but left behind more than 1,500 musical works. His 600-plus pieces for voice and piano are still the gold standard for songwriters, and they are precisely the kinds of moody, emotion-filled works one would expect from such an introspective personality. I am always amazed when some pop culture magazine or pundit publishes a list of the greatest "all-time" songwriters and doesn't include Franz Schubert. He probably belongs at the top of the list, whether the metric is quality, influence, or just sheer indefatigable effort. How, one wonders, did Schubert have any time for living— let alone political causes—given the ceaseless labor and dedication required to create this oeuvre? And then there are the masterworks for orchestra, piano, chamber ensembles, and liturgical settings, any of which alone would have earned him fame. Indeed, there isn't much to write about him beyond these works. "The dearth of information has permitted every kind of biographical fantasy," writes music critic Alex Ross. "The man is not quite there; the music is another thing altogether. Its presence and immediacy are tremendous."[9]

Yet this hasn't prevented later generations from attaching Schubert's name to every kind of movement, from Nazi totalitarianism to gay rights. Then again, perhaps he was a proto-socialist— Schubert was arrested once, along with four friends, by Austrian police seeking to root out revolutionary currents among students, but was only given a reprimand for his insulting language. Yet Vienna conservatives would also claim Schubert as their own at the close of the century, celebrating his music as a nostalgic throwback to a simpler time, before the corruption of modern ideas. But Schubert might also deserve consideration as a liberal populist: just look at his willingness to write music for both the concert hall and the dance hall, or even the humble parlor piano, defying the elitist hierarchies of cultural czars. These causes all can find some evidence to promote their claims. But the fit is never perfect, and we are left with Schubert the outsider, focused on his own concerns and defiant against interference, but mostly so he can get back to his craft.

Yet I would mislead you if I claimed that the breakdown of institutional control of music during this period was driven largely, or even primarily, by the prickly, independent personalities of the leading composers. A much larger factor was the inward turn in the cultural ecosystem, as the home and salon emerged as the main locations for music-making in the Western world. Here, outside the control of church and state, millions of amateurs and semi-professional musicians performed pieces for friends, family, and often merely for their own enjoyment, their numbers gradually rising over the course of the nineteenth century. This shift impacted every aspect of music: how it was composed; the instruments featured; the way it was published, sold, and disseminated; and the income it generated.

The first signs of this change can be traced back to the end of the Renaissance, when we find growing evidence of artisans and tradespeople owning instruments, hiring music teachers, and hoping that a few lessons might lead to a better marriage match for their children or enhance the family's reputation. As the middle class grew in size, so did homemade music. Even so, the well-traveled composer Charles Burney reported that he couldn't find a single music store in Vienna in 1770, or in any of the Italian cities he visited. But the democratization of music accelerated with unprecedented speed during the 1800s, fueled by a rise in standards of living and a drop in the cost of pianos. Making music for a king or pope might still provide acclaim and a gratifying ego boost, but composers now maximized their income by selling to the sons and daughters of butchers, bakers, and candlestick makers.

Even by Schubert's time, the impact on music is evident—the majority of his works are perfectly designed for intimate performance in humble domestic settings. With Frédéric Chopin (1810–1849), we encounter a composer who wrote almost exclusively for solo piano, a career move that would have been disastrous only a short time before his birth. But introspective music for a solitary performer was now both aligned with the spirit of the age and tailored for the demands of the marketplace. By 1850, the change was complete. London directories from that period tell us that a staggering two hundred piano manufacturers served the local market. Specialized producers emerged in response to rising demand, providing keys or cases or other parts for the name brands, thus serving to improve quality and drive down cost. The growing availability of used instruments—no longer needed after the youngsters get married—added to their affordability and helped make a home piano not just a luxury but a necessity. In these final decades before the invention of the phonograph, the home piano embodied almost the entire scope of musical culture. It's where songs were written, where they got performed, where they were heard by new listeners, where they went viral or were forgotten. If *Billboard* charts had existed back then, they would have measured keyboard activity in middle-class homes—that was now the make-or-break measure of musical success.

The classical music ecosystem in Europe seemed on the brink of an era of peaceful domestic music-making, downsized for home and hearth, and nurtured among family and friends. But these comfortable moments in music history never last for long. I suspect that some inherent instability in social psychology or an ineradicable tendency toward cultural restlessness prevents them from defining the soundscapes for more than a few years. Whenever the leaders of the musical mainstream get too soft or introspective, fiercer predators always emerge to dislodge them. I'm convinced that the sweet, sentimental songs that dominated American popular music in the early 1890s, when the insipid waltz "After the Ball" became the best-selling tune in US history, merely built the audience's hunger for the transgressive sounds of ragtime, jazz, and blues. The craze for romantic torch songs, gentle crooners, and optimistic novelty numbers at the dawn of the Great Depression probably made listeners all the more welcoming when the hot music of the Swing Era arrived in the second half of the 1930s. The same thing happened in the 1950s: the first half of the decade was the golden age of inoffensive pop music, but the second half belonged to irreverent rockers. And it happened again in the 1970s, when the age of nuanced, understated singer-songwriters lasted five years, more or less, before in-your-face punk and shake-your-ass disco took center stage. I hesitate to proclaim some recurring twenty-year cycle, but I can't deny the evidence for a constant shift of polarities: whenever the musical culture gets too easy and affable, look for a revolution on the horizon.

As the midpoint of the nineteenth century approached, this change arrived in tandem with genuine revolutionary movements as political upheavals broke out across Europe in 1848. But the intensely nationalistic fervor of the conflicts set them apart from previous battles over reform. Patriotism was aflame, and unification movements underway in Germany and Italy changed not only the map of Europe, but also its psyche and soundtrack. We are so familiar with nationalistic movements in our own time that we are hardly surprised by this turn of events. Yet few changes in Western history were less expected and violated more forecasts than the rise of patriotic emotion at this juncture. If you had convened a meeting of the great European thinkers of the eighteenth and nineteenth centuries and asked them what would drive future global politics, not one of them would have put nationalism on the list. The leaders of the Enlightenment anticipated a coming age when reason and universal values would shape the course of events. Marx and his fellow travelers trusted that class struggle and economic oppression would serve as the spur to change. The positivists in the camp of Auguste Comte championed science and progress as the driving force in future history. Social Darwinists postulated evolutionary models; political economists attributed power to Adam Smith's "invisible hand"; and neo-scholastics put faith in the hand of God. Everybody had a theory. But *none* of the thought leaders anticipated a future when war and bloody carnage would be instigated by chauvinistic impulses and love of country. The illustrious philosophers dismissed those as archaic tribal loyalties, irrational sentiments no longer useful for human society, and destined for the dustbin of history. But the theorists were wrong. No force in the world since 1848 has been more powerful, more deadly, more pervasive, or more persistent than nationalistic zeal.

Whenever there is violence on a large scale, music is enlisted in the struggle. In this instance, overheated nationalism was the new ingredient that shook up the classical music establishment around the midpoint of the nineteenth century, and it would reverberate for the next hundred years. Even so, there is something awkward in this new weaponization of well-crafted musical works, destined for combat duty at the symphony hall or opera house. Many scholars see the rise of nationalism as an inherent part of the Romanticist spirit of the century, but I would argue that the appeals to fanatical patriotism should be viewed as the arrival of a decadent stage in the Romanticist ethos. The movement was now half a century old, and it needed some new ingredient to fuel its fires. The eccentric individualism of a Beethoven, or the moody parlor sounds of a Schubert, were no longer sufficient to stir up the powerful emotions that the zeitgeist demanded. The nationalist movements provided precisely that new source of energy composers required—and audiences craved. Now was the time, it seemed, for all good composers to come to the aid of their country.

In retrospect, it's striking how little nationalism had impacted classical music in the hundred years leading up to the conflicts of 1848. Handel, who had been born in Germany, could be proclaimed a great British composer, and no one gave much of a fuss. Haydn's most famous orchestral works were labeled as the "London Symphonies," and this only added to their allure—even today, audiences tend to prefer them over his supposedly home-grown Austrian fare. Mozart opted to compose his operas in Italian (two-thirds of them are in that language) and his sacred music in Latin, including his final *Requiem*, without fretting about the political implications of these choices. Mendelssohn, despite his

Jewish roots, could gain renown as the preeminent figure in German music—something that could never have happened shortly after his death in 1847—even though his most popular orchestral works were his *Scottish Symphony,* his *Italian Symphony,* and his incidental music for the Shakespeare play *A Midsummer Night's Dream,* a story by a British playwright set in Greece. "No national music for me!" Mendelssohn proudly declared. "Ten thousand devils take all nationality!" Not much scope for German triumphalism there. And even when a German composer was accused of revolutionary affiliations, as in the case of Beethoven, the allegiance imputed was typically to France, not his own homeland. By the same token, when Beethoven made the cause of freedom a central theme of *Fidelio,* he set the story in Spain, not Germany. The principle at stake was more important than the principality.[10]

Chopin is the most obvious outlier among the early exponents of musical Romanticism, his activities as an ardent Polish nationalist predating the fervor of the late 1840s. Yet how much of this reputation has been colored by wishful thinking? Chopin avoided participation in political actions and was hardly a revolutionary—despite the fact that one of his most famous compositions is called the "Revolutionary Etude." (It's worth noting that there's zero evidence that Chopin applied this nickname to the piece—and that, in itself, is a lesson in how this process works.) He had comfortable relationships with European aristocracy and ignored pleas to compose a great national Polish opera. By one account, poet Adam Mickiewicz chastised him for ignoring Polish causes while wasting his talent on providing entertainment for Parisian society. Even when Chopin adopted Polish musical traditions, as in his mazurkas, these were performed during his lifetime without any hint of political intent—indeed, the deeply personal and intimate nature of his music makes it an unsuitable soundtrack for aggressive nation-building. The careful scholar is forced to conclude that the legend of Chopin as a fiery advocate of Polish causes is mostly a construct imposed after the fact.

But the relationship between music and nationalism changed around the time of Chopin's death in 1849, and with a vengeance.

We can already detect the new tone in a chauvinistic prediction that Friedrich Theodor Vischer, a German novelist and philosopher of aesthetics, made in 1844: "The German shall yet hear his own great history surge towards him in mighty waves of sounds. . . . We want a native world of our own, a national one in music." He didn't have long to wait. In 1850, the composer who saw his destiny as the fulfillment of these nationalist aspirations, Richard Wagner, published his article "Das Judenthum in der Musik" (Judaism in music), the most dispiriting document in the history of nineteenth-century music criticism. At the time, Wagner was residing as a political exile in Zurich, a result of his participation in the 1849 uprising in Dresden, where his activities ranged from writing incendiary articles to providing hand grenades for revolutionaries. This essay, originally published under a pseudonym, but later reissued under Wagner's own name, denounced Mendelssohn and asserted that the Jewish ethos in music was incapable of achieving the profound, uplifting spirit that audiences demand from art. Even before this, Wagner had drawn on medieval German literature for *Tannhäuser* (1845) and *Lohengrin* (1850), whose debut took place just a few days before the composer published his anti-Semitic tract. While still in Zurich, Wagner began work on *Der Ring des Nibelungen*, his epic cycle of four operas that even today represents the high point of his oeuvre and the most charged artistic symbol of grandiose nationalism in the history of Western music.[11]

I doubt that the controversy over these works will ever end. Yet Wagner clearly grasped the spirit of the age and the new direction in music. Virtually every significant composer who came of age during this period bought into the nationalistic ethos. It would be impossible to grasp the musical contributions of Antonín Dvořák (born in 1841) without taking stock of his Bohemian heritage, or those of Edvard Grieg (born in 1843) without placing them in the context of his love of Norway. The same is true of Nikolai Rimsky-Korsakov (born in 1844) and Russia; Edward Elgar (1857) and Britain; Jean Sibelius (1865) and Finland; Manuel de Falla (1876) and Spain; or Béla Bartók (1881) and Hungary. Dozens of other examples could be cited, even hundreds, if we were willing to dig into the mostly forgotten composers of the era. But the older generation also participated in this newfound patriotic fervor. Liszt composed his Hungarian Rhapsodies and published *Des Bohémiens et de Leur Musique en Hongrie* (1859), a half-baked book of ethnomusicological research. And, of course, Giuseppe Verdi, an ardent nationalist who played a key role in the unification of Italy, could match Wagner opera for opera in his patriotic zeal.

Verdi's history casts special light on the shifts underway in European music. The chorus "Va, pensiero," from his 1842 opera *Nabucco*, ostensibly represents the sentiments of the Israelites during the Babylonian captivity, but its expressed longing for a lost homeland could also serve as a coded appeal to Italian nationalists. Posterity has dealt with the song in this spirit, and stories have often been told of the audience getting so roused by its patriotic sentiments that they demanded an immediate encore of the stirring anthem. But here, as in so many other instances, the historical record was revised to match the prevailing ideology of a later day. We always do well to pay close attention to the earliest sources, which are too often dismissed out of hand by later commentators, yet often contain our most reliable information about the history of music. In the case of Verdi, there is no evidence that audiences in 1842 saw this chorus as inflammatory, or even as particularly noteworthy. They did demand an encore at the debut performance, but of a different song—the closing hymn "Immenso Jehova," an innocuous and solemn refrain in praise of God, and lacking any political overtones.

Yet rumors and legends often have more influence than facts. "Va, pensiero" took on such symbolic force that half the population of Milan lined the streets and sang the now-famous chorus for the composer's funeral procession in 1901, a real-life example of popular uprising and unity beyond anything ever staged in an opera house. You can search through Verdi's later operas for clues and symbols, interpreting them as political documents—some, such as *La Battaglia di Legnano* (1849), make their patriotic sentiments obvious, while others keep their polemical intent, if any, well hidden. Yet the image of Verdi as a nationalist didn't need deep textual analysis to capture the public's imagination. Some admirers actually believed that his name was a mystical talisman, and should be viewed as an acronym for *Vittorio Emanuele, Re D'Italia*, the King of Italy following the nation's unification. Even superstition was enlisted as a prop for revisionist music history.

The cases of Wagner and Verdi have been extensively studied, debated, interpreted, and reinterpreted. Yet the more interesting psychological question has rarely been addressed: Why did composers, so prideful and resistant to the meddling of royalty and state at the dawn of the nineteenth century, become willing pawns for power brokers before its close? We have traced the recurring figure of the composer as outsider in these pages, and seen how this prickly independence has fueled so much innovation. So we must stop and ask what unusual circumstances turned the most influential musicians of the late nineteenth and early twentieth centuries into such accommodating shills for regimes. Even in the modernist era, when composers such as Arnold Schoenberg and Igor Stravinsky reversed that trend and became political exiles—ironically, much like Wagner in an earlier day, but on the opposite side of the ideological spectrum, now escaping from the values his successors espoused—the idea of attaching national identities to musicians continued. In recent times, no discussion of Dmitri Shostakovich can last more than a few minutes without the name of Stalin entering the conversation. Track down any account of Aaron Copland, and you will find some reference to Americana within the first few sentences. I would like to believe that we have finally broken out of this reductionist attitude in the current day, when music goes viral on the web and crosses borders in a heartbeat. In the global village, composers seek the favor of a worldwide audience, not an unpaid job as national spokesperson or pats on the back from a dictator. Let's hope that continues. Yet what made the composers of late-stage Romanticism so willing to play that game in the first place, cozying up to power in a way that we can hardly envision with Bach, Mozart, or Beethoven?

The shift was psychological even more than sociopolitical, and it was insidious. Before the 1840s, musicians became insiders by serving the powerful—but even as they reaped the benefits, they rebelled against their role as servants. They chafed at slights, even imagined ones, and often schemed at how to game the system, manipulating the rulers of nations for their own artistic purposes. This attitude, for all its occasional pettiness, created a healthy tension, spurring these artists to produce many of the greatest masterworks in human history. The composer could be an insider while retaining the irritable independence of the outsider. But a new psychological model of the artist emerged with Wagner and Verdi. They no longer saw themselves as *serving* the nation; instead, they believed they *represented* the nation. They saw themselves as embodying the most powerful movement of their time, and this notion gratified their egos and inflamed their pride to a degree previously unknown in the annals of secular music. This marked a profound change. The creative tension between patron and artist was broken. There was no give-and-take. The end result could only be an art marked by grandiosity, extravagance, and self-proclaimed world significance—ego flourishing without check or balance. It's hardly a coincidence that we still use the term *Wagnerian* to describe artistic works of this sort.

Our current-day music still carries the weight of the aggressive nationalism embedded in these sounds. I've done a survey of the soundtracks to violent movies, and can attest that the higher the onscreen kill count, the more likely it is that the background music borrows from the sonic palette of the nineteenth-century Romanticist composers. Even if the film takes place in the Middle Ages or Middle Earth, you still want a dose of Beethoven, Mahler, and Wagner to stir up the combatants. Similar sounds can be heard in many first-person shooter video games—even when (somewhat paradoxically) you are hunting down Nazis, you still apparently benefit from uplifting Germanic-sounding music as accompaniment. Long after the orchestral works of this period got repackaged as effete music for highbrows, there's still something about it that calls for blood.[12]

I'm not surprised that the Nobel laureate Elias Canetti, a deep thinker on matters of human frailty, focused on the example of the orchestra conductor when trying to come to grips with destructive populist movements of the twentieth century in his seminal book *Crowds and Power*. For Canetti, the musical maestro reveals the same personality traits found in manipulative leaders who incite the populace, standing in the forefront and waving the baton while others do the dirty work. And though Canetti doesn't mention any musician by name, his descriptions of these demagogues could almost be taken out of the pages of Wagner's famous treatise on conducting. Here Wagner praises authority, firmness, self-confidence, personal power, energy, and an insistence on absolute obedience—the exact same ingredients found in the psychological profiles of tyrants and dictators. The sad truth: Wagner was probably describing himself.[13]

The debate over Wagner's complicity in the bloody and genocidal results of this overweening sense of national destiny will probably never end. There is no formula for balancing the value of an artistic work against human suffering. That equation simply doesn't exist and never will. It's the same issue we deal with, albeit in different ways and on a different scale, when assessing Roman Polanski, Woody Allen, Michael Jackson, or other artists accused of crimes and abuses. We can try to evaluate the art on artistic terms, and the human being on moral and ethical ones. But in many instances, the offenses seem to poison the artistry, preventing any such fine distinctions. That in itself is a legacy of Romanticism: the notion that the artist's works and biography blend together. In Wagner's case, the art itself may have inflamed the destructive national pride that caused many horrors to come. At a minimum, it was used to legitimize these future transgressions—a catastrophic testimony to the powers and perverse repurposings of music that are a major focus of this book. I will leave it to others to weigh the trade-offs in such matters. I don't believe there's a scale that works in these cases, or any balance that makes sense.

But there are important lessons here, crucial to the overarching goals of this subversive history. When I tell people that music is closely connected to violence, a key theme in these pages, they often reject the notion out of hand—perhaps because such a linkage seems to taint their own intimate relationship with favorite songs. Or perhaps because they sense their own vulnerability to the persuasion of the melodies. But recall that the first word that set in motion the whole canonic tradition of Western music is "rage": "Rage—Goddess, sing the rage of Peleus' son Achilles, murderous, doomed," is the disturbing opening to Homer's *Iliad*. And the rage has never stopped. Every violent group in history has its motivating songs, whether it is the Nazis and Wagner, Charles Manson's killing crew and the Beatles song "Helter Skelter," or any of the other anthems that bloodthirsty groups have used since time immemorial. Perhaps in these cases, we could describe it as the *misuse* of music. But the connection between song and bloodshed remains, and it will exist in the future just as it has in the past.[14]

Consider the symbolic violence embedded in a wide range of songs that we take for granted, whether sports team 'fight' songs or seemingly innocent children's melodies, such as "Ring Around the Rosie," or "London Bridge Is Falling Down," with their macabre overtones and sacrificial victims. From any objective historical standard, music is the most violent art form, the closest to the action when terrible deeds are done. There's a reason why painters and poets usually wait to celebrate warfare until the combat is finished, but musicians are actually invited onto the battlefield, trumpet or drum in hand, to participate in the carnage.

And this is why we probe into the rise of musical nationalism and its destructive aftermath. We need to acknowledge that this isn't an aberration in cultural history, a peculiarity, or a onetime event. Music is a mighty force, possessing far more potency than we give it credit for—especially in an age that treats songs as idle entertainment, or, even more banal and misguided, as a kind of brain stimulation, what the Harvard philosopher Steven Pinker calls "auditory cheesecake." *That is some deadly cheesecake, Professor Pinker!*[15]

Music's efficacy as a change agent is savage. Songs are weaponized, again and again, and any history of music that leaves out this chapter is woefully incomplete. Political theorist Michael Walzer has gone so far as to claim that the German Revolution of 1918–1919 was doomed because "it did not have a song," while the Bolsheviks in Russia made brutally effective use of "The Internationale." His former student Todd Gitlin suggests that the missing ingredient in communism since the fall of the Berlin Wall has been "a melody you can't get out of your head." In other cases, this melodic energy can be neutral or even good-naturedly idealistic, and we can console ourselves with the thought that every peaceful utopian scheme with a sufficient number of followers also has its favored tunes, whether it is the Shakers and their hymns or the Saint-Simonian socialists, who enlisted the composer of the "Marseillaise," Claude Joseph Rouget de Lisle, to write a song to inspire cooperative labor. In either case, militant or utopian, music has power, and we ignore its force at our own peril.[16]

19

The Great Flip-Flop

Most people assume that folk music stands for the opposite of everything we have just encountered with Mozart, Beethoven, Verdi, Wagner, and other elite composers. Even more to the point, ardent fans of folk music embrace it for that very reason. Folk music breaks down hierarchies, opposes elite institutions, and gives a voice to marginalized groups who would never get a platform at Bayreuth or La Scala. At least that's the marketing message accompanying this music at every turn, legitimizing it and establishing its credentials of authenticity.

Yet the rise of folk music collectors—those gentle enthusiasts who scour the countryside searching for songs handed down by oral tradition—took place during the same period when these famous composers flourished. The same prevailing cultural forces shaped this movement, and with similar results. Just as nationalistic sentiments inspired Wagner and Verdi, they also spurred interest in folk music, and it didn't take long before a whole ideology of national pride and racial purity got loaded onto even the simplest songs. Many musicians participated in this patriotic program, but a philosopher gets most of the credit for providing its theoretical underpinnings. Johann Gottfried Herder (1744–1803) famously declared that "every human perfection is national"—a decree that included all artistic endeavors, in his view, but especially poetry and music. Herder derided class distinctions and situated the locus of authenticity in the *Volk* (the folk), a group that encompassed every individual in the nation, from the king to the lowliest peasant.[1]

Herder published his views at the same time that the leading composers of Europe were enjoying the first perks of celebrity and seeking ways to assert their independence from church and state. At this stage, both movements—the growing cult of personality in classical music and the newfound interest in folk music—were democratizing and anti-authoritarian. Herder died a year before Napoleon declared himself emperor, and during his lifetime this idealization of the *Volk* had little connection with iron-fisted authoritarian impulses. Rather, the philosopher's sentiments aligned him with disruptive, egalitarian causes. Some are surprised that Herder supported the revolutionary movement in France in his later years; this is a strange view, one might think, for an individual so closely linked to German patriotism. Yet Herder's desire to break down hierarchies and empower the lower classes was part of the same worldview that led him to celebrate the folk song. Like classical music, the folk song movement later got co-opted by authoritarian patriots. But that took time. Here we have a familiar story: the music of the masses gets turned into a prop for the powerful. If we don't grasp the dynamics of this shift, we won't understand the whole bizarre charade of the folk music movement as it unfolded during the nineteenth and twentieth centuries.

I refer to the folk music *movement*—that loosely organized coalition of collectors, composers, and other co-conspirators who seek to elevate the songs of the common people into something more *serious*—and contrast it to the music itself. These two have often been confounded in ways that obscure and mystify rather than illuminate. Some commentators have been so disgusted by the former that they are willing to abandon the latter. Dave Harker, in his controversial book *Fakesong*—a kind of manifesto denouncing the phoniness of folk music—goes so far as to proclaim that "concepts like folksong and ballad are intellectual rubble." He adds that there is "no point" to the attempts "to rehabilitate such concepts. They are conceptual lumber and have to go." I can hardly blame Harker, even though he pushes legitimate criticisms to ridiculous extremes. The folk song movement, as we shall see, provides far too many case studies in false consciousness, institutional sell-out, kowtowing to the powerful, and out-and-out duplicity—indeed, everything opposed to the purity and innocence celebrated in the genre's public image. But that's why we must distinguish it from the folk music itself, which flourished for thousands of years before song collectors and theoreticians began imposing their dogmas on it.[2]

How did folk songs lose their innocence? Let's count the ways. Almost everyone involved in the rise of the folk song business had an agenda, usually a hidden one, and here are at least ten that influenced—and frequently distorted—songs that supposedly sprang up wholesome and unadulterated from the common people, pure as a mountain spring. First we encounter the manipulation of folk songs to advance a nationalist agenda. Some in the educational establishment even insisted on using the term "national songs" instead of "folk songs," and mangled books of traditional music, inserting recent compositions filled with approved patriotic sentiments and disseminating them to schoolchildren. Next on our list: the promotion of folk songs as a tool of nostalgic conservatism, evoking good old days and homespun values. These were countered by a third group, made up of those who promoted folk music as a spur to progressive politics, promulgating songs of class-consciousness, protest, and rebellion. Then came a fourth, the classical music establishment with its shrewdly utilitarian notions for employing folk melodies to revitalize the concert hall, often concocting tall tales to help in the process. (Antonín Dvořák's *New World Symphony* is a telling example: at the time of the work's premiere, the composer told the press that he didn't use a single American folk melody in its score—he even derided the story as nonsense and a lie—and yet that disinformation is still spread today because it makes for good marketing.) But the street singers and commercial entertainers, fifth in our police lineup of culprits, had the exact same idea, only they wanted to use these songs to energize populist music for the masses. A sixth contingent saw folk music as a new field of intellectual study that could support academic careers and secure comfortable, tenured jobs. And three other factions looked to these songs as uplifting soundtracks to a utopian vision of a purer life; or as a measuring rod for cultural authenticity; or as a way of making money with a hot trend in the music business. And let's not forget one more contingent, those gentle fans who celebrated and shared folk songs because . . . well, I guess they enjoyed listening to them.

We ought to pay particularly close attention to this last group, if only because these music lovers seem to have the purist motives of the lot. Yet the quest for enjoyment may have led to more manipulation and falsification than all the other agendas put together. In their zeal to help songs go viral (even before the Internet), various factions strived to make old tunes more *enjoyable*—a quest that led to countless altered texts, changed melodies, and bogus stories. "He may have told us lies but he gave us good songs," was a typical justification, as folk music historian Steve Roud points out in his assessment of A. L. Lloyd, one of the leading advocates for traditional music in the middle decades of the twentieth century. Lloyd had an aggressive political agenda for the music, but he understood that this would go nowhere if the songs weren't embraced by a mainstream audience. "It is not so much that he rewrote and altered songs to make them more singable or to suit the purposes and interests of the Revival, as he frequently did," Roud notes, "but that he was never clear (some would say never honest) about the extent of his tinkering." As a result, Lloyd left behind a lifetime of research, but who knows how much of it can be believed?[3]

Yet this was no isolated example. Even back in Herder's day, the zeal for 'improving' folk music overwhelmed the movement to document it accurately. Joseph Ritson (1752–1803) is rarely mentioned among the heroes of the field, but he made most of his enemies merely because he wanted to ensure the accuracy of folk songbooks. Yet his reputation among his contemporaries was that

of a spoilsport, and is best conveyed by Walter Scott's gripe: "Whenever presented with two copies of a traditional song or ballad, Ritson perversely chose the worse as the most genuine."[4]

We are forced to conclude that even the people who created
the folk music movement often feared that these songs were too
boring in their natural state. Some years later, composer Constant
Lambert would sum up this view in a cruel quip: "The whole trouble with a folk-song is that once you have played it through there
is nothing much you can do except play it over again and play it
rather louder." Lambert also penned a rhyming insult directed at
Ralph Vaughan Williams's folk-influenced classical works, in which
"both yokels and driads / are represented by triads." Nevertheless,
even Lambert was influenced by populist music in his own work,
and very inclusive in his tastes—he was one of the first establishment composers to praise jazz, and he recognized the importance
of Duke Ellington back in the early 1930s. But the sad truth here
is that the most ardent champions of the *Volk* were often the worst
offenders in tinkering with their music.[5]

Poetic license sometimes went to such extremes that it turned
into poetic fraud. In fact, the biggest literary scandal of the era was
stirred up by the marketing of a nonexistent Celtic bard named
Ossian. The Scottish poet James Macpherson gained international
fame in the 1760s as the translator of Ossian's epic works, previously unknown texts that now set off a kind of Harry Potter–style
mania among readers. Ossian's fans included Napoleon, who
allegedly carried the epic poetry into battle, and Thomas Jefferson,
who praised the imagined bard as the greatest poet in human history. Jefferson even announced his plan of learning Gaelic so he
could read Ossian in the original.

But was there an original? Scholars soon noted textual, chronological, and mythological problems with these works that undercut
Macpherson's claim that they had been written by a third-century
poet. Despite promises that he would share his sources, Macpherson never produced the original manuscripts. Most experts eventually concluded they didn't exist. Macpherson had constructed
Ossian's work out of bits and pieces of folklore, tales, and poems.

Any literary skill involved was his own, not that of a mythical long-dead bard. Perhaps if he had admitted as much, his reputation wouldn't have taken such a heavy hit. Instead, Macpherson is remembered as the most audacious literary con artist of the late eighteenth century.

But for more than half a century, starting in the 1760s, many of the leading figures in music and the arts got caught up in the Ossian mania—an enthusiasm that continued even in the face of allegations of fraud. Schubert set Ossian's poetry to music, drawing on translations that were so bad they provoked laughter when performed. Mendelssohn's visit to Scotland, which inspired some of his most famous works—although he griped that traditional Celtic music was vulgar and gave him a toothache—was spurred in part by his enthusiasm for Ossian. But the most intriguing response came from Herder, our fervent father of the folk song movement. The philosopher expressed gushing enthusiasm for Macpherson's discovery, which he saw as a support for his advocacy of the *Volk* and their sublime music, and denied all charges of fakery. "Ossian's poems are songs, songs of the people, folksongs, the songs of an unsophisticated people living close to the senses, songs which have been long handed down by oral tradition," he declared. Herder's final conclusion: "Macpherson could not possibly have invented something of this kind. Poetry of this kind could not possibly have been composed in this century."[6]

There's a lot to unpack in these words, almost all of it unpleasant. Here at the very moment when folk music was emerging as a serious subject of scholarly study, we find its leading champion caught up in the most nostalgic naïveté, asserting the sublime ignorance of the *Volk* as noble savages, and embracing a fraudulent text as emblem of his movement.

Yet the Ossian scandal was no isolated case. Even when actual manuscripts served as the basis for scholarship, they were misused with such disdain for the truth as to boggle the mind. *Reliques of Ancient English Poetry*, published by Irish bishop Thomas Percy in 1765, is often considered the foundational work in British folk music. Collections of traditional songs had appeared before, but none of them captivated the public's imagination as much as this compilation of 180 ballads in three volumes. And unlike Macpherson, Percy had an authentic source document, a collection of old poems and songs that he found "lying dirty on the floor, under a bureau in the parlour" of Sir Humphrey Pitt, a resident of Shifnal in Shropshire. Pitt's chambermaid used this scrap paper to light fires, but the astute bishop rescued the manuscript from blazing oblivion and eventually recognized the value of its contents—a collection of songs compiled by an unknown hand, probably a century earlier. Yet Percy waited more than a decade before sharing his discovery, and was only inspired to turn it into a literary work after Macpherson's Ossian 'translations' proved how lucrative the publication of old folk material could be. Cunningly assessing the opportunity before him, Percy aimed to *improve* his ballads before bringing them to the marketplace. The enthusiastic reception to his *Reliques* no doubt confirmed the commercial value of this decision, but once again at the price of honesty and accuracy. In the harsh verdict of folk song expert Steve Roud: "It can be justly claimed that the *Reliques*, as published, is completely useless in our attempts to understand ballads or folk songs in [Percy's] time or before it. He left nothing alone, and nothing in his writing can be trusted as evidence."[7]

There's both tragedy here and an invaluable lesson. Percy clearly believed he was motivated by the highest ideals—as no doubt so did Herder and Lloyd and countless others in the folk song movement. When Percy was eventually forced to share his source manuscript, in response to accusations of forgery, he had a ready-made excuse, which he shared in a new paragraph added to the preface of his collection in a later version edited by his nephew. The old manuscripts were so corrupt and defective, he claimed, "that a scrupulous adherence to their wretched readings would only have exhibited unintelligible nonsense." On the other hand, "by a few slight corrections or additions, a most beautiful or interesting sense hath started forth, and this so naturally and easily, that the editor could seldom prevail upon himself to indulge the vanity of making a formal claim to the improvement." Here again, at the very beginning of the folk song movement, a founding member—and a bishop, no less!—not only defends rewriting history, but explains that it happened so "naturally and easily" that it couldn't be helped.[8]

Perhaps you feel outraged by this. But Macpherson and Percy were simply doing the same thing we have already witnessed repeatedly in the course of this subversive history. The only difference in this case is that they operated in an age when other scholars could expose their double-dealings—although the upholders of transparency and honesty were typically attacked and ridiculed for their efforts at policing the field. When the mainstream assimilates a new kind of music, it always reconfigures its lineage and history to meet the needs of the present moment, and those who try to impose strict controls on the process rarely have much success. In a way, we ought to feel gratitude for these folk song fraudsters, who finally revealed to the light of day what previously happened behind the scenes, outside the purview of music history. By peering into the inner workings of the assimilation process in this period, we may gain a better grasp of what has occurred in other ages. We might, for example, arrive at a deeper understanding of how Pindar's lyrics were preserved for posterity, while Sappho's survive mostly in isolated fragments embedded in the works of later authors. We might be able to reconstruct the steps by which romantic love lyrics, forbidden in one era, became the intellectual property of the nobility in the next. We may discern the path by which a mysterious popular refrain, such as "L'homme armé," found its way into dozens of Catholic masses, or understand how a manuscript such as the *Carmina Burana*, a medieval equivalent to Percy's folk ballad manuscript, got distorted into a prop for nationalist ideology. Or (looking forward to our next chapter) we might grasp how W. C. Handy earned fame and wealth for his "St. Louis Blues," while the musician who inspired him at a train station in Tutwiler, Mississippi, didn't even leave his name behind for the history books. This is how the process of assimilation and dissemination works, and at no point does it require evildoers and malicious intent (although they aren't completely absent from our history). An eminent bishop, an esteemed philosopher, a brilliant poet, a revered Christian composer, even the so-called "Father of the Blues," can all play the game, and still sleep well at night.

So we need to guard against any notion that these attempts to repurpose the music of the past represent a breakdown in the system. They *are* the system. The current generation is always ruthless in repurposing songs inherited from the past, and always will be. We can strive for more transparency and honesty—that's what this book is about—and encourage a healthy dose of skepticism among onlookers when outrageous claims are made, but the repurposing will continue in the face of all exhortations to reform. Of course, the way it happens will change with the passing decades: beboppers adding new melodies (known as *contrafacts*) to old songs in the 1940s; easy listening versions of familiar tunes in the 1950s; rock cover bands in the 1960s; cassette mixtapes in the 1970s; hip-hop sampling in the 1980s . . . all the way to the remixes and pop star holograms of the current day. Back in the past, this process might have required an elaborate song-collecting mission in a distant part of the world, but in the digital age it can happen with a simple copy-and-paste on a handheld device. Yet whatever you call it, this repurposing is as much a part of the musical ecosystem as the food chain or the water cycle is to the natural ecosystem.

By the same token, we must reject the bizarre allegation that folk music doesn't really exist, that it's all just a construct of profiteers and manipulators. This is the party line, for example, of Dave Harker, with his claim that folk song is just fake song, and it is echoed in many other attacks on the concept of authenticity in music. A deep dissection of the notion of artistic authenticity is beyond the scope of this book, and I hope to write about it in another setting where I can give it the attention it deserves. Authenticity may be the most misunderstood concept in all of music at the current moment. But even if we just focus on examples already given, we can see that in every instance, a body of work exists, and often even flourishes, before the profiteers and purifiers arrive on the scene. We have seen the Venerable Bede, so struck by the impromptu singing of the herder Caedmon that he documented the lyrics— the oldest surviving lyric in Old English from a known source—in his ecclesiastical history. We encountered the same with art critic John Ruskin, who was similarly struck by the extraordinary musical memory of Beatrice Bernardi, also a herder. We have studied how Harvard scholars Milman Parry and Albert Lord worked to preserve the remarkable epic singing of a Turkish peasant, Avdo Međedović, and John Lomax doing the same with James "Iron Head" Baker, an African American inmate at Huntsville Penitentiary in Texas. The preservation and documentation of these sources might be scrupulous or inadequate, depending on circumstances and agendas. But in each of these interventions—and many others like them by scholars and ethnomusicologists over the decades—a folk practice embedded in the real world exists long before the 'experts' show up with their schemes and recording technologies.

If we want to understand the role of music in human life, we must take these documents from the past seriously, even if they come through the filter of a collector with a cause. And, frankly, it's reassuring to witness how disturbing and transgressive much of this music remains even after it is cleaned up for mass consumption. Even Percy couldn't cover his tracks completely, especially when we take into account not only his published versions of ballads, but also his source documents and correspondence (which includes many songs sent to him by readers). The obscenity and violence that survive can almost serve as guarantees that the mainstreaming and purifying process had limits. Bishop Percy's ballads are marked by accounts of murder, rape, assault, adultery, dismemberment, pillage, and other instances of lewdness and violence. Percy's embarrassment at this material may have contributed to his reluctance to share the manuscript, and he didn't hesitate to admit that much of it was trash or nonsense. He even asked readers to forgive him for the rudeness of his published work. Percy's deep sense of shame and awkwardness is perhaps our most reliable sign that some of the original animating spirit of the lyrics managed to survive the interventions of this heavy-handed editor.

This obsession with sex and violence is even more noticeable in the famous ballads that a Harvard professor, Francis James Child, collected in the late nineteenth century. This compilation of

Scottish and English traditional ballads and their variants, eventually comprising some 2,500 pages, long ago established itself as the most influential work in the history of the folk song movement. The 305 ballads included in this collection, known now as the *Child Ballads*, is the nearest thing we have to a canon of traditional songs in the English language—and many of the works have close counterparts on the continent, especially in northern Europe, testifying to the cross-border reach of this body of music. These are almost sacred texts to a folk singer.

Yet the reverence with which these works are treated and the highbrow pedigree of their Harvard imprimatur should not blind us to their subversive content. These story songs feature virtually every kind of transgressive behavior. Rape is a frequent event in these ballads, and is sometimes integrated into a romance plot, with rapist and victim eventually marrying and apparently living happily ever after. Numerous ballads deal with incest, often only discovered after the fact, and then remedied through murder or suicide. A whole litany of torture techniques and modes of brutal revenge are presented, but they are just as likely to be used against the virtuous as to thwart evildoers. In fact, anyone attempting to construct a coherent moral code on the basis of these ballads would be left with a mishmash of horrid maxims. In "Crow and Pie" (Child Ballad 111), women are advised to avoid getting raped, but if it does happen, they should get some money from the man, or at least learn his name and address. Other stories of assault and violence are capped with advice to pick a spouse from the Highlands rather than the Lowlands, or from England, not Scotland. But the lessons are little more than window-dressing, reminiscent of the token attempts of pornographers in the 1970s to avoid obscenity charges by highlighting the "redeeming social values" (in the famous words of the Supreme Court decision *Miller v. California*) of their smut. In the Child Ballads, the moralizing is formulaic, but the tawdry details kept the songs in circulation.

I tabulated the plot ingredients in the Child Ballads and found that more than two-thirds of them involve violence. Around one-third of the ballads deal with sex, and the sex is frequently paired with violence. Yet no statistical summary can convey the coarseness of the various plot details. Take, for example, "Child Owlet" (Child Ballad 291), where the protagonist resists the incestuous advances of his aunt, who exacts murderous revenge by telling her husband the young man seduced her—Child Owlet's uncle solves the problem by having his nephew torn limb from limb by a team of wild horses. In the ballad's coda, the singer notes that neighbors of the victim will find bits of Child Owlet's dismembered flesh and drops of his blood wherever they go.

Such songs may gain respect as traditional music, but they hardly advance so-called traditional values. As a result, even a revered folk ballad can still stir up outrage or demands for censorship in modern times. In a strange twist of history, a Child Ballad inspired the most controversial hit single of 1967. Newspapers at the time were filled with accounts of bad LSD trips, inner-city riots, and foreign wars, but the BBC directed its ire at "Seven Drunken Nights," released at the end of March by The Dubliners. This song, based on "Our Goodman" (Child Ballad 274), recounts a wife's implausible excuses to her intoxicated husband, who returns from his drinking binges each night to find evidence that she's taken on a lover. At that juncture, Mick Jagger could sing "Let's Spend the Night Together" on BBC radio with impunity, but a folk song dating back to the 1760s was considered taboo.

Even so, a government ban could hardly stifle the song's success, especially with the rise of pirate radio stations operating on actual ships offshore during that era. Radio Caroline, broadcasting from a 188-foot ferry ship in international waters in order to avoid British regulations, helped turn "Seven Drunken Nights" into a pop hit. The song even reached the top place on the chart in Ireland. When the TV program *Top of the Pops* begrudgingly agreed to let The Dubliners perform "Seven Drunken Nights" on its show, astute listeners noticed that only five of the seven nights were featured in the song—the other two were considered too scandalous to broadcast.

There's no evidence that Professor Child deliberately selected the most sensationalistic material for his collection, and there are examples of equally disturbing material that never made its way into his canon. The director of the English Broadside Ballad Archive, Patricia Fumerton, has called my attention to "A Lanthorne for Landlords," circa 1630, which deals with God's punishment of a landlord who evicts a woman and her children from their home after her husband dies in battle. In the course of a song of just forty-eight lines, we encounter plot twists involving dismemberment, bestiality, witchcraft, prostitution, treason, execution by hanging, burning at the stake, and suicide. Even in our tolerant age, such stories cross the boundaries that define acceptable narratives. Yet as folk music, these same themes gained not only legitimacy but even a kind of reverence as talismans of authenticity.

And we are left to wonder how many songs were censored or omitted entirely from the early song collections because of their perceived obscenity. When Cecil Sharp and Maud Karpeles were compiling their seminal work *English Folk Songs from the Southern Appalachians* (1932), they responded to such works with a clever team effort: Sharp would transcribe the music with scrupulous fidelity, while Karpeles would selectively write down the words, leaving out anything too lewd or explicit. This method provided the duo with an authentic song, suitable for publication, but not so authentic as to offend the chaste sensibilities of their readers. But even when more open-minded collectors were willing to preserve coarser lyrics, the rustics and common folk who provided them with songs must have frequently exercised restraint. If a Harvard-educated scholar from the Library of Congress shows up at your doorstep with an expensive recording device, are you inclined to belt out a rendition of "How Can I Keep My Maidenhead," or "Nine Inch Will Please a Lady"? It's remarkable that any of these outré songs were documented at all, and we can safely assume that hundreds of obscene lyrics were lost to posterity for every one that survived.

Much of our knowledge of obscene music comes not via scholars, but from the records of the criminal justice system. A nineteenth-century survey of vice suppression efforts in London reveals that "obscene songs (on sheets)" were actually more common than "impure books" or "obscene publications." British police confiscated tens of thousands of these illegal songs, yet countless others must have spread without the need for a printing press, taught by example and learned by ear. The persistent researcher can find accounts of sing-alongs at brothels and other disreputable settings, where musicians clearly knew the tunes and the patrons could supply the words. Many familiar songs had alternative lyrics that were deliberately crude and offensive, and the most vigilant legal authorities could hardly prevent their dissemination. But they certainly tried. Any fair and accurate list of song collectors must include the vice squad and criminal courts—our only regret is that they collected but did not preserve the rich folk material of the *Volk* under their jurisdiction.[9]

In an odd coincidence, highbrow music showed the same obsession with themes of sex and violence. In fact, the convergence between opera and folk ballad is rather striking. In the case of the popular ballad operas that flourished in the wake of John Gay's commercial success with *The Beggar's Opera* (1728), actual folk melodies and lowlife characters were incorporated into the proceedings. But even the most elitist operas gravitated again and again to transgressive plots. Rape figured prominently in opera from its very beginnings, with *Il Rapimento di Cefalo* in 1600, and despite intense censorship imposed on the genre, it kept recurring on the opera stage over the ensuing centuries. Take the case of Mozart, hardly a representative of the dark side—but what might we conclude if all we had to go on were the stories of his operas? At the opening of *Don Giovanni* (1787), a masked protagonist breaks into a young woman's room in the middle of the night, an apparent rapist intent on gratifying his lust. The woman screams for help and her father comes to her rescue, but is murdered by the intruder, who then escapes—perhaps already hatching plans to attempt the same with another woman. The threat of rape also drives the plot in *The Marriage of Figaro* (1786), where Count Almaviva is reluctant to give up his *droit du seigneur*, the alleged tradition allowing a feudal lord the right to deflower virgins on their wedding nights. Even earlier, in Mozart's *The Abduction from the Seraglio* (1782), women are kidnapped and enslaved in a harem. The violence and sex in these plots are strikingly similar to what we find in the folk ballads of the same period.

And they have not lost their shock value. A 2004 production of *The Abduction from the Seraglio* in Berlin came with a warning label, although that did not deter critics from denouncing it as an exercise in perversion. And controversies continue to erupt over the canonic works in the opera repertoire. In 2015, audiences at the Royal Opera House in London booed an especially graphic enactment of sexual violence in a production of Rossini's *Guillaume Tell*, and journalists peppered their reviews with denunciations of its brutality and nastiness. A 2018 production of *Carmen* in Italy went so far as to construct a different ending to Georges Bizet's famous opera. After decades of punk rock and gangsta rap, you might think we would be inured to such situations, or at least benumbed into acquiescence. But there is something about music that seems to seek out the rawest parts of our psyche and the most dysfunctional corners of our social life. The ruling institutions of opera have had to deal with that edginess since the origins of the genre, but for all their cleansing and censoring, the tension remains unresolved.

In many instances, folk music served as the viral medium for news in those days. But not just any kind of news. The more disturbing the story, the more likely it was to become attached to a melody. We don't sing much nowadays about violent crimes, battlefield carnage, natural disasters, and other such tragedies, but merely because we have other ways of sharing bad tidings. Matters were far different in earlier eras. If we can judge by the signatures on marriage documents, more than half the population of England was still illiterate well into the eighteenth century. So even a newspaper lacked the reach of a good song.

So-called *execution ballads* and *murder ballads* were especially popular with the public. I doubt if anything in our current culture can match the combination of the macabre and the celebratory achieved by these songs. The text of a ballad about the execution of John Felton—the poor fellow who posted the pope's decree excommunicating Queen Elizabeth I on the door of the bishop's residence in London in 1570—includes brutal descriptions of his quartering and hanging, but was set to a country tune that even today is used for line dancing—with exhortations to *do-si-do* and *clap your hands*. Could this really be Elizabethan *party* music? Again and again, the worst details were summoned up for the public's delectation in these ballads. In the song commemorating the 1638 execution of Edward Coleman, based on bogus accusations that he planned to assassinate Charles II, the lyrics leave nothing to the imagination.

> *His Bowels ripd out, in the flames to be cast,*
> *His Members disseverd on Poles to be placd.*[10]

Many of these execution ballads were set to the tune of "Fortune My Foe," one of the most popular songs of Shakespeare's day, and a favorite melody for conveying news of a gloomy, destructive, or merely sadistic nature. In the 1635 broadside ballad recounting the execution of the Reeve brothers, sung to this melody, listeners were not only told how the killers were hung in chains and left to rot, but assured that the disintegrating corpses were still available for viewing by passersby—a crude illustration was included on the broadside to remove any doubt. Printers often later reused the violent images that accompanied these songs to illustrate newsworthy events, and one could make a case that the old British ballads originated what we now call a *visual meme*. But the music also went viral in strange and surprising ways. Sometimes onlookers sang "Fortune My Foe" during the execution to provide an appropriate soundtrack for the slaughter. Yet this same tune frequently found its way onto the stage for song scenes, even in comedies. This minor-key song may have gotten dubbed the "hanging tune," but that didn't stop William Byrd from setting "Fortune My Foe" for the virginal, or John Dowland drawing inspiration from it for his gentle lute music. Such an unlikely repurposing of the darkest song in Elizabethan England could almost serve as a defining example of what is called 'gallows' humor.

And lest you think we have evolved beyond such crude songs, I'll point out that the execution ballad "Tom Dooley" reached number one on the *Billboard* chart in 1958, and the murder ballad "Frankie and Johnny" earned a gold record for Elvis Presley. Johnny Cash enjoyed success with "Long Black Veil," a modern commercial song with many similarities to execution ballads—and the song has been covered by a host of music megastars, including Mick Jagger, Bruce Springsteen, and the Dave Matthews Band. Other commercial recordings, from "Mack the Knife" to "Hey Joe," invoke in various ways the old murder ballad tradition.

The moralizing tone in these songs aims at conveying a simple message: crime doesn't pay. Yet at a very early stage, a subversive counter-theme emerges in the folk music annals, turning this admonition on its head. Criminals are turned into the heroes of many songs; listeners cheer them on, and sometimes they survive to commit more offenses. Robin Hood, the archetype of the heroic criminal, is the most popular figure in the Child Ballads, appearing in almost forty of these songs. Many other traditional ballads celebrate outlaws and rebels of all stripes, the enemy of the establishment becoming the darling of the common folk. But the same type of reversal figures prominently in opera as well, proving again the convergence of high and low music styles. The enduring popularity of *Don Giovanni* shows just how alluring a murderer and seducer can be, and even a final scene consigning the protagonist to the flames of Hell fails to undercut his heroic stature. The most popular operas are filled with such reversals, from the freeing of the prisoners in Beethoven's *Fidelio* to the idealized presentation of criminals and prostitutes in a host of now canonic works. The prominence of this theme across genres and national boundaries is so great that we are tempted to claim that musicians invented the concept of the antihero.

I've looked (with reluctance and dismay) at the Wikipedia entry for "Antihero" and found absolutely no mention of music. The same is true of other semi-reliable sources of information in the digital age. In these 'official' accounts, Hollywood gets most of the credit for popularizing the antihero, with some help from a diverse group of writers, including Dashiell Hammett, Raymond Chandler, Ernest Hemingway, and Jack Kerouac. But movie stars receive top billing (as always), and we are left with the notion that the golden age of the antihero started with Humphrey Bogart and ended with Jack Nicholson. Along the way, we got a dose of James Dean, Steve McQueen, Clint Eastwood, and other actors who somehow managed to embody gnarly rule-breaking and virtuous situational ethics in one more or less integrated psyche. Yet folk ballads and sung epics predate all of these swaggering celebrities, capturing the essence of the antihero many centuries before Hollywood stumbled onto the formula.

And the folk antihero was hardly restricted to Western songs and folklore. The African trickster also incorporates the main ingredients of this personality type. The trickster, much like the antihero, confidently upsets hierarchies, norms, and power structures—not just toppling them, like a thug, but reversing them and imposing a new order on the old. The same is true of myths and sung stories in many other traditions, including tales about the coyote in Native American communities, Sinbad and the genies in Arabian folklore, and the crow in Australian Aboriginal culture. In many instances, the singers and their heritages have been marginalized themselves, and that merely increases their appetite for narratives about the sly outsider who triumphs over the insiders.

Once you are sensitized to this time-honored theme embedded in the DNA of the popular song, you start recognizing it everywhere. Gangsta rap is merely the latest incarnation of the sung narrative of the outsider in commercial music. 'Outlaw' country music captures the same ethos but for a very different demographic group. Yes, both Democrats and Republicans cherish their antihero playlists. This embrace of the outsider frequently spurs controversy, censorship, and restrictions of various sorts. Mexican legislators have tried to prohibit *narcocorridos*, current-day ballads about drug lords and cartel thugs that are surprisingly similar to the now-revered Child Ballads of British culture. In the same way, *rebetiko* music was prohibited by Greek authorities in the 1930s for its glamorization of criminal behavior. Tango, in its origins, brandished the same underworld associations, and for a long time it faced pushback from authorities both political and religious. "Tango has always been related with fighting, with *roña*, with guys breaking the law," explains Argentine composer Pablo Ziegler, who defines the two essential ingredients of this genre as "*mugre* [filth] and *roña* [fight]." In the United States, classic blues music built its appeal on a similar recipe, delighting audiences with songs about no-good men, at best wandering heartbreakers, at worst violent lawbreakers, whose values disrupted the communities they visited—but rarely for long, as their personalities resisted assimilation into the sanctioned and everyday. Compared with these music styles, Hemingway and Bogart were latecomers to the antihero game.[11]

But how do we come to grips with the next stage in the process, the path by which the musicians themselves became antiheroes? This may be the most significant shift in the social history of modern music, yet it is rarely noticed, let alone studied with any degree of rigor. During the middle decades of the twentieth century, the antihero ethos moved outside the song and started shaping our images of the singer. By any definition, the blues singer Robert Johnson was an antihero, and all the efforts made in recent years to sterilize and mainstream his life story (perhaps the most futile project in contemporary revisionist music history) were doomed to failure from the outset. Robert Johnson will always be as much a folk hero as a recording artist, his mythos just as influential as his music. By the same token, Bob Dylan is an antihero. Tupac Shakur is an antihero. So are Willie Nelson, Miles Davis, and Lou Reed. The songs augment the image, but the musician looms larger than any recording. They are our glorious desperadoes, contemporary Robin Hoods who disrupt the power structure, but with guitars or microphones rather than bows and arrows, and whatever they sing about, they are always singing about themselves. We wouldn't have it any other way.

All these powerful trends and tendencies, the very lifeblood of a music business that sells rebellion the way Procter & Gamble peddles toothpaste and detergent, are based on a reversal of hierarchies that started with the folk song movement. Herder and the song collectors of the eighteenth and nineteenth centuries did not invent the folk song—any claim of that sort fails to meet the most basic sniff test. But they still changed everything. They did this by insisting that the epicenter of culture was low, not high. They forged a framework and aesthetic vision built on songs others had dismissed as crude and vulgar. And this shift in standards of excellence proved more important than the actual songs they documented. Folk music would have continued to flourish even without scholars writing them down in books. The assault on highbrow culture, however, proved fatal.

By the time of Francis James Child's death in 1896, the process was all but complete. The ragtime craze had just started in the United States, and soon would spawn the genre-defining works of Scott Joplin, the most innovative American composer of his day. The origins of jazz in New Orleans date back to this same time. In the Mississippi Delta, blues music could be heard by those savvy enough to know where to find it. Tango was starting to take over the nightlife of Argentina. Samba was gaining momentum in Brazil. In an earlier day, these musical offerings of the marginalized and oppressed would have existed in obscurity until nobles and wealthy patrons legitimized them. But the rules had changed. The singers from the underclass didn't need legitimization—in fact, their allure drew on the simple fact that they were *not* legitimized.

The great flip-flop had happened; now it was simply a matter of watching how it would play out over the decades. From this moment forward, symphonies and cantatas will still get composed; monarchs and popes might still offer opinions on music, or hire a favorite performer. Opera houses and concert halls won't disappear. They will still present their familiar fare (although increasingly requiring subsidies to stay afloat), and on rare occasions might even surprise us. But when measured in money or fame or influence, their glory days have passed. Highbrow culture now recedes into the background, exerting less and less impact on the larger music ecosystem. God bless Carnegie Hall—we will still treat you with respect—but the pulse of the music world will now emanate from the Cotton Club or Birdland or Danceteria or CBGB. From this moment on, a mass audience will dictate the priorities of the music business, and it cussedly embraces the new aesthetic of the outsider and the underclass as its guiding light. Even in the most sedate streets in the most mainstream communities, the sound of rebellion will provide the soundtrack to daily life. Music styles may morph and mix—they always have and always will—but the spirit of revolt will henceforth dictate the pace and scope of change to an unprecedented degree. Now that the *Volk*, and especially the *Jungvolk* (or what we might call teenagers), have learned the power of their own subversive music, they will insist on calling the tunes for everybody else.

20

The Aesthetics of Diaspora

'm almost ashamed to talk about the *cultivation of taste* at this
juncture. Critics in music and related fields tend to avoid that
term as an embarrassing relic of the past. Back in the nineteenth century, self-proclaimed arbiters of taste, such as John
Ruskin and Matthew Arnold, made it their mission to uplift the
artistic sensibilities of the public, and they pursued this goal with
the zeal of Moses returning from the mountaintop with aesthetic
principles carved on stone tablets.

Who can be surprised to learn that Ruskin long considered a
career as an evangelical clergyman before pursuing art criticism as
a vocation? In a way, Ruskin never abandoned his mission to proselytize and inflame souls—he simply substituted high culture for
Jesus Christ in his missionary work. Matthew Arnold, for his part,
claimed in a famous passage of *Culture and Anarchy* that his ambition was nothing less than "a pursuit of total perfection" that would
spread the "best which has been thought and said in the world."[1]

It's widely accepted that French sociologist Pierre Bourdieu
(1930–2002) killed off the project of cultivating taste. In his
deconstruction of taste, Bourdieu strived to reveal its hidden role

as a tool of "snobs and socialites," a kind of gated community of the mind where riff-raff and the working class were denied admission. Wealthy elites manipulated the concept of taste to reinforce their own privileged status, and to impose stultifying attitudes of "detachment, disinterestedness, indifference" on the audience's relationship with the arts. After Bourdieu, the notion of good taste only left a bad taste in the mouths of critics. Even the word *taste* has mostly disappeared from discussion of the arts.[2]

Although Bourdieu's model is enlightening in many fields of cultural commerce, it also has its blind spots. On the one hand, his theory of taste cultivation explains many of the problems besetting visual arts in the current day. A few hundred rich patrons exert enormous influence over the ranking and reputations of painters and sculptors, and even a world-famous artist must pay attention to their whims and fancies. But music defies this reduction of taste to class privilege. For many decades now, the "cultivation of taste" for most music consumers has been controlled by record labels, DJs, YouTube, MTV, streaming services, *Rolling Stone* and various other music magazines, bloggers, tweeters, and other such intermediaries between performers and listeners. Powerful tech companies are already laying the groundwork for a future in which this whole process is reduced to algorithms—preferably ones that feed their bottom line and expand their customer base. These organizations and their attendant tastemakers have little in common, but they mostly agree in their disdain for the cultural preferences of socialites and millionaires. In fact, the taste-formers of today pursue the exact opposite of the Ruskin/Arnold agenda. They learned long ago that the vitality of music comes from the masses, or—even better—from transgressive and disruptive subcultures within mass society. The cultivation of taste in music, for at least the past hundred years, has been a project of assimilating subversion and turning it into a mass-market product for consumers.

Even the wealthy participate in this subversion. I've seen this principle in action firsthand in my own experiences of cultural conflict and dislocation. Nothing in my early life proved more psychically disruptive than coming from a working-class family on the cusp of South-Central Los Angeles—where none of the parents in the neighborhood, mine included, had gone to college—and arriving as a scholarship student at Stanford University and later overseas at Oxford. In subsequent years, I did fundraising for Stanford, and worked in the heart of Silicon Valley, dealing on a daily basis with some of the richest people in the world. I came to learn about their tastes in music (and other matters), and these preferences almost always involved a studied imitation of those who were several steps lower in the socioeconomic hierarchy. Their attitudes weren't always as extreme as those of the scandal-ridden business executive Martin Shkreli, who paid $2 million for a one-of-a-kind hip-hop album from the Wu Tang Clan, but that incident could almost serve as an emblem for the posture of elites toward music today. Instead of launching a symphony orchestra, Microsoft cofounder Paul Allen donated $240 million to create the Museum of Pop Culture (originally the Experience Music Project) in Seattle. Heiress Doris Duke left a bequest of $1 billion to fund a foundation that supports singers, dancers, and musicians "of the entertainment world" (according to the organization's website), with no mention of orchestras or operas. Almost every other grant-giving arts foundation of any influence today has embraced populist entertainment as part of its charter. Where have Bourdieu's snobbish elites all gone?

The real passion among privileged classes in modern times, at least in music, has been *slumming*, not the cultivation of taste. The word *slum* flourished as a noun for decades before it morphed into a verb, and what an odd verb: it signified the act of visiting an impoverished neighborhood for diversion, nightlife, and perhaps a few illicit transactions. These activities frequently involved music of some sort, and the entertainment embodied a new kind of aesthetics, the exact opposite of the hoity-toity image-building cultivated by Bourdieu's donors to the local symphony. And from the start, slumming possessed a vibrancy and allure that a table at the philharmonic gala could never match. Slumming still happens today—although perhaps under different labels—and so frequently that I no longer marvel when encountering CEOs who proclaim their love of punk rock, or financiers who spout off hip-hop lyrics as easily as components of the S&P 500. In fact, these affiliations make perfect sense when you consider that these gnarly musical styles almost always rely on a rhetoric of boasting, dominance, and defiance. What could possibly serve as a better anthem for a world-beating elite? Beethoven's "Ode to Joy" can hardly compete with Sid Vicious belting out "My Way," or Freddie Mercury strutting onstage while proclaiming "We Are the Champions."

A search of more than five million books and documents in Google's database reveals that the term *slumming* first took off in the 1880s, and has continued to rise, except for a brief lull following World War II, ever since. The term typically carries negative connotations, conveying a mild reproach at the naughty nabobs who indulge in these semi-scandalous pastimes. The slummers themselves might prefer a different term for their activities, maybe *open-mindedness, philanthropy*, or even *noblesse oblige.* The jokes and criticisms leveled against them certainly do little to limit their pleasure-seeking in low places, and grotesque institutions have arisen to accommodate their treks. The most notorious were those Harlem clubs of the 1930s that delighted upper-crust white patrons with black entertainment filled with allusions to Africa or southern plantations, and packaged with appropriate songs and dances—Duke Ellington, who performed for an all-white clientele at Harlem's Cotton Club during this period, was often praised for his *jungle* music. But slumming was half a century old by this point. Back in 1884, the *New York Times* had already offered its readers guidance to the "colored colony between Twentieth and Thirtieth streets," promising that a short stroll there would lead to "some of the lowest beer saloons in the city, dingy and dirty, frequented by the vilest characters of both sexes."[3]

But this phenomenon was hardly restricted to New York, and gained even greater respectability across the Atlantic. The same year the *New York Times* offered its guide to slumming, the British periodical *Punch* published a satirical article on members of the upper class who journeyed to East London for a taste of sexual intrigue, intoxicants, and music. But in Paris, a whole new kind of business emerged to serve this clientele, creating what we now know as the modern cabaret. Over the next three decades, this form of nightlife would spread throughout Europe, delighting the respectable citizens of Berlin, Vienna, Amsterdam, Barcelona, Zurich, Kraków, Budapest, Prague, and many other cities. By 1908, the cabaret concept had even arrived in Moscow, setting up in a tiny cellar under the name The Bat, proving that this saucy style of nightlife could flourish as much in a semi-feudal, tsarist-led nation as in the Third French Republic or Kaiser Wilhelm's Germany.

Le Chat Noir (The Black Cat), which opened in the Montmartre district of Paris on November 18, 1881, established the formula for this new form of musical entertainment. Here, well-heeled patrons could drink and enjoy live music alongside bohemians and artists, criminals and prostitutes. In this gaudy and sometimes grotesque environment, slumming reached its high point, achieving the necessary balance between elegance and depravity that kept the cash register ringing. Soon other venues followed suit, and by the mid-1890s more than fifty cabarets and a dozen music halls were operating in Paris, including the famous Moulin Rouge, which opened in 1889, where the can-can dance was popularized, and the Folies Bergère, which started out in 1869 to showcase operetta and comic opera, but by the 1890s had attracted a larger following with edgy entertainment and semi-nude dancing.

Perhaps the most intriguing measure of the sociocultural role of the cabaret can be found in the sharp reduction in the number of prostitutes registering with the Paris police during the 1880s. That decline hardly indicated an improvement in French morals; it merely represented a shift in the business to these new nightclubs, where the whole economic model of sex-for-hire took on a different guise. Dancers and other employees in the cabarets often worked on the side as prostitutes, and the clubs provided a steady stream of clients, a place to strike a deal, and sometimes even the opportunity to consummate the transaction in a back room. The impact on the traditional purveyors of sex was so damaging that some brothels reinvented themselves as music venues.

Yet the cabaret also possessed a kind of cultural cachet that raised it far above a bordello. Édouard Manet painted a barmaid at the Folies Bergère—featuring as model a real-life prostitute known as Suzon—and transformed her into a glamorous and blasé female deity presiding over the patrons and glittering lights of her professional setting. Henri de Toulouse-Lautrec not only painted Moulin Rouge dancer Jane Avril, and other regulars at the cabaret, but even designed advertising posters for the club. These mass-produced marketing items, which now can change hands for up to $100,000 at auction, rank among the most significant intersections of high art and low business in the history of painting, but they could hardly have been possible without this shift in the tone of European nightlife.

The great and not-so-great writers of Paris could be found in these same settings, and not just in the audience. Long before she was nominated for the Nobel Prize in Literature, French writer Colette worked as a music-hall entertainer, and several generations of composers, of every genre and style, came of age in the Parisian cabarets—including Éric Satie and Claude Debussy, who both played piano at Le Chat Noir. In later years cabarets helped popularize almost anything that was new, different, or 'exotic' in musical entertainment, whether African American ex-pat Josephine Baker's dancing, celebrity chanteuse Édith Piaf's torch singing, or the full-fledged Cotton Club revue that took over the Moulin Rouge in 1937, re-creating the Harlem slumming experience in Paris. Avant-garde twentieth-century music also found inspiration in these settings. The group of forward-looking French composers known as Les Six—which included Darius Milhaud, Francis Poulenc, and Arthur Honegger—met regularly at the Paris cabaret Le Bœuf sur le Toit, where they sometimes joined in the music-making.

But Paris had no monopoly on cutting-edge cabarets. Zurich's Cabaret Voltaire, which opened its doors in the closing days of World War I, has sometimes been praised—or chastised, perhaps—as the wildest club in the history of nightlife. A banner above the pianist proclaiming the single word "Dada" (adjacent to a skull mask leering over the stage) made clear to all and sundry the anarchic agenda at play here. The avant-garde Dada movement, which coalesced in this hothouse environment, rejected not only the war-mongering and profit-generating institutions of modern society, but also those guiding principles of logic and coherence one might think indispensable even to revolutionaries. Long before punk shook its belligerent fists at society, Dada was trying to topple whatever it could get its hands on, and its leading exponents would have simply laughed at those spiky hairstyles in M&M candy colors, or the flamboyant usage of safety pins as an alternative to costume jewelry. "Dada doubts everything," announced poet Tristan Tzara, one of the central figures in the movement—and he quickly added that it even doubted Dada.[4]

Performances at Cabaret Voltaire involved nonsense syllables, typewriters, pot covers, rakes, and even an imaginary violin played with a make-believe bow. But the audience could be as nihilistic as the performers. In this city of war refugees and radical exiles (Vladimir Lenin lived across the street), Dadaists were just one fringe group among many. We even hear of the audience storming the stage at this cabaret—one more example, anticipating many others we will encounter in the pages ahead, of a musical performance resembling a violent, quasi-sacrificial ritual.

The self-deprecatory names of the cabarets are revealing. These fashionable European venues took their identities from animals—a bat or oxen or a cat—in ways reminiscent of early rock bands, which named themselves after beetles and crickets, yardbirds and turtles, or just simply "the Animals." A semi-earnest back-to-nature rootedness mixed with a disdain for social titles and distinctions. But very soon, outrageousness was courted for its own merits, and revered as a kind of ultimate artistic value. At the Cabaret du Néant (The Cabaret of Nothingness), which operated in Montmartre in the 1890s, customers ate and drank on large wooden coffins instead of tables, and the décor included guillotines and skeletons. At the Cabaret de l'Enfer (The Cabaret of the Inferno), the proprietors promised nothing less than an evocation of Hell—entertainment was provided by musicians dressed as devils performing in a large cauldron over a real fire. Patrons seeking redemption could go next door to Cabaret du Ciel (The Cabaret of the Sky), where attractive young women danced in the attire of angels, and the master of ceremonies pretended to be St. Peter himself. The terms *punk* and *postmodern* didn't exist back then, at least not in their contemporary meanings, but self-proclaimed decadence and nihilism were powerful cultural forces and anticipated many of the aesthetic principles that would flourish a century later.

But our main concern is with music, and we can't allow ourselves to get distracted by guillotines and surrogate St. Peters. The bold songs of the cabarets were filled with satire and sensuality. They could take on a political bent, or delve into eroticism, or aim merely for the grotesque. Only a short while before, following the collapse of the Paris Commune—which controlled the French capital for two months in 1871 with promises of collectivism and reform—the authorities had imposed strict censorship rules on the music world. The minister of public education blamed the "depravity" of the Commune on "the orgy of songs produced during that epoch"; another commentator described the café concerts as a "disgraceful invention which is spreading across our country like leprosy." Yet now the contagion had returned, and it was more virulent than ever. In the late nineteenth and early twentieth centuries, the cabaret stood out as the vital epicenter of popular music culture in European life, and everyone recognized that edginess and irreverence were the key ingredients in this successful formula.[5]

The degree of censorship imposed on cabaret and music-hall entertainment varied from city to city, and shifted with political currents. In Berlin, for example, cabaret was strictly controlled under Kaiser Wilhelm, turned lewd and outrageous during the 1920s, and eventually retreated into stale conformity under Hitler's Nazi regime. But in most settings, these venues pushed the limits, stirring up controversy and maintaining only the bare minimum of decency required to keep police from shutting them down. In some instances, laws were flouted through a pretense that the performances were private affairs for "club members" or "invited guests," and not open to the general public. In other instances, cabaret owners claimed they were exempt from censorship because they weren't operating real theaters, just pubs, or that they were quasi-artistic nonprofits, because no admission was charged at the door.

By a variety of ruses and expedients—and out-and-out bribes when necessary—these venues stayed at the cutting edge of the entertainment world for decades.

In the year 1900, if you had gathered together a group of the leading experts on popular music and asked them to predict how songs would evolve during the twentieth century, the most knowledgeable would have told you that these European cabarets would set the tone for the next hundred years. Where else would you find music so saucy and sexy, so daring and *au courant?* Paris and Berlin had developed the formula, and it was simply a matter of time before the rest of the world followed their example. Once again, rebels and outsiders were at the forefront of a dominant new style of music, and either you raced to keep up or got left behind.

But at this juncture something unexpected happened. Those experts would have been proven wrong. Cabaret was *not* the future of twentieth-century popular music. Another group of outsiders, even more disenfranchised and despised, would alter the course of modern commercial music—and then would do it again and again and again.

We now know with the benefit of hindsight that the black population of the Americas, almost all of them descendants of slaves, would reinvent popular music in the twentieth century. And they did it in so many ways: first with ragtime and the blues, then with early jazz and swing and the first stirrings of R&B, and again with soul, reggae, samba, boogie-woogie, doo-wop, bebop, calypso, funk, salsa, hip-hop, and numerous other genres and subgenres and hybrid genres. Even when white musicians stepped forward with their own distinctive popular music styles—whether it was "British Invasion" rock, disco, bluegrass, or whatever else climbed the charts for longer or shorter durations—they almost always did so with heavy borrowings from black sources of inspiration. No European cabaret, however fashionable or disreputable, could compete with this outpouring of creativity and innovation—one that continues in the current day.

We take the triumph of the black underclass over the global music business for granted, but by any sober calculation it must rank as the most amazing turn of events in the past five hundred years of music history. Is there anything more remarkable than a poor and often hated minority from the bad side of town— whether in New Orleans, the Mississippi Delta, Detroit, the South Bronx, Compton, wherever; the specific address may change but the socioeconomic reality not so much—reconfiguring the musical tastes of the entire world, and then doing it again and again with clockwork regularity for each new decade and generation? How did that happen? We have already seen the surprising ways in which slaves and other outsiders shaped the music of ancient and medieval societies, but surely the degree of difficulty increased by an order of magnitude during the twentieth century, when powerful corporations with so many vested interests and captive distribution channels controlled the mainstream music of modern life. If you are looking for superhuman feats in music history—and perhaps some insight into how new genres and styles arise—this is a puzzle worth exploring.

The history of musical creativity arising from the African transatlantic diaspora is as old as the institution of slavery in the various nations and communities of the Americas. Or, rather, it's even older, starting on the very ships that transported these captives to the New World. Singing, dancing, and drumming might happen spontaneously, but in many instances they were scheduled and enforced by the captain, who offered these 'freedoms' out of sheer self-interest. Mortality rates on these ships were high, and music was seen as a support both to the health of unwilling passengers and the economic returns of the slave-trading enterprise. On these journeys, the captives were "obliged to dance," noted British doctor Alexander Falconbridge, who took part in four slave-trading voyages in the 1780s, and "if they go about it reluctantly or do not move with agility, they are flogged." The music in this particular setting was merely a drum, accompanied by singing. No aesthetic or expressive consideration entered into the equation, yet it imposed itself nonetheless. Falconbridge could not help hearing in these supposedly restorative exercises of the "poor wretches" of the Middle Passage the "melancholy lamentation of their exile from their native country."[6]

This ability to extract musical artistry in the face of the most extreme violations of human dignity will be a recurring pattern in American music. Needless to say, cultural or aesthetic considerations played no role in the elaborate chain of transactions and incentives that brought more than ten million Africans to the Americas. In other times and places, businesses specialized in the training and sale of slaves as entertainers and performers—for example, in the Islamic world under the Abbasid Caliphate—but such notions would never have entered the mind of a transatlantic slave trader, who valued little beyond the strength and endurance of the human chattel in the hold. These slaves were intended for the American South, where they would be put to work as the foundation of an agrarian economy. Yet at every stage in the history of black enslavement in America, the power of the music emerged despite all hindrances, regulations, obstacles, or punishments. The descendants of African slaves eventually came to dominate the musical culture everywhere they settled—indeed, long before the end of slavery, black musicians were already displacing white performers. Even within the most racist communities, audiences gradually came to prefer the very population they oppressed as purveyors of musical entertainment.

As early as the 1690s, slave fiddlers were enlisted to perform for white dancers in Virginia. In subsequent years, black musicians took charge of the entertainment at virtually every kind of venue in the South. They entertained steamboat passengers on the Mississippi and Ohio Rivers. They provided dance music at elite resort hotels and private parties. When a Scottish dance teacher in Virginia took out an advertisement for his school in 1788, he specified his use of "the best white music that is to be had in these parts"—a claim that suggests many of his competitors were relying on black performers. And at some point in the 1700s, black musicians began calling out steps and movements to white dancers—a practice familiar to us nowadays as a staple of hoedowns and traditional folk dancing, but shocking to many observers at the time. English writer Frances Trollope, who encountered these bandstand exhortations during her stay in the United States, griped about their "ludicrous effect on European ears." A Swedish traveler, hearing a similar dance caller during his 1832 visit to Boston, claimed that it was "a practice which surprised me more than any other." As this anecdote indicates, dance calling had spread far beyond the South by this time. When British actress Fanny Kemble visited Philadelphia in the 1830s, she was disappointed to find that dancers no longer learned the steps but needed a caller to guide them through their motions. The freed black slave Frank Johnson, a very popular entertainer in Philadelphia at this time, may have been the dance caller in this instance. The spectacle of black slaves and former slaves barking out orders to obedient white folk may seem incongruous, perhaps even surreal, given the values of the era, but it serves as a symbol of the whole African American musical experience in the United States. Black culture provides the direction, and white audiences follow along, even as hierarchies and institutions in other spheres of society stay unchanged.[7]

The ruling elites in ancient and medieval times, who considered entertainers disreputable, easily accepted the preeminence of slaves in musical matters. The job of performing songs was, for them, *fit for a slave*. But nineteenth-century America experienced intense cognitive dissonance when confronted with a talented member of a dispossessed underclass who, without the benefit of formal training or even decent instruments, rose to the top of the music field. Recall that this was an era that idolized musical performers, attributing to them transcendent poetic and spiritual sensibilities. The star system was already entrenched in the music business, and newspaper reviews captured the prevailing ethos with words of breathless praise and reverent emoting targeted at the leading performers of the day—many of them from Europe, because Americans also suffered from a deep inferiority complex about their own cultural achievements. What a terrible shock it must have been when the African slaves and their descendants emerged as America's most precious musical resource, the antidote to subservience to Old World ways. We shouldn't be surprised that it took roughly three hundred years for this process to play out, if we measure the span starting with the arrival of the first twenty African slaves in the New World in 1619 and finally reaching critical mass with the intense public fervor for jazz, blues, and other African American musical styles in the early decades of the twentieth century.

One might say that American elites did everything possible to delay and obstruct the rise of a homegrown Africanized musical culture. But that would only capture half the story. The public simultaneously displayed a great fascination, even bordering on obsession, with the music of its disenfranchised black population. As a result, the shadow of black music constantly loomed over the musical world of nineteenth-century white America. Take, for example, the most popular song at the midpoint of the century, Stephen Foster's "Oh! Susanna." At the time of its publication in 1848, no American popular song had sold more than five thousand copies, but Foster's viral tune achieved sales of one hundred thousand copies soon after its release. This minstrel style of whites mimicking blacks frequently incorporated demeaning and racist verses, and we find those in words to "Oh! Susanna" that are usually omitted nowadays. Yet most of the song, written in a mimicked African American vernacular style, describes the romantic longing of a separated black couple. The two ingredients here, intolerant bigotry and sentimental affection, simply don't fit together. Some commentators have gone so far as to dismiss the lyrics as nonsensical or incoherent. At a minimum, they embody a paradox, the same kind of cognitive dissonance that is described above. But this internal contradiction simply echoed the conflict already present in the American psyche of the time, reflecting a citizenry that found itself drawn to the Africanized music of the New World, yet also determined to assert its cultural superiority to it.

Years ago, I wrote an essay on Stephen Foster titled "The Con Man Who Invented American Popular Music." I stand by both claims—both Foster's key role in establishing the tunesmith's trade in the United States, and the essential elements of rip-off and deception at the heart of his craft. This songwriter built his reputation on nostalgic songs about the Deep South, but had virtually no firsthand knowledge of the region. His fluency in black culture was a studied pose that makes white rapper Vanilla Ice look like a paragon of authenticity by comparison. But in this instance the appropriator also got appropriated. In the two years following the publication of "Oh! Susanna," sixteen other companies released their own arrangements of the song, and Foster could only watch as others reaped the financial benefits of his music. When he died in 1864, a resident of a Bowery flophouse, Foster had only thirty-eight cents in his pocket. But the robbery of musical intellectual property was already an established American tradition long before "Oh! Susanna." Even the country's national anthem was a rip-off on a British song, and the early music business in the United States had operated in blissful ignorance of copyright and royalties. Long after legal protections for songwriters started to be enforced, large spheres of musical activity, from traditional folk singing to scratch-and-sample deejaying, continued to play by looser rules, and sometimes none at all. It's only a slight exaggeration to say that, for most of American history, robbery is how music went viral. Some current-day observers, kicking the tires at YouTube and other purveyors of digital music, would say that's still true in our own time.[8]

Black music, faux or real, was everywhere in nineteenth-century America, even in communities where people had little or no first-hand contact with African Americans. But the perks and privileges of stardom only went to white intermediaries and imitators. As early as the 1820s, white minstrels in blackface, such as Thomas Rice (who reinvented himself under the stage name Daddy Rice—it almost sounds like an ancestor of Vanilla Ice) were tapping into the public's demand for songs that both evoked black entertainment while also mocking it. Rice's trademark skit, "Jump Jim Crow," found him dressed in patched, ragged clothing, wearing blackface, and offering a grotesque version of a song and dance he had learned by imitating the antics of a disabled black man. Could you really build a star-studded career on such stuff in nineteenth-century America? In truth, many entertainers did just that. Rice played to packed theaters and even took his show overseas to London, but faced increasing competition as minstrelsy turned into the hottest musical fad of its day.

In the 1840s, the Virginia Minstrels, led by Dan Emmett, took this style of entertainment to the next level by introducing full-fledged shows. These typically involved a group of blackface performers, as few as four or as many as fifteen or more, seated in a semicircle facing the audience. They served up songs, skits, declamations, and jokes built around hackneyed characters and situations, supplemented by other onstage spectacles—which might include a cakewalk, a one-act play, or some other diversion. Sometimes musicians accompanied from behind or from an orchestra pit, but the cast members also played on stereotypical plantation instruments, from banjos to bones. Even in the days of slavery, many considered this as low entertainment for the rabble, but in 1844 a minstrel troupe performing as the Ethiopian Serenaders received an invitation to the White House to play for President John Tyler.

Strange to say, audiences sometimes mistook this for real black music. When the Ethiopian Serenaders toured England, troupe members made a point of declaring they had no 'black blood,' and even released portraits of themselves without blackface to reinforce the point. Despite these protestations, many Londoners remained convinced that these visiting entertainers were actual Ethiopians. But Americans of the era were often just as credulous, mistaking minstrel songs for the genuine music of the black underclass. Music publishers made it hard to distinguish between the two, marketing collections of "plantation songs"—a label that could cover a wide range of material. I suspect that even today, many educated music lovers simply assume that songs such as "Oh! Susanna" and "Camptown Races" are authentic black folk melodies, with no grasp of how much contrivance and dissimulation went into their creation. How much harder must it have been in the Antebellum United States for anyone seeking real black music? Yes, minstrel troupes featuring black entertainers went on the road as early as the 1840s, but even these worked within the constraints and expectations created by the dominant culture and their blackface competitors. Where were all the followers of Herder, with their zeal for collecting the authentic songs of the folk? They had a gold mine of musical material awaiting them in the American South in the early decades of the nineteenth century. But those folk weren't their kind of folk. Even a century later, when the celebrated folk song collectors Cecil Sharp and Maud Karpeles came to Appalachia in search of rare tunes, they ignored blacks, Native Americans, and anyone else who didn't fit into their schema of folk music worthy of preservation.

Perhaps you wonder what would have happened if a talented black musician had actually enjoyed the perks of stardom, backed by professional marketing and promotion, during the middle decades of nineteenth-century America. In fact, we have a single example of exactly that situation, and it makes for a most melancholy case study. Pianist Thomas Wiggins, better known as "Blind Tom," achieved widespread fame in his day, performing for packed concert halls in the United States and overseas. His concert tours generated a steady stream of feature stories and reviews in newspapers and magazines, and Blind Tom acquired a celebrity status that no other black performer of his day could approach. His concerts brought in staggering sums—as much as $5,000 a month at his peak, the equivalent of $100,000 today—but as one journalist toward the end of Wiggins's life explained to readers, "the idiot never received a cent for his services." The family of his slave master, who conveniently became Wiggins's legal guardian after abolition, got rich off the pianist's talent.[9]

The circus-like marketing of Thomas Wiggins was as disturbing as his economic exploitation. The first star black performer in American history was promoted as an "idiot savant," a keyboard freak show for curious spectators. The *othering* of musicians is probably as old as music itself—shamanistic cultures even prized practitioners who demonstrated abnormalities—but Wiggins's exploitation represents an especially grotesque chapter in this history of marginalization in American life. Such practices would continue for at least another hundred years. Talented black musicians who were blind almost always ended up with their disability attached to their name, part of their 'branding.' After Wiggins's death in 1908, the music industry promoted Blind Lemon Jefferson, Blind Willie Johnson, Blind Blake, Blind Willie McTell, Blind Boy Fuller (a double whammy there, both blind and a boy, although Fuller didn't start recording until his twenties), and many others. When I've given talks to youngsters in recent years about the blues tradition, they are often puzzled, and certainly uneasy, about this way of referring to music pioneers. I stick with the familiar names, although I still wonder why we don't just refer to Blind Boy Fuller by his legal name (Fulton Allen), which is quite stately, even suitable for nobility. Our current-day uneasiness testifies to the progress we've made. But it's only relative. The notion that musical greatness is a kind of aberration, often accompanied by physical or mental stigmata, is too deeply ingrained to disappear entirely. For good or bad, musicians are deemed chosen people, and it's a tossup whether that leads to idolization and celebrity or fear and exclusion.

Blind Tom experienced both almost from the start. In addition to his blindness, Wiggins demonstrated signs of autism. But the harsh circumstances of the pianist's upbringing no doubt contributed to his disability. During his childhood in Georgia, he was often confined to a high-sided wooden box—in the days of slavery, that was a childcare option for a youngster who might wander off and get hurt while parents were working. This sensory deprivation may have heightened the child's perceptions of sounds, but it also left lasting damage to his psyche and emotions. Around the age of four, the youngster started showing signs of his extraordinary skill in imitating what he heard others play on the piano. He was a well-traveled performer even before his teens, and a carnival atmosphere surrounded his public appearances. The musician's genuine talents were channeled into various stunts to demonstrate his skill at mimicry. But a key goal of a Blind Tom concert was also comedy, and surviving accounts stress how audiences often responded with cruel laughter to his onstage stunts.

Yet it's worth considering what Wiggins might have done in a different time and place. An observer who heard him playing at age eleven noted the "startling beauty and pathos" of his "strange, weird improvisations." You can't help but be reminded of jazz from this description—yet that genre wouldn't even exist for another half century. This side of Wiggins's musical talent evidently shook up listeners. One critic dismissed the performances as "wild barbaric, racial laments" and another, searching for a descriptor, could only explain that they sounded like "echoes of plantation songs." Other accounts hint at the supernatural and quasi-clairvoyant powers they thought Blind Tom possessed. Newspaper stories testified to his ability to describe landscapes he couldn't see with uncanny accuracy, or to learn music from birds and the natural world. His reputation for psychic powers spread so widely that Harry Houdini, the famed magician who worked to debunk the claims of spiritualists, felt compelled to denounce Blind Tom as a fraud. Yet it's clear that many observers believed that Wiggins had genuine spiritual powers, and talents that went far beyond playing the piano. In another culture, he would have become a shaman or a mystic. In a later day, he could have flourished as a jazz or blues icon. But in his own time and place, this first black star of American music was permitted only two roles: he was a gimmicky stunt for audiences, and a money-maker for his bosses.[10]

Yet American music in the nineteenth century desperately needed what only black music could offer. It's hard to convey the banality and repression of mainstream white America's popular songs from that era. You would have to sift through stacks of parlor tunes to grasp how mind-numbingly the nation's music was compromised by a clichéd primness and a blatant lack of originality. During colonial times and the early days of the United States, formulaic patriotic songs were churned out and recycled, and the marketeers of nationalistic pride showed no shame in stealing melodies from overseas for this purpose. Not just the "Star Spangled Banner," but a host of other patriotic melodies had European antecedents. "Yankee Doodle" probably originated as a Dutch harvest song. "My Country, 'Tis of Thee" rips off "God Save the King" almost as brazenly as the Sex Pistols would do in a later day. "The Liberty Song" was adapted from "Heart of Oak," the official anthem of the British Royal Navy. "War and Washington" came straight out of "The British Grenadiers." When would Americans, so proud of their independence, actually demonstrate it in their music?

During the second half of the nineteenth century, the American public's taste shifted markedly to love songs, but they hardly deserve the name. Based on the insipid content of these works, they ought to be called "songs of gentle affection," or "songs of sentimental feeling." Don't expect to encounter a kiss or a hug or any other physical contact in these lyrics. Even the slightest hints of desire were purged from this music. A bland expression of tender regard takes the place of passion, and is wrapped up in the most polite terms. Only two variants of love songs existed, happy or sad, and both were written according to formula, repeating the same tepid feelings with little variation in tune after tune. Even another *person* as the object of affection was optional here. Almost anything old or familiar would do. "The most frequent recipients of affection were a family or mother's Bible, a church, schoolhouse, tree, flower or home," writes Nicholas E. Tawa, a scholar who has specialized in this music. Even Billie Holiday or Frank Sinatra would be hard pressed to extract emotional significance from songs such as "The Old Arm Chair" or "The Cottage of My Mother." But this was the sheet music that Americans purchased, learned, and sang. The contrast with the bold cabaret music of Europe could hardly be more pronounced. And Americans themselves were acutely aware of the gap—when performers from overseas were booked for tours in the United States, they were warned in no uncertain terms to clean up their songs and avoid any lyrics that might offend the delicate sensibilities of the New World.[11]

I can't blame the songwriters or music publishing companies. They were responding to the demands of the marketplace. The music business in this period was built on peddling reams of sheet music for the home market, where millions of parents saw playing an instrument as a mark of refinement for their children. Songs could provide entertainment, but it was even better if they raised a family's social status or helped an eligible daughter find a good match. Never before or since had love songs been sung with less hope of seduction. In fact, the exact opposite was the intended effect. Sex came after the marriage; before that, a suitor could simply sit in the parlor and listen, with Mom and Dad closely watching over the proceedings, while the beloved sang of sweet and tender feelings.

Even if these songs had continued to find buyers, they would have effectively prevented the American music business from evolving into a true entertainment industry. Songs would have been sold as status symbols or matchmaking accessories, but not much more. This is why the injection of African American sounds into popular music proved to be so important. Without it, the cabaret model would have prevailed during the twentieth century, and popular music would be dominated by European composers and performers. The United States was saved from this fate by its most reviled underclass.

Put simply, black Americans were allowed to sing for reasons other than status, and permitted to address all those taboo subjects that weren't allowed entry into the parlors where parents kept up their vigilant control of matters musical. The slave, the refugee, the dispossessed, and the displaced have few reasons to uphold cherished community values, and their music always reaches out for truths unspoken in other settings, even if they require expression in coded terms. This is the aesthetics of diaspora, the power of innovation that only the outsider possesses, a principle no different in nineteenth-century America than it was when the ancient Greeks named their most dangerous modes after Lydian and Phrygian slaves. This creative potency of the underclass would not only reshape artistic standards—and the sounds of songs emanating from the parlors of the citizenry—but also put the United States into a dominant position in the growing global recording business of the twentieth century. The American steel industry had its Andrew Carnegie. The oil industry had its John D. Rockefeller. Still other industries benefited from their pathbreaking, future-oriented leaders. But for the music industry, the descendants of slaves played this seminal role, providing the vision and direction, that spark of innovation that drives commerce. The leaders of the music publishing companies and the nascent recording business didn't realize it yet, in those closing years of the nineteenth century, but they would find out soon enough.

21

Black Music and the
Great American Lifestyle Crisis

A hint of the sexual revolution of the 1960s can already be detected in American music at the turn of the twentieth century. Instead of the tame expressions of affection that characterized the love songs of previous decades, couples now hugged and kissed in sheet music hits, and sometimes dared to do even more. For the first time, American tunesmiths embraced eroticism as a tool of self-expression—and even more, as a way to sell their wares.

But only black couples, for the most part, showed up in these salacious songs. If you were to judge turn-of-the-century American morals by the lyrics or the pictures on the covers of popular sheet music, you might assume that fornication in the United States was limited to the African American populace. Yet many of these songs were big sellers, testifying to an audience whose tastes cut across racial divides, especially when sexy music was involved. "The Warmest Baby in the Bunch," by George M. Cohan, was highly suggestive for 1897, with its description of a "baby" who made the other "wenches take a chill" and was "such a hot radiator" that "steam comes from her shoes in cold December." Body contact, taboo in the parlor songs of previous decades, had now entered the vocabulary of the American love song, but no one complained, because the illustration of a black couple on the cover of the sheet music made clear that such excessive body heat was limited to *dark* bodies. The same was true of "Honey on My Lips," composed by Charles E. Trevathan, from the following year. Here, illustrations of a black couple kissing and groping made an edgy song acceptable for commerce. Hughie Cannon's "Won't You Come Home Bill Bailey," from 1902, even hinted at adultery, but again, the sheet music artwork let consumers know that the philandering Mr. Bailey, a dapper man with a leering gaze and wearing a stylish fedora hat, was black. So of course it was okay to put his infidelities into a tune.

This song became a huge hit and inspired many spin-off compositions. Bill Bailey grew into a brand franchise (in the contemporary parlance). You could almost describe him as a kind of black folklore hero, akin to John Henry, working not with a hammer but a far less burdensome tool in his tireless bedroom vocation. In fact, the actual couple who inspired the song, Willard and Sarah Bailey, were white residents of Jackson, Michigan, but at this point in American music, the marketplace simply assumed that anything sexual or tawdry in a song had to refer to the black underclass.

Take, for example, the song now known as "Frankie and Johnny," originally published by Cannon in 1904 as "He Done Me Wrong," with the subtitle "Death of Bill Bailey." This song contains a scandalous story of adultery followed by cold-blooded murder. The historical antecedents of the story are still debated—its origins may date back to the early nineteenth century—but there is nothing in this tale that requires the protagonists to be black. The sheet music, however, again presents an image of an African American couple. In a revealing incident from 1936, artist Thomas Hart Benton included a saloon scene featuring these famous lovers in his murals for the Missouri State Capitol Building. Here an angry woman is shown firing a gun at close range into a man's hindquarters. Some state legislators were so shocked by this image that a bill was introduced to paint over the offending couple. Although the mural was saved, it's worth noting that the complaints had nothing to do with the rude subject matter or the allusions to sex and violence. Leading citizens were simply indignant that a painting of black people had appeared on the wall of a government building. The indecorous aspects of their doings, in contrast, were simply taken for granted.

These songs came from white composers, who continued to serve as the channel by which most popular music about African American topics reached the general public. In the years following the end of slavery, black music started to find platforms for expression that presented it with a modicum of dignity, but this newfound respect was restricted almost entirely to religious music that reinforced the values of the mainstream culture. We see this shift almost immediately after the end of the Civil War with the release of *Slave Songs of the United States* (1867), compiled by three white abolitionists, and the publication that same year of an influential article on "Negro Spirituals" by Unitarian minister Thomas Wentworth Higginson in *The Atlantic Monthly*. These song collectors seemed to believe that black music rarely departed from Christian themes. "Almost all their songs were thoroughly religious in tone," Higginson insisted in his description of black music, drawing on his experience leading the first authorized African American regiment in the Civil War. The editors of *Slave Songs of the United States* apologized for not including more secular songs in their collection, but explained that these were very rare. They also assured their readers that "negro music is *civilized* in character" because it is "partly composed under the influence of association with whites," and very little of it is "intrinsically barbaric."[1]

The enormous success of the Fisk Jubilee Singers in the 1870s proved that the spiritual side of black music performed by actual African American ensembles could also flourish in concert halls. Yet at a very early juncture, some critics questioned the authenticity of these songs. An article in the *Peoria Journal* in 1881 complained that concert hall spirituals had "lost the wild rhythms, the barbaric melody, the passion" of real black music and "smack of the North." The debate continues to this day on the legitimacy of this music, as to both its origins and its purposes, although without the pejorative insinuations. I doubt we will ever reach full consensus on how much of Africa shows up in African American spirituals. But the notion that these songs simply reflected the values of the dominant culture can't really be taken seriously. You don't need to be an expert in decoding hidden messages to find the latent meanings in spirituals that referenced the recurring themes of slavery, suffering, and liberation in sanctioned biblical texts. In various times and places, these scriptural passages have conveyed very different significations to ruling elites and oppressed groups—for example, when Catholic composers William Byrd and Thomas Tallis could reference biblical passages that described the suffering of the despised 'papists' in England without displeasing their anti-Rome patron Queen Elizabeth. These complaints against oppression are pervasive in the traditional African American spirituals.[2]

Sometimes the sociopolitical symbols in black spirituals were obvious to all hearers. When the words of "Go Down Moses" resounded with the demand "Let my people go," listeners didn't need to apply advanced code-breaking skills to grasp that the lament rose above historical concerns with pharaohs and ancient Egypt. The spiritual "Steal Away" is ostensibly about leaving earthly constraints behind and joining Jesus in a better place, but that better place was obviously also any reachable destination outside the control of slave-drivers and overseers. Other spirituals were subtler in their alternative meanings. Songs such as "Swing Low, Sweet Chariot" and "Wade in the Water" have been interpreted as coded references to the Underground Railroad, that system of safe houses and secret routes that brought slaves to freedom in the North. Of course, these songs also served as heartfelt expressions of faith and religious sentiment in many, perhaps even most, situations. But even if we can't determine with any precision the motivations and intentions of specific singers, it's clear that two levels of meaning coexisted, and did so very comfortably. Given the long history of downtrodden individuals doing double duty as musical innovators, we should hardly be surprised by this flexibility. Protest songs do not always advertise their protestations, and often reveal extraordinary adaptability to the dictates and values of the authorities.

But American music at the dawn of the twentieth century required more from black musicians than religious songs and encrypted messages. The United States might have been flexing its military and economic power on a global scale—the recent Spanish-American War proved that Yankees could triumph over a former Old World colonizer in just ten weeks—but the musical culture of its ruling class was still a tepid mixture of stale formulas and clumsy imitations. Around this time, black performers started encountering audiences receptive to more jarring and rebellious music, but this had little to do with tolerance and racial harmony. Mainstream America craved the excitement that only this new music—first ragtime, and later jazz and blues—could provide. This early breed of (what we might now call) 'alt music' had existed before, but only on the fringes or hidden from view. Consider the curious case of composer Basile Barès (1845–1902), a black man who wrote classical music in nineteenth-century New Orleans. For the public he composed sentimental waltzes of little distinction, but more recently, an unpublished work titled "Los Campanillas" has come to light. This extraordinary piece, still little known, features a hauntingly melancholy melody and the same habanera rhythm W. C. Handy would later employ in his huge hit "St. Louis Blues." We can only guess at the circumstances under which Barès created it, but who can wonder that a black composer born as a slave would keep his less conventional music under wraps? It is ironic that a white New Orleans composer of the same era, Louis Moreau Gottschalk, had more freedom to draw on Africanized sources of inspiration than Barès did. But that would soon change, and for the most powerful of reasons: consumer demand.

I can't help recalling an anecdote shared by the Roman diplomat Priscus, who visited the court of Attila the Hun in the year AD 448. This seasoned representative of the Roman emperor was shocked when, in the midst of these fierce enemies to everything he held sacred, he was greeted by a man in rude Scythian attire who was fluent in Greek. Priscus learned, to his befuddlement, that his interlocutor was a merchant who had been born and raised among Romans, but had decided that life was better with the "barbarians" than in "civilization." The two proceeded to debate in passionate exchanges the comparative advantages of these opposed ways of life. This phenomenon, rare in the ancient world, would become so common among later empires and colonizers that it even received a name: *going native*. And few things are more feared by dominant powers even today than this sort of switch of allegiance at the grassroots level. Rulers do well to combat it, because it represents nothing less than a highly contagious psychic treason to prevailing values. People are aligning themselves with the views and manners of the colonized rather than those of the colonizers. Once this infection begins to spread, all the military strength and economic clout in the world is powerless to halt its influence.

Something of this sort entered into American musical culture at the turn of the century. Black music, once ridiculed for its crudeness, now openly enticed listeners—especially young ones—with its promise of an alternative to established conventions. We have now gone beyond slumming and arrived at a kind of *lifestyle* crisis, although that word didn't exist back in 1900. The epicenter of this shift, in its early stages, was *ragtime*. This label, much like *hip-hop*, *punk*, or *country* in later decades, represented more than just a music genre, encompassing a wide array of cultural signifiers and activities. At least as far back as the 1890s, the word *rag* started taking on new meanings. Sometimes it referred to a kind of music; in other instances, to a dance. In the words of the writer Rupert Hughes in 1899, the rag was "a sort of frenzy with frequent yelps of delight from the dancer and the spectators." These meanings linked up with a whole history of terms derived from the Old English *raggig*, which had spawned words such as *raggedy*, *ragpicker*, *ragamuffin*, and others suggesting degradation, roughness, poverty, and outright evil. *Ragamoffyn* in the fourteenth-century allegory *Piers Plowman* is the devil himself—and Satan will show up in many unexpected contexts in twentieth-century black music, not least as a person you could negotiate with if you wanted to play the blues. Even before the end of the 1890s, *rag* could refer to an actual event, a kind of rave for *fin de siècle* American delinquents. A Kansas City news report from 1893 describes a shooting that took place "at a rag" that left both a white man and a black man dead. The racial mix here is interesting. Even in a highly segregated world, some segment of white society felt the allure of *ragging.*[3]

Rag (or ragtime, as it was now called) exerted its greatest commercial influence as a style of music typically played on piano, but its influence quickly spread to ensembles featuring string or wind instruments. This music perhaps sounds quaint or old-fashioned to many listeners today, suitable for the soundtrack of a period historical movie. But that wasn't how ragtime was heard in its early days. Practitioners of this new genre took a simple rhythmic device known as syncopation, which involves placing heavy accents between the beats rather than on the beat, and pushed it to extremes not previously heard in Western music. In ragtime, syncopation is happening constantly. Many ragtime melodies are extremely difficult to whistle or hum, but that hardly mattered to the performers or their audiences. The goal was to keep the rhythmic displacements coming, imparting a restless, off-kilter energy to the music that no waltz or quadrille could match.

The origins of new musical styles resist precise dating in almost every instance. They arise from the fringes and outliers, away from the limelight and the scrutiny of experts (who always arrive late on the scene). But ragtime almost certainly followed the recurring pattern of innovation emerging from centers of scandal and forbidden activities. The conventional accounts tell how early stirrings of ragtime could be heard at the World's Columbian Exposition, a massive fair that spread over six hundred acres and two hundred buildings in Chicago in 1893. Yet this genealogy casts an undeserved luster of respectability on ragtime, which is not mentioned in any official documents or accounts of the exposition. You probably could hear ragtime in Chicago at this moment in history—after all, musicians of every style and genre flocked to the city to make money off fair attendees—but your best chance would have been at a saloon or a brothel, and especially in the Levee, the red-light district in the city's South Loop neighborhood. A few years later, when ragtime emerged as a noteworthy regional style in Missouri, the same nightlife associations predominated. The ragtime expert Edward A. Berlin, who created street-by-street maps of Sedalia and St. Louis during the period of the music's ascendancy, found that rags frequently served as a soundtrack to prostitution and intoxication, and probably a host of other social vices as well, in its early days.[4]

This connection is celebrated in the very name of the most famous ragtime composition of the era, Scott Joplin's "Maple Leaf Rag," which helped turn the new music style into a nationwide phenomenon in 1899. Many people assume this piece is named for the maple trees native to Missouri, or perhaps honors Canada, and references the leaf emblazoned on that country's flag. The truth is less decorous. The Maple Leaf Club, where Scott Joplin entertained patrons, is almost certainly the source of the composition's title. This social club was a controversial establishment in Sedalia, stirring up protests by black preachers, who wanted the city to close this center of drinking, dancing, gambling, and, in the words of one critic, "other immoral practices, too disgraceful to mention." Authorities eventually shut down the operation in 1900, but it's worth noting that even during its brief tenure this African American social club also attracted white customers. I doubt that a zeal for racial tolerance and equality inspired their patronage—which testified more to ragtime's allure than to enlightened social attitudes prevalent in Sedalia. Thus, even at this early stage, we get a hint of the role that innovative black music could play, sometimes inadvertently, in furthering integration in the United States.[5]

The composition "Maple Leaf Rag" enjoyed a much longer—and greater—fame and influence than the club that spawned it. Joplin's publisher, John Stark, boasted that the sheet music sold a million copies. He may have exaggerated, but the "Maple Leaf Rag" was a huge success by any measure. Yet Stark himself had originally doubted the composition's commercial appeal. "It's too difficult," he allegedly responded at first hearing it. "Nobody will be able to play it." Even rudimentary piano rags present technical challenges, both in the fast leaping motions required of the left hand, which typically stays on the beat, and the complex syncopated patterns superimposed by the right hand. But Joplin's breakthrough piece was more difficult than your garden-variety ragtime workout, and many who purchased the sheet music must have failed miserably in their attempts to play it. Yankee ingenuity, however, came to the rescue. Demand for player pianos, a mechanical substitute for a flesh-and-blood performer that anticipated many of our current-day obsessions with robots taking over human jobs, was rising rapidly during the glory years of ragtime music. It's hard to imagine ragtime having the same cultural impact without this technological boost.[6]

Were the great African American composers of ragtime praised for their innovations? That did happen, but here again, legitimization only took place long after the fact—a recurring theme in these pages. Scott Joplin, who died in 1917, got a posthumous Pulitzer Prize in 1976. During his lifetime, ragtime music was a scandal. But that was what mainstream America wanted from black music: a taste of the forbidden. In 1900, the prominent music magazine *The Etude* denounced ragtime as a "virulent poison" and "malarious epidemic" damaging the "brains of the youth to such an extent as to arouse one's suspicions of their sanity." A host of other accusations were hurled at ragtime. Ragtime was just noise, claimed upholders of establishment values. Its very sound was monotonous and depressing. Its presence in respectable settings was a sacrilege. Trained musicians were losing jobs to untutored pretenders. And if you listened to ragtime long enough, you might even go insane. But the greatest fears aroused by musical upheavals of this sort are almost always sexual in nature. These concerns usually went unspoken, but a writer for the *Musical Courier* spelled them out for his readers: Ragtime, he declared, "is symbolic of the primitive morality and perceptible moral limitations of the negro type. With the latter, sexual restraint is almost unknown."[7]

These complaints didn't hurt the commercial prospects of ragtime music, and probably even gave them a boost in some circles.

But this offered little consolation to Scott Joplin. That Pulitzer looks good on his Wikipedia page, but Joplin wanted legitimization during his lifetime—and even more, he craved the chance to write music on a larger scale than the market for ragtime allowed. He was forward-looking by any measure. He even managed to negotiate a royalty agreement for "Maple Leaf Rag," and we can see from the surviving contract that he secured his own lawyer to defend his interests—an extraordinary move for a black musician of his generation. And immediately after the success of that work, Joplin started hatching even more ambitious plans. As early as 1899, he formed a troupe to perform a ragtime ballet with sung narration, and rented a local opera house to showcase his musical vision. Alas, the only surviving documentation of his vision is the piano sheet music for "The Ragtime Dance," published by Stark in 1902. Joplin's next project, the opera *A Guest of Honor* (1903), is entirely lost to us. But the scope of his ambition can be gauged by surviving news accounts. They tell us that Joplin composed music, wrote lyrics, hired and rehearsed a cast, and took his show on the road under the banner of "Scott Joplin's Ragtime Opera Company." Even that name is amazing in the context of America circa 1903. The tour collapsed when someone stole the box-office receipts, but it's hard to imagine Joplin getting very far in any case with this defiant assault on highbrow music pretensions.

True, black theater was going mainstream at this very moment. The year 1903 saw the successful Broadway debut of *In Dahomey: A Negro Musical Comedy*, written by an African American creative team consisting of Will Marion Cook, Paul Laurence Dunbar, and Jesse A. Shipp. That production marked a major breakthrough in the history of black music, paving the way for a host of later stage projects by other composers. But *In Dahomey*, with its obvious linkages to minstrel and vaudeville formulas, was hardly as ambitious as Joplin's attempt to reinvent the opera idiom as a vehicle for black pride and African American musical expression. The plot of *A Guest of Honor* revolves around black educator Booker T. Washington's 1901 visit to the White House to dine with President Theodore Roosevelt—an event widely denounced in the press during that era

331

of widespread segregation. You could hardly imagine two more different works of African American theater than *In Dahomey* and *A Guest of Honor*. This quixotic project represented Joplin's corrective to the demeaning tone of most black music constructed by white interlopers—an anti-minstrel show for the most progressive members of American society at the dawn of the twentieth century. I am hardly surprised that no copy of the musical score has survived.

Joplin was even willing to leave ragtime behind in order to improve his status as a composer. His boldest surviving project, the opera *Treemonisha*, only makes the most sparing use of rag phrasing. Instead, Joplin aimed at nothing less than establishing a black equivalent of the Wagnerian tradition, with African American history and folklore substituting for Teutonic mythology. At this stage in music history, operas about women were usually expected to focus on their sexuality and sinfulness, but Joplin's *Treemonisha* defied these expectations. The title character is a proud black woman who champions education while battling superstition and ignorance. Did our composer really believe America was ready for this? Should we lament Joplin's naïveté, or applaud his single-minded determination? In any event, the end result was all too predictable. Despite the years he devoted to this project, Joplin failed to find the backing necessary to mount a professional production. In his final days, his other grand plans also came to naught—including work on a rumored (but almost certainly lost) piano concerto and symphony. At his death in 1917, he was remembered, if at all, as the exponent of a lowbrow style of piano music suitable for honky-tonks and bordellos.

The almost insurmountable obstacles Scott Joplin faced in his attempts at legitimization should make clear that the opponents of musical innovation have been just as stodgy and unforgiving in fast-moving modern times as they were in ancient and medieval societies. When we seek something new and exciting in music, we inevitably turn to those taboo-violating outsiders with their dangerous, illicit wares; we don't want this music legitimized, not at this stage, and will even denounce as sell-outs any musical rebel's attempt to enter the mainstream. Of course, this all changes with time. We will eventually allow these rebels into Carnegie Hall—where, by the way, the complete piano works of Scott Joplin were performed for the first time in 2017 to commemorate the one hundredth anniversary of his death—but only after a sufficient *cooling-off period* has elapsed. By that late stage, we have moved on to new subversive sounds, and can let the old ones age into respectable classics.

22

Rebellion Goes Mainstream

Of course, it's pure coincidence that the first jazz record was released just a few days before Scott Joplin's death in 1917. The same is true of Ethel Waters's decision, that same year, to include W. C. Handy's "St. Louis Blues" in her performances—she may have been the first black woman to feature this now iconic song, but soon many others would follow her lead. The real instigator of this shift in America's musical tastes might actually have been World War I, another milestone moment in the long history of mass violence exerting a second-order impact on songs. Even as America left behind its isolationist ethos to intrude into geopolitical conflicts, it became more inward-looking in its music. A movement to purge American concert halls of German composers and performers and replace them with homegrown talent, as a kind of snub to the nation's military adversary, was the most visible manifestation of this shift. But even more momentous indicators of the growing Americanization of American music would soon be evident elsewhere, outside the realm of concert halls and orchestra programs. Popular entertainment was changing rapidly at this historic juncture, and with virtually no deference to Old World role models.

Major wars always disrupt traditional customs and familiar patterns of living, especially when they transpire over a period of years and involve exposing thousands—or in some cases, millions—of soldiers to different cultures far away from home. Someday a shrewd multidisciplinary scholar will probe more deeply into the history of these bloodshed-driven modifications in musical practices. But even a cursory glance brings out the ongoing linkage between the violence of war and the sublimity of song in Western culture, starting with Homer singing about the rage and brutality of the Trojan War, recurring when the Crusaders brought back 'exotic' instruments from their travels, and then again with the complex musical after-effects of the French Revolution, and in modern times with the intimate connections between rock music and the Vietnam War and beyond. If it isn't the combatants returning from the battlefield to rewrite music history, it's the refugees, protesters, or family members taking on that responsibility. In any event, the American soldiers coming back from the Great War, as it was known back then, discovered completely different songs awaiting them on their homecoming. (And the influence went both ways: black soldiers left their mark on European music, especially through the intervention of the aptly named James Reese Europe, an African American bandleader whose ensemble of "Harlem Hellfighters," drawn from a military unit known both for its fighting prowess and jazz-oriented instrumentalists, performed widely in France, changing continental culture before returning home to the United States in 1919.)

The ways music went viral were also shifting during this period. The most powerful change came with the growing influence of the phonograph record—and we will talk more about that soon—but even live performance venues were altering how music was disseminated and consumed. The minstrel show now proved far less popular than vaudeville, a format of theatrical production featuring an endless variety of touring acts, each given from ten to twenty minutes to display their talents. And what an odd assortment of talents: vaudeville theater might present magicians, musicians, ventriloquists, acrobats, comedians, pet tricks, jugglers, dancers, and practitioners of various stunts, impersonations, and other routines. In virtually every significant population center in the United States, audiences could sit down and over the course of a few hours see the full range of American talent, from crude to highbrow, paraded before their eyes. Separate vaudeville theaters served black audiences in major cities, elevating the careers of many African American entertainers who, in earlier decades, would have lacked any platform for touring. More than at any previous point in history, audiences in different communities were listening to the same songs, and even the same performers. This star-driven entertainment business was creating a mass market, and vice versa.

Yet at the very moment when vaudeville was evolving into a coast-to-coast network for mass entertainment, the next revolution in song—perhaps the greatest in modern times—was getting its start in almost complete isolation from the music business. In time, vaudeville impresarios, record labels, and radio stations would discover the blues, and would accelerate its dissemination into the broader culture. But the earliest manifestations of this brazenly transgressive idiom first appeared outside the notice of the power brokers in American entertainment. In fact, if you drew a scatterplot of the birthplaces of important blues musicians from the early twentieth century, the resulting pattern would show a surprising avoidance of the major centers of corporate culture. This music, in its first blossoming, seems correlated with black poverty, and especially black rural poverty.

The rise of the blues may offer the most powerful test case we could devise for assessing a key thesis of this book, namely, the assertion that musical innovation comes from the underclass. This hypothesis, if it could be proven, would show how different music is from other art forms. Innovation in painting and sculpture, for example, has almost always happened in close proximity to rich patrons—even today, a couple hundred affluent collectors set the tone for the visual arts economy. The rise of the novel drew momentum from the wealth-creating enterprises of the Industrial Revolution. The new artistic mediums of today—video games, virtual reality, and probably whatever is coming next—appear inextricably connected to profit-generating businesses in Silicon Valley. Only music plays by different rules, almost defiantly so.

Let's ask ourselves this question: Which locale in the United States was the most isolated and impoverished and least well equipped to launch a cultural revolution in the early decades of the twentieth century? The answer would have to be the state of Mississippi. It suffered from widespread poverty and enjoyed the lowest per capita income of any state. As new technologies came on the market, Mississippi was the last to enjoy their benefits. During the glory days of the Mississippi Delta blues, it had the lowest penetration of automobiles, telephones, and radios of all the states. Even electricity was in short supply in Mississippi: as late as 1937, when Mississippi blues legend Robert Johnson made his final recordings, only 1 percent of the farms in that state had access to it.

We should stop and ponder how these oppressive circumstances spawned the most transformative radicals in American music, again and again, during the whole half-century period from the dawn of the twentieth century to the rise of (Mississippi born and bred) Elvis Presley and rock 'n' roll. This center of 'backwardness' also spawned Muddy Waters, Howlin' Wolf, Sam Cooke, Charley Patton, Son House, B. B. King, Albert King, John Lee Hooker, Skip James, Elmore James, Bukka White, Bo Diddley, and a host of others, who set in motion repeated revolutions in song. In aggregate, these innovators would not only establish the significance of Mississippi blues, but also provide the key ingredients that led to the rise of Chicago blues, R&B, rock 'n' roll, and other mainstream styles.

Of course, Mississippi had some help in this regard. You can't prove with any certainty that blues music was invented in Mississippi—in fact, I'm not sure the term *invented* is at all relevant to a style that seems to bear such strong signs of an ancient lineage going back to Africa. But the other centers of early blues, from Texas to Appalachia, reveal similar demographic patterns of poverty and isolation. In fact, the early history of this music is so hard to trace because of this very fact. The first stirrings of the blues took place in areas with no recording devices and comparatively low rates of literacy. Occasionally a researcher would show up on the scene and note the innovative music at hand—as did Charles Peabody, a Harvard scholar, who was mesmerized by the black music he heard during an archaeological dig in the Mississippi Delta in 1901, or Howard Odum, a sociologist, who collected songs in the region between 1905 and 1908. In many instances, early researchers did not even use the word "blues" to describe what they heard. That in itself is a measure of how outside the mainstream this music was at the time. Can you imagine a music genre that doesn't even have a name? How isolated must you be from commercial markets and the formulas of the entertainment industry to exist in that degree of purity?

Howard Odum and his colleague Guy Johnson preferred to describe these melodies as "workaday sorrow songs," writing in 1926 that they had been documented "decades ago from camp and road in Mississippi before the technique of the modern blues had ever been evolved." Peabody, for his part, made no attempt to define the songs he heard under a label or genre category, but mentioned all the key ingredients that would eventually become codified as blues music. He described the bending of notes, and pointed out that it was intentional and not the result of poor singing ability. He identified the reliance on three chords. He noted the fixation on themes of hard luck, love, and violence. In perhaps the most eerie anticipation of the future, Peabody recounted the details of an especially haunting performance he heard from a "very old negro employed on the plantation of Mr. John Stovall of Stovall, Mississippi." But he struggled to convey its essence in words. After trying and abandoning various comparisons—the music was weird, Japanese, monotonous, resembled a bagpipe or a Jew's harp, and the like—he left us with this simple summation: "I have not heard that kind again nor of it." Consider the fact that Muddy Waters, the pioneer of Chicago blues and proto–rock 'n' roll, was discovered residing on that *same* Stovall Plantation by a Library of Congress emissary, Alan Lomax, forty years after Peabody's visit, and then try to guess the age and musical education of the "very old negro" who performed the blues for Peabody at the dawn of the century. It's hard not to conclude that the roots of this music date back to a time long before the music industry decided to give it a label and support it with a marketing campaign.[1]

In fact, it's hard to imagine how the blues ever got the backing of the American music industry during the first half of the twentieth century. Muddy Waters is an appropriate name for a purveyor of such *dirty* music. That's truth-in-advertising for you. The explicit references to sex and violence in blues lyrics went far beyond anything the mainstream music business had previously permitted. Only the fact that the early recordings were targeted at the African American market—and assigned the commercial label of *race records*, a category within which previous notions of obscenity apparently no longer applied—explains the leeway given performers to shock and alarm. In some instances, the sexual references were hidden behind crude symbolism. But was there really any listener who didn't know what blues musician Bo Carter was singing about in his songs "Please Warm My Weiner" or "Banana in Your Fruit Basket"? Did Bessie Smith fool anyone with "Need a Little Sugar in My Bowl"?

The record labels went along with the charade. When Blind Lemon Jefferson released his "That Black Snake Moan," Paramount promoted it with an ad campaign featuring "black snakes— weird, slimy, creepy" (according to the marketing copy). But music fans were advised: "You'll never stop playing this one when you hear that moan." For the follow-up, "Black Snake Moan No. 2," Paramount decided that the innuendo hadn't been clear enough, and now featured an illustration of an aroused sleeper, still in bed, confronting a huge black snake rising from between his legs, whose head is in a markedly erect posture. Sometimes even this slight degree of pretense was thrown aside, as when Jane Lucas declared on a 1930 recording: "You can play with my pussy, but don't dog it around; if you're going to mistreat it, no pussy will be found." Yet blues in live performance was even more explicit. "You could sing anything at them Saturday night balls," declared blues icon Son House. "I don't care how dirty you made it; they liked to hear it."[2]

Descriptions of violence in early blues lyrics were just as extreme. Songs about guns were surprisingly common, and these adopted the style of praise odes, a lineage that stretches from ancient bards and Pindar all the way to contemporary hip-hoppers extolling their Gucci and Nike accessories. Robert Johnson praised the superiority of his .32-20 Winchester over his lover's .38 special, and promised it would cut his no-good woman in half. Johnson was obviously inspired by Skip James, who had made a similar claim for his .22-20, which he planned to use whenever his gal got unruly. Women were often victims in these songs, but some could play this game even better than the men. Ma Rainey bragged about her expertise with a Gatling gun, a deadly forerunner of today's automatic weapons, and clearly superior to anything Johnson or James would bring to a fight. And these were more than just threats. In her song "Broken Hearted Blues," Rainey confesses in court to a mass murder—not just her no-good lover, but everyone else in the vicinity was taken down in her killing spree. The amount of gun lore, both true and imagined, in these songs is striking, but blues singers didn't just sing about firearms. Mary Butler, according to her lyrics, kept a razor in her bosom, and planned to cut up her man before finishing him off with a pistol. Georgia Tom (the blues name of gospel music pioneer Thomas Dorsey) preferred to cut his woman's head off with a butcher knife. Victoria Spivey opted for a dose of poison in her lover's drink. And there's a whole subgenre of blues songs about drinking gasoline.

These tunes may well have posed a threat to public morals, yet even the musical ingredients, the very notes of the blues, were an outrage. And for the simple reason that they refused to be notes. After more than two thousand years of the Pythagorean paradigm, blues declared that music no longer needed to remain subservient to mathematics. Indeed, the musicology of the blues was a scandal in the face of everything that had been done to codify and schematize Western music. Its melodies refused to fit into the accepted system of music notation, the acknowledged framework for composition since the time of Guido of Arezzo. The musical pitches of the blues, its most basic building blocks, similarly resisted all conventional notions of playing in tune—even back in 1903, Peabody had advised his readers that Mississippi musicians weren't ignorant of how to sing in tune, but simply *refused* to do so—and returned song to its origins in unconstrained sound.

We also need to take note of the curious fact that the classical music world was rebelling against Pythagorean constraints at the very same moment that the blues emerged, reassessing the boundaries between tuned notes and noise that had prevailed for centuries—and doing so in ways that reflected a clear grasp of the role African American artists were playing in this project. Music for the 1917 ballet *Parade,* composed by Erik Satie, with a scenario (and input on sound effects) from Jean Cocteau, as well as costumes and sets by Pablo Picasso, featured noise-making implements that included a typewriter, foghorn, pistol, and clanking milk bottles alongside musical bits and pieces evocative of ragtime. The African element was even more explicit in George Antheil's *Ballet Mécanique,* performed with siren and propellers. Antheil explained that the work was designed to "express America, Africa and Steel." This composer was certainly aware of the blues—Antheil even hired W. C. Handy's orchestra to perform his *Jazz Symphony*—and frequently described his endeavors in the context of black culture. At this critical juncture in modern music, even the most progressive members of the European classical music world saw the enterprise of moving outside tuned notes into the realm of 'noise' as a project led by African American performers.[3]

The same rule-breaking extended to the larger structures of musical form. Despite what is usually taught about the twelve-bar blues, the early practitioners didn't follow a twelve-bar pattern. In many instances, they didn't follow *any* set pattern: sometimes a blues chorus might last eleven bars or thirteen, or even include partial bars, stray beats that didn't adhere to any organized metric. Even more outrageous, the same song, when repeated by the same performer, might make different deviations the next time around. The very blues harmonies that defined the idiom, those proverbial three chords of the blues song, were equally resistant to codification. They didn't look anything like their textbook voicings as presented in the current day. They were unruly textures of sound that often bore only a loose resemblance to I, IV, and V chords. This would all change over time—Western music eventually forced blues into a standardized form. But that tells you less about the blues and more about the relentless mainstreaming forces that try to rein in all musical innovations. In their earliest manifestations, blues songs were nothing less than an affront to the very heart and soul of Western music.

That's why I have to laugh at the recurring attempts to clean up the history of the blues. In recent years, revisionists have worked tirelessly to construct alternative lineages for this music, struggling to trace its origins to vaudeville shows, or imagining a fanciful alternative universe in which blues pioneers learned how to play by listening to records and the radio. The very origins of the blues in the most isolated and impoverished communities in America should make clear how little this music relied on record-industry conventions.

Yet, in a way, these peculiar attempts to clean up the blues are inevitable, because that's what always happens with subversive styles of music—both with the songs and their history. And in the case of the blues, the purified songs were the first to gain widespread visibility in mainstream America. W. C. Handy heard an unknown blues singer playing the guitar with a knife at a train station in Mississippi, and this moment of inspiration eventually led to the "St. Louis Blues." That Handy song, which squeezed out most of the irregularities of the blues and made it suitable for mass consumption, became one of the biggest hits of the twentieth century, but its raw antecedent at the Tutwiler train station never got the chance to go viral. The great classic blues singers of the 1920s—Bessie Smith, Ma Rainey, Mamie Smith, and others—drew on a whole posse of helpers to turn blues into a commercial property. They worked with professional songwriters, highly skilled accompanists, costume and set designers, record producers, impresarios, and others in crafting a blues sound that played by rules and formulas unknown in the Mississippi Delta or rural Texas. These performers were great artists in their own right, and innovators as well, but their work has to be viewed in light of the tremendous forces of acculturation already incorporated into the blues by this stage in its history. Commercial businesses may not have invented the blues, but they certainly knew how to package it.

In the introduction to this book, I listed the ingredients of songs that are most embarrassing to the dominant musical establishment, and thus are always the target of 'sanitation' efforts. This list includes explicit sexual references, celebrations of violence, allusions to altered mind states (whether produced by intoxicants or shamanistic-type visions), magic and superstition, and other indecorous matters. The blues posed a particular threat because it embodied *all* of these things. The elements of superstition have been especially painful for modern commentators, who have worked assiduously to remove them, or—when removal is impossible, because they are too deeply embedded into the songs—to find alternative explanations. That's a tall order, because these elements show up almost everywhere in the blues tradition. In fact, the most famous story in the entire history of the blues tells of Robert Johnson selling his soul to the devil during a midnight meeting at a crossroads in exchange for his legendary mastery of the guitar. Similar stories are recounted of other, lesser-known blues musicians, such as Tommy Johnson and Peetie Wheatstraw (whose nickname was the "Devil's Son-in-Law"). The past two decades have witnessed a movement to demythologize the blues, especially the legends surrounding Robert Johnson, and these stories about the devil are especially embarrassing to those involved in this process of mainstreaming and legitimization.[4]

A popular response is to blame blues fans for this embarrassment. According to revisionists Barry Lee Pearson and Bill McCulloch, a 1966 article by a blues enthusiast, Pete Welding, "formally launched the notion that Johnson was a twentieth-century incarnation of the legendary Faust, a sixteenth-century astrologer who supposedly sold his soul to the devil to gain knowledge and magical power and who thus incurred God's anger." Under this hypothesis, a whole generation of foolish fans bought into this notion, which was "more than a little dubious," but got embellished and turned into a staple of blues mythology.[5]

Could this account be true? Did the story of Robert Johnson selling his soul to the devil really emerge only in the 1960s, long after his death? This sanitizing theory collapses when put under the microscope. The late blues scholar Mack McCormick told me that he personally had heard stories of Johnson selling his soul back in the 1940s, and had found them both among record collectors and in the black communities where he conducted field research. In the Library of Congress, I discovered a previously unpublished transcript of an interview with Robert Johnson's friend and associate David "Honeyboy" Edwards that dates back to the early 1940s. Here he tells interviewer Alan Lomax that Johnson had lost his soul because he was involved in the "Devil's business." But even the reference in the 1966 article isn't Pete Welding's invention, but a direct quote from Son House, Robert Johnson's real-life mentor. Of course, Johnson's music itself explicitly references the devil and hell—these ingredients can't be missed in songs such as "Hellhound on My Trail" or "Me and the Devil Blues." Even apart from these allusions, what we know of Johnson's life makes it plausible, perhaps even likely, that he believed his choice of music and lifestyle put his soul at risk. At a minimum, he knew that the image of devil-haunted musician made for a good marketing story (just as many metal bands discovered a few decades later).[6]

None of this should be surprising to a student of southern black culture of the early twentieth century or of the African belief systems that influenced it. During the same years that Robert Johnson played the blues, Harry Middleton Hyatt, an Anglican minister and folklorist, conducted extensive research into prevailing notions about magical spells, folk medicine, witchcraft, and conjuring in Alabama, Arkansas, Florida, Georgia, Illinois, Louisiana, Maryland, Mississippi, North Carolina, South Carolina, Tennessee, and Virginia. He interviewed 1,600 people in the South and compiled 13,458 spells and superstitions—all published in a five-volume study that spanned 4,766 pages. Here we find the actual roots of the culture and belief systems that spawned the Robert Johnson legend, which has nothing to do with the ideas of 1960s music fans, but arose directly from the attitudes and metaphysical systems prevalent in the Mississippi Delta at the time when blues musicians started making records. Misguided attempts to remove these belief systems from the life stories of blues musicians constitute nothing less than a rewriting of history. Purified blues is falsified blues.[7]

But Robert Johnson also contributed, in no small part, to the process of legitimization. In fact, this is a key part of his legacy. Johnson played a leading role in reconciling the inherent African elements of the blues with the Pythagorean, mathematical paradigm of the dominant Western music culture. He codified the techniques he mastered and reined in the more unruly elements of the blues, imposing a crystal clear harmonic sensibility and a sharply delineated vocabulary—figures, passing chords, boogie patterns, grooves—onto the prickly Delta idiom. Each song he performed came across as holistically conceived and aesthetically rounded. His music wasn't as raw as the blues of, say, Son House, Blind Lemon Jefferson, Charley Patton, and many of his other predecessors. Johnson's oeuvre, in contrast, embodied a system—and, as such, was more suitable for transcribing, studying, and emulating. I would almost be tempted to call it a science of the blues, if that term didn't imply coldness and dispassion. No one could accuse Johnson of artistic aloofness. But he brought a clarity of conception and precision of execution that transformed a quasi-folk practice into a new kind of Western art song.

For all his greatness, Robert Johnson isn't my favorite blues artist. I am more drawn to the shamanistic excesses of Son House or the dark moodiness of Skip James. But I understand full well why later generations of guitarists—even superstars, such as Eric Clapton, Bob Dylan, and the Rolling Stones—idolized Johnson above all others. He somehow managed to reconcile the demands of the music business with the signifying irascibility of African performance practices. He wasn't alone in this mission. We also must give credit to W. C. Handy, Bessie Smith, Buddy Bolden, Muddy Waters, Howlin' Wolf, B. B. King, and a host of others. But Johnson is the most exemplary member of this elite group, offering the most striking example of a musician at a crossroads—and I'm not talking about a meeting place with the devil. He had one foot in folkloric practice and the other in commercial entertainment, and his fluidity in forcing them together into inspired three-minute songs has never been surpassed. It's hard to imagine the next half century of popular music unfolding in quite the same way without his intervention.

23

Funky Butt

I f you persist in believing that musical tastes are shaped by
elites, you might consider it a mere fluke that a regional song
style from the most marginalized population in American
society somehow managed to change the course of global entertainment. But jazz did the exact same thing, and managed this
world-conquering triumph during almost the same time period as
the blues, at almost the same pace. Here again, scorned outsiders
set the tempo for mainstream culture with music too hot to handle,
at least at first. Powerful institutions, from Harvard to the Pulitzer Prize, eventually embraced it—but only after another lengthy
cooling-off period.

The two idioms may often borrow from each other, but jazz
and blues are essentially different in their inner dynamic. Jazz is
an urban music that came out of the hustle and bustle of the most
multicultural city in the Western world at the dawn of the twentieth
century, New Orleans. The jazz idiom thrives in melting-pot situations, because it is outwardly focused and hungry for new sources
of inspiration. The blues, in contrast, first emerged in the most
isolated rural areas, and its aesthetic beauty has more to do with

traditions and legacies preserved from the past. You can still hear the griots of Africa, those community storytellers and preservers of cultural lore, in the blues. These influences also reverberate in jazz, but with more of an Afrofuturist vibe, a greater receptiveness to the possibilities of synthesis and metamorphosis.

From its earliest days, jazz demonstrated a remarkable ability to devour and digest other performance styles, a trait that would distinguish it from all other folk arts. Jazz assimilated the syncopations of ragtime with such success that many listeners believed, at least at first, that the two styles were identical. Yet unlike the ragtime music of Scott Joplin, the rag-influenced jazz of New Orleans placed great emphasis on improvisation, on spur-of-the-moment alterations in the composition. Jazz artists were eventually evaluated on their skill in making these spontaneous changes, and though they would play the melody, they just as often *played around* with the melody, or abandoned it completely, in the free play of personal expression.

Jazz musicians also mastered the bent notes and twelve-bar structures of the blues. This may seem an obvious move until you realize that New Orleans jazz players somehow learned about the blues decades before their peers in New York and other major cities. Jelly Roll Morton claimed he heard blues in the Garden District of New Orleans while still a child, probably not long after the year 1900. And Buddy Bolden, often credited as the first jazz bandleader, may have been performing blues even before the turn of the century. Most music historians take this for granted, yet we ought to consider the anomaly of New Orleans embracing blues at a time when other urban musicians were blissfully unaware or openly scornful of this humble rural idiom.

Yet Bolden was just as willing to draw inspiration from religious music, which he heard while attending services at the Baptist church on Jackson and Franklin. "I know that he used to go to that church, but not for religion," later explained Kid Ory, a trombonist who met Bolden around the year 1900. "He went there to get ideas on music. He'd hear these songs and would change them a little." Ory also specified that trombones, trumpets, and even drums would sometimes join in with singers at church services—suggesting that influences between jazz and religious music went both ways. The first generation of jazz musicians, omnivorous in their tastes, mixed these ingredients with songs and styles they heard at dances, brass band parades, funerals, and picnics and other social events. In fact, many of them learned their trade in such settings. Yet they also drew from idioms rarely considered as part of the jazz tradition, whether songs performed in the New Orleans opera houses or the music of visiting ensembles from Latin America. From the start, the jazz idiom was built on transgressing musical boundaries.[1]

And other boundaries as well. The oldest original jazz song known to us is a nasty piece of work called "Funky Butt." This song was Buddy Bolden's trademark, but it could change each time it was played. Sometimes the words were lighthearted, at other times obscene. Depending on the circumstances, it might serve as comedy or insult or even political commentary. The authorities did not look kindly on such improvisations. "The police put you in jail if they heard you singing that song," explained New Orleans clarinetist Sidney Bechet. He recalled hearing Bolden play it in person at one event: "Bolden started his theme song, people started singing, policemen began whipping heads." Here again we find that a respected musical idiom of the current day originated on the fringes, infuriating power brokers with its audacity and even inciting violence. The next time you hear jazz in a concert hall, recall that its documented history began with an illegal and riot-provoking song.[2]

Jazz musicians took pride in their boldness, but already at this early stage they also wanted to entertain their audiences. So much respectability has been piled upon this music over the decades that we can easily lose sight of how jazz conquered the world through sheer joy and delight. Buddy Bolden never made records (or if he did, they haven't survived), but firsthand accounts testify to his skill as a showman and a crowd-pleaser. In this regard, he set a pattern for the jazz stars who came after him.

By all rights, Louis Armstrong ought to be best remembered for his extraordinary recordings of the late 1920s and early 1930s, when he established a new gold standard for jazz on tracks such as "West End Blues," "Potato Head Blues," and "Heebie Jeebies," among others. Armstrong constructed a whole new music vocabulary, inventing countless original phrases that musicians still imitate almost a century later, and turned the jazz genre into a true soloist's idiom. Yet for the general public, Armstrong's enormous fame had little to do with trumpet hijinks, and drew instead on his consummate skills as an entertainer and his charismatic personality—assets that ensured his crossover success in radio, movies, and (eventually) television. Some serious jazz fans perhaps dismiss Armstrong's hit recordings "Hello Dolly!" and "What a Wonderful World" as commercial fluff, musical antics that don't do justice to his artistry. Yet they miss the point: jazz from its inception wasn't a respectable highbrow affair for knowledgeable insiders. It had more in common with an ecstatic religion that aimed to proselytize, a ritual that converted nonbelievers through rapture and enchantment. Armstrong's heroics could never have changed the music world if he hadn't delivered his personal beatitudes and exaltations to the masses in an environment of participative euphoria.

The same pattern recurs repeatedly in the evolution of jazz. Consider the case of Duke Ellington, the only innovator of the early decades of the idiom who could rival Armstrong's impact and influence. Ellington is now considered an elite American composer, and his name is often mentioned alongside the paragons of the concert hall. He deserves this acclaim, and his greatest works invite comparisons with his contemporaries, such as Igor Stravinsky, Aaron Copland, Dmitri Shostakovich, and Béla Bartók. I especially admire Ellington's recordings from the late 1930s and early 1940s, which achieve a radiant balancing of form and content unsurpassed by other jazz composers. But here's the most remarkable aspect of this period in his music: Ellington was also a celebrity entertainer during this same era, and one of the biggest-selling popular music stars in the world. We cannot give full credit to his mastery without factoring in this crowd-pleasing mass-market angle.

The same is true of the hottest bandleader of the late 1930s, Benny Goodman, a clarinetist who commissioned classical works from Copland and Bartók, yet also led the most popular dance orchestra of the period. Or consider the case of jazz star Woody Herman, whose band performed the debut of Stravinsky's *Ebony Concerto* at Carnegie Hall in March 1946, but a few months later served up lighthearted dance music in the Hollywood film *New Orleans*. Of course, not every jazz performer of that era collaborated with a famous European composer. Count Basie, Billie Holiday, Ella Fitzgerald, Glenn Miller, Artie Shaw, and other hit-parade bandleaders of the World War II years had different agendas that didn't require the participation of a Hindemith or a Schoenberg, but they never wavered in their determination to maintain a high level of artistry while also pleasing audiences and selling records.

Yet we also must marvel at how much social protest, disruption, and irreverence got embedded into these entertaining songs. Benny Goodman used his preeminence as a pop culture hero to promote desegregation a full generation before Congress passed the Civil Rights Act. In 1935, his commercial success ushered in the Swing Era, setting off a stirring decade during which hot big-band jazz stayed at the forefront of popular music in America. The very next year, Goodman hired African American pianist Teddy Wilson for his trio—more than a decade before Jackie Robinson joined the Brooklyn Dodgers, breaking down the color line in professional sports. Clarinetist Artie Shaw, Goodman's biggest rival, hired vocalist Billie Holiday in 1938, and other jazz bandleaders, unwilling to be left behind as the jazz world embraced this new attitude of tolerance, followed suit with their own anti-segregation efforts.

In the context of American society, these were earthshaking moves. Popular music was the first important sphere in American society to desegregate, and superstar jazz musicians led the way. And they continued to play a key role in the desegregation battles at every step during the years ahead. In 1957, Louis Armstrong made headline news with his criticism of President Dwight D. Eisenhower's refusal to enforce school integration in Little Rock, Arkansas. The trumpeter's words stung all the more because of his reputation as a happy-go-lucky entertainer who didn't get involved in politics. Armstrong now faced an intense backlash—some critics even burned his records and called for a boycott of his concerts. But a week after Armstrong's explosive interview, Eisenhower changed his policy and ordered the National Guard to intervene in Little Rock. We can't, of course, assign Ike's change of heart to the off-hand comments of a jazz star, but the *Chicago Defender* wasn't far off when it claimed that Armstrong's words "had both the timing and the explosive effect of an H-bomb. They reverberated around the world."[3]

All world-changing music styles, no matter how far outside the mainstream their origins, eventually achieve legitimization and respect. In most instances, this shift is not announced in newspaper headlines, but takes place gradually in the attitudes of audiences and the policies of institutions. In the case of jazz, the music itself both anticipated and accelerated the shift. Even before the general public embraced jazz as a kind of art music, the musicians nurtured grand ambitions. An experimental, almost avant-garde sensibility emerged in the jazz world at an early stage, and never left it—you can still hear it in the genre today—despite an ecosystem that turned musicians into workaday commercial entertainers. We see this in the bifurcated career of cornetist Bix Beiderbecke (1903–1931), who could delight dancers with his sweet-toned solos, but also compose piano music in a prickly, neo-modernist style. We encounter a similar paradox in the saxophone work of Coleman Hawkins (1904–1969), who could achieve a jukebox hit with "Body and Soul," yet simultaneously push ahead the harmonic frontiers of the jazz idiom. Or consider the case of Art Tatum (1909–1956), whose musical roots lay in ragtime, blues, boogie, Harlem stride piano, and Tin Pan Alley tunes—but his improvisations were so virtuosic and extravagant that they invited comparisons with the iconic masters of classical keyboard music.

Two figures stand out in this history of jazz straddling popular entertainment and art song ambitions: Duke Ellington and George Gershwin. If Benny Goodman sought legitimization by hiring Aaron Copland—"I paid two thousand dollars and that's real money," the clarinetist later boasted—Ellington and Gershwin aimed to prove they were on the same level as the 'serious' composers of their day.

352

Ellington, perhaps more than any other figure from the early days of jazz, anticipated with almost telepathic clarity the eventual destiny of this new style of popular music. He understood that jazz would gain widespread acceptance as art music, and wouldn't have to give up its commitment to swing and spontaneity as part of the bargain. In fact, the peculiar path of jazz to respectability required it to maintain its own core values, holding onto the blues, syncopation, hot solos, and all the other calling cards of its craft.[4]

Yet Ellington was perhaps cursed for seeing this destiny before the rest of society. When he introduced his most ambitious extended work, the almost one-hour-long kaleidoscopic tone poem *Black, Brown and Beige*, at Carnegie Hall in 1943, he was rewarded with sharp-tongued, unsympathetic responses from both inside and outside the jazz community. John Hammond, an influential advocate of black music, attacked Ellington in print for abandoning jazz, and composer Paul Bowles chimed in with a diatribe that dismissed not only *Black, Brown and Beige*, but *all* attempts to transform jazz into art music. A host of other critics called out the work as confused, fulsome, self-conscious, even corny. Of course, the consensus view today is that *Black, Brown and Beige* is a masterpiece of American music. But at the time, these criticisms stung. Ellington, for his part, stopped performing the work in its entirety, and never again attempted an extended piece on this scale. We are fortunate that this setback did not place a heavy burden on his confidence or genius—Ellington hardly needed an hour-long time slot to perform a masterpiece, and was perfectly capable, or perhaps even uniquely qualified, to turn out extraordinary works of three or four minutes' duration. Yet we can't help wondering at the strange process of musical legitimization that honors these visionaries as true artists, but only decades after the fact—first punishing their attempts to rise above the status of mere entertainers. Scott Joplin, Duke Ellington, and other preeminent black composers could see the eventual endpoint, and worked to accelerate the process, but society doesn't allow any shortcuts for outsiders, whose rebirth as insiders almost always takes place over a period of decades, and sometimes long after they are dead.

George Gershwin presents an even stranger contradiction. He gained fame in his own abbreviated lifetime as a musical prestidigitator who fused jazz and classical idioms, yet he had a background in neither field. This son of Russian Jewish immigrants, born in 1898, dropped out of school at age fifteen to pursue a career in Tin Pan Alley, the name given to New York's commercial song publishing industry, then centered on West Twenty-Eighth Street in Manhattan. Gershwin wrote his first hit in 1919, "Swanee," a late-vintage minstrel tune that would become a trademark number for singer Al Jolson, and went on to compose around thirty Broadway shows and produce dozens of songs now considered classics of American popular music, often in collaboration with his lyricist brother Ira. Tin Pan Alley was already under the spell of black music during this era, even if the songwriters themselves were usually white. Hit songs such as Irving Berlin's "Alexander's Ragtime Band" (1911), Jerome Kern's "Ol' Man River" (1927), and Hoagy Carmichael's "Star Dust" (1927), for example, drew on rag, spirituals, and jazz, respectively, for inspiration. But they were targeted at the mainstream American audience, which demanded catchy melodies, danceable rhythms, and memorable words. Gershwin's skill in this musical marketplace was unsurpassed; he could easily have spent his entire career as a tunesmith, creating pop songs for the widest general public.

But an unusual commission from a bandleader—Paul Whiteman, who wanted to showcase an impressive work mixing jazz and classical influences at a February 1924 concert at New York's Aeolian Hall—changed all this. The tremendous success eventually enjoyed by *Rhapsody in Blue*, the work Gershwin produced for this event, would transform our Tin Pan Alley songwriter into the hottest young classical composer in America. Gershwin seized on this opportunity to reinvent himself, pushing ahead with his follow-up orchestral showpieces *An American in Paris* and *Concerto in F*, and eventually staging the folk opera *Porgy and Bess* before his death in 1937. Yet the huge success of these works should not blind us to the fact that few other composers of the day had much commercial success following Gershwin's crossover path. The symphony orchestras of the United States may have made an exception for George Gershwin, but they were hardly ready for symphonic jazz as a regular part of their mission. You might think that the canonization of Gershwin's jazzy classical works would have opened the door for an entire generation of black jazz musicians to establish themselves as orchestral composers, but nothing of that sort took place. This is no knock against Gershwin, whose works deserve acclaim and enshrinement in the standard repertoire. But we ought to recognize the larger incongruity of the Jazz Age, the name now assigned to the era that produced *Rhapsody in Blue*. The emblematic figures of that period in the minds of the general public (F. Scott Fitzgerald, Paul Whiteman, George Gershwin) were often those who served as conduits for the jazz spirit to enter the mainstream, rather than actual jazz musicians themselves—the latter were still excluded from the highest rungs of fashionable society. This tense and unstable situation, underpinned by many socioeconomic fault lines, testified both to the power of early jazz, which the mass audience clearly craved, and to its outlaw status. And this outlaw status was more than just image: when the young and dissolute went to places where illegal activities took place (drinking during the Prohibition era, gambling, prostitution), they expected to hear real jazz, not *Rhapsody in Blue*.

Music historians should probe more deeply into Ellington's apparent rivalry with Gershwin, a subject rarely addressed in scholarship on these figures. After the premiere of *Porgy and Bess*, Ellington offered up testy words to a journalist, asserting that Gershwin had pilfered key elements of his music from a hodgepodge of sources ("he borrowed from everyone from Liszt to Dickie Wells' kazoo band"), and suggesting that his own ambitions were constrained by the demands of earning a living and pleasing audiences. After these comments appeared in print, Ellington disavowed them, but it's an open question whether they misrepresented his views or just weren't meant for public airing. Ellington occasionally recorded and performed Gershwin songs in subsequent years, although not very often, and quite likely without much enthusiasm. After Gershwin's death, Ellington would make polite comments and observations about his rival, but politeness was always the Duke's way of deflecting issues he preferred not to discuss in public. More revealing is clarinetist Barney Bigard's claim that Ellington refused Gershwin's proposal to collaborate on songs. As that anecdote suggests, the rivalry probably only went one way. By all indications, Gershwin had great reverence for Ellington, and learned from the bandleader's example. And in all likelihood, this merely inflamed Ellington's irritation, as the above comment about Gershwin's borrowings implies. At the time of his death, Ellington was working on a quasi-operatic stage musical titled *Queenie Pie*—a project he had first conceived almost forty years earlier, back in the 1930s, and was now crafting as his final opus. I don't think it's going too far to say he was still stewing over *Porgy and Bess*, perhaps nurturing a grudge over Gershwin having staged an African American opera while Ellington was still playing in dance halls.[5]

As noted, Ellington's politeness and propriety in public settings were legendary. When the Pulitzer board rejected its music jury's recommendation that Ellington receive the honor in 1965, the bandleader's measured comment was typical of this well-honed facade: "Fate is being kind to me. Fate doesn't want me to be too famous too young." But the next generation of jazz innovators had tougher, edgier attitudes, and showed little interest in pleasing dancers on the ballroom floor or attracting nickels and dimes at the jukebox. The modern jazz movement of the 1940s openly embraced its outsider status. Tempos got faster—often too fast for comfortable dancing. Melodies and rhythms took on new complexity, and set in motion a separation between jazz and popular music that would widen in subsequent decades.[6]

The early leaders of *bebop*, the onomatopoeic label that would get attached to this sound, were embraced by the counterculture, not the mainstream. Saxophonist Charlie Parker, trumpeter Dizzy Gillespie, and pianists Thelonious Monk and Bud Powell would never have the pleasure of watching one of their hit singles climb the charts. Instead, they reasserted jazz's outlaw status at a time when the music had gone mainstream. And their very willingness to walk away from crossover acceptance served to accelerate the pace of experimentation and innovation in the idiom. The twenty years following the end of World War II thus marked both a tremendous burst of jazz creativity and a simultaneous withdrawal of the genre's leading artists from popular culture. Jazz flourished as an art form despite—or perhaps because of—its shrinking audience. Even today, various lists of the jazz classics most cherished by serious fans are dominated by the artists whose careers peaked during the period from the late 1940s through the late 1960s, not just the beboppers but the next generation that they mentored, including Miles Davis, John Coltrane, Charles Mingus, and others.

This was a different path of legitimization, one that required no acquiescence from the ruling institutions of the music world. Eventually the institutions would follow along—in time, jazz would even be rebranded as "America's classical music"—but that was late in the game, almost an after-effect. Miles Davis didn't need an honorary degree to prove how dead serious he was about his art; nor did John Coltrane or Ornette Coleman or a host of other jazz icons who rose to the top of their craft during the second half of the twentieth century. Even when they embraced elements of popular culture, as, for example, Davis did with rock in his seminal *Bitches Brew* (1970), a certain prickly *otherness* pervaded the music. *Bitches Brew* sold half a million copies, a new milestone for Davis, but you would never have mistaken him for an entertainer. The three most famous aspects of his onstage demeanor were playing with his back to the audience, walking offstage mid-performance, and keeping a serious demeanor—rarely did he let even a hint of a smile appear on his face. Needless to say, no one dared ask to see his Juilliard transcript.

Perhaps I am conveying the idea that musical innovations of the twentieth century never came from white elites with institutional backing. That would be misleading. In fact, a whole flurry of subversive music-making arose from symphony orchestras and composers schooled in the traditions of Western concert hall music. And in some instances, these highbrow excursions managed to channel the same kind of raw energy propelling popular culture— for example, when audience members allegedly got out of control at the debut of Stravinsky's *Le sacre du printemps* in 1913, and at George Antheil's *Ballets suédois* performance in 1923. (The latter tumult was even captured on film by Marcel L'Herbier, who may have actually incited the riot to create an appropriate scene for his movie *L'Inhumaine*.) Our schemas of music genre and social stratification would separate works such as "Funky Butt" and *Le sacre du printemps* into separate spheres, lowbrow and highbrow, that in theory have nothing to do with each other, but in practice, the zeal for subversion and transgression in twentieth-century culture would recognize no boundaries and cut across all traditional class lines. In a later chapter, we will look at the striking connections between rock performances and acts of ritual violence, yet even here, in the midst of the classical music world of the early twentieth century, we already see anticipations of Altamont and the Sex Pistols' final concert at Winterland. Composers are increasingly viewed as provocateurs, and their music is now expected to disrupt and agitate.

In still another way, the classical music innovators of the twentieth century reveal a surprising resemblance to the originators of ragtime, jazz, and blues. We have already highlighted the importance of diaspora in the creation of new forms of musical expression, but previously we focused on the black diaspora—and in particular, on the supersized influence the descendants of African slaves exerted on modern popular music. Yet in classical music as well, political exiles and émigrés spearheaded the most progressive movements of the century. Arnold Schoenberg, a Vienna native, had to resettle in California after the rise of Nazism. Russian-born Igor Stravinsky spent most of his life in Switzerland, France, and the United States, and resided in Los Angeles for a longer period than in any other city. Paul Hindemith also relocated to the United States, as did Kurt Weill, Sergei Rachmaninoff, Béla Bartók, Erich Wolfgang Korngold, Ernest Bloch, and many others. The circumstances varied in each case, and sometimes better opportunities in a new locale, rather than political oppression at home, motivated a move. But we do well to consider these migrations in a larger context, recalling that outsiders have always played a prominent role in classical music—for proof, you merely need to consider the popularity of Handel and Haydn in England, the successes of Chopin and Liszt in Paris, and the many other cases of itinerant or relocated artists. Perhaps someday, a scholar will undertake a statistical analysis of the masterworks of the Western concert hall tradition, and determine what percentage were composed or made their debut outside the geographical boundaries of the composer's native land—it will certainly represent a significant portion of the classical repertoire. In the twentieth century, these strangers in a strange land gained special influence, and remind us that the mystique of the outsider is just as great whether we are considering academic music departments and concert halls or jazz nightclubs and blues juke joints.

Yet in another regard, modernist classical music diverged sharply from these popular idioms: namely, in its pathway to respectability. All successful outsiders in music eventually gain the luster of esteemed insiders, but in the case of classical music innovators of the twentieth century, this could now happen without any real mainstreaming of the compositional techniques involved. In the twelve-tone row music of Arnold Schoenberg and his followers, or the experiments of various composers with microtonal techniques, or even the radical silence of John Cage, we encounter something very unusual: movements gain acclaim and legitimization, often through the intervention of academic and grant-giving institutions, without ever crossing over into the broader culture. Black musical innovations gain respect in very different ways—notably by selling records, attracting fans, and getting imitated (and frequently ripped off) by various commercial interests. In both cases, the transgressive innovator eventually finds acceptance as an admired cultural hero, and each subversive movement and their leaders secure respectability and iconic status, but the paths they take on this journey could hardly be more different.

The winners of the Pulitzer Prize in music during the second half of the twentieth century exemplify the classical model: try to find the hit record in the bunch. It's not there, and hardly by chance. More than any previous generation, these composers resisted assimilation. This is something new. Mozart and Haydn were crowd-pleasers. Even the fierce spirits of Romanticism, such as Beethoven, Chopin, and Tchaikovsky, eventually had their musical vocabulary taken over by pop culture, and sometimes their melodies have been ruthlessly pilfered and repackaged as radio hits. But that will never happen with Arnold Schoenberg, Alban Berg, Anton Webern, and the vast majority of other academic composers of the post–World War II years. Perhaps this represents the height of subversion—What could be more radical than an innovation that can never be assimilated? Or perhaps it's a kind of "end of history" moment in elite Western music.

What happens at the end of history? Well, as Friedrich Nietzsche would admonish us, with his theory of eternal recurrence, we have no choice but to return to the beginning. Relocation, recurrence, rebirth—these three forces seem to confront us at every turn as we grapple with the disruptive currents of classical music during the tumultuous twentieth century. It's all too fitting that, at almost its midpoint, Olivier Messiaen followed up his seminal *Quatuor pour la fin du temps* (Quartet for the end of time), first performed at a Nazi prison camp where the composer was in captivity, with works inspired by birdsong, the starting point for all music, according to Darwin. This shift from ends to beginnings propels many of the most provocative musical projects of this era, especially during the second half of the twentieth century. (And not just classical music: What is rap but a resurrection of the pure expressivity of monophonic chant? What is the EDM-driven rave but a return to the trance-inspiring rituals of prehistory?) And in such instances, the eternal recurrence frequently demands homage to Africa—acknowledged as the ultimate source of human migrations and mythologized as the ultimate root of roots music—whose contributions are now embedded in the DNA of concert music no less than of pop. Here, again, the narratives of black and white music converge, even in a sociocultural context marked by extraordinary measures to keep these two spheres separate and incommunicado.

When we turn our attention to the early masterworks of modernist agenda, both this African element and symbols of rebirth and recurrence already demand our attention. At the dawn of the 1920s, Darius Milhaud crafted his *La création du monde* (1923)—its very name (literally "the creation of the world") signals a return to first premises—on the basis of African folklore. This remarkable work anticipated *Rhapsody in Blue* to an uncanny degree two years before the Aeolian Hall concert that marked the debut of Gershwin's masterwork. Even earlier, in *Le sacre du printemps* (1913), Stravinksy built his modernist sound structures on evocations of ancient sacrificial and fertility rites. George Antheil served up his *Sonata Sauvage* (1922) and *A Jazz Symphony* (1925) at a time when European interest in jazz had become permeated with odd notions of primitivism and noble savages. These concepts haven't worn well with the passing years, and in truth, the African and world music ingredients in these works were often overwhelmed by the onrushing currents of European experimentalism. The stratified music scene was still some distance away from a real dialogue between cultures in which both could be on an equal footing. But from an ideological standpoint, the agenda has already been laid out for our inspection at this early stage. We are clearly witnessing the first stirrings of the pan-global approach that has come to the forefront of all music, highbrow or lowbrow, in recent decades. Perhaps we just needed to reach the end of history—or at least conventional tonality—before we could accept these traditions on their own terms.

When that more vibrant dialogue finally started to take place, with Africanized musical structures mixing on almost equal terms with European elements in Western classical music, the turning point demanded both a new name and a new agenda of rebellion. It arrived on the scene in the guise of *minimalism*, marked by the ascendancy of Steve Reich, Philip Glass, Terry Riley, and La Monte Young in the 1960s and 1970s. These new rebels not only drew on vital non-Western traditions, but also forged a dynamic point of contact between forward-looking classical music and mass-market popular culture—finally on speaking terms again after a long period of almost total isolation. Listeners didn't need to take a music appreciation class in order to trace lines of influence between these minimalist composers and the trendy currents in New Wave rock, funk, jazz, and disco. It jumped out at them in the music, with its insistent pulsations and vamp-styled patterns, ingredients that now seemed just as suitable for the dance hall as the concert hall. In the early 1970s, Philip Glass might have been labeled a classical composer and Brian Eno a rock musician, but that discrepancy simply pointed out how misleading such labels could be. They both participated in the zeitgeist. Terry Riley's albums were kept in the classical music section of the record store, but anyone who actually listened to his oeuvre heard everything from South Asian influences to DJ-style tape loops. This music just couldn't be pigeonholed. More to the point, minimalism represented a vital return to the musical values that predate the whole enterprise of Western classical composition, standing out with a populist celebration of rhythm and trance. And again we find our way back to the diaspora and the black underclass, here in the concert hall just as on the jukebox. It's hardly a coincidence that Terry Riley could have made a living as a badass jazz pianist, or that the Philip Glass Ensemble deliberately emulated Duke Ellington's band, or that La Monte Young initiated his music career by playing with Los Angeles jazz musicians, or that Steve Reich cited John Coltrane's *Africa/Brass* album as a significant influence. Even as this music promised—and often delivered—sounds that were fresh and new, the old dialectic reasserted itself: the soundscape of the outsider (as in so many instances, African or African American) laying the groundwork for what would turn into the sanctioned, legitimized music of the symphony hall and opera house.

In truth, radical realignments of music during the late twentieth century almost always required, at least in some degree, an African or African American infusion of creativity—even experimental electronic music, which at first glance seems perhaps immune to national and racial markers. These new high-tech sounds may have originated in research laboratories and academic settings, but soon the key innovations were coming from funk, jazz, and soul artists and forward-looking DJs. Only a few months after the Minimoog synthesizer came to market, this exciting new black vibe could be heard on projects such Sun Ra's *My Brother the Wind* (1970), Isaac

Hayes's soundtrack to *Shaft* (1971), and Stevie Wonder's *Talking Book* (1972). Here was one area in which elitists did get assimilated, perhaps to their chagrin. The innovations of Karlheinz Stockhausen (1928–2007), a pioneer in integrating electronic sounds into classical compositions, reverberate in current-day dance music, ambient soundscapes, and the various chill-out genres whose names are legion. Stockhausen's heirs range from Aphex Twin to Frank Zappa, and a full assessment of his influence on commercial music would encompass such disparate figures as the Beatles, Björk, David Bowie, Miles Davis, Pink Floyd, and Daft Punk. When reminded of his influence on some of these artists in a 1990s interview, Stockhausen complained about his acolytes' "post-African repetitions," and griped about musicians who aimed at achieving a "special effect in dancing bars, or wherever it is." But it was too late; the classical music establishment had been bypassed in this matter. Even if some electronic music innovators disdained crossover success, others would bring their trademark sounds to the masses.[7]

With all due respect to these musical agitators, I must point out that jazz musicians had been experimenting with electric instruments, specifically the vibraphone and electric guitar, back when Stockhausen was still in swaddling clothes. Today, these instruments are considered everyday ingredients of mainstream music, but they were little more than novelties when Lionel Hampton started playing the vibraphone in 1930 or Charlie Christian recorded on electric guitar with the Benny Goodman Sextet in 1939. In this instance, black jazz musicians served as the legitimizers for the innovations of white technologists, an odd reversal of their traditional role—but soon to become standard operating procedure for new music gear.

Jazz bandleader Raymond Scott, a quirky composer whose works became best known as cartoon soundtracks, set up a tech company to create new electronic music systems in 1946, and his work from this period anticipates key elements of the *musique concrète* movement, which embraced a similar aesthetic in France during the post–World War II era. Yet Scott was a forgotten figure in his later years, and even today has only started to receive his due. In truth, he bears much of the blame for this. This innovator worked with an obsession for secrecy that bordered on paranoia. Under slightly different circumstances, his Electronium, a combined synthesizer and algorithmic composition tool, might have displaced the Moog and shaped the course of popular music. But even now, long after Scott's death in 1994, the specifics of the technology are still very much a secret. Despite these self-imposed obstacles, his collaborations with disparate pop culture institutions, ranging from the Motown record label (which purchased an Electronium and even hired Scott as a technologist) to the Muppets, make clear that his innovations had the potential to move outside of academia and research facilities and enter the mainstream.

This same path of dissemination has been repeated with every subsequent innovation in music technology, from the plugged-in instruments of the jazz-rock fusion movement to the most up-to-date digital music tools of the current day. Commercial musicians, from jazz to hip-hop and all points in between, have turned into forces of mainstreaming and validation for the innovations of others. When Intel, the semiconductor powerhouse of Silicon Valley, hired will.i.am of the Black Eyed Peas as its "Director of Creative Innovation" in 2011, many observers wondered what possible role a rapper and DJ could play in advancing a tech-driven agenda. But as we have already seen with Hampton and Christian, this kind of symbiosis has been going on for decades now, and any real history of technology in modern culture would have to address figures as disparate as Miles Davis, Sun Ra, and Grandmaster Flash—although none of them ever earned a STEM degree. The outsider becomes the source of a different pathway to legitimization.

At first glance, this trend seems to represent a total reversal of thousands of years of music history. But even as outsiders gained a certain kind of social power during the course of the twentieth century—call it coolness or hipness or street cred—they still operate within a larger socioeconomic context controlled and shaped by others. This situation creates a distinctive tension in modern music, which we will see manifested at different times and places in the closing chapters of this book. As a result, institutions and gatekeepers are increasingly conflicted over what gets included or excluded from any given setting.

So far in our narrative of twentieth-century music, white folks haven't fared too well—at least not as self-sufficient pioneers who can make the transition from outside-the-box innovation to mainstream pop culture acceptance. And when we have encountered a visionary figure of this sort, such as George Gershwin or Benny Goodman, we've often found them drawing explicitly upon sources of inspiration from the black community. But modern music history offers one huge exception, and we need to address it now. We must wrangle with country music, which for almost a century has consistently ranked among the most popular genres in the United States, and long ago went global in its appeal. I still recall my shock as a young man, when a scholarship allowed me to leave behind the rough-and-tumble neighborhoods of my youth and study at Oxford University in faraway England. Here I uneasily adapted to a world and culture completely different from my American origins, but one thing was the same, very much to my surprise: even at Oxford, I heard country music—over and over again—and found it possessed a following and popularity that seemed incongruous in this elite setting. This was an unlikely success story, especially when I considered that the rural cowboy lifestyles that had defined this genre had almost disappeared even within the United States, making country a kind of anachronism in its country of origin. At that point in my life, I was immersed in my beloved jazz music, and playing piano to supplement my scholarship funds. I resented this rival export, which was hardly as authentic, or so I thought, as the more radical and disruptive music I favored. But nowadays, I'm not so sure about that way of differentiating music genres.

From another perspective, country music isn't an exception at all from the processes we have traced in the evolution of black music. In truth, the vernacular black and white music styles of the South were never as far apart as their public images might suggest. Bluegrass banjo music may be branded as the ultimate hillbilly music (Hollywood certainly thinks so—just check out the soundtracks to *Deliverance* or *The Beverly Hillbillies*), but its syncopations are often identical to those found in ragtime. Country singers bend their notes just like the blues singers, and can even operate comfortably within the standard twelve-bar form. When the country star Jimmie Rodgers recorded with Louis Armstrong on a seminal track back in 1930, ignoring the segregated ways of mainstream society, no genre clash could be detected by discerning ears. But more to the point, if I needed a closing argument to prove my contention that music innovation inevitably comes from outsiders and marginalized communities, this down-home genre provides the clincher. How else can we explain the peculiar circumstance that even white culture needed to turn to its most impoverished communities and despised citizenry to find its emblematic sound? Here again, New York and Los Angeles and Chicago fell short. So-called hillbillies, cattle wranglers, and moonshiners took precedence over Harvard and Yale graduates. Once again, to go high, the first step was to go low.

Country music and blues share so many similarities in their origins, to an extent that can hardly be mere coincidence. They emerged at almost the same historical moment, and for the most part in the same down-and-out locales. In many instances, the very same record producers were responsible for their history-making early recordings—take, for example, Ralph Peer, who supervised the recording of Mamie Smith's "Crazy Blues," the breakout hit that established the market for blues, and then organized the Bristol sessions, often praised as the "birthplace of country music," launching the careers of Jimmie Rodgers and the Carter Family. For both genres, record labels had to mount field trips to the South to find their biggest stars, a humiliating admission for big-city music moguls who liked to think that aspiring artists should make the journey to them, not the other way around.

And consider the even odder conjunction of circumstances that brought both Jimmie Rodgers and Robert Johnson, the most iconic figures in early country music and early blues, respectively, into the exact same retail store in Jackson, Mississippi, to audition for the exact same person, H. C. Speir. Speir was the lowliest talent scout you could find in the music world of his day, a small-town operator who tried out unknown wannabes in the back room of his Farish Street retail store, and occasionally referred the more promising singers to those higher up the food chain in the record industry. To his later chagrin, Speir passed on Rodgers and told him to go back to Meridian, Mississippi, and work on his songwriting. But he did give the nod to Johnson, and helped launch the blues legend's career. Yet what are the odds against these two genre-defining stars arriving at the same humble address in the same black neighborhood in the poorest state in the country during the Great Depression on their very different world-shaking trajectories?

No, this can't be coincidence, but in its very unlikelihood we find a kind of statistical proof of the troublesome nature of musical innovation. Even after the rise of a powerful, global music industry built on the whiz-bang technologies of the modern era, the old dynamic was still in place. The insiders might very well run the wheels of commerce, but they had no choice but to rely on outsiders—and to do so over and over again—to keep them turning.

24

The Origins of Country Music in the Neolithic Era

M any years ago, I noticed a puzzling pattern in my research into the music of herding societies. Cultures with no direct contact with each other had embraced strikingly similar musical practices and values. I could hear it in the style of their songs, in their choice of instruments, even in their attitudes about the role of music in everyday life. I had just completed a comprehensive survey of hunting economies and their songs, and the contrast could hardly have been more sharply delineated. Herding communities in every part of the world had renounced the musical practices of their hunting ancestors and opted for a completely different body of techniques and platforms for expression. Was this just happenstance, or did the shift from hunting to herding in the Neolithic age fundamentally change musical practices—perhaps in ways that still impact our songs today?

Seeking guidance, I contacted a leading ethnomusicologist who had undertaken fieldwork in a current-day herding community and pressed him for answers. How did he account for these similarities and convergences? He had spent a considerable amount of time in one of these herding villages and had firsthand knowledge I lacked. What did he see as the connection between livelihood and music in these societies?

Rather than answering my question, he showed some irritation at it. Musical cultures were unique and incommensurable, he indicated, and generalizations of the sort I was pursuing failed to respect this fact. To explain one person's song by looking at another individual across the world in a different context and community was a dangerous methodology, and ought to be discouraged.

The irony of this encounter only became apparent to me later, when I concluded that the similarities in the music of herding societies had nothing to do with people. It was determined, in large part, by the *animals*. Herders around the world had become adept at performing songs that soothed their livestock. By the same token, they avoided music that agitated the animals. Even today we use the term *pastoral music*—its etymology literally tells us that it is *music for herding*—to refer to gentle, relaxing sounds that summon up images of the pastures, soundscapes that evoke nature or rural settings. Musicians in these settings do *not* favor drums; instead, we find string instruments and plaintive wind instruments, such as panpipes and flutes. The music rarely channels aggression, but more often calms and subdues. These performers bequeathed that tradition to later generations, even those who abandoned the herding profession. Without the legacy of the shepherds, there would be no *Pastoral Symphony* from Beethoven, and perhaps no country music either.

Once you grasp this, it seems so obvious. And so many otherwise inexplicable choices and traditions are suddenly clarified. Yet even experts immersed in the music of the herding communities can fail to understand it—if their ideology is so rigid that they refuse to look beyond their own pasture.

Hunting societies had very different musical needs. If renegade historian Joseph Jordania is correct (see Chapter 2), our hunting ancestors were primarily scavengers and relied on loud, boisterous music to scare away other predators. Their music is more assertive, more aggressive, more likely to rely on drums and other declamatory instruments. We have inherited these practices as well. It's perhaps an oversimplification to say that country singers are herders, and rock stars are hunters. But there's an important truth here that deserves recognition. We have nurtured two sharply contrasting musical cultures over thousands of years. One celebrates conciliation and the settled life of the rural world, while the other revels in the nomadic triumphs of the fierce and passionate human predator. (Recall, in this context, our recognition in the opening chapter that the two dominant theories for the origin of music link it, respectively, to love and violence—and our conclusion that these hypotheses may not be incompatible, but mirror images of each other, explicable both in terms of aesthetics and body chemistry.)

Surviving documents from the long history of herding reveal how much music contributed to that way of life, not only shaping its emotional texture but also supporting its economic viability. In different times and places, these songs stood out for their comforting melodies. "Shepherd's pipes bring rest to the flocks in the pasture," announced Macrobius, a Roman writer of the fifth century. In his studies of medieval herding practices of more than five hundred years later, historian Emmanuel Le Roy Ladurie notes that "a flute was a necessary part of every shepherd's equipment, and of one who was ruined it was said that he no longer had *even a flute*." In more recent times, cattle herders and cowboys in the American West learned to rely on soothing songs to control livestock long before this vocal tradition got turned into a music-industry genre.[1]

During the course of the twentieth century, country music grew into a multibillion-dollar business, but the herder's marked animosity to drumming remained. For many years, the Grand Ole Opry in Nashville went so far as to impose a formal rule prohibiting the use of drums in performance. Long after electric guitars and rock-influenced acts found their way onto this venerable stage, musicians still had to fight for even a simple snare drum, and stories are told of drum kits played behind curtains to protect the delicate sensibilities of (no, *not* the cattle now) the audience. Even superstars were forced to change their arrangements to please their persnickety Nashville patrons. When Carl Perkins enjoyed a huge hit with "Blue Suede Shoes" in 1955, the Grand Ole Opry had no qualms featuring this spirited rock 'n' roll tune, provided the band's drummer stayed at home. Country music eventually made its peace with the drums, but even today if you listen closely you will hear the rhythm guitar still driving the beat on many Nashville tunes while the drummer keeps a low profile in the background. Long after the cows have come home, to reverse an old proverb, we still seem to match our countrified music to their tastes.

Even the lyrics of country music seem to have their roots in the Neolithic period. Country music still adheres to the ethos of settled life that entered human society with cultivating and herding—in sharp contrast to the nomadic imperative of hunting and gathering societies. You couldn't wander very far if you wanted to raise a crop while breeding livestock. Maybe that's why country songs still celebrate static lives, sticking with your job 9-to-5, even if it's lousy, and standing by your good-for-nothing man, even if he's worse. Blues songs are different. They deal with ramblers leaving on the next train and evading the hellhound on their trail, but that's not country music. In country, you endure and abide, make the payment on the dented pickup truck, and go back to that same sad bar you went to last week, last month, last year.

That's also true on the macro level: country first gained commercial success as the preferred music genre of those who refused to participate in the migration to the cities. Tens of millions of Americans left rural life behind during the course of the twentieth century, looking for new opportunities and ready to shed the traditional values of their origins. They ended up in Chicago, New York, Los Angeles, Detroit, and other bustling urban centers. Those folks were never the core audience for country music. Eventually, demographics prevailed, and country music became citified. But that didn't change the ethos of the genre, which still held fast to time-honored values and viewed urban trends with a large dose of skepticism. When the Carter Family brought their popular touring show of country music to town, the poster announcing their performances declared: "The Program is Morally Good"—a promise never made, since the beginning of time, by any famous blues band. The sober singing style of Sara Carter, purged entirely of the sensual sonorities of a Bessie Smith or Billie Holiday, reinforced the message. Buy your ten-cent admission ticket, and leave your lust behind. Later country stars didn't always live up to this standard in their private lives, or their public personas, for that matter, but the connection between this music genre and a settled, traditional way of life has never been completely sundered.

A direct historical lineage can be constructed tracing today's country music back to the rural folk music of the distant past. There's a good reason why British folk song collector Cecil Sharp came to the Appalachian region of the United States. "The people are very interesting, just English peasants in appearance, manner and speech," he explained in a 1916 letter from North Carolina. "Their songs are marvelous. I have only been here 17 days and I have collected between 90 and 100 songs. Many have long since become obsolete in England." Representatives of the music industry journeyed to this same region a decade later in their search for country recording stars. And the songs they found here retained some of the most distinctive elements of Old World herding music.[2]

Yodeling, for example, has been employed by herding communities for more than a thousand years, both as a call to animals and as a communication tool that reaches across pastureland to nearby villages. It's a charming sound, with its alterations between low chest tones and high-pitched or falsetto notes, but not really a song in any true sense of the term. Yet yodeling started showing up on country records almost from the start. We hear it in the recordings of Emmett Miller, Riley Puckett, and especially Jimmie Rodgers, who turned it into a trademark of his down-home country style. "Everyone who could pick a guitar" was soon yodeling like Jimmie Rodgers, according to musician Herb Quinn, who performed in Mississippi in the 1920s. The music was now popular entertainment, no longer a functional tool in the management of livestock, but its pastoral origins still reverberated in the radio hits.[3]

Make no mistake, however: the country genre from the very start was more than just a revival of old folk songs. Talent scout

Ralph Peer offered what might be the best description of the difference between the two idioms. When a researcher approached him late in his life, seeking to find details of Peer's advocacy of new music genres, the veteran producer claimed that he had been seeking out "*future* folkloric songs." Country music fans may have celebrated the values of the past, but they always demanded new songs. This craving for novelty created an inevitable rupture with folk musicians, who had a "greatest hits" mentality long before that became a music-industry album concept. Folk singers wanted to live off the back catalog (as we might describe it nowadays), not create new songs. As such, they were less adept at dealing with the music business, which constantly needs fresh material to peddle, than this new breed of country singer. "I made it a rule," Peer clarified in his letter, "not to use any artist for a recording who could not compose."[4]

Perhaps you are surprised—or even dismayed—that country singers can keep on writing new songs about the same old subjects for going on a century, and never lose their audience. But recall that constant reassertion of old values is the *modus operandi* of traditional societies. The weekly homily from the pulpit isn't supposed to break new ground. The blueprint for down-home living isn't a future utopia—it's holding onto the *good ol' days*. But country music's ability to survive the urbanization and suburbanization of America is nonetheless a puzzling phenomenon. Country was the first lifestyle music, and was marketed that way a full generation before the strategists at the Rand Corporation invented lifestyle marketing. In fact, that brand-building strategy shaped the image of country music long before the word *lifestyle* entered the English language. But how do we explain the puzzling anomaly that country music not only survived but actually thrived even as herding and cultivating lifestyles disappeared from the economy? Perhaps that was the real stroke of genius behind the marketing of country music: the realization that lifestyles are about projecting a fantasy, not living in reality. From this perspective, our favorite songs and genres are less like a mirror to our actual lives and more like photoshopped images presenting the lives we wish we led. So just as cunning minstrels still sang about knights and their oaths of fealty long after the collapse of feudalism, country singers celebrated a world in their music that had disappeared, or in many cases, for most of their listeners, never existed. The pickup truck must symbolize the horse that never was; and instead of rounding up the cattle, you just grab a six-pack from the fridge.

And in this way, too, the country audience was staying true to their Neolithic ancestors. Recall that the rupture of the Neolithic revolution wasn't really inspired by a love of farming or herding; it was driven by the preference for a stable, settled life, despite its boredom and repetition, over the risky, rambling ways of the nomad. From that perspective, country music is perhaps relevant even in a high-tech digital age, all the more so if our new technologies seem disruptive or threatening.

The rise of the singing cowboys in Hollywood movies during the years leading up to World War II showed just how far country music was willing to go to promote the lifestyle fantasies of its core audience. In this regard, country music was simply a few steps ahead of the game: eventually all music genres would rely on film and video to establish a larger-than-life ethos. Country was doing this back in the 1920s and 1930s, long before MTV and YouTube. Gene Autry made so much money from his singing cowboy career in Hollywood that he parlayed it into a position on *Forbes'* list of the 400 richest Americans. As a real estate and business tycoon, Autry lived in a palatial residence in Southern California, but if you went into his closet—which was larger than many people's homes—you would have found 250 western-style outfits, 50 cowboy hats, and 75 pairs of boots. He knew his riches were built on keeping the fantasy alive. A host of other screen cowboys, from Ken Maynard to Roy Rogers, flourished as country singers, and even those with little natural talent for music got prodded into vocalizing. Check out the many (failed) attempts to turn John Wayne into a singer.

Even after World War II, country singers adopted the attire and persona of cattle rustlers and ranch hands. Hank Williams dressed like a gentleman cowboy when he sang his lonesome songs, and Patsy Cline posed for publicity photos as though she were a budding rodeo star. This playacting continues today. You can spend an entire afternoon strolling around Dallas, Houston, Nashville, and other centers of western music without seeing a single cowboy hat. But no self-respecting country music luminary would go on tour without one. (To this day, country music is the only genre where a singer can go bald without fans ever finding out.) The same is true of accents. Those Texas twangs and Mississippi drawls have mostly disappeared from the younger generation in those states. Who can be surprised? For years, they have been learning their language skills from TV and movies, and today's toddlers will probably spend more time talking to artificial intelligence assistants than conversing with blood relatives. In the future, we will all speak with a Cupertino or Seattle accent. But listen to the latest country music hit songs, and you will still hear all the countrified articulations of the past carefully preserved as the ultimate signs of authenticity. In the old days, a cowboy needed a fast draw; today, a slow drawl is the first requirement to pass the audition.

All these ingredients—attire, accent, and attitude—make country music the perfect soundtrack for traditionalists, and they have embraced the genre with fierce loyalty. Yet what does it tell us that even country music eventually needed to celebrate rebels and renegades? Here again we find compelling proof that innovation in music almost always requires an outsider's stance. By the late 1950s, everyone in the music industry had figured this out. Rock 'n' roll led the way, but every commercial genre was following in the same path. Whether they were promoting Glenn Gould or Ornette Coleman or Jerry Lee Lewis, the labels marketed their rising stars as eccentric, wild, and unconventional. Even Las Vegas, the epicenter of tame and packaged entertainment for tame and packaged people, needed to build its allure on Rat Pack indiscretions and bad behavior. How could country fight this trend? Somehow the music of settled ways and old-fashioned values needed to discover its own rebel streak.

From this pressing need, the new genre of *outlaw country* was born. Perhaps it started out as a subgenre, but it came to dominate the country music field. The new stars in the field almost always had spent at least some time behind bars or in rehab to burnish their image. The smallest transgressions got exaggerated in order to feed the audience's hunger for bad behavior from their new icons. We all know about Johnny Cash's outlaw past—in "Folsom Prison Blues," he sang those well-known lines: "I shot a man in Reno just to watch him die." In truth, Cash never had to spend more than one night in jail, and his crimes were as wimpy as they come—his 1966 run-in with the law resulted from the country star picking flowers late at night on private property, and he ended up in the Starkville city jail for just a few hours. *I picked some flowers in Starkville, just to watch them wilt.* No, you can't market that. But dress Mr. Cash all in black, and record live albums at maximum-security penitentiaries . . . well, that's an entirely different proposition. Even mainstream audiences took note.

Times were changing even in the never-changing genre. When Hank Williams got arrested for public drunkenness and disorderly conduct in 1952, his reputation suffered. But a generation later, Willie Nelson could turn his history of busts for marijuana possession into a key part of his public persona—and eventually a business opportunity, when he launched his own commercial brand of pot, named Willie's Reserve, in 2016. A serious rap sheet was now compatible with a pristine country music reputation. Merle Haggard was actually in the audience as an inmate when Johnny Cash performed at Folsom Prison, but just a few years later, country audiences embraced him as an exemplar of patriotism and decency. His song "Okie from Muskogee" was a defining anthem of settled ways.

But the ultimate measure of the outlaw movement's success came at the cash register. Bad behavior, whether real or imagined by a marketing department, sold records in huge quantities. When country music celebrated its first platinum album, the title told the whole story. This compilation, featuring Waylon Jennings, Willie Nelson, Jessi Colter, and Tompall Glaser, was called *Wanted! The Outlaws.* The cover was designed to look like a wanted poster from the Wild West. The album sold as fast as they could press it.

This was no anomaly. Rock 'n' roll had forced these changes on other genres. It was the first major movement in the history of commercial music that resisted legitimization. It's tempting to explain this shift purely in economic terms. Under this hypothesis, the music business finally realized in the late 1950s that it made more money by marketing renegades than from promoting role models. In previous eras, you got rich by going mainstream, but as censorship laws were overturned and social norms came under fire, a different option presented itself. A musical movement could set itself up as a constant scourge to the mainstream and still reach the top of the charts. When individual musicians within the movement opted for legitimization (the term *sell-out* would quickly enter the lexicon of rock fans), they could be replaced by edgier new talent—the process repeating itself in a kind of *permanent revolution*, if I can borrow a loaded Trotskyite phrase that seems rather appropriate here.

Perhaps this explanation gives too much credit to the music business. Many execs at the leading labels were probably more surprised by the staying power of rock than anyone else. They hadn't read their Trotsky. These leaders of the *ancien régime* probably saw rock 'n' roll as a passing fad, a detour in the pop culture highway, a novelty sound that would come and go like so many others before it. But eventually even the laggards and close-minded figured out that the rules had changed. If they needed a reminder, they just had to turn on the radio.

Fans and experts have long debated which musician released the first rock 'n' roll record, the instigator of the permanent revolution. I've been dragged into these heated and pointless arguments, debating the pros and cons of Fats Domino, Ike Turner, Big Joe Turner, Big Mama Thornton, Little Richard, Bill Haley, and other claimants to the title. But that question is, frankly, quite irrelevant. The real revolutionary change wasn't in the music; it happened in the audience. Plenty of records from the pre-rock era anticipated the future. Those who were hip to the sounds of electric Chicago blues or black R&B in the late 1940s and early 1950s were already hearing the shape of rock hits to come. But most white American teenagers (and almost all of their parents) lived in blissful ignorance of their clarion call. Many black households also disapproved of these songs, setting off clashes between parents and teens that anticipated what sociologists would later call the *generation gap*. But long before rock 'n' roll emerged on the scene, these anticipatory sounds started showing up in unexpected places. Jukebox operators found they could make money by placing black R&B singles in white neighborhoods. Record stores in these same locales started stocking more black music—young buyers insisted on it. The dividing line segregating the audiences of black and white radio stations, at best a weak barrier, got overturned without requiring the assistance of court orders and the National Guard. The stage was set.

Maybe rock 'n' roll would have ignited the youth under any circumstances. But the complacency and conformity of the prevailing culture, both in music and other matters, gave it an extra edge. Mainstream radio DJs in the early 1950s were peddling sentimental love songs and novelty tunes to bored teenagers who craved a stronger brew. Where would they find it? We shouldn't be surprised that they did the same thing their parents and grandparents had done before them, looking to African American music for cutting-edge sounds.

Savvy musicians seized the opportunity. When Chuck Berry came to Chicago in 1955, he caught the attention of Muddy Waters, who referred the newcomer to his label Chess Records, where Berry would be groomed as another rising blues/R&B star. In a different environment, Berry's single "Maybellene" might have been just another R&B hit on black radio stations; instead, it sold a million copies with a groove that was just a little more danceable (and with a more streamlined backbeat) than your typical Chess vinyl. A few months later, in his declamatory hit "Roll Over Beethoven," Berry declared his new allegiance, using the words "rock" and "roll" in his lyrics—these turbocharged verbs were now talismans of the zeitgeist. Chuck Berry was no longer an R&B star, but a genuine *rock 'n' roller*. By the time he released his chart-climbing hit single "Johnny B. Goode," the transformation was complete. The beat here is pure rock 'n' roll, chugging along like a hot-rodder's V-8 engine, and ready for the high school sock hop.

You didn't have to go to the nasty part of town to hear these tunes anymore—the nasty tunes came to you. The 1956 Sears Christmas catalog featured a $9.75 children's record player, marketed with a photo of sweet, smiling adolescents listening to their favorite nursery songs. But if the moms and dads of white mainstream America had known what they were getting into, they would have blocked the chimney and sent Santa packing. In their ignorance, they were *letting black people into their homes*, even into their children's bedrooms. That cheap turntable wasn't the Internet or a smartphone; even so, a kind of worldwide web was getting woven in the 1950s. Before long, the first wave of semiconductor innovation would accelerate these changes in the music world. In fact, the first transistor radios were hitting the stores at the very moment that rock 'n' roll rose to ascendancy. Coincidence or causality? Teenagers might be angels or deadbeats, college-bound or dropping out, model citizens or juvenile delinquents, but each and every one of them was also a consumer, and their aggregate dollars and cents increasingly drove the music business.

Music critic Chuck Klosterman has predicted that future generations will look back at Chuck Berry as the key innovator and dominant force "when rock music is retroactively reconsidered by the grandchildren of your grandchildren." Little Richard, whose hit single "Long Tall Sally" came out a few weeks before "Roll Over Beethoven," would bristle at that verdict, countering that he invented rock 'n' roll. Either of these assertions may well be correct, but in the context of the United States during the Eisenhower administration, *white* superstars were essential to establish rock 'n' roll as the dominant genre in the commercial music business. In so many ways, this juncture in the mid-1950s brings us back to the dynamic of mainstreaming that we've studied before, whether we're looking at medieval troubadours, nineteenth-century minstrels, or other assimilators. But in one significant way, something new was happening with the ascendancy of rock. Even the assimilators and mainstreamers now had to be rogues and rebels, outsiders from the fringes of society. Even the legitimizers craved illegitimacy. When the Decca label promoted white rock 'n' roll star Bill Haley, whose hit single "Rock Around the Clock" played a key role in launching the movement, the marketing copy went overboard in stressing his impoverished upbringing, and made sure fans knew he survived on one meal a day while learning his craft. This was the first rock song to reach the top of the *Billboard* pop music chart, and it stayed there for eight weeks. But the tune's placement in *Blackboard Jungle*, a gritty 1955 Hollywood film about a violent multiethnic school, starring Sidney Poitier, increased its allure. The marketing message left no doubt: the musicians might be white, but the ethos was black and disruptive.[5]

At the close of 1955, the rock 'n' roll world wasn't just ready for a white superstar, it desperately needed one. Bill Haley, already in his thirties with a receding hairline and the look of a used-car salesman, couldn't fill that role. Pat Boone, who was battling "Rock Around the Clock" on the charts with his own cover version of Fats Domino's "Ain't That a Shame," lacked the rogue quality teens craved. Boone diluted the impact of every rock song he performed—he would even change the lyrics if he feared they were too edgy. For a brief spell, Carl Perkins was the great white hope, and the success of his song "Blue Suede Shoes" in early 1956 looked like a genuine game-changer. But destiny intervened on March 22, when Perkins got into a serious auto accident that left him sidelined at a decisive moment. Perkins had actually been driving to New York to perform on a high-profile TV show that might have launched him into the stratosphere of pop culture. Instead, he was still recuperating in Tennessee on April 3 when Elvis Presley performed "Blue Suede Shoes" on *The Milton Berle Show*. That same month, sales of Presley's single "Heartbreak Hotel" reached a million copies and earned the singer his first gold record. Carl Perkins would never have another number-one hit. Presley would enjoy a stunning eighteen chart toppers, and he dominated the airwaves for the rest of the decade.

I have an old jazz musician friend who was hanging out with Jack Kerouac and other beatniks in Big Sur at this turning point in music history (he even shows up as a character in Kerouac's novel *Big Sur*). He assures me that the prevailing attitude among these leaders of 1950s counterculture was that rock 'n' roll was a passing fad. It would come and go, like all those other short-lived music-business fads—boogie-woogie, mambo, female ukulele players, and other trends of that sort. These jazzheads couldn't take rock 'n' roll seriously, not the simple music, not the silly band names, not the sillier dances (between 1955 and 1965, teenagers embraced the Twist, the Watusi, the Shake, the Mashed Potato, and the Frug, among other dance steps). How odd that the 1950s beatniks, who in many ways anticipated the whole hippie movement of the 1960s, should miss such a huge trend even when it was at their doorstep.

But who knows? Maybe without Elvis and his off-the-charts charisma, things might have played out differently. Perhaps in some magical alternative universe, jazz really did come back, or a more sophisticated kind of pop ruled the airwaves. But that's not our world. By the late 1950s, journalists started calling Presley the "king of rock 'n' roll," soon abbreviating it to the simple honorific *The King.* As it turned out, his monarchy was short-lived. But all the leaders and pretenders to the throne who followed in his wake, for more than three decades, would claim they were successors in his lineage. And even the genre itself got a new, simpler name. It was no longer rock 'n' roll, just *rock*, a harsh guttural sound that perfectly captured the take-no-prisoners ethos of the music. By 1960, rock had taken over the commercial music business, and far from burning out as a fad, announced itself as the new status quo.

25

Where Did Our Love Go?

Social theorist Marshall McLuhan announced, virtually at the peak moment of rock triumphant, that the "medium is the message"—a valuable warning that the public's perceptions of reality were getting altered, even back then, by screens and devices. But the prescient Mr. McLuhan might just as well have claimed that the "medium makes the music," because that adage is just as true, and not only in the modern day. For more than a thousand years, each major shift in technology has altered the way people sing. Elvis Presley, for his part, was the first genuine singing superstar of the TV era, and his rise to fame is inextricably linked to the peculiar intimacy of that 1950s centerpiece of household evening ritual. But Presley was merely the latest in a long lineage of medium-made stars, dating all the way back to the rise of music notation and the introduction of the printing press, and probably even further to the days of cuneiform and cave drawings.[1]

But it's hard to deny that these technology-driven shifts accelerated during the twentieth century. Advances in microphones and recording equipment in the 1920s made more conversational ways of singing possible and led to the rise of torch songs and crooners. The introduction of talking films exerted a similar impact—it's no coincidence that the first talkie, *The Jazz Singer*, elevated Al Jolson to a new level of stardom and helped define what we now call the Jazz Age. A few years later, the emergence of radio as the dominant form of family entertainment boosted the popularity of charming vocalists with a genial sense of humor, masters of diversion from the woes of the Great Depression, such as Bing Crosby, Fats Waller, and Eddie Cantor. Each platform defines its own rules of engagement.

But TV demanded a different persona. By this stage, visual impact was far more important than singing skills or instrumental prowess. Presley delivered—so much so that his performances on *The Ed Sullivan Show* rank among the most significant cultural events of the twentieth century. Sixty million people watched Presley on his first guest appearance, a stunning 82 percent of the TV viewing audience, and this was a moment many of them would remember for years to come.

Those tiny boxes in American households seemed too small to contain Elvis's visceral singing, full-body performances that were more eroticized than anything previously featured on network television. The story is told of CBS censors refusing to show what Presley was doing below the waist, afraid those gyrating hips would arouse uncontrollable teenage concupiscence. That oft-told tale isn't entirely accurate, but the truth is even more revealing. The cameras cut off Elvis's famous pelvis only on his third appearance on *The Ed Sullivan Show*. Network executives had learned the hard way that a full-body Presley was too strong a brew for mainstream audiences. His rendition of "Hound Dog" on his second visit had crossed a line, violated some unwritten law of public decency; adding to the controversy, uninhibited screams from the studio audience made it sound as if a bacchanalia were taking place in the aisles of the Ed Sullivan Theater. In the aftermath, outraged citizens burned Presley effigies, along with records and photographs, in Nashville and St. Louis. (In the next chapter, we will look at rock music from the perspective of René Girard's hypotheses about public rituals of sacrificial violence, but note how early these burnings, which recur on a regular basis, appear in the history of the genre.) The FBI, for its part, opened an investigation into Presley's performances, which an informant described as "sexual gratification on stage" and "a strip-tease with clothes on." Only at this juncture did censors intervene. But it was too late; the contagion had spread, and could not be contained.[2]

If you were constructing the perfect crossover star for early rock 'n' roll, the blueprint would look just like Elvis Presley. Elvis was strong and sexy—he came across as a more testosterone-charged version of Hollywood star James Dean, who had died in a car crash just a few weeks before Presley's first national television appearance. In fact, Dean's character in the 1955 film *Rebel Without a Cause* can almost be viewed as a prototype of the Elvis persona. (By the way, another promising Elvis alternative, the great rock icon Buddy Holly, would briefly challenge Presley before dying in a plane crash in 1959, and around this same time, both Chuck Berry and Jerry Lee Lewis faced intense backlash when newspapers covered their relationships with underage women—all adding to the uncanny pattern of rivals' deaths, scandals, and injuries clearing the way for the supremacy of the King.) With all the other contenders pushed aside, Elvis faced no real competition except his own impersonators—and that would turn into a cottage industry still thriving today. But let's be fair to Elvis. No one of his generation, whether singer or movie star, could have matched Presley's charisma and stage presence. And he was likable as well as lovable—those two qualities may seem pretty much the same, but in the world of superstars they rarely coexist. Yet Presley could also exude the flippancy and tough attitude of the perennial bad boy; he was the guy other guys envied and emulated, but would never introduce to their sisters. That dangerous quality, like a bomb ready to go off, was essential to his stardom in a genre built on transgressions, symbolic or otherwise. But above all, Presley had the right pedigree, and I'm not talking *Burke's Peerage*. In the topsy-turvy world of commercial music, that lineage meant humble origins in Tupelo, Mississippi, immersed in the sounds of blues, country, and gospel music.

Have you noticed the pattern? When Cecil Sharp was seeking out authentic folk music, he traveled across the Atlantic and went to the poorest regions in the American South. When record labels went on the hunt for country music talent, they did the same thing. Robert Johnson and the legendary blues guitarists of the 1920s and 1930s came from those same impoverished southern rural roots. As did the stars of gospel music and other genres. And now rock 'n' roll followed the same formula. Consider the curious fact that all this happened during the period of mass migration out of southern rural areas and into the major cities of other regions of the country. Why did music reverse the trend, forcing talent scouts to journey into these poverty-stricken locales to find innovative new styles and genres? This recurring correlation makes little sense unless we grasp the dilemma of insiders and elites in the music business. They crave exciting sounds that shake the paradigm, but they *are* the paradigm. As a result, they must always look far outside their preconceptions and comfort zones for the next new thing. Are we surprised, then, that the same South whose self-made mythos proclaimed it the Land of the Rebel now had morphed into the land of rebellious music?

The same pattern emerges elsewhere in the Americas. In Brazil, the state of Bahia has exerted enormous influence over the musical direction of the nation, serving as a launching pad for the stars of bossa nova, tropicalismo, and other exciting new genres. Why Bahia? It is just one of Brazil's twenty-six states, and contains roughly 8 percent of the population. You could describe it as the Brazilian equivalent of the American South, more Africanized than the rest of the country, and still living with the legacy of a tragic history built on exploitative plantations and forced labor. The Bahia Revolt of 1835 is the only documented instance of a Muslim slave rebellion in the New World, and played a key role in spurring the nation's abolitionist movement. Bahia is still one of the poorer regions in Brazil, but that has hardly constrained its musical riches, which it shares generously with the rest of the world. We find a comparable situation with the rise of tango, which flourished in the poor neighborhoods of Buenos Aires before turning into the dance of Parisian elites. In Jamaica, reggae is closely connected with the Rastafarian community, which set itself up in opposition to British colonial culture and gained adherents among the poor and dispossessed. The specifics of sound and style are different in each instance, but they all built their allure on the defiant stance of outsiders and outcasts.

Rock 'n' roll turned this defiance into a huge money-maker for the music business, but its very success posed a problem: What do you do for an encore? Rock was the music of permanent revolution, and peace was breaking out all over. By the early 1960s, Elvis Presley was already getting assimilated into the mainstream of pop culture. Hollywood came knocking and cast him in a series of hit movies—but check out the shift in his cinematic persona. In *Jailhouse Rock* (1957), Presley plays a convict in prison serving time for manslaughter. By the time we get to *G.I. Blues* (1960), Elvis stars in a formulaic romantic comedy as a charming and polite singing soldier in the US Army. This was the new Elvis, the nice guy you could introduce to your sister. With each passing year, it got harder to view him as an alienated rebel in the mold of James Dean; Presley was more like a young, virile alternative to Dean Martin and Rock Hudson.

His music was changing too. In 1960, Presley released his first album of religious music, *His Hand in Mine*, and followed it up the next year with a project whose name could almost serve as a motto for the new Elvis: *Something for Everybody*, a sweet, sentimental mishmash of pop and country with occasional touches of watered-down rock. All this might have been great for Elvis, but it was lousy for rock 'n' roll. Rock would die if it got assimilated. Yet that seemed likely in 1961 and 1962, when the *Billboard* album charts were filled with Broadway cast albums, movie scores, folk songs, gentle pop, and easy listening projects. Rock 'n' rollers were fitting into that bland music scene with surprising, if dispiriting, ease. If rock wanted to maintain its credibility, the music of permanent revolution needed to find a new battlefield with gnarly new combatants to take up the cause.

I'm hardly surprised that when the next new thing arrived in the rock world, it was actually described by the mainstream press as an invasion—in this case, a *British Invasion*, which turned the whole music business on its head in the mid-1960s. In retrospect, this all makes perfect sense. If musical innovation comes from the outside, why shouldn't it arrive as a kind of military assault, a D-Day type beachhead from another shore? Mulling over the tumultuous impact of the Beatles in February 1964, *Life* magazine compared the band's advent to a World War II bombing: "Like the Blitz, it began with shrieks, sirens and total panic." The bottom line, according to the popular weekly: "In '76 England lost her American colonies. Last week the Beatles took them back."[3]

This felt like something new and strange to those living through it. Yet the arrival of the Beatles merely repeated the same dynamic process that had been driving change and innovation in Western song since the days of the ancient Greeks, when they decided to name their most dangerous musical modes after slave performers from other cultures. Even within Britain, elites in the entertainment world were now displaced by unruly outsiders. This British Invasion wasn't coming from Buckingham Palace or Ten Downing Street, but originated far outside the centers of prestige and power. Liverpool, home of the Beatles, gained notoriety as the emotional epicenter of the movement. But how uncanny that the band members had spent their earliest days amidst constant German air strikes, real battle attacks preceding the symbolic invasion to come. In fact, Liverpool was the most targeted city in Britain after London, and John Lennon was actually born during an air raid. Locals bragged after the war that the area around the Gladstone Dock—located midway between the birthplaces of John Lennon and Paul McCartney—was the most bombed place in all of England during the Blitz.

To some extent, Liverpool never really recovered after the war. The Germans had hoped to take out the port, the mainstay of Liverpool's economy; but what it failed to do, the rise of container shipping almost achieved during the postwar years. This was hardly a propitious environment for an artistic revolution—until you start thinking about all the other musical innovations that have arisen in working-class port cities, from Mytilene in Lesbos to New Orleans on the Mississippi, with their ingrained openness to multicultural influences. If musical innovation comes from outsiders, it makes perfect sense that these gateways to the outside world should serve as breeding grounds for new sounds and styles.

This upheaval in mid-1960s rock 'n' roll was hardly restricted to Liverpool bands, but almost every one of the leading groups originated outside the traditional centers of British musical culture, in working-class neighborhoods and cities more famous for factories than philharmonics. Mick Jagger and Keith Richards, now rising to fame as members of the Rolling Stones, came out of Dartford, an industrial area southeast of London struggling to adjust to declines in local manufacturing. The Animals hailed from Newcastle, famous for coal mining, but the last pit had closed in 1956. Manchester, a center of labor unrest dating back to the Industrial Revolution—both Karl Marx and Friedrich Engels studied the city firsthand while formulating their communist agenda—spawned Herman's Hermits. Tottenham, an ethnically diverse North London neighborhood with a heavy concentration of African and Caribbean residents, produced a whole subgenre known as the "Tottenham Sound" and served as the breeding ground for the Dave Clark Five. Britain presented a very different ethnic and cultural situation from the United States, of course, yet the rise of rock 'n' roll in England seemed to demand a similar socioeconomic setting, defining itself outside the established centers of power and prerogative and beyond the purview of the London-centric entertainment business.

Not every British Invasion rocker rose from the proletariat. Mick Jagger hailed from a family of teachers, and was preparing for a career in business at the London School of Economics when the Rolling Stones first started touring—he didn't drop out until the band secured a recording contract. But even when the families of these musicians were comfortably middle class (or higher) in the social pecking order, these artists' lineages as performers drew on the most rebellious practitioners of black and blue-collar

American music. Mick Jagger and Keith Richards bonded over their shared enjoyment of Chuck Berry and Muddy Waters—and even named their band after the latter musician's 1950 recording "Rollin' Stone." All six cover songs on the Beatles' debut studio album, *Please Please Me*, had been recorded previously by black musicians. The Animals rose to fame on the strength of their hit recording of "The House of the Rising Sun," a traditional folk song about a New Orleans brothel. The Yardbirds—a band that helped launch the careers of Eric Clapton, Jimmy Page, and Jeff Beck—rose to fame as a British Invasion rock group, but started out as a blues/R&B combo and only gradually adapted to the formulas of the new movement. In virtually every instance, the British Invasion was constructed on the foundation of African American influences.

You might think American audiences wouldn't need guidance from England to tap into these currents of homegrown vitality. But the British Invasion bands not only possessed the benefits of their outsider status—always a plus in bold new musical idioms—complete with foreign passports, but added their own homegrown personalities and reference points to the musical mix. The black influences can be heard, but they are transformed. Paul McCartney thought he could sing like Little Richard, but he never really pulled it off—he sounded like Paul McCartney. Mick Jagger drank deeply from Mississippi Delta sources, borrowing heavily from Muddy Waters and Howlin' Wolf, but you would never mistake him for these role models. We should celebrate these failures: Keith Richards may have emulated the rhythm guitar playing of Chuck Berry, but ended up with something exciting and different and all his own. Eric Clapton would never really solo like B. B. King, but that's no cause for complaint either. Joe Cocker tried to sing like Ray Charles, but what came out the loudspeakers was pure rock 'n' roll. Even as they drew on old sounds, these British bands crafted a provocative new vocabulary of their own devising.

American audiences responded with a fervor that has never been surpassed in modern popular music. The Beatles' arrival at JFK Airport in New York on February 7, 1964, set off a crowd reaction that can only be described as mass hysteria. When the band performed on *The Ed Sullivan Show* two days later, some seventy-three million Americans tuned in—at that time a record for televised entertainment. The screaming teenagers in the audience were as much part of the story as the music. Track down the video of that charged moment on YouTube and marvel at the delirium of the onlookers, even more revealing than the performance by the band. And mania meant money. On April 4, 1964, the Beatles held all top five spots on the *Billboard* Hot 100—the only time that has ever happened in the history of the chart. The magazine noted that disk jockeys were tired of playing Beatles songs, but listeners refused to accept anything else. If this had been an actual invasion, the war would have been the shortest on record. The Beatles and their many imitators—new ones would arrive on the scene every month—vanquished all challengers from the moment they stepped off the airplane.

But here something delightfully unexpected happened. I have perhaps conveyed the impression, over the course of this book, that music evolves by means of discernible rules and predictable historical forces. But the processes outlined here are not iron-clad laws; rather, they are adaptive patterns of behavior. They are flexible, multifarious, human—above all, human, which is to say, beyond simple predictive cause-and-effect calculations. Sometimes the entire history of music can shift because of a key figure's whim or personality quirk. And that's exactly what happened with rock music after 1964.

Almost everyone in the music business wanted to imitate the Beatles, but the Beatles proved cussedly hard to pin down and impossible to anticipate. They started changing the style of their music every few months, each new album revealing a different aesthetic stance. By 1965, the Beatles were already a moving target for copycats and wannabes, and seemingly intent on abandoning many of the trademarks of the British Invasion sound. At this juncture, NBC decided to feature a Beatles knock-off on a weekly television show, and signed the Monkees, an appealing construct suitable for mass marketing to the general public. The show *The Monkees*, featuring the eponymous band, launched on September 12, 1966, and offered a fairly convincing simulacrum of the Beatles' movies *A Hard Day's Night* (1964) and *Help!* (1965). The legitimization process already seemed underway, ready to turn the Beatles' sound mainstream just as it had done to Elvis and others. But the Beatles eluded all attempts at pigeonholing. They had already released *Rubber Soul* and *Revolver* with their eclectic mix of experimental pop-rock concepts drawing on a range of influences, from Indian sitar music to the *Tibetan Book of the Dead*. In fact, *Revolver* hit the stores just a few days before the Monkees made their TV debut, making the gap between the imitators and the original all too obvious. Then in November, when the Monkees were basking in the glow of their rapidly eroding half-life of fame, the Beatles started hatching plans for *Sgt. Pepper's Lonely Hearts Club Band*, a kind of psychedelic vaudeville concept album that would initiate an entirely new phase in their career.

This cat-and-mouse game would continue until the end of the decade, and for perhaps the only time in the modern history of popular music, there was no clear role model to imitate for a period of five full years. For many artists (and labels), this proved tremendously frustrating, and entire careers went by the wayside. But for a handful of visionaries, the exhilarating sense of freedom in a music scene without rules launched them on exciting trajectories. New subgenres and styles were emerging in a quasi-anarchic free-for-all, and even old genres were morphing under the influence of a music business operating without clear direction or accepted guidelines. Brian Wilson gave up writing formulaic songs about surfing and, inspired by the Beatles, prodded his reluctant Beach Boy colleagues into recording *Pet Sounds* and *Smile*; the latter, a long-unfinished project, aimed at nothing less than serving up, in Wilson's words, "a teenage symphony to God." The Velvet Underground appeared at this very same moment, refracting influences ranging from the pop art of Andy Warhol (the producer of their debut album) to the avant-garde concepts of John Cage and La Monte Young—all channeled into songs that dealt with formerly taboo commercial music subjects, such as drug addiction, prostitution, and sadomasochism. A few weeks later, Janis Joplin, virtually unknown until she took the stage of the Monterey Pop Festival, shook the audience to its soul with a raw, emotional force that redefined the role of female singers in the rock era. She walked off the stage that day as a new superstar. Frank Zappa, a counterculture guitarist recently released from San Bernardino County Jail—where he had served time for making an audiotape deemed pornographic by the local authorities—was now storming the music world with his band Mothers of Invention, an irreverent ensemble that mixed camp, performance art, and high-powered rock in hitherto unheard ways. At this same juncture, the Doors, another rising Southern California band, climbed to the top of the charts with "Light My Fire," a song that sounded more like the soundtrack to a pagan ritual than a pop tune. Meanwhile, across the Atlantic, the Jimi Hendrix Experience released its incantatory debut album, *Are You Experienced*, a quasi-shamanistic aural brew that marked a new high point in psychedelic hard rock.

And all that was just 1967!

Even Bob Dylan, the poster child for the folk revival movement, found it impossible to resist the new imperative to plug in, rock out, and push the limits. When Dylan arrived on the New York scene in 1961, he impressed listeners as a bard for modern times, mesmerizing audiences with his mix of traditional ballads, old blues, protest songs, and smart acoustic originals that somehow managed to sound both folksy and biting at the same time. You could hear Dylan's ties to older singers, especially Woody Guthrie and the first generation of acoustic blues performers, but he resisted the retro nostalgia that made so many other folk music acts sound like background music for grandpa's shuffleboard party. Dylan, in contrast, offered proof positive of Ralph Peer's prediction that the marketplace really wanted "future folkloric songs." That almost could have served as Dylan's motto, pre–British Invasion. But this same forward-looking stance now forced Dylan to adapt to the supercharged musical landscape of the mid-1960s. For his fifth studio album, *Bringing It All Back Home*, released in March 1965, Dylan incorporated elements of electric rock on the first side, before returning to an all-acoustic format for the B-side tracks. But any doubts about Dylan's allegiances were cleared up

in July, when he released "Like a Rolling Stone," a spirited electric rock anthem that would dominate the airwaves for the rest
of the summer. Even the title of the song seemed to announce a
realignment in the Dylan universe and the artist's determination
to follow the new trails blazed by the prominent British bands of
the era.

Dylan's next step stands out as the most controversial moment
in a career that never lacked for newsworthiness. A few days later,
Dylan decided to play with a plugged-in band, featuring electric
guitar and organ, at the Newport Folk Festival. Attendees still argue
over what really happened that day, whether the boos from the
audience were a response to the music or the poor sound quality or
the short performance set. But the details are less important than
the mythology, which quickly transformed the actual circumstances
into a kind of morality play for music purists. Folk music icon Pete
Seeger was displeased by the proceedings, but he didn't really take
an axe and chop through the cables that powered the electric
instruments onstage. Folk song collector Alan Lomax didn't really
get into a backstage fistfight with Dylan's manager Albert Grossman
(well, he actually did, but that was two days before, at a different
plugged-in concert). Many such tall tales were told after the event.
But even after toning down the exaggerations and distortions, the
larger truth remained: the great Bob Dylan now felt he needed
to adapt to the pop culture zeitgeist, although it meant leaving
behind many of his most devoted fans. And there was heavy irony
in the fact that, at this same moment, the Beatles were now turning more to acoustic folk-flavored songs, many of them inspired by
Dylan's earlier work. Just a few years later, a whole movement of
acoustic singer-songwriters would emerge on the scene, climbing
the charts with songs more like early Dylan than anything from
the electric rock playbook. Yet in the spirit of the second half of
the 1960s, none of that really mattered. The zeitgeist demanded
constant reinvention. No one could afford to stand still or revisit
past successes, and the leading artists stood out for their very willingness to burn the bridges that had launched their careers in the
first place.

In retrospect, all this seems implausible. Could you really build a mass entertainment movement on musicians who continually subverted their own styles and undermined the very sounds that had raised them to the pinnacle of fame? Could you construct a commercial music genre on the notion of permanent revolution? As if this weren't enough, the end of the 1960s brought about the most unrealistic chapter in the whole story, a moment when the history of music seemed ready to veer into the realm of fantasy. It was strange. It was bizarre. And I'm almost ashamed to admit how charmed I am by it. I want to deride it, but I can't.

I'm talking about the moment when the leaders of the rock movement decided that songs would now bring about a *new global culture of peace and love.* As if that wasn't crazy enough, their fans actually started working to make it happen—millions of them taking to the streets, transforming their own lives, and confronting the rest of society with mantras of a love supreme. If you were writing a movie script, this ending would get rejected as too far out. Even in a chronicle such as this one, devoted to the notion that music repeatedly transforms and enchants and changes the world, defying power brokers and ruling institutions, such ambitions seem beyond the scope of what songs can actually deliver.

The war in Vietnam had galvanized the rock community. Rock was the soundtrack of protest, and even before the Summer of Love—the name now given to this culture-changing midpoint of 1967—served as a rallying cry for those who opposed the conflict. Yet protest music is one thing; this new phase in rock offered something more visionary, even spiritual: nothing less than an alternative view of society and daily life, complete with its own philosophy, ethical code, and (most of all) musical anthems. As early as 1965, the peculiar term "flower power" entered the popular discourse—perhaps inspired by Allen Ginsberg's proposal that protesters hand out flowers to police officers and politicians. The popular press was soon writing about "hippies"—advocates of a new rock-inspired lifestyle that embraced almost every aspect of the counterculture, from LSD to ragtag multicolored clothing, but especially the notion of protest, now morphing beyond a mere commentary on war in Southeast Asia to embody a distrust of all conventional values. Rock was no longer a music genre; it was, depending on your perspective, a transformative social movement or a deadly threat to established ways.

On June 25, 1967, the Beatles commandeered the whole world, creating the first-ever global television broadcast via satellite out of the Abbey Road studio in London. This was the worldwide web before the World Wide Web, and an estimated four hundred million people watched. Other celebrity rockers, from Eric Clapton to the Rolling Stones, were invited to the happening. The occasion was a message in the form of a song: "All You Need Is Love." From one perspective, this was nothing new—popular music had always dealt with love. But the love celebrated in commercial music at this moment in history was something different from the romantic and carnal varieties of previous pop tunes. The love movement of 1967 wasn't about sex—or wasn't *only* about sex; it was certainly not a time for chastity—but also celebrated a platonic love of quasi-spiritual or societal dimensions, a vision not just for spooning couples but for everyone.

By this stage, media outlets were reporting regularly on strange new gatherings, called *love-ins* or *be-ins* or *happenings*, mass events inspired by the new vibe. At the great London Love-In of July 1967, held at Alexandra Palace, attendees were each given a flower at the door, and every kind of counterculture movement seemed to coexist peacefully amidst the high-volume rock sounds. Thirty thousand people attended the Human Be-In at Golden Gate Park in San Francisco, and even a power failure that interrupted the music couldn't disrupt the groovy atmosphere—after all, the real show took place among the attendees, many of whom had brought their own chemical entertainment for the day. Music was reshaping society, and the record industry was struggling to keep up with a force beyond its control, and mostly beyond its comprehension. In just a matter of months, the whole British Invasion sound became outmoded, and pop hits were now referring to this new kind of cosmic love. The hippest radio stations of the period were spinning records such as "Groovin'," "Happy Together," "Good Vibrations,"

"The Happening," "Mellow Yellow," and perhaps the most emblematic song of the movement, "San Francisco," which advised listeners to head to the City by the Bay, but make sure to "wear flowers in your hair." Many listeners must have taken this advice seriously: one hundred thousand young people arrived in the Haight-Ashbury district of San Francisco during the Summer of Love on a kind of vision quest to tap into the trippy, transcendental feelings sung about on the radio.

This story, of course, ends badly. But it's worth probing exactly why it ends badly. This will help us understand the paradoxical nature of music as a force of social change. We have already seen so many examples of songs inciting violence even as they promote love in their lyrics. The late 1960s presents the most glaring examples of this contradiction. The groovy atmosphere of 1967 flowed seamlessly into the social upheavals of 1968, and rock music was the soundtrack of both movements. The Weather Underground, a revolutionary group that detonated bombs at government buildings, banks, and other public places, took its name from a Bob Dylan lyric. Charles Manson, the leader of a ruthless gang that committed some of the most high-profile murders of the late 1960s, adopted the Beatles track "Helter Skelter" as his personal theme song. Manson was an aspiring rock singer himself, and it's disturbing to learn how seriously many people in the music business took him before he went on a killing rampage. (But perhaps that's not as strange as it seems at first blush: the demographic profile of superstar singers during this period—young, male, single, and possessing a Nietzschean will to power—shows an eerie similarity to that of convicted murderers.) By 1969, the world of love and happenings was already becoming a dim memory. The biggest news story in San Francisco that summer focused on the Zodiac Killer, a lunatic who liked to murder young couples out on romantic dates, and then send encrypted messages about it to the local press, occasionally quoting song lyrics. The most infamous rock event that year was the Altamont Free Concert, which drew three hundred thousand people, but is remembered for its violence and deaths. Within moments of arriving by helicopter, Mick Jagger was punched by an enraged fan, and things got worse during the Rolling Stones' performance, when a group rushed the stage and spurred reprisals from the Hells Angels gang members handling event security. One of the attendees, Meredith Hunter, drew a revolver, then was stabbed and beaten to death by a member of the security crew. That took place on December 6, 1969—but it was more than the end of a decade; it was the unofficial end of the most optimistic era in popular music. How did things change so quickly? How did we go, within a few months, from "All You Need Is Love" to the rage of Altamont?

In Altamont's aftermath, participants and commentators sought explanations. Perhaps the strangest was speculation, circulated in the underground newspaper the *Berkeley Barb* and other less-than-official sources, that Hunter's murder was a ritual sacrifice presided over by Mick Jagger himself. Even *Rolling Stone*, a more reliable periodical for counterculture news, announced incorrectly that the killing had taken place while Jagger was singing "Sympathy for the Devil" (actually it happened four songs later, during "Under My Thumb"). This may have been shoddy journalism, but also represented a kind of "magical or religious thinking," or "form of wish fulfillment," according to Altamont historian Saul Austerlitz. "The fans," he notes, "really did want Mick Jagger to be powerful enough to summon the Devil."[4]

No more summering in love—people were now worried about summoning Beelzebub! And this shift wasn't just the result of bad karma or a bad acid trip, although body chemistry does play a role. Back at the beginning of our history, we looked at that intriguing hormone oxytocin, which is released into the body's bloodstream via a message from the hypothalamus in response to certain crucial stimuli, including music. When we sing, this hormone makes us feel emotional bonds with those in our group. That's why countries all have national anthems, and sports fans sing their team songs. Some people even call oxytocin the "love hormone" or the "cuddle hormone." And not without reason: your parents probably went on their first date to some event that involved the performance of music, bonding at a concert, a dance or school prom, or romantic movie with some sentimental song over the closing credits. But all this is only half the story. Oxytocin also mobilizes people to fight against other groups. This hormone emerges in situations of stress, and can send people into riots or battles. That explains why military organizations also have their music—marches instead of sentimental songs. And it's why those sports team melodies mentioned above are often called "fight songs," or why protesters express their anger by singing or chanting. In other words, the double role of the hormone is a platform for the double role of music. We will never understand the real role of songs in society if we don't grasp this seeming paradox. Poets tell us that music is the food of love, but they also ought to warn us that songs can stir up violence and brutality. This may be an unpleasant truth—and perhaps this unpleasantness explains why the relationship of music and violence is rarely explored in scholarly studies—but not one a historian of music can afford to ignore.

That's why our Summer of Love couldn't last. But it's also why it will come back again, in some different manifestation and under a new name. It always does. And each time it brings a new soundtrack with it when it arrives on the scene. I suspect we crave that blissful vision all the more because of our inevitable detours into the dark side.

26

The Sacrificial Ritual

ere is a puzzle for you to solve. I will write down a list
of names, and you need to figure out what they have in
common.

Let me start with these two:

- The Beatles
- The Rolling Stones

Perhaps you already have a hunch what this list contains. But let's
add a few more names:

- The Beatles
- The Rolling Stones
- Led Zeppelin
- Grateful Dead
- The Doors
- The Who
- The Beach Boys

By this point, there can be little doubt. I am listing the most influential bands in rock music. Maybe these were even the initial inductees of the Rock and Roll Hall of Fame, or the top vote-getters on one of those recurring magazine polls of all-time greats.

But if you guessed this, you would be wrong. Let's continue the list, but with the addition of some more details.

- The Beatles (John Lennon, dead at age forty)
- The Rolling Stones (Brian Jones, dead at age twenty-seven)
- Led Zeppelin (John Bonham, dead at age thirty-two)
- Grateful Dead (Ron "Pigpen" McKernan, dead at age twenty-seven)
- The Doors (Jim Morrison, dead at age twenty-seven)
- The Who (Keith Moon, dead at age thirty-two)
- The Beach Boys (Dennis Wilson, dead at age thirty-nine)
- The Jimi Hendrix Experience (Jimi Hendrix, dead at age twenty-seven)
- Buddy Holly and the Crickets (Buddy Holly, dead at age twenty-two)
- The Sex Pistols (Sid Vicious, dead at age twenty-one)
- The Allman Brothers Band (Duane Allman, dead at age twenty-four)
- Big Brother & the Holding Company (Janis Joplin, dead at age twenty-seven)
- Nirvana (Kurt Cobain, dead at age twenty-seven)
- Etc.

An actuary studying this list would be forced to conclude that rock star is the world's most dangerous occupation. *I'm sorry, we can't underwrite your life insurance policy because you play electric guitar.* How can so many superstar bands lose founding members at the age of forty or younger? Even more disturbing, not one of these deaths can be attributed to "natural causes." None of these superstars died quietly in bed surrounded by family. You don't need a statistician to tell you that this cannot be a matter of coincidence.

The odds against that would be astronomical. Some might dismiss these deaths as little more than *bad luck*—John Lennon was in the wrong place at the wrong time; Dennis Wilson had a swimming accident that could happen to anyone; and so on—but the cumulative evidence resists such simplistic narratives. (By the way, even if you eliminate Lennon from consideration, we are still left with the tragic case of the Beatles' first bassist, Stuart Sutcliffe, dead at age twenty-one from the effects of a beating after a 1961 gig. Rock is a dangerous muse.)

Various explanations can be offered, but every one of them is disturbing to consider. Perhaps rock fans are sick in the head, attracted to the most self-destructive personalities in society—they elevate to fame the very characters who will destroy themselves. Maybe that's what fans want from their favorite rock stars. Consider the revealing case of keyboardist Ian Stewart, who was forced out of the Rolling Stones in 1963 because he looked too *normal*. What would the actuaries say about that? Or perhaps the profession changes people once they experience success, turning them into daredevils, drug addicts, maniacs hell-bent on destruction. Or ponder the possibility that creating music at the cutting edge brings extreme danger along with it, like a career involving exposure to radiation or deadly pathogens. The risk of early death is simply part of the job description of visionaries who operate beyond the boring boundaries that constrain the rest of us. Or maybe God just doesn't like rock 'n' roll. Take your pick, and consider the implications.

But the recurring connection between musical performance and violence, dating back to the very origins of instruments as killing tools and pieces of the dismembered bodies of prey—the hunter's bow, the animal's horn, the hidebound drum, the bone flute, the gut strings—suggests that rock 'n' rollers dying young is just one more manifestation of a long-standing linkage. Music has always been a risky business, the art form most closely linked to spilled blood. So many traditional rituals combine music and violence, manifested in so many different ways: warfare, martial arts, victim sacrifice, walking on hot coals, piercings, extreme self-mutilation, and on and on. You find these in the Sun Dance in the Americas, the *Kavadi Attam* in India, the *Anastenaria* in Bulgaria, *capoeira* in Brazil, and everywhere else you look in the world. In modern times, the brutality is typically latent rather than actualized: the danger has been turned into a symbol. In most instances, the ritual has so completely tamed the risks that the latter are almost unrecognizable. But on occasions of particular intensity, whether Altamont or the premiere of Stravinsky's *Le sacre du printemps* or the Sex Pistols' last concert at Winterland, symbols and rituals can no longer contain the powerful emotions aroused by the performers onstage. The crowd seeks a channel for uncontrollable impulses, perhaps even an actual sacrificial victim, whether in a quest for catharsis gone beyond reasonable bounds or as a scapegoat for violence they would otherwise inflict upon each other. The essence of rock, as the music of permanent revolution, is to approach that liminal point where symbol turns into actual violence, but without crossing over the dividing line. Sometimes the rhetoric of rock seems to demand actual sacrifice, but that is more a posture than a genuine proposal. "Rock and roll is so great, people should start dying for it," Lou Reed once announced. "The people just have to die for the music. People are dying for everything else, so why not the music? Die for it. Isn't it pretty?" Reed was exaggerating, of course, but he wasn't far off the mark. The real goal of rock is to play with fire without getting burned. But who can really master that game of brinkmanship?[1]

The sacrificial imperative becomes most clear in the ritualistic destruction of musical instruments at moments of calculated frenzy during performances. Rock didn't invent this spectacle, but quickly recognized its power as a substitute for actual physical violence directed at the band or audience members. "I was one of the first people to destroy an instrument onstage," boasts La Monte Young. "I burned a violin at the YMHA, and people were shouting things like 'Burn the composer!'" As such words make explicit, the instrument is a kind of substitute for the musician, and its ritual destruction has a potent effect on the audience. As early as 1956, virtually at the birth of rock 'n' roll, a performer parodying Elvis Presley on *The Lawrence Welk Show*, a TV series specializing in sweet music for sentimental old-timers, smashed an acoustic guitar on his knees. But it didn't take long for actual rock stars to grasp the value of such gestures. The tale is often told of Jerry Lee Lewis, irritated at having to serve as lead-in act for Chuck Berry at a 1958 concert, pouring lighter fluid on the piano and setting it ablaze—all the while playing his hit song "Great Balls of Fire." The audience (so the story goes) had been getting out of control, and police were struggling to keep them offstage, but they settled for a sacrificial substitute. Did this really happen? Over the years, Lewis has some-times denied the incident, and other times confirmed it. In the mythology of rock, that hardly matters. When Hollywood made a movie out of Lewis's life, the 1989 biopic *Great Balls of Fire*, the burning piano was the highlight of the film. This is how rock stars are expected to act, and if it didn't really happen we must pretend that it did.[2]

With the next generation of rock stars, there could be no doubt about their instrument-destroying rituals. Peter Townshend of The Who claimed that he started this practice by happenstance. He accidentally cracked his guitar when lifting it up at a club with a low ceiling, then decided on the spur of the moment to smash the now damaged instrument to pieces. Audiences at the band's follow-up gigs expected him to do it again—that's the essence of ritual: anticipated repetition—and he frequently obliged. The bro-ken bits of his guitars are now collectors' items, the rock equivalent of saints' relics. But such a powerful routine invited imitation, and soon The Who's drummer, Keith Moon, got into the act. When the band made its US television debut, Moon packed his drum kit with explosives. By some accounts, the resulting blow-up caused Town-shend's subsequent hearing problems, but Moon moved up a rung in the rock pantheon. When the Yardbirds appeared in Michelan-gelo Antonioni's 1966 film *Blow-Up*, the guitarist Jeff Beck tapped into the same zeitgeist, destroying his guitar on camera and caus-ing a riot at the club where the band is playing. Around this same time, the Kinks actually got into an onstage fight during a con-cert in Wales when drummer Mick Avory pummeled guitarist Dave Davies with a drum pedal—Davies ended up in the hospital, and

Avory spent the next three days hiding from the police. Even today, fans of the band talk in breathless terms about the "tiff in Cardiff."

It's surprising how many of the iconic photos of rock artists capture them in the act of destruction. When Jimi Hendrix set fire to his guitar at the 1967 Monterey Pop Festival, this incendiary (literally) performance not only helped launch his career into the stratosphere, but got commemorated as a defining rock moment. The photo of the burning, which starkly emphasizes the ritualistic nature of the incident—Hendrix is on his knees over the flames, raising his hands, seemingly in a kind of invocation to the gods of rock—would appear twice on the cover of *Rolling Stone.* But when *Q* magazine picked the best rock 'n' roll photo of all time, Hendrix lost out to the cover image from *London Calling,* which shows Paul Simonon of the Clash smashing his Fender Precision Bass on the stage of the Palladium in New York—a photograph now prominently displayed at the Rock and Roll Hall of Fame next to the busted instrument.

You could devote a whole book to rock musicians destroying things, as well as each other, and (too often) themselves. Over time, the concept of ritualized rock violence went beyond the concert stage into a range of other settings. Rock musicians became so well known for wrecking hotel rooms that this almost turned into a cliché. In 2010, *The Guardian* even ran an article titled "Why Don't Rock Stars Trash Hotel Rooms Anymore?"—a nostalgic lament for the days when guitar heroes spray-painted the walls, threw TVs out the window, and puked on the sofa. Yet even by the end of the 1960s, the spiral of ritualistic destruction seemed (no pun intended) to burn itself out. The story circulated of Brian Wilson, presiding muse of the Beach Boys, finally going off the deep end when he decided to start a fire during a recording session for the aborted album *Smile.* To enhance the realism of the moment, he handed out red firefighter helmets to the band members. The session was a fiasco, but how fitting when another rumor started making the rounds, later discredited, that Brian Wilson eventually set fire to the tapes of the songs. Just erasing a tape would hardly be good enough for a true rock fan—the music must be offered up as a burnt sacrifice.[3]

This is a book of music history, not sociology or psychology. Even so, it's worth considering why rock music from this era reveals so many resemblances to sacrificial rituals. It's true that songs have been connected to violence as far back as we can trace, but there was something about the tumultuous period between the assassination of John F. Kennedy in 1963 and the Watergate break-in of 1972 that seemed to push commercial music into uncharted, dangerous waters. René Girard, the great theorist of sacrificial rites, may point the way toward an explanation. He notes that these rites, whether real (a human being or animal is sacrificed) or merely symbolic (a guitar is destroyed), impart a powerful social and psychological benefit. They defuse the violence rampant in a society by focusing it on a special victim, usually innocent, and in some instances even treated as a hero or quasi-deity, although this special status may not exempt the proxy figure from mockery and derision.[4]

Girard's description of the ideal target eerily matches the defining characteristics of the musical innovators we have discussed throughout this book: "Ritual victims tend to be drawn from categories that are neither outside nor inside the community, but marginal to it. . . . This marginal quality is crucial to the proper functioning of the sacrifice." The individuals chosen for this dubious distinction are both honored and feared—sometimes their sexual favors are sought, so great is their attraction, but in other instances they find themselves accused of violating taboos or channeling dark powers. Yet after their death, and calm returns to the community, veneration almost completely erases all earlier feelings of negativity. Music stars at this exalted level may even see their recordings reach a new peak of popularity in the week following their demise. The previous lightning rod for destructive emotions is now revered, and relics linked to the victim are treated as special objects cherished by devotees (even to the extent of buying bits and pieces of destroyed guitars on eBay). All musicians should consider these matters with some trepidation. Yes, you are special—but special isn't always a good thing. The very factors that set the performer apart from the audience also stir up powerful emotions both worshipful and destructive. It's only in retrospect, after the dangers have passed, that canonizations, if any, take place.[5]

The participants or audience members are, almost as a rule, unaware that any transference of darker impulses has taken place; in fact, the power of the ritual, according to Girard's model, depends on this lack of awareness. But in a curious side note, he admits that these rites are less important in societies where government officials and legal institutions are trusted and respected—for the simple reason that individuals in these stable environments delegate to authorities a monopoly on violence (declaring war, punishing crimes, etc.), and this replaces more traditional outlets for aggression. By the same token, a loss of that trust in ruling elites thrusts responsibility for violent reprisals back on the individual. In these contexts, rituals and festivals that channel this dangerous energy in the direction of a quasi-sacrificial act may be necessary to prevent the situation from spiraling out of control. Should we be surprised, then, that the Vietnam era—the most destabilizing period in twentieth-century America, at least when measured in terms of loss of confidence in government legitimacy—should have triggered the emergence of the rock concert as sacrificial rite?

That same era witnessed a similar destabilization outside the United States—just consider the Parisian street riots of 1968, the Soviet tanks in Czechoslovakia a few months later, the 1969 riots in Northern Ireland, the Cultural Revolution in China, and many other incidents of mass violence in various locales. By the way, this was the exact same period when Girard was writing his seminal book on sacrificial rites, *Violence and the Sacred*, which he published in 1972. He doesn't deal with music in this work, but we are perhaps justified in concluding that the same events that opened Girard's eyes to the sacrificial crisis of his time were also echoed in the rock culture of the era—which, in its own distinctive way, may have helped defuse the rampant emotions. (And it's worth noting that a Girardian analysis of musicians as quasi-sacrificial victims, although especially helpful in grasping 1960s rock, might be applied in other contexts and situations, for example, with regard to opera, minstrelsy, children's song games, TV reality show singing contests, Robert Johnson and traditional blues, liturgical music, etc.) Put another way, the volatile attitudes evoked by musical performances—whether aroused by a superstar on stage or merely by the losing party in musical chairs or "London Bridge Is Falling Down"—are not just signs of fans' fickle allegiances, but essential parts of the ritual, and even a way groups 'let off steam.'

The success of the sacrificial ritual is typically measured, according to Girard's theory, by its ability to curtail rampant violence in a community and allow individuals to return in a calmer frame of mind to their own individual concerns. This creates a peculiar paradox: the same ritual event that accompanies a dangerous destabilization of society and stirs up violent emotions is also cherished as a source of peace and love. It's a strange combination—a hybrid of aggression and groovy togetherness—yet that's almost exactly how Woodstock and the other counterculture music events of the late 1960s made their mark on modern history. Also, if this hypothesis is correct, both the broader culture and the music scene should lose their violent energies in the aftermath of these rituals. Events such as Hendrix setting fire to his guitar or Keith Moon blowing up his drums with an explosive charge are, from this perspective, much more than publicity stunts or crowd-pleasing antics; they serve rather as potent interventions with cathartic effects, a kind of Aristotelian purging of emotions for those involved. So we should expect that the tumult of the 1960s would be followed by a cooling-off period in the early 1970s. This is, after all, what invariably happens after the resolution of a sacrificial crisis: aggression gives way to conciliation, and collective action is replaced by individual initiatives.

And that's precisely what took place in music during the early 1970s, as counterculture rockers gave way to low-key singer-songwriters and a less aggressive pop sensibility. The year-end *Billboard* list of top singles in 1972 showcased a very different musical landscape: the top twenty included Wayne Newton's "Daddy Don't You Walk So Fast," Sammy Davis Jr.'s "The Candy Man," Gilbert

O'Sullivan's "Alone Again (Naturally)," and other examples of sickly sweet fare, with no instruments harmed in the making of these tracks. Not all the hit songs were aural confectionaries. This era also witnessed the ascendancy of a more intimate artistry in the works of true modern troubadours such as Joni Mitchell, Carole King, Elton John, James Taylor, Nick Drake, Harry Chapin, Neil Young, Randy Newman, Don McLean, Cat Stevens, Carly Simon, and others. But the shift to a more introspective, individualistic ethos could be seen everywhere on the commercial music scene. Even the Beatles, whose advocacy of peace and love apparently couldn't heal their own rifts, were now forging separate careers after their breakup, formally announced in April 1970. Almost at the same moment, Paul Simon dissolved his partnership with Art Garfunkel—although this duo had just released a megahit about togetherness and overcoming differences, the Grammy-winning anthem "Bridge Over Troubled Water"—and both joined the growing ranks of solo acts on the circuit. At this turning point, even a superstar working band seemed too confining, and the next phase seemed to demand the clarity and prerogatives of an *auteur*, not the coming together of a collective.

Black music was making a similar transition. The group-oriented vocal harmony, doo-wop, and traditional R&B sounds of African American commercial radio were now pushed aside by a funkier variant of the singer-songwriter movement. In 1970, Diana Ross separated from the Supremes, Curtis Mayfield departed from the Impressions, and Eddie Kendricks left the Temptations. Star singers increasingly saw bands as impediments, and now craved a place by themselves in the spotlights—and perhaps an excuse to stop sharing royalties and paychecks with less famous colleagues. In 1971, Michael Jackson released his first music as a solo artist (although he continued to perform with the Jackson 5). In 1972, Smokey Robinson departed from the Miracles, and in 1974, Sly Stone left his "Family" to start recording as a solo act. Stevie Wonder took this prevailing spirit of individualism to the next level, dismissing the Motown label studio musicians and songwriters who had accompanied his rise to fame, and playing *all* the instruments on many tracks.

Solo artists were the new face of soul music, and never before had it been easier for black performers to cross over into mainstream Top 40 radio. Just a few years earlier, black artists of extraordinary talent, such as Aretha Franklin, Nina Simone, and James Brown, had encountered countless obstacles in their attempts to reach audiences outside the African American community. Everything from music genres to hotel rooms on the road had been segregated into separate black and white categories. But now the traditional marketing barriers were collapsing in the face of the new tone of the 1970s scene. Even B. B. King could enjoy a crossover hit with "The Thrill Is Gone" (1970), after decades of relegation to the R&B charts. Rock and pop stations were helping to spread the fame of Roberta Flack, Bill Withers, Isaac Hayes, Bob Marley, Marvin Gaye, Minnie Riperton, and dozens of other rising black artists. Society was changing, and so was the music. The spirit of the age demanded self-expression, lyricism, and intimacy and cut across many boundaries that had previously pigeonholed and ghettoized commercial black music.

For a while, it appeared as if music fans had left the over-the-top intensity of the 1960s behind them—but appearances can be misleading. Before the end of the decade, sexual preening and violence would reemerge as the inescapable gravitational poles of the commercial music scene, manifesting themselves this time in the guise of, respectively, disco and punk rock. And soon hip-hop would join to form a triumvirate of sassy, in-your-face genres that collectively toppled the short-lived reign of lyrical troubadours and soulful balladeers.

As we have seen, similar shifts had already taken place during the 1930s and 1950s (and no doubt earlier). It's almost as if fans crave disruption, and when the upheavals in popular music come to an end, peacetime can only last a few short years before audiences demand a new insurgency. Recall how, by the dawn of the 1930s, the hot jazz of the 1920s had fallen out of favor, replaced by moody torch songs and upbeat novelty numbers. Yet this proved just a passing interlude: the Swing Era brought intense dance music back to the forefront during the second half of the decade. In the 1950s, the pattern repeated. The decade started with dreamy pop music and (again) novelty songs dominating the charts, but they gave way in the second half of the decade to hotter dance music, this time in the guise of early rock 'n' roll. The transition in the 1970s was the same. After the rock revolution, a low-key, nuanced aesthetic came to the forefront of popular music with the under-produced singer-songwriters—who sometimes relied only on a guitar or piano for accompaniment—and they gained enthusiastic followings. But, as the lessons of history tell us, this could not last. Fans would soon demand something hotter, something sexier, something more danceable.

When it arrived, this new dance music came with a new name: *disco*. The name, a shortening of the term *discothèque* (a French word originally signifying a collection of phonograph records), also indicated a change in the technology. Disco nightlife didn't need actual musicians, and thus signaled a decisive break with the past—one that still defines the dance scene of the current day. Economic reality facilitated this shift: hiring musicians to play dance music was expensive, but a DJ spinning records in a disco format cost a fraction of a name band. Yet new attitudes and lifestyles also contributed to the rising disco culture. The real action in the club was no longer on the bandstand but out in the crowd. When they made the definitive disco movie, *Saturday Night Fever* (1977), the director never considered putting the musicians in the film—even though the Bee Gees' accompanying dance music generated the biggest-selling soundtrack album of all time, sitting on top of the chart for more than four months. Real-life discos were no different: attendees were checking each other out, assessing dance moves, and advancing romantic—or merely sexual—conquests. Music has always been connected with sex, as far back as the fertility rites of yore, but never had the music business been so openly interventionist in facilitating liaisons. (I recently heard one melancholy dance club owner complaining that the Internet had destroyed his business, *not* because of streaming music, but due to the ease with which sexual hookups can now be arranged online. *Go to the disco to get laid? Nah, they got an app for that now.*) Disco was Tinder before there was Tinder.

The music itself could hardly have been simpler. The tempos rarely deviated much from 120 beats per minute. Even when the music relied on a real flesh-and-blood drummer, the beat had to maintain a quasi-machine-like predictability. Fancy chord changes or arrangements were unnecessary, even distractions. As for lyrics, a slogan could suffice, often little more than a banal exhortation to the dancers: "You Should Be Dancing," "Get Up and Boogie," "Get on the Floor," "Shake Your Booty," "Get Down Tonight," and other mantras of disco date advice. Old-school music fans often ridiculed the formulaic tracks, and musicians lamented the replacement of live bands with cheaper disco formats. A backlash gradually emerged over the course of the 1970s, reaching its peak at the infamous Disco Demolition Night held at Comiskey Park in Chicago between the games of a July 1979 baseball double-header. Organizers anticipated a crowd of twenty thousand, but fifty thousand people actually showed up to watch the explosion of a huge crate of disco records. Attendees were so roused by the detonation—a new variant of the old sacrificial ritual—that they stormed the field and wouldn't leave until riot police intervened.

Around this same time, the Rand Corporation was developing an innovative new theory of marketing based on lifestyle categories. Advertisers had long used demographic data to target their campaigns, but they had focused on income levels, age, and traditional assumptions about gender roles. One of the Rand pioneers told me that the breakthrough moment for lifestyle marketing came when Merrill Lynch relied on the think tank's advice in crafting its "bullish on America" TV commercials, with their images of actual bulls, often in incongruous settings—the most famous featured the proverbial bull in an actual china shop. Lifestyle analysis showed that an influential group of consumers saw themselves as individualists who thought for themselves and took pride in getting ahead of the crowd; they wanted to view themselves as leaders, not followers, just like the free-spirited bull in the marketing campaign. Merrill Lynch's ensuing success proved that companies could gain consumers' trust by tapping into their psyches before targeting their wallets. In time, almost every first-rate consumer brand would try to identify lifestyle triggers and cues, but this shift was slow in developing. Old habits die hard, especially in big corporations.

But not in the music business. Record labels knew about lifestyle marketing long before it had a name. The creation and cultivation of commercial music genres—a major preoccupation of record labels at least since the 1920s—had essentially been a task of lifestyle definition almost from the start. Loyalty to country and western, jazz and blues, classical music, and other categories often depended more on a fan's self-image, fantasy life, and aspirational projections than on the brute measurable facts of census data. When the rock revolution arrived, labels quickly realized that this genre, too, was driven largely by lifestyle considerations—and even if the industry was sometimes clumsy in applying this insight, it was still light-years ahead of the automobile and appliance manufacturers, with their simple-minded notions of status and income. So we shouldn't be surprised that emerging lifestyles, especially those related to sexual liberation and nontraditional gender roles, found a platform in the music business long before corporations in any other significant sector of the economy dared to acknowledge them. This isn't because record labels were especially progressive, or even because they anticipated the changes to come. Rather, the astute managers in the industry mostly just got out of the way and let musicians lead the charge. Industry execs had learned (often the hard way, through mistakes and miscalculations) that their profits depended on the charged and sometimes mysterious psychic relationship between performer and audience. Even if they didn't understand it, they didn't mess with it. Tolerance was simply a smart business practice.

That's why stories about the so-called visionaries of the music industry are often surprisingly banal. The Chess brothers distributed liquor before starting the label that launched Chicago blues, a shift that might be viewed as the simple substitution of one intoxicant for another. Long before Colonel Tom Parker steered Elvis Presley onto his path to fame, he had worked as a carnival barker. The three Mafia investors in the Stonewall Inn, a focal point of the gay rights movement in the late 1960s, wanted to make a buck, and didn't have much respect for police and city regulations. These pioneers succeeded because they knew nothing about corporate marketing, but had a shrewd grasp of human nature not taught at Harvard Business School.

So at least the business interests didn't interfere when alternative lifestyles moved to the forefront of the music scene in the 1970s. No manager could have ever concocted David Bowie's Ziggy Stardust persona of 1972—which combined crossdressing, gender fluidity, science fiction concepts about extraterrestrials, and a strong ass-shaking backbeat into something never seen before onstage. But in retrospect, Bowie, too, stands out as a far-sighted sociologist, mapping lifestyle changes long before they entered the mainstream. The same is true of *The Rocky Horror Picture Show*, which started as a stage musical in 1973 and was turned into a low-budget movie in 1975. At the time, few paid much attention, and many who did dismissed *The Rocky Horror Picture Show* as a failed exercise in camp humor. One commentator described the film as "a cross between a Busby Berkeley musical and a drag version of Frankenstein." *Newsweek* summed up the prevailing view in a three-adjective dismissal: "tasteless, plotless and pointless." Yet the film soon started appearing at art-house cinemas in midnight screenings, where it showed remarkable staying power. In its celebration of freeform gender identities and reversal of stereotypes—the mainstream couple now emerges as the misfits, while outsiders set the norms—this seemingly lightweight musical comedy proved positively oracular, offering a glimpse into the shape of sexual personae to come. Other rising music acts, whether disco artists, such as the Village People, or hard rockers in the mold of the New York Dolls, confirmed that this was a genuine movement. Music had been the first field to embrace racial integration, and it was now doing the same in a new sphere, alerting mainstream society via the airwaves to changes that would soon come out of the shadows in their communities.[6]

It was all too easy, at the time, to underestimate the subversive elements in much of this music. Many in the media labeled it as *glam rock* or *glitz rock*, names that made the whole movement seem like a pose, a stage construct not much different from the clichéd light shows and props that tired rock bands were using to justify rising ticket prices for warmed-over radio hits. Elton John might show up onstage wearing anything from a Disney princess dress to a bumblebee costume. The Village People put on the workaday uniforms of the most banal professions (cowboy, cop, construction worker), somehow managing to turn them into gay cultural archetypes. Freddie Mercury adopted a dazzling range of theatrical stances onstage—at his last concert, he took on the persona of a monarch, wearing a golden crown and royal robe while performing "God Save the Queen." At the other extreme, the band Kiss specialized in creepy clown makeup suitable for a low-budget black-and-white horror film. Many onlookers may have dismissed these moves as stunts or jokes, not the first stirrings of a radical social movement. But these rockers probably did more to instill notions of tolerance and diversity than any legislators of the era. Here again, music showed its hidden power to champion human rights and expand personal autonomy.

At this same juncture, other forms of musical rebellion were shaking up the cultural landscape. They appealed to fans who craved something edgier than disco. For a time, heavy metal bands, with their ultra-loud, ultra-aggressive music, emerged as standard-bearers for a more confrontational rock stance. These varied in tone and degree of gnarliness, and connoisseurs would eventually make fine distinctions between dozens of subgenres, including doom metal (slower, despairing, a gloomy trip down the river to hell), black metal (fast, with shrieking vocals, sometimes flavored with fascist allusions), pirate metal (hardass, but with occasional sea shanty overtones), industrial metal (what your factory job would sound like if it came with guitar riffs), satanic metal (a nasty soundtrack for worshipping the dark lord), and Christian metal (a saintly soundtrack for subduing the dark lord), among others. As the idiom evolved, even the name of a band could serve as a kind of warning, or at least a guarantee that the uninitiated would stay away—especially when the marquee at the local concert hall announced the arrival of Anthrax, Black Death, or Carcass (and we haven't even gone beyond the ABCs of metaldom). Do you buy a ticket or set up a quarantine zone? As even these thumbnail descriptions indicate, this music came with agendas as ponderous as the huge loudspeakers that loomed onstage, blasting metal sounds to auditoriums packed with true believers.

At its best, metal music lived up to its billing. It snubbed its nose at parents and authority figures. Its leading exponents knew their instruments, and sometimes even achieved a raw and vulgar virtuosity that exhilarated audiences. At a minimum, those in rapt attendance at concerts by Black Sabbath, AC/DC, Metallica, and other star metal acts were assured of immersive performance art of the highest level of theatricality.

Even so, the rise of metal couldn't hide the pervasive sense that rock was losing its edge during the middle years of the 1970s. Just a few years before, rock 'n' roll had stirred up an earthshaking social movement, mobilizing millions of young people and channeling their demands for radical change in society at large. Metal music seemed to maintain that radical stance, but now only for a much smaller niche of devotees—fringes within fringes beset by infighting and constant denunciations of *poseurs* in their midst, wannabes who didn't deserve true metal acolyte status. If rock was seen as the music of a new generation taking to the streets, metal was the genre of disaffected teens sulking in their bedrooms. Their impact was mostly restricted to annoying parents with the loud music coming from behind a locked door. Eventually pop culture would turn metalheads into jokes, parodying their in-bred zeal in comedies such as *Beavis and Butt-Head* and *Wayne's World*. But long before clueless metal fans became a meme, the mainstream culture had decided it could safely ignore these antics. If rock hoped to maintain its status as the music of permanent revolution, it needed something stronger, even more defiant, a lifestyle formula scarier and less hokey than Ozzy Osbourne and Kiss clown makeup.

When punk rock arrived on the scene, in all its bloody glory, fans loved it or hated it, but no one doubted that this was something dangerous and volatile. I was living in England in the late 1970s and early 1980s, immersed in my own niche culture experiences as jazz musician (by night) and philosophy grad student (by day), but even I had to pay attention to the punk ethos. When punk gangs showed up in my neighborhood, they wanted people to feel their presence as disruptive and threatening. I once got caught up in a standoff between punks and police, the stage was set for a riot, and I counted my blessings that I escaped before things got out of control. Just a few years before, when Carole King and James Taylor had ruled the charts, no one suspected that a new music genre would come along that could mobilize something like this. Even my cherished jazz seemed a pale thing by comparison.

Music writer Jerry Portwood has gone so far as to claim that punk rock deserves more credit than politicians for bringing down the Berlin Wall—a view that may seem like mere punk braggadocio until you examine the documents he has gathered. They show the maniacal obsession of East German secret police with this rebellious youth movement. "I couldn't believe, when I was reading the Stasi files, the level of paranoia," Portwood explains. "The deeper you go into it, you realize, well actually, they were right. It was a genuine threat to the dictatorship because they were trying to take control of the basic decisions in their lives." Yet punk was simply fulfilling the time-honored tradition, one we have now traced back thousands of years, linking new ways of singing with the expansion of personal autonomy and threats to those in positions of authority. Punks thrived (and some died) by that linkage.[7]

This new subversive movement called into question almost every core value of the rock world. Previously, bands strived for hits and judged their success by radio airplay and TV appearances, those measuring rods that had validated the stardom of Elvis, the Beatles, and other rock elites of earlier days. Now, the highest achievement was a song that radio stations were *afraid to play*. When the BBC imposed a total ban on the Sex Pistols' "God Save the Queen"— a mild response when you consider that some citizens were calling for a public hanging of band members—sales took off. Even though many retailers refused to stock the single, 150,000 copies per day got snatched off the shelves by eager fans. In the past, bands celebrated when they saw their name on the charts, but the Sex Pistols could boast of an even more amazing accomplishment: the official UK hits chart put a blank entry where their song should have been listed. Even Satan-worshiping rockers had never inspired that degree of institutionalized loathing.

During the previous decade, leading rock bands had raised the standards of musicianship by several rungs. Metal bands took pride in their shredding, and progressive rock groups, such as Yes and Emerson, Lake & Palmer, incorporated virtuoso techniques from the music conservatory into their explosive performances. But the new generation of punk stars not only rejected all that, but strutted in pride over how little they practiced, how much they didn't know about their craft. "I had no idea how to tune a guitar and only knew the E chord," boasted Dee Dee Ramone of the Ramones. "No one else was any better." When Paul Simonon joined the Clash, he didn't play an instrument, and learned his bass guitar parts through rote imitation. That didn't stop CBS Records from signing the band to a £100,000 contract after the Clash had only played a few gigs, most of them as a warm-up act. Countless copycat bands were emulating the Sex Pistols at this juncture, but their bassist, Sid Vicious, couldn't even handle the simple parts on the group's debut album—bandmate Steve Jones had to play those very rudimentary bass lines. Jones, after all, had three months of actual experience with a guitar before the Sex Pistols formed, making him a polished pro by punk standards. (In Vicious's defense, some of his fans quipped that bass wasn't his preferred instrument—it ran a distant second to the syringe.)[8]

But who needed musicianship when what rock fans really craved was a sacrificial victim? And no one in the music world of the late 1970s was better suited to play that role than Sid Vicious (born John Simon Ritchie in London, 1957), the poster child for punk rebellion. A public hanging wouldn't be necessary; anyone could see that. Vicious was hell-bent on self-destruction. Here's a thumbnail CV of his formative years: Vicious played his first gig with the Sex Pistols in April 1977, shortly after his release from the Ashford Remand Centre. He already had a reputation for violent outbursts in clubs—his latest moment of public rage had left a young woman blinded in one eye, and Vicious entertained himself during the resulting detention by reading a book about Charles Manson. Over the next six months, the Sex Pistols got fired from two record labels, created a controversy by swearing on national TV, were banned in much of Britain, and provoked almost the entire establishment, from media pundits to leading politicians, into paroxysms of loathing. Their first album came out in October, but the Sex Pistols were *already* the most notorious rock band of their generation.

The band's rising fame did nothing to soften either Vicious or his public image. Performances by the Sex Pistols were less like rock concerts and more akin to frenzied cult rituals out of Euripides's *Bacchae*. Usually, fans show up to adulate and applaud, but the punk audience seemed just as likely to taunt and assault the heroes onstage. Yet the Sex Pistols relished the dangerous energy they roused, and by any fair assessment, they instigated much of the violence unleashed upon them. When the band performed in San Antonio during their ill-fated US tour, fans threw beer cans and other objects—this was now a part of the punk performance ritual— and Vicious got into an altercation with a taunting fan, swinging his guitar at the transgressor. He only grazed a roadie's shoulder, yet soon another story was making the rounds, spreading like wildfire from punk to punk: Vicious, the rumor went, had bashed in a fan's head with his ten-pound Fender bass. In Dallas, things got even stranger. The Sex Pistols brought their punk act to a country music ballroom previously managed by Jack Ruby (yes, *that* Jack Ruby, the man who shot Lee Harvey Oswald, who in turn shot President John F. Kennedy), and here the fans threw tomatoes, beer cans, bottles, and other objects at the stage. Vicious played covered in his own blood, probably from multiple causes, including self-inflicted injuries with a razor and a broken Heineken bottle. Photos of the event show the words "Gimme a Fix" carved into his chest.

When the band showed up in San Francisco on January 14, 1978, for the final stop on its US tour, there were some expectations that the Sex Pistols would attract a more sophisticated audience than at its previous stops in Baton Rouge, Dallas, and Tulsa. Here at Winterland—where I went to hear fan-friendly music as a college student and my mother had visited a generation before for skating when it was home to an actual ice rink, a true *Winter*-land— things would be different, no? Scads of media people were in attendance, many them traveling on assignment from Los Angeles or elsewhere, to assess the hot new band. But from the start they could tell this would not be a typical rock road show. In Dallas, Sid Vicious had greeted the audience with "Ya cowboy faggots"; in San Francisco, Johnny Rotten's first words to the fans were "You're a queer lot." Things got worse from there. Greil Marcus, the leading chronicler of the punk ethos, describes the scene:

> One had heard that, in the U.K., audiences "gobbed"—spit—at punk performers; in San Francisco the Sex Pistols were greeted with a curtain of gob. One had heard that, in the U.K., there was violence at punk shows (the storied event told of a woman losing an eye to a shattered beer glass; Sid Vicious was said to be responsible, though he denied it, but not that he had beaten a journalist with a chain); in San Francisco a man in a football helmet butted his way through, smashed a paraplegic out of his wheelchair, and was himself beaten to the floor. . . . [Johnny Rotten] hung onto the microphone stand like a man caught in a wind tunnel; ice, paper cups, coins, books, hats, and shoes flew by him as if sucked up by a vacuum. . . . Sid Vicious was there to bait the crowd; two fans climbed onto the stage and bloodied his nose. . . . For decades, pulp rock novels had ended with a scene out of *The Golden Bough*, with the ritual devouring of the star by his followers, and Sid Vicious was begging for it, for absolute confirmation that he was a star.[9]

This band would never perform again in concert, and, in truth, it's hard to imagine how the Sex Pistols, or any performers, could take the rock ritual of sacrificial violence any further without devolving into pure riot and orgy. Even so, the offstage coda to the Sex Pistols legend is far more brutal than anything they did on tour. In the band's last US radio interview, Sid Vicious even gave a glimpse of that postscript. Asked about what the future held in store, he predicted he would probably be dead within two years. That proved an optimistic assessment. It took roughly half that time.

You could write a book about the following year, but here is the thumbnail sketch: In October, Vicious would get charged with murdering his girlfriend, Nancy Spungen, with a knife. Ten days later, he attempted suicide, slitting his wrist with a broken lightbulb. During the resulting confinement at Bellevue Hospital, he tried to jump out a window. In December, the punk rocker was arrested for assaulting Todd Smith, brother of singer Patti Smith, and placed in Riker's Island for detention and detox. Within hours of his release, on February 2, 1979, Sid Vicious died of a heroin overdose.

He was twenty-one years old. And it was surprising he had lasted that long.

27

Rappers and Technocrats

S id Vicious belongs to my generation; I was born just a few weeks after him. The whole punk ethos was constructed by my contemporaries, those of us who arrived too late for Elvis and the Beatles, but had front-row seats for this new spectacle that promised to push everything to the limit. Even so, the Sex Pistols' worldview is so far afield from my own that I struggle to find any common ground. Much of it is horrific, sometimes repulsive. Nonetheless, I admit I am riveted and chastened by the band's abbreviated career. In a disquieting sort of way, Sid Vicious & Co. gave rock fans exactly what they wanted—and, after all, isn't that the definition of success for an entertainer?

A useful dictum: If you really want to understand a new type of popular music, turn away from the stage and gaze at the audience. The Sex Pistols taught us much about these onlookers. Perhaps rock, in its most extreme manifestations, is really not so different from the gladiator games of yore, or the bullfights and cockfights and other blood spectacles of today. I wish I could dismiss all this— Altamont, Charles Manson, Sid and Nancy, Mark David Chapman, rockers dying young, fans out of control, etc.—as a string of evil coincidences, the dispensation of a quirky and unpredictable fate. But I can't. There was something definitive and revealing and deeply unsettling about the Sex Pistols that nothing in later installments of rock stardom will ever either erase or surpass. And though it would be wrong to say that rock or even punk rock ended at Winterland and Hotel Chelsea, there's really no suitable encore, nothing that can take the genre's ethos of rebellion any further. What started with Elvis Presley ended with Sid Vicious.

Should we be surprised, then, that the 1980s started with the same kind of retrenching that had previously occurred at the dawn of the 1930s, the 1950s, and the 1970s? The rising tides of corporatization played a key part in this shift, as every aspect of the industry, from band discovery to radio formats, became increasingly streamlined and micromanaged. Of course, this was like trying to capture lightning in a bottle. Could you really reduce the permanent revolution of rock to a corporate business model? The music bosses were willing to spend the money to find out. One billion albums were sold in 1981, and there was plenty of cash to go around. But the two biggest changes of that era were easy to miss at the time: the invention of the audio compact disc in 1980 and the launch of MTV in 1981. Both seemed like small and insignificant events at the outset, but they would change everything in music during the course of the decade.

A darker truth was hidden there. This was the moment when music technology started evolving faster than musical styles themselves. The songs would change at a glacier's pace over the next several decades. A Lady Gaga song of thirty years later would be quite recognizable to a Madonna fan of the 1980s. The hip-hoppers of the Reagan era would nod knowingly at many of the beats and attitudes of new-millennium rappers. Jazz after the 1980s became increasingly obsessed with its own heritage, and the quest for respectability often got confused with mimicry of the past. Rock today is mostly a nostalgia business. Country radio, for its part, hasn't invented a new trope in a horse's lifetime (roughly twenty-five to thirty years, for your information). In several commercial genres, the exact same song from yesteryear would get sampled—or, in a surprising number of cases, actually plagiarized—by the hit-makers of a future day. Marvin Gaye died in 1984, but he would earn more from copyright lawsuits a generation later than he ever did during his lifetime. What's old is new, and what's new is old.

The songs are timeless, and artistry, now as always, defies generational barriers. But the technology of Internet-age music would be unrecognizable to a time traveler from the 1980s. Streaming, YouTube, peer-to-peer sharing, torrents, music from your phone or wristwatch, music blogs on the Internet, algorithm-generated playlists—each and every one of these would mystify a fan from that earlier era, even if the songs that all this tech delivers sound vaguely familiar. How dispiriting to consider that the real revolutions in music would increasingly take place in corporate offices and Silicon Valley research departments, not in Mississippi jukejoints and Liverpool clubs. That is the lasting legacy of the 1980s and 1990s, but who dared imagine it at the time?

The prevailing ethos back then was, in fact, a sense of unlimited freedom and unconstrained possibilities. Punk had pushed the limits, and it had overcome threats of censorship and criminal prosecution. With the benefit of hindsight, the two corporate entities with bland alphabet-soup names (A&M and EMI) that had dropped the Sex Pistols before their apotheosis looked like close-minded fools. By the 1980s, record companies had finally learned their lesson: anything goes so long as it sells. Even as the punk ethos lost some of its edge in the early 1980s, creativity flourished with the rise of various indie, post-punk, and New Wave sounds. In truth, much of this music resisted labels or pigeonholes. Talking Heads and their star singer, David Byrne, are considered pioneers of New Wave music, but with their mix of a surreal performance art stance with danceable beats, along with an eccentric onstage posturing bordering on self-parody, the band defies easy categorization. The British rising star Sting and his power trio the Police earned a similar New Wave label, but if you listen long enough to his music you hear bits of everything from reggae to jazz, all streamlined and laser sharp, and with a very unfashionable allegiance to musicianship and poetic expression that bristle inside the slick packaging.

Bruce Springsteen had launched his recording career during the era of singer-songwriters, and his producer, John Hammond, had hoped to groom him as a successor to Bob Dylan—in an interview from 1972, he described the artist as a "young folksinger." But Springsteen had different plans and in the early 1980s was crafting a populist arena rock sound that blended working-class Americana, progressive social commentary, and old-school rock 'n' roll tropes in hitherto unheard ways. There was no playbook. The spirit of the age was diverse enough to embrace the post-punk songwriting of Elvis Costello, the artsy synthpop of Cyndi Lauper, the androgynous neo-funk of Prince, the glittery dance grooves of Blondie, the dark melancholy of Morrissey and his band the Smiths, and countless other unique takes on musical self-expression.

Yet, as the decade went on, the emerging technology of the music video and the growing influence of MTV rewrote the rules of the record business. The notion of short music-driven films built around a single song had been around for decades. Hollywood had tinkered with this format since the beginning of talking movies, but without much conviction or consistency. Companies made various attempts to introduce jukeboxes that combined film and music, but the grand promises that accompanied the launch of the Cinebox and the Scopitone never were fulfilled. Then cable television came along in the 1980s, creating the perfect platform for a new generation of music videos. By the close of the decade, more than fifty million US households were subscribing to cable, and almost eighty cable channels were competing for cheap programming to fill up airtime. What could be more affordable than music videos, especially if the record labels covered the cost of production? MTV—its name originally served as an abbreviation for *music television*—took full advantage of this new state of affairs.

The effect on the commercial music business was extraordinary. Almost from the start, record stores in areas with high cable penetration were forced to stock music by MTV acts, even bands that were getting almost no radio airplay at the time. The network could single-handedly turn a previously little-known band, such as Men at Work or the Human League, into a major act. By 1983, even Hollywood started to take notice. Paramount decided to boost the visibility of the film *Flashdance* by editing portions of the movie into cable-ready material for MTV. Many critics panned the film, but MTV helped turn *Flashdance* into the third highest-grossing movie of the year. In the aftermath, Hollywood studios began creating custom-made music videos to promote their new films, even if they lacked suitable scenes. But the biggest beneficiaries were forward-looking artists who grasped the new reality: namely, that songs were no longer self-sufficient on this new tech platform. Success required support from experts and specialists rarely consulted by record labels in the past: dancers, choreographers, cinematographers, makeup artists, costume designers, and the like. In an earlier day, a solitary artist with a guitar, a Robert Johnson or Bob Dylan, could conquer the music world. Now, a whole support crew was required.

The defining artists of the decade, Michael Jackson and Madonna, anticipated the late twentieth-century rules of audience engagement with prescient clarity. Just a few years before, rock megastars would have laughed in derision had anyone suggested that knowing slick dance steps would be essential to their career. But these new-era MTV stars spent more time working on their dance routines than studying music theory, and they surrounded themselves with teams of dance professionals who could ensure that every move and gesture was as well crafted and rehearsed as those in a Broadway routine or Busby Berkeley spectacle. With his 1983 music video "Thriller," Jackson pushed this aesthetic vision to the next level, creating a fourteen-minute plot-driven dance extravaganza that stands out as the most innovative short film of the period. Although it failed to achieve an Oscar nomination—a puzzling oversight, but perhaps a sign of Hollywood's fear of competition from MTV—audience response was so enthusiastic that MTV started playing "Thriller" twice every hour. Yet the impact on record sales was still more dramatic. *Thriller* became the best-selling album of all time: it generated seven hit singles, won eight Grammy awards, and established Michael Jackson, now dubbed the King of Pop, as the leading male music star of his era. But never before had so much ancillary talent gone into making a hit record. Perhaps no one could surpass Jackson's stage presence and dance steps, but by the same token, no other singer had a support team that could match his. It included legendary producer Quincy Jones, film director John Landis, choreographer Michael Peters, Oscar-winning makeup expert Rick Baker, and the combined marketing muscle of CBS, MTV, and Pepsi, among others.

Superstardom in music now relied, to an unprecedented degree, on tapping into the cinematic potential of songs. When Madonna reeled off a list of stylish predecessors in her music video "Vogue," almost all of them were Hollywood actresses—Rita Hayworth, Jean Harlow, Ginger Rogers, and other movie queens. No musician made the list, and it's not hard to see why. Madonna had more in common with these screen stars than with the celebrity singers of the past. Her obsession with Marilyn Monroe would be a recurring theme in her career—some even claim she dated John F. Kennedy Jr. for the purpose of emulating Monroe's involvement with his father. Her video for "Material Girl" is filled with allusions to Monroe's "Diamonds Are a Girl's Best Friend" performance from the film *Gentlemen Prefer Blondes*, down to the dress and jewelry. In the 1987 movie *Who's That Girl*, Madonna even gets made up with a fake beauty mark to match the one Marilyn had above her lips. Selling music was still the main thrust of Madonna's career—despite many attempts, most of them unsuccessful, to gain renown as a Hollywood box-office draw—and her songs were well-crafted vehicles, propelled by danceable beats, insistent melodies, and saucy lyrics. But the music itself was now only one ingredient in a larger whole. Even the lavish music videos seemed subservient to the larger mission of crafting a persona. To some extent, the marketable product here was neither an album nor a concert tour, but Madonna herself.

The whole commercial music scene adapted to these new metrics of career success. Visual impact was everything, and opened up new career paths that allowed, for example, Paula Abdul to make the transition from cheerleader for the Los Angeles Lakers to music video star, and Vanessa Williams to go from Miss America beauty contestant to R&B diva. Olivia Newton-John managed to rejuvenate her career with the campy song "Physical": the flesh-strutting video was perfectly suited to the MTV format at a time when many other established stars hadn't adapted to the new platform. By the same token, Prince could shift easily into the role of movie star in the film *Purple Rain*, and it seemed like an extension of what he had already been doing in his compelling music videos. When you consider that the album *Purple Rain* generated more revenue than the movie, you might even be tempted to view the latter as an elaborate music video designed to sell recordings.

This new dominance of a visual medium in the world of music did not come without a heavy cost. Many otherwise talented musicians felt shut out by an industry that craved a certain look and persona. I sometimes wonder whether Michael Jackson, in an earlier day, would have developed his quasi-pathological obsession with plastic surgery if his own career hadn't been so closely linked with the video format. Jackson understood full well how important his *look* was to his renown, and probably felt he was protecting his business empire every time he went under the knife. But the biggest risk here was the increasingly corporatized nature of the music business under the influence of MTV. Record labels paid the bills for these now lavish videos and faced the harsh truth that launching a new superstar act might easily require a million dollars or more. Could renegade and outsider musicians—the lifeblood of music since ancient times—still rise to the top in this world of big-budget productions? Or would record labels grow more cautious, chasing after proven formulas while avoiding risk-taking and unconventional artists?

MTV, for its part, wanted to appear progressive and cutting-edge, but the reality was that it was a multibillion-dollar enterprise run by middle-aged, bottom-line-driven executives. It's hard to stay edgy and experimental when you are generating 40 percent cash-flow margins, growing at 50 percent per year, and getting compensated for delivering profits, not for enhancing the music ecosystem. These stewards of shareholder equity had no qualms about banning videos, forcing the removal of objectionable content, or doing whatever else it took to please a mainstream audience. They loved sexy singers, and after Madonna's success they embraced Whitney Houston, Mariah Carey, and other attractive performers. But not all sexy videos met with their approval. Rick James's "Superfreak," or Motely Crue's "Girls, Girls, Girls," got axed. Cher's "If I Could Turn Back Time" was allowed on MTV only after 9:00 p.m., and the network eventually forced edits so that Cher shared a little less flesh with cable viewers. Around this same time, more adventurous fans started talking about their preference for "indie rock" or "indie music"—those terms didn't exist until the late 1980s, but within a few years emerged as definable genres with large followings. This shift suggested a growing sense that the major labels and their friends at MTV had become too corporatized and less skilled at promoting exciting new talent.

The rise of grunge music exposed all the fault lines in the new order of things. This movement emerged in Seattle in the 1980s and went mainstream in the early 1990s with the tremendous success of Nirvana, Pearl Jam, Soundgarden, and other like-minded bands. Nirvana's album *Nevermind* had started life as a low-budget affair by a still unproven band. The group's previous full-length album *Bleach* hadn't even made the charts on its initial release, although it had gained some traction with college radio stations. The initial budget for *Nevermind* was $65,000, but it ran over and eventually cost $120,000, still modest by the standards of the day. The band's new label, a subsidiary of Geffen Records, saw promise in the finished project and hoped it might sell 250,000 copies, a significant success for a raw outfit that resisted the slickness of MTV-ready fare. But audiences seemed to crave precisely this less polished, more urgent sound. Sales took off, first in the Pacific Northwest and then in other markets. Three months after launch, *Nevermind* dislodged Michael Jackson from the top spot on the *Billboard* chart. The album eventually sold 30 million copies worldwide, and for many listeners would stand out as the defining music of the era. Pearl Jam's *Ten*, released almost at the same moment, found a receptive audience in the aftermath of Nirvana's crossover success and would sell 10 million albums. Once again, a red-hot movement had risen up outside the major urban centers of the music industry, but even the accountants and lawyers, who increasingly called the shots from their LA and New York offices, could grasp the significance of those numbers.

MTV wanted to play a part in this new zeitgeist, but you could hardly imagine an artist less suited to the network's ethos than Nirvana's lead singer, Kurt Cobain. In the late 1980s, MTV was already reducing its dependency on music videos and trying to forge a broader identity as the upbeat and glamorous voice of youth culture. The network's Spring Break broadcasts from Daytona Beach, Florida, captured the new spirit, represented by a heady mix of music, bikinis, beautiful people, and a carefree party-time attitude. Nothing could be further from this ethos than Cobain and his grunge aesthetic, and I am not just referring to the coast-to-coast distance from sunny Daytona Beach to overcast Seattle. Cobain was physically frail, clinically depressed, and plagued by addictions he couldn't overcome. Nirvana's success thrust him into a limelight he did not enjoy and put him under unwanted pressure to redefine himself as a pop culture leader and a public voice for a generation. Cobain definitely wasn't a Spring Break kind of guy, and even the skills he could contribute to MTV and the pop culture vultures—above all, his creativity as a musician and powerful presence as a performer—were out of alignment with the persona now demanded of him. The grunge aesthetic was dark and edgy, sharp-tongued and inward-looking. Its songs dealt with rape, abortion, violence, dysfunctional families, and the incomprehension of outsiders, or even devoted fans, the latter increasingly seen as a burden as grunge went mainstream.

In a more sensible world, grunge would have remained an outsider movement. Kurt Cobain was well equipped to operate in the renegade fringes of indie music; his sardonic attitudes and hypersensitivity made him a perfect foil to taunt and critique the mainstream, but a poor candidate to join it. The bosses at MTV must have realized this, too, but they had learned the key lesson of rock profiteering—namely, that outsiders and disruptors set the tone and pay the bills for the execs at the home office. In an earlier time, the process of legitimization and mainstreaming of musical innovations took decades, but everything was happening faster in modern life. If the stakes were high enough, why couldn't that drawn-out process get compressed into just a few months? Grunge could enhance the network's street cred at a time when it needed to look like something other than a profit-driven corporation cashing in on adolescent lust.

At first MTV played Nirvana's "Smells Like Teen Spirit" video with caution, quarantining it on its alternative rock show *120 Minutes*. The video itself had been shot in a single day on a shoestring budget, and Cobain derided the first cut as akin to a commercial for aspirin or AT&T. Even so, the song stood out as a potent antidote to the increasing slickness of format-driven MTV hits, and both the execs and fans embraced Nirvana as the hot new trendsetter. But Cobain & Company resisted assimilation. When Nirvana was invited to perform on the MTV Video Music Awards, Cobain told horrified network representatives that the band would play the song "Rape Me" instead of its world-famous hit. Cobain eventually compromised and agreed to substitute the less prickly "Lithium," but as a prank played the opening of "Rape Me" during the broadcast before shifting to the agreed-upon number. The network eventually loosened its restrictions on Nirvana, and even "Rape Me" got its moment on the network's New Year's Eve special in 1993. But the inherent tensions between the grunge worldview and the commercial dictates of pop culture would never be adequately resolved.

Something had to give here, and what gave was Kurt Cobain. As the band's popularity escalated, his private life spiraled out of control. On March 3, 1994, he almost died from an overdose in Rome—in what might have been a suicide attempt. Two weeks later, Seattle police responded to a call from Cobain's wife, Courtney Love, who reported that the rock star had locked himself in a room with a .38-caliber revolver and was threatening to kill himself. When the officers arrived, Cobain denied the claim and surrendered his gun to them. But his problems only escalated from there. At the end of the month, Cobain checked into a rehab center near the Los Angeles International Airport, but first purchased a 20-gauge shotgun and ammunition. Rehab lasted only two days before Cobain jumped a fence and escaped.

On April 8, Kurt Cobain's body was found at his home in Seattle, with a suicide note nearby. The official cause of death was a self-inflicted gunshot wound to the head. The note itself was rambling, less an explanation than a lament, and in the aftermath many theories were offered about why grunge's first and last superstar had taken his own life. Cobain's battles with addiction and depression may have provided sufficient reasons, but the note itself dwelled at length on his vocation as a musician. "I haven't felt the excitement of listening to as well as creating music along with reading and writing for too many years now," Cobain wrote. "I feel guilty beyond words about these things."[1]

As with punk and the death of Sid Vicious fifteen years earlier, grunge survived this loss, but just barely. Their respective moments at the forefront of pop culture had passed, and their violent ends raised legitimate questions about whether fiercely subversive musical movements could ride a fast track into the cultural mainstream. Fault lines reached a breaking point when, almost overnight, music-industry executives repackaged the deep-seated antagonisms and hostilities brewing in punk and grunge as mass-market commercial products. These tensions don't always result in something as visible as a superstar's suicide, and in the earlier cases—with Buddy Bolden and jazz, Robert Johnson and blues, and Charlie Parker and bebop, or later, with Tupac Shakur and the Notorious B.I.G. and hip-hop—different causes of death show up on the official documents. But no impartial assessment of the sources and courses of musical innovation can avoid taking a long hard look at the potential for destruction and violence that seems embedded in so many decisive shifts in musical culture. We should perhaps reach for the obvious conclusion—obvious, yet typically forgotten, in an age that prefers to view songs as escapist entertainment— that music is an awe-inspiring force of disruption and upheaval, with more similarities to a riot or guerrilla warfare than we usually choose to acknowledge. Casualties and collateral damage are inevitable, especially when vast sums of money and corporate destinies are also at stake.

In the post-Cobain world, rock remained a big business, but struggled to live up to its promise as the music of permanent revolution. I still recall my shock when I first heard a radio station devoted to a nostalgia-driven classic rock format—this seemed like a betrayal of the whole rock vision. You might as well open a restaurant that served old, stale food as launch a radio station built around old rock. But you could already see the future of rock as a retro movement back in 1983, when Tom Cruise, rising to stardom in the film *Risky Business*, danced in his underwear while lip-syncing the words to "Old Time Rock and Roll." In the late 1980s and the 1990s, rock bands rose and fell like stocks—it might be Huey Lewis and the News for a spell, then Hootie and the Blowfish, or some other short-lived momentum play. But few artists possessed much staying power. The best bands tended to resist commercial expectations, perhaps wisely learning lessons from the fallout of previous 'partnerships' between business interests and rock rebellion. Radiohead's influence, for example, was enhanced by its embrace of art-rock concepts and its willingness to take unexpected shifts in direction—sometimes even fans complained that the band was making its songs intentionally difficult. The Irish group U2 deliberately turned away from the formula that produced its stratospheric hit *The Joshua Tree*, which topped the charts in twenty countries, and entered the 1990s with a darker sonic palette and more introspective moods—leading some to quip that these ungrateful bandmates seemed intent on chopping down the Joshua Tree. To hold onto anything meaningful in rock now required a battle against all the accumulated forces that pushed incessantly for sticking-to-the-formula and cautious brand building. In this environment, the notion that a rock band could change your life, let alone the direction of society, now struggled to pass the sniff test. Rock was becoming one style among many in the battle for genre loyalty, and as its core audience aged, its potential for stirring up revolutionary social movements waned in proportion. How could rock disrupt the status quo when it was the status quo?

But the music industry still needed disruptive outsiders—they are always its lifeblood—and by now had found them elsewhere. Rappers and the hip-hop lifestyle provided a new subversion, an alternative music of permanent rebellion. Here again, the global entertainment corporations deserve very little credit for nurturing this music, which rose up on its own without the accountants and lawyers paying any notice. It's extraordinary to consider that even in the late twentieth century, when a cash-rich music business willingly threw millions of dollars at unproven bands, the real innovations were taking place without the major labels knowing about them. Indeed, all the ingredients of subversive music we have seen over a period of thousands of years were repeated again with the rise of hip-hop. The outsider again emerged as the source of innovation. *The last shall be first and the first shall be last.* And to find these catalysts for change, we need to turn our attention to the most influential metropolis in the world, New York City, but not to its elites and rich arts organizations, rather to its most impoverished neighborhoods.

The executives at the largest record labels in the world worked less than ten miles from the birthplace of hip-hop, but they might as well have been living on a different planet. How do you get from the RCA Building to South Bronx? The answer: You don't. "The South Bronx is a necropolis—a city of death," declared the head of a local health clinic to the *New York Times* shortly before rap emerged from the neighborhood. Twenty percent of the homes lacked running water, and half sometimes went without heat. Life expectancy was lower there than in Panama. Infant mortality was twice the rate of the rest of the country. Some 600,000 manufacturing jobs had disappeared from the neighborhood, and youth unemployment was a staggering 40 percent. Per capita income was just $2,430, less than half the national average. Banks wouldn't lend money here, and businesses often shut down or left for better prospects elsewhere. The only thriving organizations were gangs,

and by some estimates, a hundred different ones, boasting aggregate membership of more than 10,000 young people, carved up
control of the Bronx. The main responsibility of police was to look
the other way. This was the culture that created hip-hop.[2]

The term *Afrofuturism* didn't exist back then, but the origins of
hip-hop anticipate its celebration of forward-looking technology as
an expressive tool for black culture. Don't be fooled by the impoverished neighborhoods: at almost every juncture the roots of this
genre repurposed old technologies and invented new ones. The
DJs whose raps and manipulation of recordings laid the foundation for hip-hop were ghetto techno mavens, and their setup at gigs
looked like a tricked-out Mission Control from a hipper alternative-
world NASA. Kool DJ Herc, the moniker for Jamaican American
Clive Campbell—the idiom's performers typically adopted new
identities that sounded less like names and more like superhero
alter egos—gained acclaim not just for his raps but also for humon-
gous speakers that out-blasted all rivals. Grandmaster Flash (born
in Barbados as Joseph Sadler) developed or popularized a host of
sound manipulation techniques, many of them anticipating with
analog tools the digital studio software of a later age. Spinning
records back and forth on two turntables, he could extend portions
of a song, keeping a propulsive instrumental break going without
losing the beat, a prefiguring of the drum loops of the next generation. The humble drum machine, originally invented as a gimmick
for electric organ players to use at home or on the cheesiest lounge
gigs, was still despised during this era by most professional bands,
but Grandmaster Flash and others repurposed it into a flexible
beat box that intensified the groove and supplemented the sounds
coming from the turntables. A kind of cut-and-paste mentality predominated, even before commercial digital tools and sampling culture legitimized it. Much like the early blues singers, who brazenly
borrowed what they heard and adapted it freely as if copyright laws
didn't apply to them, the pioneers of rap mixed and matched whatever served the purposes of the moment. Records now weren't just
played, they were also *scratched*, moving the needle back and forth
across a record to create a range of percussive effects, or used as

backing for the spontaneous rap of the presiding DJ. In essence, the turntable was transformed into a musical instrument in its own right, the medium again becoming the message.

No one called this rap or hip-hop at the start, and for many listeners this was still just dance music. But the lyrics would give this new idiom even more bite than the accumulated weapons of mass percussion mobilized by DJs on their incursions into the neighborhoods. You can trace the lineage of rap in many ways—back to soulful 1970s disk jockeys speaking rhythmically over intros to radio hits, or to the chanted refrains of work songs; to the patter songs of Gilbert and Sullivan, or the jazz poetry of Gil Scott-Heron; or further back to African griots and Gregorian chant. The intensification of signification via semi-musical chanting is as old as human society itself. But by the time the first rappers came onto the scene, the music world had mostly forgotten the power of monophonic chant. It was as if these South Bronx upstarts were bypassing a thousand years of polyphonic tinkering and returning to powerful first principles. But those who associated rhythmic chanting with religious devotion, hitherto its primary use in the Western world, were in for a shock. The new rapping emphasized the music's outsider status, opting instead for exhortation, boasting, taunting, denunciation, erotic and romantic posturing of all stripes, autobiographical commentary, harsh sociopolitical critiques, various calls to action, and the widest range of swear words accessible in the English language.

For many listeners, the Sugarhill Gang's 1979 hit single "Rapper's Delight" served as introduction to this iconoclastic new sound. But even after the commercial music world took notice, many in the industry no doubt viewed rap as a short-term fad, much as 1950s talent scouts had looked upon the first rock 'n' roll hits. The incomprehension of the major labels provided opportunities for rap entrepreneurs to fill the void. Sugar Hill, the label behind "Rapper's Delight," would declare bankruptcy in 1986, and Enjoy Records, another early entrant in hip-hop, shut down in 1987; but these pioneers set the tone for commercial rap and laid the pattern for later 'golden age' entrepreneurial businesses such as Profile (1980), Jive (1981), Def Jam (1984), Cold Chillin' (1986),

Ruthless (1986), Delicious Vinyl (1987), and Death Row (1991). Huge careers were launched, with almost no traditional marketing and little involvement from the big players in the industry, who sat by and watched Run-D.M.C., Public Enemy, Beastie Boys, LL Cool J, and others push their more conventional soul and R&B stars off the charts. Nelson George recalls the incomprehension of the major labels during his tenure as black music editor at *Billboard* in the early days of rap's ascendancy. The general attitude was "'How long will this last?' They saw rap records, at best, as a fad and, at worst, a blotch on African America."[3]

But instead of retreating, rap was soon crossing over into the mainstream. Aerosmith collaborated with Run-D.M.C. on the 1986 hit album *Raising Hell*, which sold three million copies and placed the single "Walk This Way" in the top five of the *Billboard* chart—the highest ranking of a hip-hop song to date. Around this time, the Beastie Boys started showing up on MTV, with a frat-friendly anthem, "Fight for Your Right to Party," that fit perfectly with the network's fun-oriented youth culture ethos. The band's album *Licensed to Ill* sold four million copies, setting another new record for rap. A few months later, LL Cool J enjoyed a mega-hit with his *Bigger and Deffer* album, and proved, with the hit single "I Need Love," that rap could also serve as a vehicle for romantic ballads.

We have already seen with punk rock and grunge how market forces attempted to compress the process of legitimization that all outsider music genres eventually experience if they last long enough. In previous eras, this mainstreaming might require an entire generation or longer, but could profit-hungry corporations really stand by and wait, letting others—less squeamish about swear words and edgy lyrics—make money off hip-hop? In retrospect, hip-hop presents a fascinating, and sometimes ludicrous, case study that highlights all the tensions and incongruities resulting when a new movement, still proud of its rebellious outsider status, faces powerful interests determined to monetize it. One of the first signs of this incongruity came via the many novelty rap songs performed by familiar celebrities, many of them woefully lacking in street cred. Rodney Dangerfield released his *Rappin' Rodney* record in 1983—enlisting the same songwriters who worked with Kurtis Blow on "The Breaks"—and earned heavy rotation on MTV at a time when genuine rap artists were kept off the network. Other celebrity rappers of the 'golden age' included David Hasselhoff, Joe Piscopo, Chevy Chase, Lou Reed, Tom Hanks, Dan Aykroyd, and the entire 1985 Los Angeles Rams. Rap was a fashionable meme, and everyone wanted a piece of it.

But you didn't need to make a record to make a buck. A wide range of consumer product companies were jumping on the bandwagon. In 1986, Adidas cut a shoe deal with Run-D.M.C., rewarding the band for a song it had recorded in praise of its German footwear. Every major soda brand would eventually seek out a hip-hop advocate: Kurtis Blow rapped for Sprite; Run-D.M.C. brandished Coca Cola cans in a print and TV campaign; MC Hammer didn't feel he was too legit to turn down a Pepsi deal. The brand-friendly ethos of hip-hop, whose exponents praise high-status products even when no endorsement deal has been cut, made this genre a perfect vehicle for corporate marketing to the youth demographic. Rap seemed like a ready-made platform for aspirational brands and status-enhancing lifestyle products.

Was it really going to be this easy? Could hip-hop go mainstream without a backlash or boycotts? Many must have believed just that in the late 1980s and early 1990s. Even Walt Disney Corporation's record business, originally launched to promote the "Ballad of Davy Crockett" and virtue-inspiring songs for youngsters, was moving aggressively into rap—its early offerings included an album by Lifers Group, consisting of performances by men serving life prison sentences in New Jersey, and *Coming Down Like Babylon,* a hip-hop album by Nation of Islam exponent Prince Akeem. Goodbye Mickey Mouse; hello Louis Farrakhan. But the execs in the corporate suites clearly underestimated the resistance within the hip-hop community itself, which took questions of authenticity very seriously.

Even as corporate America began to embrace the genre, a new generation of tougher, grittier performers was rising to the forefront of hip-hop. Almost at the same moment that Disney discovered rap, the term *gangsta* entered the lexicon—a label that encompassed lifestyles and attitudes that had been brewing in the black community for years and was now about to make the front pages of newspapers. When measured by memes and mentions, sneaker affiliations would soon get eclipsed by gang affiliations. Hip-hop might still sell merchandise, but its true destiny was to serve as the focal point for outrage and protest in the inner city— something it did with a vitality and immediacy no political spiel or party platform could match.

N.W.A.'s *Straight Outta Compton* album managed to reach platinum status with virtually no airplay and without a national tour. But media coverage was intense, most of it alarmist. Songs about street gangs, police brutality, racial profiling, and life in South Central Los Angeles mixed protest with a glamorization of violence. Some saw this as a new level of realism in music; others denounced it as a fraudulent distortion, a misguided promotion of age-old stereotypes of black culture that glorified those doing the killing rather than their victims. In some instances, police officers refused to provide security at the N.W.A.'s appearances. In Detroit, cops actually rushed the stage and ended up in a scuffle with hired security; later they detained the band at their hotel. Church groups got into the act, mobilizing protests among their constituencies, much as they had previously with Elvis and other music stars. As the coup de grace, an assistant director at the FBI sent a denunciatory letter to the group's record label—a move soon announced on the cover of *The Village Voice*, which proclaimed, in block capitals and large red type: THE FBI HATES THIS BAND. You can't buy that kind of publicity, and all these efforts merely boosted N.W.A.'s sales and fame.

How times had changed. Just a few years earlier, the Parents Music Resource Center had publicized the "Filthy Fifteen"—a 1985 list of the most objectionable songs of the day. Not a single rap song made that list. But in the late 1980s and early 1990s, rap displaced all other forms of subversive music. It wasn't just the gangsta lifestyle that got headlines, or the obscenities and epithets, but increasingly, a frank sexuality, often misogynistic in tone. A few weeks after the release of *Straight Outta Compton*, the Miami group 2 Live Crew, known for its raunchy raps, launched *As Nasty As They Wanna Be*, a headline-grabbing album eventually branded as obscene by a federal judge. The group was acquitted at a subsequent trial, but here again the publicity helped the album go platinum—the first rap album from the South to earn that distinction.

All this seemed shocking and new at the time, but celebrations of the gangsta lifestyle and sexual exploits were surprisingly congruent with the age-old traditions of folk music. As we have seen, two-thirds of the cherished and ultra-respectable Child Ballads deal with sex or violence, and some address topics (incest, graphic descriptions of torture, etc.) that even the most rebellious rappers would hesitate to embrace, at least until the rise of horrorcore rap in the mid-1990s, when those last taboos of necrophilia, cannibalism, and other grotesqueries were crossed. Recall also how many Child Ballads celebrate the exploits of Robin Hood—he appears in more than 10 percent of those songs—who was the most notorious gangsta of British folklore, leader of a turf-defending posse that alienated the FBI-equivalents of his world. To some extent, the rappers themselves took on the role of folk heroes, increasingly so in the post-golden-age era of the 1990s and afterward. A kind of mythology of rap was now on the rise. The life of Tupac Shakur seems like something out of a British broadside ballad, albeit modified for modern times and technologies. Eminem went so far as to create an onstage persona, Slim Shady—even the name sounds like something out of a traditional ballad—who was an exemplar of the violent protagonist. But in the most striking cases, in a genre that valued authenticity above everything, the rappers maintained the same personas onstage and off. When rapper 50 Cent made the transition to film in *Get Rich or Die Tryin'*, he played a character based on himself. That was the ideal.

But still more fascinating is how even the parts of rap that seemed completely resistant to mainstreaming eventually got legitimized. Consider what a quarter century did for N.W.A.'s *Straight Outta Compton*, the album that riled up everyone from parents to the FBI in its day. In 2015, Hollywood released its Oscar-nominated N.W.A. biopic, also called *Straight Outta Compton.* In 2016, *Straight Outta Compton* was honored as the first hip-hop album inducted into the Grammy Hall of Fame, and in 2017 was chosen by the Library of Congress for preservation in the National Recording Registry, a distinction limited to works of cultural, historical, or artistic significance. As in so many previous cases, a single generation sufficed to turn even the most subversive music into an institutional monument. By the way, the threatening letter sent by the FBI is now on display at the Rock and Roll Hall of Fame, a monument to the futility of authorities' attempts to control the evolution of song.

Of course, by this time, the whole hip-hop genre had found many paths to the mainstream. Some were purely commercial— for example, the many collaborations between hip-hop artists and pop singers that emerged as a familiar formula in the new millennium. Others were personal but highly symbolic—as when President Barack Obama started recommending tracks by Kanye West, Kendrick Lamar, Jay Z, Chance the Rapper, and Drake on his Oval Office–approved playlists. Others were institutional, such as the Smithsonian's 2017 decision to form a committee of fifty scholars and practitioners to create an official *Smithsonian Anthology of Hip-Hop and Rap.* And in a landmark moment, Lamar took home the Pulitzer Prize for Music in 2018 for his album *Damn*—unprecedented for an honor previously restricted to classical composers and the occasional jazz artist. The overarching picture is clear: hip-hop has followed the same path as every previous musical scandal, and found itself declared *respectable.* And this raises the obvious question: Is any permanent revolution in music possible? Is there any forbidden sound sufficiently subversive to resist mainstreaming? Or do all significant musical revolutions eventually find their way inside museums and institutions?

The power brokers at the top of the music business rarely worry about such matters. Even if one genre loses its edge, another one rises up, sometimes in the most unexpected place, to start the process all over again. If they wait long enough, a new disruption will appear, a new revolution—with all its attendant opportunities to monetize and commercialize. In the 1990s, the masters of corporate entertainment were simply awaiting the next outsider, the new force of change. And, in a way, they were correct—there was a revolution on the way. But it wasn't coming from musicians this time; rather, a new generation of technologists had their own notions about disruption. They also had plans to monetize and commercialize, and frankly, didn't care what the music sounded like. They wanted to disrupt the industry, not the songs.

28

Welcome Our New Overlords

In the mid-1980s, I found myself working with some of the smartest people in Silicon Valley, and I watched as they hatched a plan to change how people consume music. The leader of this group, a former Rhodes scholar with a PhD from Harvard, envisioned a high-tech digital delivery system that would allow music fans to create customized playlists and download the songs for personal use. At the time I expressed my skepticism, not because of the concept—which was very exciting and far more consumer-driven than any of the existing music retail platforms back in those before-the-web days—but due to my fear that record labels would view this new technology as a threat rather than an opportunity. All my experiences with the music business had taught me to expect hostility toward outsiders and bold concepts. But the team persisted and eventually secured $25 million in venture capital, a sizable amount at the time. Flush with cash, and full of high hopes, they launched Personics.

A few months later, Personics began installing large kiosks in Tower Records stores. These big clunky hardware systems were the first music download devices, but back then the only viable medium for storing a customer's playlist was a cassette tape. Even so, this new system was a breakthrough in many ways. Users could browse a catalog, choose songs they liked, input their selections at the kiosk, and have a custom mixtape created on the spot. Personics had solved a host of technological problems, from data compression to noise reduction. But record labels were, as I predicted, reluctant to license their songs. Without access to all the new hits, Personics was doomed to failure. The visionaries behind the company had anticipated, with uncanny accuracy, the future of music consumption—a future built on personalization, customization, digital access, and playlist curation. But the world—and especially the technophobic music business—wasn't ready for this in the 1980s.

Yet with each passing year, Silicon Valley got bigger and stronger, with deeper pockets, better technology, and greater cultural influence. Meanwhile, the music business gave up on R&D. In an earlier age, almost every breakthrough in audio technology had been invented or commercialized by a record company, including the long-playing record, the 45 rpm single, the ribbon microphone, the Sony Walkman, the 8-track tape, stereo and quadriphonic sound, and other hits and misses. RCA was so good at launching new technologies that it could be called the Apple equivalent of the middle decades of the twentieth century—not just a major record label, but also a leader in consumer-driven technologies and inventor of the coolest 'devices' on the market. But by the late 1990s, consumer electronics and music had splintered, each going its separate way. You could even view it as a geographical divide: the music business flourished in Southern California, taking its cues from Hollywood and thriving on glamour, whereas new consumer technologies increasingly came out of Northern California, drawing on the accumulated expertise and ambitions of Silicon Valley.

No one dared describe this as a war between North and South, but it increasingly looked like one to those who could see the fault lines and antagonisms beneath the surface. And like the Civil War of an earlier day, the North would prevail here. Too set in their ways, the entertainment companies of SoCal were ill prepared for industry disruption. By the dawn of the new millennium, Silicon Valley was choosing the platforms and priorities and dictating the pace of change. Fast-forward to the current day: the most powerful forces in music are all technology-driven companies—Apple, Google, Spotify, Amazon, and others who view songs as mere content, one ingredient in a larger business model.

It's not accurate to say that record labels did *absolutely nothing* while tech companies ate their lunch. They did put money—and an immense amount of undeserved faith—into the three L's of their business: litigation, legislation, and lobbying. Even as record labels ignored the biggest revolution in the history of consumer entertainment technology, their lawyers kept busy issuing threats and cease-and-desist letters. And they did enjoy some successes during their downward spiral. The Sonny Bono Copyright Extension Act of 1998 created an extraordinary situation in which corporate control of a creative work, originally 14 years in the early days of the United States, with an option for a renewal for an extra 14 years, could now last 120 years or more, depending on various criteria. By comparison, a US patent expires after 20 years—hence the absurd situation that a cure for cancer would be granted only a fraction of the protection that a Milli Vanilli song or Mickey Mouse cartoon receives. But we can safely predict at this juncture that no more copyright extensions will come from the United States Congress. Just a few years after passage of the Sonny Bono Act, the dominant tech companies—Apple, Google, and others with a vested interest in limiting copyrights—would have more powerful lobbyists than the entertainment companies.

The record labels' victory over Napster, a very popular Internet music-sharing platform, can now be viewed as a final battlefield triumph in a losing war. The industry put its full legal muscle into this fight, managing to get a court injunction in 2001 that led to the music service's eventual bankruptcy. The Recording Industry Association of America (RIAA), the industry trade group leading the attack, would have been much wiser taking over Napster and expanding its platform as a direct distribution channel from music labels to consumers—thus possibly preventing the later dominance of iTunes, YouTube, Amazon, Spotify, and other intermediaries. But that would have required an industry culture based on meeting consumer needs, instead of the legalistic, threat-driven, head-in-the-sand worldview that prevailed within the corporate offices of the music moguls.

As it turned out, music sales reached their peak in 1999—the very year that the RIAA launched its legal attack against Napster. Industry revenues would drop by roughly half over the next decade, and even the blips of recovery would never approach the glory years of the twentieth century. The Napster and Bono victories would be the last hurrahs of an antiquated business model. When Apple released the iPod in 2001, record labels found themselves in a quandary. Apple had more political clout than they did, and more consumer loyalty to boot; the iPod, and the company's other products, were the result of reams of research into customer preferences that no record label would ever 'waste' money on studying or meeting. And no one could match Apple's hardass legal staff, either (today Apple employs more than five hundred lawyers). And yet the iPod was only a harbinger of things to come. The launch of YouTube and its subsequent acquisition by Google signaled that the most powerful Internet platform in the world aimed to dominate the distribution of music over the web, and *pay as little for it as possible.*

Think for a moment of what this meant from a business standpoint. For RCA, in the old days, music showed up on the income statement in the sales lines, as a source of growth and profits; for Google, it is a cost that needs to be squeezed, kept to a minimum, perhaps even pushed to zero if possible. The streaming service Spotify, for its part, declared, in its 2015 annual report to shareholders, "We don't sell music." The company sells subscriptions and access; music is just the cost of doing business. But this shift in economics only begins to capture the damage to the music ecosystem caused by this changing of the guard. When RCA and Columbia invented new music platforms in previous decades, they still saw themselves first and foremost as champions of creative talent. Most of the leading musicians in the world were under contract to these labels, and a symbiotic relationship had existed between the performer and the platform. That now ended, as people got their songs from companies that had no emotional commitment, let alone financial commitment, to developing musicians' careers. These tech giants would even give music away for free if it served to advance other corporate strategies—for example, selling devices or advertising—and they sometimes did just that. Devaluing music was, to some extent, a core strategy.[1]

The major record labels thought they loved revolution, subversion, and disruption, but it didn't feel quite so good when they were on the receiving end. And this time the new overlords from Silicon Valley might very well achieve that dream of a permanent revolution, a toppling of the old guard that can never be reversed. The challenge Elvis and the Beatles presented was nothing in comparison to the incursions made by Apple and Google, the wealthiest enterprises in the history of capitalism. Once they take over, can anything dislodge them?

When these new threats first appeared, the masters of music needed a revolution of their own, something so powerful and exciting that they could dictate terms and insist on their prerogatives. What they came up with would be funny if it weren't so sad: the reality TV singing competition was the biggest innovation in music coming out of the entertainment industry in the early twenty-first century. Of course, this was hardly a new idea. The Eurovision Song Contest had been an annual event in Europe since 1956, and the "amateur night" competition at the Apollo Theater in Harlem dates back to the 1930s. In fact, even the ancients had their singing contests. But these competitions became an out-of-control fad in the new millennium, with dozens of reality TV shows featuring wannabe stars trying to please judges and the viewers at home. For all their banality, these shows offer a different twist on the sacrificial ritual, with a constant stream of musicians granted a brief taste of modern media stardom, first as heroes then as victims, just as Girard's theory dictates, before a final winner (or survivor) emerges from the pack. Such contests are fairly simple to stage and imitate, and every TV market in the world soon had its own variants—in China, the audiences grew so addicted to these shows that the government eventually stepped in to limit their influence. Some have suggested that the Chinese authorities' real fear is that the example of viewers voting for their favorite singer will inculcate a dangerous preference for democratic processes. But that interpretation underestimates the subversive potential of songs themselves, which continue to face prohibitions and censorship all around the world in the current day, just as they have in the past. Letting people pick their favorite music will always be a dangerous liberty with political ramifications.

As events turned out, no intervention has proven necessary to curtail the singing contest fad; it has destroyed itself by saturating the market with deadening formulas and look-alike formats. The shows haven't quite disappeared, but increasingly take on an absurd, self-parodying quality—evident, for example, in *The Masked Singer*, launched on the Fox network in early 2019, a competition between second-tier celebrities wearing ridiculous costumes. Here the contestants take the stage in the guise of a poodle, a hippo, a rabbit, a unicorn, or some other equally buffoonish alter ego. Perhaps we have reached the animal sacrifice stage in the concept's evolution, but that always comes late in the game when the ritual observances have already started to lose their mojo.

Only a tiny number of superstar acts have emerged from all this sound and fury. Kelly Clarkson and Carrie Underwood both parlayed victory in the *American Idol* TV show into genuine stardom, just as in an earlier day the Eurovision contest helped turn ABBA and Céline Dion into platinum-selling recording artists. But most of the victors of these TV contests have pursued lackluster careers despite the mass media exposure. In many instances, the losers have enjoyed more success than the winners. One Direction finished third on *The X Factor*, but five years later this pop boy band was earning more than $100 million per year. At age twelve,

Beyoncé Knowles got eliminated along with her group Girl's Tyme (which later became Destiny's Child) on *Star Search*, one of the forerunners of the later reality shows, but she would later rise to the top of the music world. In truth, it's hard to envision any real innovator or renegade emerging victorious in these artificial settings. Edgy performers occasionally find their way onto TV screens as contestants, but are invariably voted off the show long before the final round. Even a single intemperate remark to a judge can be sufficient to quell audience enthusiasm and guarantee early departure. Anyone who really aspires to becoming the next John Lennon or Bob Dylan, let alone Sid Vicious or Kurt Cobain, probably won't survive the first cut. And for an obvious reason: these shows don't change the musical tastes of mainstream audiences; they simply reflect ingrained preferences of stay-at-home voters. A student of music history is inevitably reminded of the singing contests of the Meistersingers back in the Renaissance, which rewarded blandness, lack of mistakes, and an inoffensive demeanor.

Even so, the rise of the singing contest reflected a genuine need. The music business had always relied on outsiders and new blood. To some degree, these nationwide competitions weren't much different from the recording field trips the labels had undertaken back in the 1920s. In both cases, business interests aimed to create a standardized process for music innovation. This same desire, the ambition to develop a quasi-objective system for launching new commercial acts, has inspired talent managers in recent decades to build their own bands out of auditions—an approach increasingly embraced by the music industry as it became more cautious and formula-driven. And some of these acts, such as New Kids on the Block, the Backstreet Boys, and the Spice Girls, enjoyed tremendous commercial success for a time, although without much staying power after their initial core audience of adolescents and teens grew up. As the accumulated examples of the previous decades—even centuries—attest, true innovation in music comes from disruption, not standardization. Any attempt to mount a genuine revolution in music out of a reality TV show or a formula-constructed band is almost doomed to failure from the start.

In the past, music has always revitalized itself through the emergence of a new genre—it happens every few years. During the course of the twentieth century, blues, jazz, rock, hip-hop, and other insurgent styles redefined and reenergized a scene that might otherwise have stagnated. Yet in the early years of the digital age, the opposite seemed to be happening: there were simply too many emerging genres and subgenres, and none with sufficient clout to mount a revolution in mainstream society, certainly not at the level experienced during the Jazz Age of the 1920s or the Summer of Love. In fact, when the streaming service Spotify decided to define every music style, the company came up with a list of 1,387 categories. (Some examples: Electro-Latino, Neo-Mellow, Christian Dance, Cinematic Dubstep, Laboratorio, Stomp and Whittle, Neurofunk, and Pop Christmas.)

This proliferation of musical styles is no different from the brand extensions in other product categories, from potato chips to toothpaste, in which consumer preferences are sliced and diced in constant attempts to identify a demographic group willing to pay a premium for something more customized. But the very success in micromanaging niche markets, which instills a comfortable complacency and a narrowing of focus among end-users, undermines opportunities for transformative change on a larger scale. When pushed to an extreme, audience decisions about listening to music start to resemble patrons at a pub reviewing an endless list of microbrewery beers. There's an illusion of unconstrained choice in a circumscribed environment where the whole selection process is stringently controlled and surprises are kept to a minimum.

At the dawn of the twenty-first century, four commercial music categories still dominated the marketplace, despite the constant addition of micro-niches in the ecosystem: rock, pop, country, and hip-hop. Other traditional genres might innovate and create artists of the highest tier—as continued to happen in classical music, jazz, and other fields—but they could neither generate profits nor change society the way they had during their glory days.

Could any other style of music challenge the four leaders? Electronic dance music, or EDM, stood out as the most promising candidate. Rising from the ashes of the old disco movement, the dance club scene had embraced a host of digital-age innovations, and each new software package or hardware setup put on the market expanded the tools at hand for practitioners. This fertile field for experimentation had already created vibrant urban habitats for new lifestyle-driven genres, leading to the rise of Detroit techno music, Chicago house music, London dubstep, and other local and regional scenes. Almost every season seemed to bring another trendy style into the mix, and as new technologies undermined old practices, they created a potent force of change in commercial music, repeatedly expanding the sound palettes of those at the cutting edge.

Yet the technologies here often proved less important than the ritualistic activities surrounding their dissemination and use. Indeed, it's a cause for wonder how much EDM, despite its futuristic trappings, re-creates the ecstatic trance rituals of music's earliest origins. The rave parties and club scenes where it comes to life stand out as the latest demonstration of music's power as a gateway to transcendence and altered mind states. It's hardly a coincidence that the illegal drug most associated with the EDM scene carries the street name Ecstasy—the exact same term used to describe the traditional mystic's mindset and the hypnotic state of the participant at an ancient bacchanalia. When Mircea Eliade published his seminal study *Shamanism* in 1951, he even subtitled his book *Archaic Techniques of Ecstasy*. The rave is the modern alternative. Then again, every major music genre today echoes, at least in part, some of the imperatives of prehistoric song. The rock star evokes the scapegoat from ancient rituals of symbolic violence. The country artist re-creates the pastoral strains of the herders, who relied on music to soothe domesticated animals, and celebrates the stable life of home and hearth. The hip-hopper returns to the monophonic chant that served to unite the first human communities, the oldest 'hoods of them all. The pop star draws an audience with erotic stylings and dance moves that remind us of the fertility rituals that gave birth to the love song. The EDM gathering, in this context, is the modern application of music to the most persistent human dilemma: how to rise out of the humdrum here-and-now and achieve bliss, or at least its short-term, song-inspired, chemically assisted equivalent.

Of course, each of these genres does much more than repeat old patterns. Lavish superstructures of signification and sound are layered onto these timeless foundations. But they also return to first principles, for the simple reason that music is *always* more than mere entertainment. Even in the twenty-first century, music serves as a dynamic tool for dealing with the fundamental challenges of our lives, both as individuals and as members of larger communities. Media and business interests may treat songs as idle escapism, but every advanced form of purposive activity—from high-performance athletics to brain surgery—aims to harness music to improve results. EDM performers (or producers and DJs, as they are more often called) are surrounded by all sorts of high-tech gear when they show up onstage or work in their studio, but song itself is the oldest technology of all, and hardly to be scorned for its antiquity. In the twenty-first century, as in every previous stage in human development, music is a reliable source of transformative power.

But even as EDM shows promise for mobilizing a new young audience, record labels aren't well equipped to take advantage of this opportunity. This music exerts its greatest impact when embedded in an event, not as a digital track. You can't deliver the real EDM experience via a streaming platform or smartphone app. Fans must make a pilgrimage instead. Certain global destinations—Ibiza, Goa, Las Vegas—have touted their associations with EDM and use it as a lure for tourism. But visitors come to Ibiza for more than an artist or song: they want a total lifestyle immersion experience that resists commodification and sale over the Internet. Even superstar EDM producers, such as Skrillex, Calvin Harris, David Guetta, and deadmau5, sometimes get treated as one ingredient in a much larger enterprise. Or, when enlisted by record labels, they find themselves serving as tech support for rap and pop artists—elite and highly paid, but nonetheless requiring the participation of a bigger name, a Rihanna or Justin Bieber, to reach those coveted billion-plus YouTube views. In a different sociocultural environment, the masters of electronic music might rise up as modern-day shamans, mobilizing a whole generation and defining new ways of life. But in the cash-hungry and trend-devouring music world of the new millennium, they are more likely to find themselves squeezed into a narrow box as beatmakers for hire, wandering troubadours like those of yore, but carrying a laptop rather than a lyre.

The commodification of music as physical albums or digital content was once an opportunity, but increasingly it's a burden. It's hard to see songs as magic when you have monetized them in micro-transactions, turned them into low-priced products or services, or sometimes just giveaways to sell a subscription or device. But the magic remains, despite these degradations, at least for those who know how to tap into it. And we can't disregard those transactions entirely, not if we care about the songs. The dramatic shift in the economics of music creation in the new millennium impacts more than cash flow—it also changes the tunes themselves. In some ways, the alterations are exciting. The collapse of intermediaries and the rise of global connectivity allow music to move around the world with unprecedented speed. Pop songs from Korea and Japan find fans in Europe, forging paths of dissemination impossible to imagine just a few years ago. A desert blues sound from Mali or an electrified *molam* band from Thailand can gain an unexpected following in the United States— sometimes even more acclaim than they enjoy at home. A music video uploaded in New Zealand or Australia can be viewed across the globe moments later. Bands that previously played only to imaginary audiences in someone's garage can go viral without ever having to pass an audition or sign a record contract. All of this is a kind of magic, too, when you think about it.

We have seen repeatedly, in the preceding pages, how music thrives in cultural melting pots and port cities. The glory of the Internet is that it has placed all of us in the midst of this melting pot. Wherever we live now, our vantage point is a portal facing the entire world and all it has to offer. Even if the digital economy threatens so much of the music ecosystem, this at least is something to cherish and celebrate.

But, alas, the threats are real. The disruptions in the economic and technological spheres have created enormous hurdles for those who seek to make a livelihood out of music. The Internet has made it easier for new artists to release and distribute their music, but the rewards for success have diminished markedly. Revenues from recorded music have collapsed. Nightclubs have closed their doors in the face of virtual competition from so many directions. The rise of new income sources, via streaming and licensing, hardly begins to compensate for the disappearance of the old ones. True, it has always been hard to make a living as a musician, but it's almost impossible in an age when tens of millions of fans decide they no longer need to own an album or even purchase a digital download. Some look to music subscription services as a savior, but can musicians really pay the rent with micro-shares of micro-transactions? In this new environment, economic models tend to reward tech companies more than music creators—who are now branded with the uninspiring title of "content providers." Musicians watch from the sidelines, their fate in the balance, as tech behemoths battle over turf, and even the most talented artists must live with the consequences. But how will they manage to thrive in a system that increasingly views songs as loss leaders given away for free in order to sell something else?

The most successful artists tend to follow the lead of Apple and Google—they turn themselves into multipurpose brands, sometimes earning more money as entrepreneurs than they ever could as performers. When *Forbes* publishes its annual list of the wealthiest musicians, music sales now have surprisingly little impact on the rankings. Jay-Z recently rose to the top of that list, but mostly because of his equity stakes in various business, including Armand de Brignac champagne and D'Ussé cognac. He narrowly beat out fellow rapper Sean Combs, better known as Puff Daddy, who generates most of his income from fashion and liquor. When Beyoncé overtook Taylor Swift to become the highest-earning female musician in the world, shortly after the launch of her lauded *Lemonade* album, fans might have assumed that her financial success was built primarily on recordings. But Beyoncé's business empire is actually a highly diversified portfolio involving a fashion line, a shoe brand, perfumes, acting gigs, ticket sales, shares in the Tidal streaming service (which her spouse Jay-Z acquired for $56 million in 2015), and various partnerships with Pepsi, Emporio Armani, American Express, Tommy Hilfiger, and other companies. In just the world of fragrances, Beyoncé has sold around half a billion dollars' worth of product.

Not every musician has the skills to succeed as an entrepreneur. Kanye West ran up more than $50 million in debt in his attempts to launch various businesses. Even as he released his successful *Yeezus* album and embarked on a supporting tour that brought in $25 million for just eighteen concerts, West needed to rely on bank loans and investors to pay his bills. In an earlier day, a musician in a tight financial spot would look to album sales and touring to fix the problem, but those often *cause* the financial problems in twenty-first-century music economics. West even tweeted a request for Mark Zuckerberg, founder of Facebook, to invest a billion dollars in his struggling business empire. It seems absurd, but really isn't. In a world where tech titans control music, performers who hope to rise to the top must act like tech titans themselves. In some instances, even a superstar musician has to view songs as financial write-offs, sunk costs necessary to keep the brand alive in other, more lucrative categories.

No period in history has seen so much technological and economic disruption in the music field. Yet in the midst of this chaos, artistry still somehow manages to emerge and flourish—although an increasing divide can be detected between the exciting and diverse activities of musicians around the globe, armed with technological tools and distribution platforms of unprecedented power, and the narrowing focus of the commercial power brokers who believe they run the music world. Considering only the latter, one might conclude that a pop sensibility is devouring the entire world of song. Taylor Swift first made her mark as a country star, but hit the heights of stardom after embracing pop. Katy Perry was recording Christian rock, but switched to pop and sold a hundred million records.

The highest-earning hip-hop artists and EDM producers seek out the crossover audience that comes from collaborations with top-tier pop stars. Asian music rarely connected with audiences in the West until the stars of J-Pop from Japan and K-Pop from Korea showed they could play this game as well as Americans. Even jazz and classical music aren't immune to this demand for pop-oriented music. In every idiom, purists lament the push for audience expansion, but it's not just money and power that are pushing for crossover. A whole school of music criticism known as *poptimism* has emerged to nurture and celebrate the dominant new sensibility.

"The smooth is the signature of the present time," philosopher Byung-Chul Han recently announced. "It connects the sculptures of Jeff Koons, iPhones and Brazilian waxing." Han sees this smoothness everywhere and links it to the same ideology of positivity that reduces social interactions to "likes" on Facebook and promotes the use of photoshopped images, with their fantasy of blemish-free visages and perfectly contoured bodies. He doesn't mention contemporary music in his account of the cult of the smooth, but it also participates in the zeitgeist, at least judging by the most heavily promoted artists and the imperatives of the marketplace. After decades of Africanized bent notes and complex timbres, hit songs are returning to pure Pythagorean tones, sometimes delivered dead-on the center of the pitch by the singer or, in many instances, later manipulated into perfection by Auto-Tune tinkering. At times, it's almost as if producers have forgotten the whole African revolution in singing, and the vocal ideals of the 1890s have returned. Harmonies have undergone a comparable whitening. The current-day pop sensibility hasn't just abandoned blues chords, but often operates without any reliance on tritones, that biting interval that has driven functional harmony for centuries. Syncopations have mostly disappeared from melodies and supporting rhythms, the latter now tending to seamless patterns, smooth and repetitive. If you were redesigning music from a blank page, with the goal of achieving maximum smoothness, these are precisely the choices you would make.[2]

Yet the most futile notion in the history of aesthetics is the concept that creative impulses can be tamed into patterns of neat precision and frictionless regularity. It's simply not true, and our growing awareness of the human brain's reaction to art demonstrates just how wrongheaded it is. The neural circuits in the prefrontal cortex are excited by musical ingredients that are *unexpected*. We crave the repetitive pattern, but we also hunger for its disruption. Subversion, from a musical standpoint, is actually hardwired into our bodies. Yet the quest for musical symmetry has rarely been more intense than in the current day. Even the hottest studio session drummers are now routinely asked to play along with a click track—a steady metronome pulse that ensures no deviation from a mathematically pure tempo. Sometimes the drummer's whole contribution is reduced to a few seconds of music, a couple bars of percussion that are repeated with a copy-and-paste function throughout the entire track. We have reached a point where an absolutely perfect beat, unchanging and precise, can propel all our songs. In an odd way, this practice repeats a trend from a century ago, when the engineers at the Aeolian player piano company attempted to impose a similar regularity on musical performances. This technology, sometimes called *quantization*, proved to be a disastrous constraint back then—the song simply didn't sound as good when it was controlled by mathematics—but it has reemerged today in a new digital guise.

As the player piano example shows, previous generations also tried to maximize smoothness in music. But the smooth songs have always been displaced, sooner or later, by more subversive sounds. In the nineteenth century, publishers peddled parlor songs that aimed to please everybody with inoffensive, sentimental themes, but African American music changed all that. During the course of the twentieth century, a series of music genres—jazz, rock, hip-hop—did the same, each new entrant disrupting singing styles and the broader society in decisive interventions that could never have been predicted in advance. In each instance, the smooth music was swept aside by something stronger, less polite, more controversial. Will the story end differently this time? Probably not. Four thousand years of music history tell us otherwise.

At times it seems as if every pressure point in the music ecosystem wants to turn songs into mere entertainment. (Or even worse, *nostalgic* entertainment—note the proliferation in recent years of reunion tours, retirement tours, tribute albums, and late-career triumphs.) This may be the only issue on which record labels and the technocrats running the digital platforms agree, despite all the superficial conflicts between Hollywood and Silicon Valley. Both those adversaries also want everything as smooth as possible. And they can even summon up academic research to back up their position. When they treat songs as 'content' for mass entertainment, they aren't really all that different from Harvard psychologist Stephen Pinker and his reductionist claim that music is just "auditory cheesecake" for the brain, akin to a recreational drug or a six-pack of Budweiser. The very term *content* implies that music is something generic, a fungible commodity without social significance or larger purpose—with "no survival value," in Pinker's terms—except (of course!) to generate a profit for its purveyors.[3]

To some extent, the human element in music is even treated as an obstacle, replaced whenever possible with an algorithm. Indeed, the second stage of the digital revolution in music is built on the application of software and data analysis at virtually every decision point in the music ecosystem. True, the algorithm, for all its high-tech sheen, is little more than a feedback loop, charting the future by looking into a rearview mirror. The songs recommended for you next week will resemble the songs you enjoyed last week—hardly a promising approach for disruptive change, but what could be smoother? The idea that songs might be evaluated without anyone actually listening to them might strike some as strange, but it's an irresistible proposition for the high-tech enterprises that increasingly dominate the music business. They now use artificial intelligence to compose music, perform it, curate it, analyze it for commercial potential, and finally sell it to a customer. Robots even serve now as consumers of songs. Musicians are already hiring bots to click on their online tracks—for $299 you can purchase 100,000 listens for your music. In a strange self-reinforcing process, these 'listens' convince the all-powerful algorithms that a song is worth hearing. "Will androids dream of electric guitars?" asks tech journalist Nic Fildes. If so, a whole closed loop emerges, encapsulating music from creation to consumption, without any human being required—the smoothest business model of them all.[4]

But as soon as we turn our gaze away from Hollywood and Silicon Valley, this vision collapses. Songs are just as disruptive now as they have ever been, and the connection between music and violence has proven impossible to eradicate. It's hardly a coincidence that so many acts of terrorism and large-scale violence are targeted at musical performances. On October 1, 2017, the deadliest mass shooting in American history took place at the Harvest Music Festival in Las Vegas, where a gunman fired more than a thousand rounds from a hotel window, killing 58 people and leaving 851 others wounded. The killer appears to have scouted out various concerts in preparation, even reserving rooms overlooking other festivals. Just six months earlier, a bomb exploded after an Ariana Grande concert in Manchester, England, killing 22 people and injuring 120 others. Less than a year before that incident, a shooter took the lives of 50 people at Pulse, a nightclub in Orlando, Florida. Seven months earlier, terrorists in Paris targeted a rock concert at the Bataclan theater, killing 90 and wounding 200. Other music-related bombings, from Indonesia to Sweden, reinforce the pattern. Music is a powerful force that stirs up the most intense feelings and violent passions, but not always for good—that's just as true today as when ancient warlords brought musicians into battle. Even as corporate interests package it as escapist entertainment, nightclubs are training their bouncers to double as terrorism experts; the weekend festivities at the Grammys recently included a "counterterrorism briefing"—a full-day session for musicians and their entourages to prepare them for those moments when songs unleash a deadly response.

Anger and backlashes against music are hardly restricted to terrorists. Even in the new millennium, governments fear the power of song. In China, authorities have blocked hip-hop artists from performing on TV. In Egypt, pop stars were recently jailed for their suggestive music videos. In Russia, members of the feminist punk rock group Pussy Riot have emerged as focal points for protest; they were convicted in court for "undermining the social order." A subsequent campaign to eradicate rap music proved impossible to implement, but Vladimir Putin announced a fallback plan to "lead" and "direct" Russian hip-hop—a mystifying declaration that seems destined to failure from the start. In Ethiopia, singer Teddy Afro became the biggest pop star in the country only to have his album launch shut down by police. In Thailand, the government was so unnerved by a rap song that it responded not only with threats and denunciations, but with its own music video response. Nobody seems to have told the rulers of these nations that music is just auditory cheesecake. They see it as subversive—and, based on the long history of song, they are probably right.[5]

But music's disruptive force is just as often embraced for its positive effects. When I talk to people about music's powers of enchantment and transformation, I often encounter skeptical responses. That's just superstition, many believe. Yet with each passing year, the magic of music is further validated by science and implemented by visionary practitioners in a host of fields. Sports trainers have learned that syncing the tempo of a music playlist to an athlete's heartbeat can improve stamina, speed, and performance. Psychologists have proven that people who attend concerts and dance events score higher on a wide range of metrics, finding greater satisfaction in their relationships, communities, and life paths. A growing body of evidence confirms that music alters body chemistry, increasing T-cell levels and strengthening the body's immune system. In fact, doctors have been the most enthusiastic in embracing music as a tool in enhancing their own performance: 90 percent of surgeons play music in the operating room—rock is the favored genre—and there's a widespread belief that songs improve their concentration and procedure results. In some instances, the surgical tools themselves are high-tech musical instruments, applying sound waves to counter everything from cataracts to kidney stones. Orpheus healed with a lyre while the modern doctor relies on a lithotripter, but in both instances sonic power is the source of their wizardry.

Even in the privacy of our homes, we trust in the catalytic capabilities of song. When sociologist Tia DeNora studied how people prepare for romantic dates and intimate moments, she learned that almost everyone places enormous faith in music as a transformative force in love and sex. The right musical accompaniment is invariably enlisted to seal the deal. "It's a kind of magical, mystical type thing," explained one woman, when discussing her choice of background music for an amorous encounter—almost the same words a participant would have used to describe the song-filled fertility rituals of our ancestors. A growing body of research supports these views, showing that music not only brings couples to bed but even enhances pleasure when sex is accompanied by the right playlist.[6]

Music may, in fact, be our most reliable aphrodisiac. But its efficacy is validated in many other settings outside the bedroom, even in a high-tech age when there's seemingly an app or pill for each human need or desire. John Sloboda, a psychologist specializing in the integration of music into day-to-day life, has proven in dozens of research studies that people employ songs as change agents in almost every conceivable manner. In one experiment, participants were interrupted at random moments in their day and asked to document their most recent activities. In 44 percent of these instances, music was involved, but almost never as entertainment or diversion—instead, songs were integrated into a variety of activities, which were pursued with greater vigor and success because of the aural ingredient. Participants were "more positive, more alert, and more focused on the present" in these engagements, which encompassed an extraordinary range of pursuits, including sports and fitness, writing and desk work, commuting and travel, running errands, housekeeping, meditating, recovery and healing, planning future events, washing and getting dressed, reading and study, cooking, eating, sleeping, walking, and almost any other activity you can name. Again and again, people reported "greater positivity, arousal, and attention" when they employed songs in these moments—no pill or prescription required.[7]

So we are faced with a paradox. Two different visions of music flourish, and they seem incompatible. On the one hand, we encounter powerful interests who want music to exist within the predictable formulas of the entertainment industry—and those formulas are increasingly embodied in algorithms that promise to remove all difficulty and obstacles from music consumption. Artificial intelligence will pick the perfect song, adapted to your mood, taste, and lifestyle. Nothing discordant or disruptive will intrude on your self-contained music ecosystem, which tech companies prefer to envision as a single-person habitat, an individual connected to a digital device. In an age that aspires to an aesthetics of smoothness, nothing could be smoother. At the same time, the lived reality of music resists this whole reductionist process, this profit-driven imperative to package songs for commerce in micro-transactions targeted at a receptive, finely defined audience. Instead, people insist on putting music to use in unexpected and unruly ways, tapping into its diverse energies, many of them resistant to commodification. Sometimes that potency is a dark magic, dangerous and uncontrollable. In other cases, it is uplifting and positive, truly life-changing. Every power broker—authoritarian rulers, religious leaders, technocrats at Facebook and Google—acknowledges this truth. They want to control music, and use its power to advance their own interests. But they also fear it, knowing that disruptive or revolutionary movements can turn the songs against them.

So take your pick: music as soothing lifestyle accessory, or music as subversive force of change. But that's always been the choice. The conflict between these two visions has served as the engine of change throughout the entire history of human song. Even when we believe we have arrived at a blissful age of music as pure entertainment, a new era of disruption is usually waiting just around the corner—and robots and artificial intelligence will prove incapable of stopping it. But when that new revolution in song arrives, its power to shake up society is short-lived. It will eventually get legitimized and mainstreamed, adopted by the same institutions that previously fought against it. Songs will be repurposed as the backstory is rewritten to fit a new agenda. So make your choice and pick your music, but don't get too comfortable with it. There's almost certainly some song already out there—another big bang in that endless series of big bangs constituting music history—that will start the process all over again.

EPILOGUE

This Is Not a Manifesto

I dislike manifestos. And I realize that the list of forty precepts below appears, at first glance, to be just another example of one. But this is not a manifesto—which is an attempt to impose a belief system on the world. This list represents the reverse: these are the truths that music imposed on my beliefs.

I never sought them out. They were never hypotheses I formulated and tested. They forced themselves onto my attention, requiring my allegiance by the vehemence with which they asserted themselves during the course of my research and studies. They are guiding principles that I only came to grasp gradually, over a period of years, as a result of my efforts to trace the essence and evolution of songs in human history.

In almost every instance, understanding these precepts forced me to alter my beliefs. To that degree, they ought to be deemed an anti-manifesto, or a kind of intrusion of brute reality on the realm of theory. They can also serve as a foundation for efforts to apply the core learnings from this book in other contexts.

1. Music is a change agent in human life, a force of transformation and enchantment.

2. Music is universal to the same extent that people have comparable needs, aspirations, biological imperatives, and evolutionary demands on their behavior. Refusing to acknowledge the universal qualities in a community's music is akin to denying it membership in the broader human community.

3. Songs served as the origin for what we now call *psychology*—in other words, as a way of celebrating personal emotions and attitudes long before the inner life was deemed worthy of respect in other spheres of society.

4. Over the centuries, freedom of song has been just as important as freedom of speech, and often far more controversial—feared because of music's inherent power of persuasion. Songs frequently embody dangerous new ideas long before any politician is willing to speak them.

5. Charts of best-selling songs can be read as an index of leading social indicators. What happens in society tomorrow can be heard on the radio today.

6. For communities that don't have semiconductors and spaceships, music is their technology. For example, songs served as the 'cloud storage' for all early cultures, preserving communal history, traditions, and survival skills. Songs can also function as weapons, medicine, tools, or in other capacities that channel their inherent potency.

7. Each major shift in technology changes the way people sing.

8. Musical innovations almost always come from outsiders—slaves, bohemians, rebels, and others excluded from positions of power—because they have the least allegiance to the

prevailing manners and attitudes of the societies in which they live. This inevitably results in new modes of musical expression.

9. Diversity contributes to musical innovation because it brings the outsider into the music ecosystem. Consider how port cities and multicultural communities, from Lesbos to Liverpool, have played such a key role in the history of song.

10. Musical innovation spreads like a virus, and usually by the same means—through close contact between groups from different places. The concept of a song going viral is more than just a poetic metaphor. New approaches to music often arise in unhealthy cities (Deir el-Medina, New Orleans, etc.).

11. If authorities do not intervene, music tends to expand personal autonomy and human freedom.

12. Authorities usually intervene.

13. Over the short term, rulers and institutions are more powerful than musicians. In the long term, songs tend to prevail over even the most authoritarian leaders.

14. Kings and other members of the ruling class are rarely responsible for breakthroughs in music. When such innovations are attributed to a powerful leader—as with the Song of Songs, the *Shijing*, Gregorian chant, troubadour lyrics, and so on—this is usually a sign that something important has been hidden from our view.

15. We still need to study these powerful figures in music history, not for what they did, but for what they hid.

16. The unwritten (or erased or distorted) history is a measure of their successful intervention. Gaps in the documented

history are often demonstrations of power. This is why stray and isolated facts that run counter to the sanctioned narrative deserve our closest attention.

17. Whenever possible, try to go back to original or early sources. If someone insists that you can safely ignore a primary source or traditional lore, that's probably a sign you should take it seriously.

18. Nothing is more unstable in music history than a period of stability. The signal for new disruption in performance styles is usually that things are going smoothly.

19. Around the time of Pythagoras and Confucius, an epistemological rupture took place that attempted to remove magic and trance from the sphere of acceptable music practices. This agenda is always doomed to failure—you can't reduce music to purely rational rules (or algorithms, as they are usually called nowadays)—but its advocates never give up trying. We are still living with the after-effects of the Pythagorean rupture today.

20. The battle continues to rage over two incompatible views: whether music is constructed from notes or from sounds. The arguments over analog versus digital music are just the latest manifestation of this conflict. It can also be described as an opposition between European and African traditions, and in many other ways. To some degree, this is the fundamental tension in all musicology.

21. Music is always more than notes. It is made out of sounds. Confusing these two is not a small matter.

22. Musical sounds existed in the natural world as creative or destructive forces (sometimes latent, other times already

actualized) long before human societies put their power to use. As such, the pentatonic scale, circle of fifths, functional harmony, etc. were not invented by musicians, but *discovered* by them—much like calculus was discovered.

23. The recurring structures and patterns in compositions invite analysis, yet music cannot be reduced to a pure science or a type of applied mathematics. Powerful aspects of emotion, personality, and deliberate subversion resist this kind of codification. Even in the most restrictive and controlling environments, these elements persist—and, if given the chance, will dominate.

24. We can learn about music from neuroscience, but music does not happen in the brain. Music takes place in the world.

25. Historical accounts often tell us more about the process of legitimization and mainstreaming than about the actual sources and origins of musical innovation.

26. Insiders try to rewrite history to obscure the importance of outsiders—or to redefine the outsider as an insider.

27. The very process of legitimization requires distortion—obscuring origins and repurposing music to meet the needs of those in positions of power.

28. Legitimization is ongoing and cumulative. In other words, music history is no different from other types of history: each generation rewrites it to match its own priorities, of which truth-telling often ranks low on the list.

29. The process of legitimization typically transpires over a period of between twenty-five and fifty years—or what we might call a *generation*. Attempts to accelerate the mainstreaming of

radical music at a faster pace (e.g., in order to make money from it) will bring irresolvable tensions to the surface. Sometimes people will die as a result.

30. Music has always been linked to sex and violence. The first instruments were dripping in blood. The first songs promoted fertility, hunting, warfare, and the like. Most of music history serves to obscure these connections and to suppress elements judged shameful or undignified by posterity.

31. The 'shameful' elements in music history—sex, superstition, bloody conflicts, altered mind states, etc.—are usually closely linked to the process of innovation itself. When we cleanse them from the historical record, we guarantee our ignorance of how new ways of music-making arise.

32. Even love songs are political songs, because new ways of singing about love tend to threaten the status quo. All authority figures, from parents to monarchs, grasp this threat implicitly, even if they can't express it clearly in words.

33. Institutions and businesses do not create musical innovations; they just recognize them after the fact.

34. They usually strive to hide this—with the goal of exaggerating their own importance—and sometimes succeed.

35. If you really want to understand music in the present day, turn away from the stage and study the audience.

36. Music was once embedded in a person's life; now it projects a person's lifestyle. That may seem like a small difference, but the distance between the two can be as large as the gap between reality and fantasy.

37. Music entertains, but it can never be reduced to mere entertainment.

38. The audience is never passive, and it always puts music to use.

39. Songs still possess magic, even for those who have forgotten how to tap into it.

40. Those who devote themselves to music as a vocation—whether as performer, teacher, scholar, or in some other capacity—can ignore this magic, or they can play a part in restoring its potency. In other words: with music, we can all be wizards.

Acknowledgments

I could never adequately acknowledge—or even trace—the many sources of inspiration, enlightenment, and guidance that underpin this book. This work has been in the making since the early 1990s, and it all started when I asked a simple question that led to some very complicated outcomes: How does music change people's lives? That question enticed me into a labyrinth that, for a long time, I feared I might never exit. I have now come out the other side, but don't ask me for a map of how I did it.

For a more detailed accounting of influences on my work, see the lengthy bibliographies, notes, and personal thanks included in my three previous books on the social history of music (*Work Songs*, *Healing Songs*, and *Love Songs*). These amount to hundreds of scholars and thousands of books, documents, and articles, and even this is hardly exhaustive. I will, however, offer one generalization: the further I strayed from conventional music history and into other fields and disciplines, the more I benefited.

It is a simpler task to list the individuals who assisted me in the writing and improvement of this manuscript. I am grateful to the many experts in a wide range of areas who read portions of this book and offered invaluable feedback. These include Saul Austerlitz, Andrew Barker, Mark Changizi, Barry Cooper, Anthony M. Cummings, Barbara Eichner, David Fallows, Kitty Ferguson, Dana

acknowledgments

Gioia, Greg Gioia, David George Haskell, John Edward Hasse, Lynne Kelly, Allen Lowe, Michael Marissen, Giulio Ongaro, Melissa Pettau, Louise Pryke, Patrick Savage, George Sawa, Nicholas Stoia, Scott Timberg, and JJ Wright. I would also like to acknowledge assistance from Laurence Dreyfus and John Haines, who pointed me in the direction of important resources. I thank all these individuals even as I exempt them from responsibility for the shortcomings and excesses of the finished book.

I have been blessed with the help of a whole team of talented people at Basic Books. I am especially grateful to my editor Lara Heimert, who supported this book from the outset and gave me every possible assistance as I worked to complete a project far more daunting than anything I've previously attempted. I also benefited enormously from the guidance, advice, and support of Liz Wetzel, Katie Lambright, Carrie Majer, Nancy Sheppard, Allie Finkel, Melissa Raymond, Roger Labrie, Brynn Warriner, and Kathy Streckfus.

Finally, I offer public thanks to my wife, Tara, and my sons, Michael and Thomas, who are the foundation for everything good and beautiful in my life.

Notes

Chapter 1: The Origin of Music as a
Force of Creative Destruction

1. Natalie Curtis, *The Indians' Book: Songs and Legends of the American Indians* (New York: Dover, 1968), xxiv; Bruce Chatwin, *The Songlines* (London: Picador, 1988), 2; George Leonard, *The Silent Pulse* (Salt Lake City: Gibbs Smith, 2006), 14.

2. Bernie Krause, "Bioacoustics, Habitat Ambience in Ecological Balance," *Whole Earth Review* 57 (Winter 1987): 14–18.

3. Ibid.

4. Lynne Kelly, *The Memory Code: The Secrets of Stonehenge, Easter Island and Other Ancient Monuments* (New York: Pegasus, 2017), 6–7.

5. Ed Yong, "Trees Have Their Own Songs," *The Atlantic*, April 4, 2017.

6. Charles Darwin, *The Descent of Man* (Amherst, NY: Prometheus Books, 1998), 592–593; Drake Bennett, "Survival of the Harmonious," *Boston Globe*, September 3, 2006.

7. Dawn Hobbs and Gordon Gallup, "Songs as a Medium for Embedded Reproductive Messages," *Evolutionary Psychology* 9, no. 3 (September 12, 2011): 390–416.

8. William Forde Thompson, Andrew M. Geeves, and Kirk N. Olsen, "Who Enjoys Listening to Violent Music and Why?," *Psychology of Popular Media Culture*, March 26, 2018.

9. See John Noble Wilford, "Playing of Flute May Have Graced Neanderthal Fire," *New York Times*, October 29, 1996, B-5.

Chapter 2: Carnivores at the Philharmonic

1. Eric Charry, *Mande Music* (Chicago: University of Chicago Press, 2000), 75.

2. Pascal Quignard, *The Hatred of Music*, trans. Matthew Amos and Fredrik Rönnbäck (New Haven, CT: Yale University Press, 2016), 18.

3. Henry Raynor, *A Social History of Music from the Middle Ages to Beethoven* (New York: Schocken Books, 1972), 45.

4. Scott Timberg, "Halt, or I'll Play Vivaldi," *Los Angeles Times*, February 13, 2005. See also Theodore Gioia, "Bach at the Burger King," *Los Angeles Review of Books*, May 17, 2018.

5. Björn Vickhoff, Helge Malmgren, Rickard Åström, Gunnar Nyberg, Seth-Reino Ekström, Mathias Engwall, Johan Snygg, Michael Nilsson, and Rebecka Jörnsten, "Music Structure Determines Heart Rate Variability of Singers," *Frontiers in Psychology*, July 9, 2013; Scott S. Wiltermuth and Chip Heath, "Synchrony and Cooperation," *Psychological Science* 20, no. 1 (January 1, 2009).

6. Mickey Hart and Jay Stevens, *Drumming at the Edge of Magic* (New York: HarperCollins, 1990), 240.

7. Iegor Reznikoff, "Sound Resonance in Prehistoric Times: A Study of Paleolithic Painted Caves and Rocks," *Journal of the Acoustical Society of America* 123, no. 5 (2008): 4136–4141. See also Iegor Reznikoff and Michel Dauvois, "La dimension sonore des grottes ornées," in *Bulletin de la Société Préhistorique Française* 85, no. 8 (1988): 238–246.

8. Steven Errede, "Prehistoric Music and Art in Paleolithic Caves" (Champaign: University of Illinois, Department of Physics, 2006).

9. Ursula K. Le Guin, "The Beast in the Book," in *Words Are My Matter: Writings About Life and Books, 2000–2016* (Easthampton, MA: Small Beer Press, 2016), 33.

10. Mircea Eliade, *Shamanism: Archaic Techniques of Ecstasy*, trans. Willard R. Trask (Princeton, NJ: Princeton University Press, 1964), 459.

11. Gilbert Rouget, *Music and Trance: A Theory of the Relations Between Music and Possession*, trans. Brunhilde Biebuyck (Chicago: University of Chicago Press, 1985), 325, 17.

12. Andrew Neher, "Auditory Driving Observed with Scalp Electrodes in Normal Subjects," *Electroencephalography and Clinical Neurophysiology* 13 (1961): 449–451; Andrew Neher, "A Physiological Explanation of Unusual Behavior in Ceremonies Involving Drums," *Human Biology* 34, no. 2 (1962): 151–160; Rouget, *Music and Trance*, 33.

13. Tam Hunt, "The Hippies Were Right: It's All About Vibrations, Man," *Scientific American*, December 5, 2018.

14. Sherwood Washburn and C. S. Lancaster, "The Evolution of Hunting," in *Man the Hunter*, ed. Richard B. Lee and Irven Devore (Hawthorne, NY: Aldine de Gruyter, 1968), 293–303.

15. Joseph Jordania, *Why Do People Sing? Music in Human Evolution* (Melbourne: International Research Center for Traditional Polyphony at the University of Melbourne, 2011), 103.

16. Ibid., 182.

17. For more information on the songs of these cultures, see the chapter "The Hunter" in my book *Work Songs* (Durham, NC: Duke University Press, 2006), 13–34.

Chapter 3: In Search of a Universal Music

1. Peter Dronke, *Medieval Latin and the Rise of European Love-Lyric*, vol. 1, *Problems and Interpretations*, 2nd ed. (Oxford: Clarendon Press, 1968), 17.

2. A. P. Elkin, *Aboriginal Men of High Degree: Initiation and Sorcery in the World's Oldest Tradition*, 2nd ed. (St. Lucia, Queensland, Australia: University of Queensland Press, 1977).

3. Bruno Nettl, "An Ethnomusicologist Contemplates Universals in Musical Sound and Musical Culture," in *The Origins of Music*, ed. Nils Wallin Björn Merker and Steven Brown (Cambridge, MA: MIT Press, 2001), 463, 471; Steven Brown and Joseph Jordania, "Universals in the World's Musics," *Psychology of Music* 41 (2011): 229.

4. Samuel A. Mehr, Marvin Singh, Luke Glowacki, and Max M. Krasnow, "Form and Function in Human Song," *Current Biology* 28, no. 3 (January 2018): 356–368. For responses from music scholars and others, see Alex Marshall, "Can You Tell a Lullaby from a Love Song? Find Out Now," *New York Times*, January 25, 2018.

5. Anthony Seeger, "Styles of Musical Ethnography," in *Comparative Musicology and Anthropology of Music*, ed. Bruno Nettl and Philip V. Bohlman (Chicago: University of Chicago Press, 1991), 350; E. J. Michael Witzel, *The Origins of the World's Mythologies* (New York: Oxford University Press, 2012), 212.

6. Witzel, *Origins*, 212.

7. Sara Graça da Silva and Jamshid Tehrani, "Comparative Phylogenetic Analyses Uncover the Ancient Roots of Indo-European Folktales," *Royal Society Open Science*, January 14, 2016.

8. Vittorio D. Macchioro, *From Orpheus to Paul: A History of Orphism* (New York: Henry Holt, 1930); A. H. Gayton, "The Orpheus Myth in North America," *Journal of American Folklore* 48, no. 189 (1935): 263–293; Åke Hultkrantz, *The North-American Indian Orpheus Tradition: A Contribution to Comparative Religion* (Stockholm: Ethnographic Museum, 1957).

9. Jayne M. Standley and Carol A. Prickett, eds., *Research in Music Therapy: A Tradition of Excellence* (Silver Springs, MD: National Association of Music Therapy, 1994).

Chapter 4: Music History as a Battle Between Magic and Mathematics

1. Plutarch, *Plutarch's Morals*, ed. William Goodwin, trans. John Philips (New York: The Athenaeum Society, 1870), 130.

2. For both Leibniz and Schopenhauer, see Arthur Schopenhauer, *The World as Will and Representation*, vol. 1, trans. E. F. J. Payne (New York: Dover, 1966), 256, 264.

3. Vladimir Nabokov, *Lectures on Literature*, ed. Fredson Bowers (New York: Harcourt Brace Jovanovich, 1980), 374; Nelson Goodman, *Languages of Art: An Approach to a Theory of Symbols*, 2nd ed. (Indianapolis: Hackett, 1976).

4. Brad Inwood, ed. and trans., *The Poem of Empedocles* (Toronto: University of Toronto Press, 2001), 211.

5. For an account of the attempts by van Groningen, Diels, and others to eliminate shamanistic elements from Empedocles, see Peter Kingsley, *Ancient Philosophy, Mystery and Magic* (Oxford: Clarendon Press, 1995), esp. 218–232.

6. J. B. Kennedy, *The Musical Structure of Plato's Dialogues* (Durham, NC: Acumen, 2001), esp. 52–60.

7. J. J. Bachofen, *Myth, Religion, and Mother Right*, trans. Ralph Manheim (Princeton, NJ: Princeton University Press, 1973); Marija Gimbutas, *The Civilization of the Goddess: The World of Old Europe* (San Francisco: HarperCollins, 1991); Marija Gimbutas, *The Language of the Goddess* (New York: Harper and Row, 1989). See also my discussion of the relationship between the goddess hypothesis and music history in Ted Gioia, *Healing Songs* (Durham, NC: Duke University Press, 2006), 82–85.

8. David A. Campbell, ed. and trans., *Greek Lyric: Sappho and Alcaeus* (Cambridge, MA: Harvard University Press, 1990), 53.

9. Ibid., 67.

Chapter 5: Bulls and Sex Toys

1. Mircea Eliade, *Shamanism: Archaic Techniques of Ecstasy*, trans. Willard R. Trask (Princeton, NJ: Princeton University Press, 1964).

2. For early theories about animals in ancient Sumerian music, see Marcelle Duchesne-Guillemin, "Music in Ancient Mesopotamia and Egypt," *World Archaeology* 12, no. 3: *Archaeology and Musical Instruments* (February 1981): 287–297; F. W. Galpin, "The Sumerian Harp of Ur, c. 3500 B.C.," *Music and Letters* 10, no. 2 (April 1929): 108–123; Curtis Sachs, *The History of Musical Instruments* (New York: Norton, 1940), 90.

3. John P. Peters, "Notes and Suggestions on the Early Sumerian Religion and Its Expression," *Journal of the American Oriental Society* 41 (1921): 132.

4. Ezra Pound, *The Literary Essays of Ezra Pound* (New York: New Directions, 1968), 85.

5. Russell Nieli, *Wittgenstein: From Mysticism to Ordinary Language* (Albany: State University of New York, 1987), 175.

6. Sierra Helm, *The Passion for the Goddess: A Comparative Study on the Reverence of the Goddess in Contemporary America and Ancient Mesopotamia* (Honors Thesis, Roger Williams University, 2011), 4.

7. Gwendolyn Leick, *Sex and Eroticism in Mesopotamian Literature* (London: Routledge, 1994), 21, 49. For the "Bob Fosse meme," see Ted Gioia, *Love Songs: The Hidden History* (New York: Oxford University Press, 2015), 248.

8. Yitschak Sefati, *Love Songs in Sumerian Literature: Critical Edition of the Dumuzi-Inanna Songs* (Jerusalem: Bar-Ilan University Press, 1998), 224–225.

9. Noah Kramer, *Aspects of Faith, Myth, and Ritual in Ancient Sumer* (Bloomington: Indiana University Press, 1969), 59.

10. Homer, *The Odyssey*, trans. Robert Fagles (New York: Penguin, 1996), 193.

11. Johan Huizinga, *The Waning of the Middle Ages*, trans. Herfsttijd der Middeleerwen (New York: St. Martin's Press, 1984), 88.

12. Quintilian, *The Institutio Oratoria of Quintilian*, vol. 1, trans. H. E. Butler (New York: G. P. Putnam's Sons, 1920), 175.

Chapter 6: The Storyteller

1. For this and below, see Shelley MacDonald, Kimberly Uesiliana, and Harlene Hayne, "Cross-Cultural and Gender Differences in Childhood Amnesia," *Memory* 8, no. 6 (November 2000): 365–376; Elaine Reese, Harlene Hayne, and Shelley MacDonald, "Looking Back to the Future: Māori and Pakeha Mother-Child Birth Stories," *Child Development* 79, no. 1 (January–February 2008): 114–125; Ed Yong, "The Desirability of Storytellers," *The Atlantic*, December 5, 2017.

2. For these and other examples, see Lynne Kelly, *The Memory Code: The Secrets of Stonehenge, Easter Island and Other Ancient Monuments* (New York: Pegasus, 2017), 3–14.

3. Ibid., 12, 19.

4. Ibid., 13.

5. Dio Chrysostom, Discourse 53, "On Homer," in *Discourses 37–60*, trans. H. Lamar Crosby (Cambridge, MA: Loeb Classical Library, 1946), 363.

6. Albert B. Lord, *The Singer of Tales*, 2nd ed., ed. Stephen Mitchell and Gregory Nagy (Cambridge, MA: Harvard University Press, 2000), xi.

7. Christopher Cannon, "Was Chaucer Really a 'Writer'?," Oxford University Press Blog, February 8, 2017.

8. Lord, *Singer of Tales*, 99, 127 (emphasis in original).

9. Ibid., 14.

Chapter 7: The Invention of the Singer

1. For more on the Turin papyrus and Egyptian eroticism, see Ted Gioia, *Love Songs: The Hidden History* (New York: Oxford University Press, 2015), 18–24.

2. Peter Dronke, *Medieval Latin and the Rise of European Love-Lyric*, vol. 1, *Problems and Interpretations*, 2nd ed. (New York: Oxford University Press, 1968), 10–11.

3. David Carter, *Stonewall: The Riots That Sparked the Gay Revolution* (New York: St. Martin's Press, 2004), 1.

4. Ted Gioia, *How to Listen to Jazz* (New York: Basic Books, 2016), 77–78.

5. Barbara Wilcox, "Stanford Archaeologist Leads the First Detailed Study of Human Remains at the Ancient Egyptian Site of Deir el-Medina," *Stanford Report*, November 17, 2014.

6. Michael V. Fox, *The Song of Songs and the Ancient Egyptian Love Songs* (Madison: University of Wisconsin Press, 1985), xxiv.

Chapter 8: The Shame of Music

1. Plato, *Republic*, trans. C. M. A. Grube and C. D. C. Reeve, in *Plato: Complete Works*, ed. John M. Cooper (Indianapolis: Hackett, 1997), 1056. Ginsberg's quote is the title of his 1961 essay "When the Mode of the Music Changes, the Walls of the City Shake," in *Poetics of the New American Poetry*, ed. Donald Allen and Warren Tallman (New York: Grove, 1973), 324–330.

2. Plato, *Republic*, 1047.

3. Aristotle, *Aristotle's Politics*, trans. Benjamin Jowett (New York: Carlton House, 1950), 332–333.

4. Allan Bloom, *The Closing of the American Mind* (New York: Simon and Schuster, 1987), 71.

5. Aelian, *Historical Miscellany*, ed. and trans. N. G. Wilson (Cambridge, MA: Harvard University Press, 1997), 369.

6. Athenaeus, "Sophists at Dinner," in *Source Readings in Music History*, vol. 1, *Greek View of Music*, ed. Oliver Strunk (New York: Norton, 1988), 89.

7. E. R. Dodds, *The Greeks and the Irrational* (Berkeley: University of California Press, 1956), 194.

Chapter 9: Unmanly Music

1. Plato, *The Laws*, trans. Thomas L. Pangle (Chicago: University of Chicago Press, 1908), 192.

2. Plutarch, *Moralia*, vol. 14, trans. Benedict Einarson and Philip H. De Lacy (Cambridge, MA: Harvard University Press, 1967), 385–387 (emphasis mine).

3. Craig A. Williams, *Roman Homosexuality*, 2nd ed. (New York: Oxford University Press, 2010), 164; Quintilian, *The Institutio Oratoria of Quintilian*, vol. 1, trans. H. E. Butler (New York: G. P. Putnam's Sons, 1920), 175; Pliny, *Letters*, trans. William Melmoth (New York: Macmillan, 1915), 147.

4. H. D. Jocelyn, *The Tragedies of Ennius* (New York: Cambridge University Press, 1967), 21; Sander M. Goldberg, *Constructing Literature in the Roman Republic: Poetry and Its Reception* (New York: Cambridge University Press, 2005), 119–120.

5. Williams, *Roman Homosexuality*, 154.

6. J. J. Winkler, "The Ephebes' Song," in *Nothing to Do with Dionysos*, ed. J. J. Winkler and F. I. Zeitlin (Princeton, NJ: Princeton University Press, 1990), 20–62. See also Marcel Lysgaard Lech, "Marching Choruses? Choral Performance in Athens," *Greek, Roman and Byzantine Studies* 49 (2009): 343–361.

7. Seneca, *Dialogues and Essays*, trans. John Davie (Oxford: Oxford University Press, 2007), 138.

8. John Jory, "The Masks on the Propylon of the Sebasteion at Aphrodisias," in *Greek and Roman Actors: Aspects of an Ancient Profession*, ed. Pat Easterling and Edith Hall (Cambridge: Cambridge University Press, 2002), 238.

9. Ruth Webb, "Inside the Mask: Pantomime from the Performers' Perspective," in *New Directions in Ancient Pantomime*, ed. Edith Hall and Rosie Wyles (Oxford: New York, 2008), 51.

10. Eric Csapo and William J. Slater, *The Context of Ancient Drama* (Ann Arbor: University of Michigan Press, 1994), 324.

11. Edith Hall, "Introduction: Pantomime, a Lost Chord of Ancient Culture," in *New Directions in Ancient Pantomime*, ed. Edith Hall and Rosie Wyles (Oxford: New York, 2008), 27.

12. John G. Landels, *Music in Ancient Greece and Rome* (New York: Routledge, 1999), 199.

13. Dave Hickey, *Air Guitar: Essays on Art and Democracy* (Los Angeles: Arts Issues Press, 1997), 15.

14. Lucius Annaeus Seneca, *Seneca's Letters from a Stoic*, trans. Richard M. Gummere (Mineola, NY: Dover, 2016), 112.

15. Walter Burkert, *Ancient Mystery Cults* (Cambridge, MA: Harvard University Press, 1987), 113.

Chapter 10: The Devil's Songs

1. Mozi, *Basic Writings*, trans. Burton Watson (New York: Columbia University Press, 2003), 114, 119.

2. *The Book of Songs*, trans. Arthur Waley (London: Routledge, 2005), 20.

3. Tamara Chin, "Orienting Mimesis: Marriage and the Book of Songs," *Representations* 94, no. 1 (Spring 2006): 71; *Book of Songs*, 81.

4. Ephesians 5:19, Colossians 3:16 (King James Version).

5. Johannes Quasten, *Music and Worship in Pagan and Christian Antiquity*, trans. Boniface Ramsey (Washington, DC: National Association of Pastoral Musicians, 1983), 60.

6. Jacques Attali, *Noise: The Political Economy of Music*, trans. Brian Massumi (Minneapolis: University of Minnesota Press, 1985), 12.

7. Quasten, *Music and Worship*, 60.

8. Joscelyn Godwin, ed., *Music, Mysticism and Magic: A Sourcebook* (New York: Routledge and Kegan Paul, 1987), 94.

9. Psalms 33:2, 149:3, 68:25 (King James Version).

10. Tim Wilson's interview with Alfred Tomatis was published in Tim Wilson, "Chant: The Healing Power of Voice and Ear," *Music: Physician for Times to Come*, 2nd ed., ed. Don Campbell (Wheaton, IL: Theosophical Publishing House, 2000), 14.

11. Abbott Justin McCann, OSB, trans. and ed., *The Rule of Saint Benedict in English and Latin* (Fort Collins, CO: Roman Catholic Books, 1951), 69.

12. John Haines, *Medieval Song in Romance Languages* (Cambridge: Cambridge University Press, 2010), 55, 6.

13. Ibid., 150.

14. Ibid., 162–163. For Caesarius, see William E. Klingshirn, *Caesarius of Arles: The Making of a Christian Community in Late Antique Gaul* (Cambridge: Cambridge University Press, 2004), 185.

15. Ibid.

16. For Haymo, see Haines, *Medieval Song in Romance Languages*, 165. For Caesarius, see Klingshirn, *Caesarius of Arles*, 185. For the Councils of Auxerre and Chalons, see Anne L. Klinck, ed., *Introduction to Anthology of Ancient and Medieval Woman's Song* (New York: Palgrave Macmillan, 2004), 4. For Charlemagne, see Peter Dronke, *The Medieval Lyric* (Suffolk, UK: D. S. Brewer, 1996), 91.

17. Guido of Arezzo, "Epistle Concerning an Unknown Chant," in *Source Readings in Music History*, ed. Oliver Strunk and Leo Treitler (New York: Norton, 1998), 214–215.

18. Maribel Dietz, *Wandering Monks, Virgins, and Pilgrims: Ascetic Travel in the Mediterranean World, A.D. 300–800* (University Park: Pennsylvania State University Press, 2005), 36; Helen Wadell, *The Wandering Scholars of the Middle Ages* (Mineola, NY: Dover, 2000), 270.

19. *Dum caupona verterem*, in *Love Lyrics from the Carmina Burana*, ed. and trans. P. G. Walsh (Chapel Hill: University of North Carolina Press, 1993), 59.

20. *Si quis Deciorum*, in George F. Whicher, *The Goliard Poets: Medieval Latin Songs and Satires* (New York: New Directions, 1965), 265.

21. *Cur suspectum me tenet domina*, in *Love Lyrics from the Carmina Burana*, 129–130.

22. Whicher's quote and the translation of *Estuans intrinsecus* from Whicher, *The Goliard Poets*, 6, 111.

23. *Grates ago Veneri*, in *Love Lyrics from the Carmina Burana*, 44.

24. Betty Radice, ed. and trans., *The Letters of Abelard and Heloise* (London: Penguin, 1974), 67–68, 75.

25. Ibid., 68, 115.

26. Some scholars have suggested that Abélard's lyrics may have survived anonymously in the *Carmina Burana*—for example, in the song "Hebet Sidus."

Chapter 11: Oppression and Musical Innovation

1. C. S. Lewis, *The Allegory of Love* (London: Oxford University Press, 1936), 4.

2. Fuad Matthew Caswell, *The Slave Girls of Baghdad: The Qiyān in the Early Abbasid Era* (New York: I. B. Tauris, 2011), 15–16.

3. Everett K. Rowson, "The Effeminates of Early Medina," *Journal of the American Oriental Society* 111, no. 4 (October–December 1991): 692, 683.

4. Ibid., 69.

5. Henry Louis Gates, *The Signifying Monkey: A Theory of African-American Literary Criticism* (New York: Oxford University Press, 1988); Caswell, *Slave Girls of Baghdad*, 63.

6. Ezra Pound, *The Cantos* (New York: New Directions), 1996, 32; Julian Ribera, *Music in Ancient Arabia and Spain*, trans. Eleanor Hague and Marion Leffingwell (Stanford: Stanford University Press, 1929), 9.

7. Benjamin Liu and James Monroe, *Ten Hispano-Arabic Songs in the Modern Oral Tradition* (Berkeley: University of California Press, 1989), 31.

8. Caswell, *Slave Girls of Baghdad*, 223.

9. Lewis, *Allegory of Love*, 2.

Chapter 12: Not All Wizards Carry Wands

1. From "The Rules of Sir Raimon Vidal," trans. Marianne Shapiro, in Marianne Shapiro, *De Vulgari Eloquentia: Dante's Book of Exile* (Lincoln: University of Nebraska Press, 1990), 114.

2. L. T. Topsfield, *Troubadours and Love* (Cambridge: Cambridge University Press, 1975), 247.

3. Meg Bogin, *The Women Troubadours* (New York: Norton, 1980), 127.

4. "Farewell to Ventadorn," trans. W. D. Snodgrass, in *Larks in the Morning: The Verses of the Troubadours*, ed. Robert Kehew (Chicago: University of Chicago Press, 2005), 93.

5. John Haines, *Medieval Song in Romance Languages* (Cambridge: Cambridge University Press, 2010), 157.

6. Ted Gioia, *Work Songs* (Durham, NC: Duke University Press, 2006), 8–9. For Austin, see J. L. Austin, *How to Do Things with Words* (Cambridge, MA: Harvard University Press, 1962).

7. Mitchell Hartman, "Employees Like Music at Work, Survey Finds," *Marketplace*, November 22, 2018; Tibi Puiu, "How People Use Music as a Sleeping Aid," *ZME Science*, November 14, 2018.

Chapter 13: The Invention of the Audience

1. From Dorothy Sayers's introduction to *The Song of Roland*, ed. and trans. Dorothy Sayers (New York: Penguin, 1957), 17.

2. Emmanuel Le Roy Ladurie, *Montaillou: The Promised Land of Error*, trans. Barbara Bray (New York: Vintage, 1979); Greil Marcus, *Lipstick Traces: A Secret History of the Twentieth Century* (Cambridge, MA: Belknap Press of Harvard University Press, 2009), esp. 371–374.

3. Edmondstoune Duncan, *The Story of Minstrelsy* (New York: Charles Scribner's, 1907), 37–38.

4. Maria Dobozy, "Creating Credibility and Truth Through Performance: Kelin's Encomium," in *The Stranger in Medieval Society*, ed. F. R. P. Akehurst and Stephanie Cain Van D'Elden (Minneapolis: University of Minnesota Press, 1997), 92.

5. H. J. Chaytor, *From Script to Print: An Introduction to Medieval Literature* (Cambridge: Cambridge University Press, 1945), 3.

6. Rob C. Wegman, *The Crisis of Music in Early Modern Europe* (New York: Routledge, 2005), 22.

7. Charles Rosen, *The Classical Style: Haydn, Mozart, Beethoven,* expanded ed. (New York: Norton, 1997), 58.

8. Robert Mullally, *The Carole: A Study of a Medieval Dance* (Burlington, VT: Ashgate, 2011), xv.

Chapter 14: Musicians Behaving Badly

1. Benvenuto Cellini, *My Life,* trans. Julia Conaway Bondanella and Peter Bondanella (Oxford: Oxford University Press, 2002), 125. Some believe Cellini exaggerated his violent exploits to enhance his reputation, but that would simply reinforce the main point made here: extreme behavior now contributed to an artist's renown.

2. Alex Ross, "Prince of Darkness: The Murders and Madrigals of Don Carlo Gesualdo," *The New Yorker,* December 19, 2011, 84–92.

3. Heinrich Glarean, "Dodecachordon" in *Source Readings in Music History,* vol. 3, *The Renaissance,* ed. Oliver Strunk and Leo Treitler (New York: Norton, 1998), 151–157; Lewis Lockwood, *Music in Renaissance Ferrara, 1400–1505: The Creation of a Musical Center in the Fifteenth Century* (New York: Oxford University Press, 2009), 227.

4. Allan W. Atlas, *Renaissance Music* (New York: Norton, 1998), 189.

5. Terry Roth, "Street Cries and Criers of New York," *Federal Writers' Project,* an eight-page document dated November 3, 1938.

6. Jacques Le Goff, *Time, Work, and Culture in the Middle Ages,* trans. Arthur Goldhammer (Chicago: University of Chicago Press, 1980), 46.

7. Alain Corbin, *Village Bells: Sound and Meaning in the Nineteenth-Century French Countryside,* trans. Martin Thom (London: Papermac, 1999).

8. Johan Huizinga, *The Waning of the Middle Ages,* trans. Herfsttijd der Middeleerwen (New York: St. Martin's Press, 1984), 2–3; *Torquay Directory,* August 9, 1899, cited in *Devon & Cornwall Notes & Queries,* vol. 1, ed. P. F. S. Amery, John S. Amery, and J. Brooking Rowe (Exeter, UK: James G. Commin, 1901), 18.

Chapter 15: The Origins of the Music Business

1. Michel Foucault, *The Order of Things: An Archeology of the Human Sciences* (New York: Vintage, 1973), 50–55.

2. Jon Paxman, *A Chronology of Western Classical Music, 1600–2000* (London: Omnibus, 2014), 50; Massimo Ossi, *Divining the Oracle: Monteverdi's Seconda Prattica* (Chicago: University of Chicago Press, 2003), 36.

3. Gary Tomlinson, *Monteverdi and the End of the Renaissance* (Berkeley: University of California Press, 1987), 110.

4. Richard Taruskin, *The Oxford History of Western Music,* vol. 2 (Oxford: Oxford University Press, 2005), 5. For the text of the letter, see *The Letters of Claudio Monteverdi,* trans. and ed. Denis Stevens (Cambridge: Cambridge University Press, 1980), 189–193.

5. Graham Freeman, "The Transmission of Lute Music and the Culture of Aurality in Early Modern England," in *Beyond Boundaries: Rethinking Music Circulation in Early Modern England,* ed. Linda Phyllis Austern, Candace Bailey, and Amanda Eubanks Winkler (Indianapolis: Indiana University Press, 2017), 51.

6. Tim Blanning, *The Triumph of Music: The Rise of Composers, Musicians and Their Art* (Cambridge, MA: Belknap Press of Harvard University Press, 2008), 89.

7. For the importance of singular and plural constructions in the evolution of music during this period, see Mauro Calcagno, *From Madrigal to Opera: Monteverdi's Staging of the Self* (Berkeley: University of California Press, 2012), 109–120.

Chapter 16: Culture Wars

1. Rob C. Wegman, *The Crisis of Music in Early Modern Europe, 1470–1530* (New York: Routledge, 2005), 33.

2. Michael John Noone, *Music and Musicians in the Escorial Liturgy Under the Habsburgs, 1563–1700* (Rochester, NY: University of Rochester Press, 1998), 346.

3. Wegman, *Crisis of Music*, 21, 17, 28.

4. Kuang Yu Chen, "The Book of Odes: A Case Study of the Chinese Hermeneutic Tradition," in *Chinese Hermeneutics in Historical Perspective: Interpretation and Intellectual Change*, ed. Ching-I Tu (New Brunswick, NJ: Transaction, 2005), 53.

5. Deborah Baker, "For the Sake of the Song," *The Caravan: A Journal of Politics and Culture*, May 1, 2011.

6. Franklin D. Lewis, *Rumi, Past and Present, East and West: The Life, Teaching and Poetry of Jalâl Al-Din Rumi* (Oxford: Oneworld, 2008).

7. Ibid., 28.

8. Charles Burney, *The Present State of Music in France and Italy* (London: T. Becket, 1773), 312.

9. Chiara Bertoglio, *Reforming Music* (Berlin: Walter de Gruyter, 2017), 175.

10. Paul Nettl, *Luther and Music* (New York: Russell and Russell, 1948), 5.

11. Bertoglio, *Reforming Music*, 212.

12. Gayle Dean Wardlow, interview with author, April 22, 2006.

13. Bertoglio, *Reforming Music*, 170, 188.

14. Ibid., 345.

15. Robert J. Zatorrea and Valorie N. Salimpoora, "From Perception to Pleasure: Music and Its Neural Substrates," *Proceedings of the National Academy of Science of the USA* 110, no. S2 (June 18, 2013): 10430–10437.

Chapter 17: Subversives in Wigs

1. John Eliot Gardiner, *Bach: Music in the Castle of Heaven* (New York: Vintage, 2015), xxviii; Laurence Dreyfus, "Bach the Subversive," a lecture given in London on May 14, 2011. My thanks to Professor Dreyfus for providing me with the text of his talk.

2. Gardiner, *Bach*, 222, 528, 220; from the city council minutes included in *The New Bach Reader: A Life of Johann Sebastian Bach in Letters and Documents*, ed. Hans T. David and Arthur Mendel, rev. Christoph Wolff (New York: Norton, 1998), 149.

3. Matthew Dirst, *Engaging Bach: The Keyboard Legacy from Marpurg to Mendelssohn* (Cambridge: Cambridge University Press, 2012), 49–50.

4. Joseph Kerman, *Write All These Down: Essays on Music* (Berkeley: University of California Press, 1994), 16.

5. Charles Rosen, *The Classical Style: Haydn, Mozart, Beethoven*, expanded ed. (New York: Norton, 1997), xvi.

6. Antoine Lilti, *The Invention of Celebrity*, trans. Lynn Jeffress (Malden, MA: Polity Press, 2017), 7.

7. H. C. Robbins Landon, *Vivaldi: Voice of the Baroque* (Chicago: University of Chicago Press, 1996), 32, 48, 27; Jan Swafford, *Beethoven: Anguish and Triumph* (London: Faber and Faber, 2015), 64; Karl Geiringer with Irene Geiringer, *Haydn: A Creative Life in Music*, 3rd ed. (Berkeley: University of California Press, 1982), 62, 107.

8. David Wyn Jones, *The Life of Haydn* (Cambridge: Cambridge University Press, 2009), 127.

9. *The Letters of Mozart and His Family*, 3rd ed., ed. Emily Anderson, rev. Stanley Sadie and Fiona Smart (London: Macmillan, 1997), 372.

10. Peter Culshaw, "Mozart Was a Political Revolutionary," *The Telegraph*, July 3, 2006.

11. Paul Johnson, *Mozart: A Life* (New York: Viking, 2013), 151.

12. *Letters of Mozart and His Family*, 828.

13. Ibid., 716.

14. Geiringer, *Haydn*, 97.

15. Rosen, *Classical Style*, 155.

Chapter 18: You Say You Want a Revolution?

1. Vincent d'Indy, *Beethoven: A Critical Biography*, trans. Theodore Baker (Boston: Boston Music Company, 1913), 66; Alexander Thayer, *Thayer's Life of Beethoven*, vol. 1, rev. and ed. Elliot Forbes (Princeton, NJ: Princeton University Press, 1967), ix; David B. Dennis, *Beethoven in German Politics* (New Haven, CT: Yale University Press, 1996), 179.

2. *Beethoven: Impressions by His Contemporaries*, ed. O. G. Sonneck (New York: Dover, 1967), 20–21, 31.

3. These responses to Beethoven's symphony can be found in Jan Swafford, *Beethoven: Anguish and Triumph* (London: Faber and Faber, 2015), 396–400. Beethoven scholar Barry Cooper tells me that *kreuzer* is the correct term for the coin in question, but I retain here the *kreutzer* cited in traditional accounts.

4. Isaiah Berlin, "Two Concepts of Liberty," in *Four Essays on Liberty* (Oxford: Oxford University Press, 1969), 118–172.

5. Swafford, *Beethoven*, 114.

6. Percy Bysshe Shelley, *A Defence of Poetry* (Indianapolis: Bobbs-Merrill, 1904), 90.

7. Daniel Beller-McKenna, *Brahms and the German Spirit* (Cambridge, MA: Harvard University Press, 2004), 31; Michael Musgrave, *The Music of Brahms* (Oxford: Clarendon Press, 1994), 80.

8. Brian Newbould, *Schubert: The Music and the Man* (Berkeley: University of California Press, 1999), 8.

9. Alex Ross, "Great Soul," *The New Yorker*, February 3, 1997, 70.

10. R. Larry Todd, *Mendelssohn: The Hebrides and Other Overtures* (Cambridge: Cambridge University Press, 1993), 50.

11. Barbara Eichner, *History in Mighty Sounds: Musical Constructions of German National Identity, 1848–1914* (Woodbridge, UK: Boydell Press, 2012), 1.

12. Ted Gioia, "Music to Shoot You By: Taking Beethoven on a Ride-Along in First-Person-Shooter Games," *Daily Beast*, February 21, 2015.

13. Elias Canetti, *Crowds and Power*, trans. Carol Stewart (New York: Seabury, 1978), 394–396. Compare with Richard Wagner, *Wagner on Conducting*, trans. William Reeves (New York: Dover, 1989), 5–10.

14. Homer, *The Iliad*, trans. Robert Fagles (New York: Penguin, 1991), 77.

15. Steven Pinker, *How the Mind Works* (New York: Norton, 1997), 534.

16. Todd Gitlin, "The Missing Music of the Left," *New York Review of Books*, May 28, 2018.

Chapter 19: The Great Flip-Flop

1. Robert T. Clark Jr., *Herder: His Life and Thought* (Berkeley: University of California Press, 1969), 194.

2. Dave Harker, *Fakesong: The Manufacture of British 'Folksong,' 1700 to the Present Day* (Philadelphia: Open University Press, 1985), xii.

3. Steve Roud, *Folk Song in England* (London: Faber and Faber, 2017), 55, 181.

4. Ibid., 59.

5. Stephen Lloyd, *Constant Lambert: Beyond the Rio Grande* (Woodbridge, UK: Boydell Press, 2014), 34.

6. Johann Herder, "Extract from a Correspondence on Ossian and the Songs of Ancient Peoples," in *German Aesthetic and Literary Criticism: Winckelmann, Lessing, Hamann, Herder, Schiller, Goethe*, ed. H. B. Nisbet (Cambridge: Cambridge University Press, 1985), 155.

7. Roud, *Folk Song in England*, 51, 53–54.

8. Thomas Percy, *Percy's Reliques of Ancient English Poetry* (Philadelphia: Porter and Coates, 1873), ii.

9. William W. Sanger, *The History of Prostitution* (New York: Harper and Brothers, 1858), 334.

10. "The Plotter Executed," Ballad 30386 in the British Broadside Ballad Archive, hosted at the University of California, Santa Barbara, and accessible online at https://ebba.english.ucsb.edu/ballad/30386/xml.

11. María Susana Azzi, "The Tango, Peronism and Astor Piazzolla During the 1940s and 1950s," in *Tejano to Tango: Latin American Popular Music*, ed. Walter Aaron Clark (New York: Routledge, 2002), 38.

Chapter 20: The Aesthetics of Diaspora

1. Matthew Arnold, *Culture and Anarchy: An Essay in Political and Social Criticism* (Cambridge: Cambridge University Press, 2011), viii.

2. Pierre Bourdieu, *Distinction: A Social Critique of the Judgment of Taste*, trans. Richard Nice (Cambridge, MA: Harvard University Press, 1984), xi, 34.

3. Chad Heap, *Slumming: Sexual and Racial Encounters in American Nightlife, 1885–1940* (Chicago: University of Chicago Press, 2009), 18.

4. C. W. E. Bigsby, *Dada & Surrealism* (New York: Routledge, 1978), 7.

5. Regina M. Sweeney, *Singing Our Way to Victory: French Cultural Politics and Music During the Great War* (Middletown, CT: Wesleyan University Press, 2001), 31. See also Greil Marcus, *Lipstick Traces: A Secret History of the Twentieth Century* (Cambridge, MA: Belknap Press of Harvard University Press, 2009), 137.

6. Alexander Falconbridge, *An Account of the Slave Trade on the Coast of Africa* (London: J. Phillips, 1788), 23.

7. Phil Jamison, *Hoedowns, Reels, and Frolics: Roots and Branches of Southern Appalachian Dance* (Urbana: University of Illinois Press, 2015), 50–53.

8. Ted Gioia, "The Con Man Who Invented American Popular Music," *Radio Silence*, no. 18 (July 1, 2015).

9. "Is Blind Tom Alive? Curious Story Concerning the Black Music Wonder," *Indianapolis Journal*, January 1, 1894, 5.

10. Deirdre O'Connell, *The Ballad of Blind Tom, Slave Pianist* (New York: Overlook Press, 2009), 55, 40.

11. Nicholas E. Tawa, *Sweet Songs for Gentle Americans: The Parlor Song in America, 1790–1860* (Bowling Green, OH: Bowling Green University Popular Press, 1980), 140.

Chapter 21: Black Music and the Great American Lifestyle Crisis

1. Thomas Wentworth Higginson, "Negro Spirituals," *Atlantic Monthly* 19, no. 116 (June 1867): 687; William Francis Allen, Charles Pickard Ware, and Lucy McKim Garrison, *Slave Songs of the United States* (New York: A. Simpson and Company, 1867), vi (emphasis in original).

2. Bob Darden, *People Get Ready!: A New History of Black Gospel Music* (New York: Continuum, 2004), 120.

3. Lynn Abbott and Doug Seroff, *Out of Sight: The Rise of African American Popular Music, 1889–1895* (Jackson: University Press of Mississippi, 2002), 443.

4. Edward A. Berlin, *King of Ragtime: Scott Joplin and His Era* (New York: Oxford University Press, 1994), 15, 164.

5. Ibid., 40.

6. Ibid., 53.

7. Ibid., 88.

Chapter 22: Rebellion Goes Mainstream

1. Howard W. Odum and Guy B. Johnson, *Negro Workaday Songs* (Chapel Hill: University of North Carolina Press, 1926), 6; Charles Peabody, "Notes on Negro Music," *Journal of American Folk-Lore* 16, no. 62 (July–September 1903): 152.

2. Stephen Calt, *Barrelhouse Words: A Blues Dialect Dictionary* (Urbana: University of Illinois Press, 2009), xiv.

3. Carol J. Oja, *Making Music Modern: New York in the 1920s* (New York: Oxford University Press, 2000), 92.

4. For attempts to demythologize the biography of Robert Johnson, see Elijah Wald, *Escaping the Delta: Robert Johnson and the Invention of the Blues* (New York: HarperCollins, 2004), and Barry Lee Pearson and Bill McCulloch, *Robert Johnson: Lost and Found* (Urbana: University of Illinois Press, 2003).

5. Pearson and McCulloch, *Robert Johnson*, 30–31.

6. Alan Lomax, interview with David "Honeyboy" Edwards, Folder 4 in the Library of Congress's *Delta Project* collection.

7. Harry Middleton Hyatt, *Hoodoo Conjuration Witchcraft Rootwork*, 5 vols. (Hannibal, MO: Memoirs of the Alma Egan Hyatt Foundation, 1970–1978).

Chapter 23: Funky Butt

1. Bill Russell, *New Orleans Style*, ed. Barry Martyn and Mike Hazeldine (New Orleans: Jazzology, 1994), 175.

2. Donald M. Marquis, *In Search of Buddy Bolden: First Man of Jazz*, rev. ed. (Baton Rouge: Louisiana State University Press, 2005), 111.

3. Daniel Stein, *Music Is My Life: Louis Armstrong, Autobiography and American Jazz* (Ann Arbor: University of Michigan Press, 2012), 241.

4. Albert R. Rice, *Notes for Clarinetists: A Guide to the Repertoire* (New York: Oxford University Press, 2017), 43.

5. Mark Tucker, ed., *The Duke Ellington Reader* (New York: Oxford University Press, 1993), 115.

6. Ibid., 362.

7. Dick Witts and Karlheinz Stockhausen, "Advice to Clever Children…, " *The Wire* 141 (November 1995): 33–35.

Chapter 24: The Origins of
Country Music in the Neolithic Era

1. Macrobius, *Commentary on the Dream of Scipio*, trans. William Harris Stahl (New York: Columbia University Press, 1952), 195; Emmanuel Le Roy Ladurie, *Montaillou: The Promised Land of Error*, trans. Barbara Bray (New York: Vintage, 1979), 259 (emphasis in original).

2. Michael C. Scoggins, *The Scotch-Irish Influence on Country Music in the Carolinas: Border Ballads, Fiddle Tunes & Sacred Songs* (Charleston, SC: History Press, 2013), 47.

3. Nick Tosches, *Country: The Twisted Roots of Rock 'n' Roll* (New York: Da Capo, 1996), 110.

4. Barry Mazor, *Ralph Peer and the Making of Popular Roots Music* (Chicago: Chicago Review Press, 2015), 90 (emphasis in the original).

5. Chuck Klosterman, *But What If We're Wrong?* (New York: Blue Rider, 2016), 84.

Chapter 25: Where Did Our Love Go?

1. Marshall McLuhan, *Understanding Media: The Extensions of Man* (Cambridge, MA: MIT Press, 1994), 7.

2. Joel Williamson, *Elvis Presley: A Southern Life* (New York: Oxford University Press, 2015), 47.

3. Gail Cameron, "We've Got 'Em, Luv, and It's All Gear," *Life* 56, no. 8 (February 21, 1964), 33.

4. Saul Austerlitz, *Just a Shot Away: Peace, Love and Tragedy with the Rolling Stones at Altamont* (New York: Thomas Dunne, 2018), 204. My thanks also to Saul Austerlitz for providing information about the *Berkeley Barb* story.

Chapter 26: The Sacrificial Ritual

1. Legs McNeil and Gillian McCain, *Please Kill Me: The Uncensored Oral History of Punk* (New York: Grove, 1996), 24.

2. Ibid., 4.

3. Caroline Sullivan, "Why Don't Rock Stars Trash Hotel Rooms Anymore?," *The Guardian,* January 3, 2010.

4. René Girard, *Violence and the Sacred,* trans. Patrick Gregory (Baltimore: Johns Hopkins University Press, 1977), 6–27.

5. Ibid., 271.

6. Caroline Joan Picart, *Remaking the Frankenstein Myth on Film: Between Laughter and Horror* (Albany: State University of New York Press, 2003), 62.

7. Jerry Portwood, "How East German Punks Helped Destroy the Berlin Wall," *Rolling Stone,* September 17, 2018.

8. McNeil and McCain, *Please Kill Me,* 182.

9. Greil Marcus, *Lipstick Traces: A Secret History of the Twentieth Century* (Cambridge, MA: Belknap Press of Harvard University Press, 2009), 79.

Chapter 27: Rappers and Technocrats

1. Brad Morrell, *Nirvana & the Sound of Seattle* (London: Omnibus, 1996), 131.

2. Martin Tolchin, "South Bronx: A Jungle Stalked by Fear, Seized by Rage," *New York Times,* January 15, 1973, 1.

3. Nelson George, *Hip Hop America* (New York: Penguin, 2005), 59.

Chapter 28: Welcome Our New Overlords

1. *Spotify Annual Report* (2015), 3.

2. Byung-Chul Han, *Saving Beauty,* trans. Daniel Steuer (Medford, MA: Polity Press, 2018), 1.

3. Steven Pinker, *How the Mind Works* (New York: Norton, 1997), 534.

4. Nic Fildes, "Rise of the Robot Music Industry," *Financial Times,* December 2, 2016.

5. Owen Jones, "Pussy Riot: A Beacon of Hope in Russia's Dark Days," *The Independent,* December 18, 2013. For Vladimir Putin's plan to lead and direct Russian rap music, see Andrew E. Kramer, "Putin on Rap Music: It's the Drugs That Really Bother Him," *New York Times,* December 16, 2018.

6. Tia DeNora, *Music in Everyday Life* (Cambridge: Cambridge University Press, 2000), 116.

7. John Sloboda, Susan A. O'Neill, and Antonia Ivaldi, "Functioning of Music in Everyday Life: An Exploratory Study Using the Experiences Sampling Method," *Musica Scientiae* 5, no. 1 (Spring 2001): 9–32.

Index

index

index

index

Ted Gioia is a music historian and the author of eleven books, including *How to Listen to Jazz*. His three previous books on the social history of music—*Work Songs, Healing Songs,* and *Love Songs*—have each been honored with the ASCAP Deems Taylor Award. Gioia's wide-ranging activities as a critic, scholar, performer, and educator have established him as a leading global guide to music past, present, and future.